D1609197

CHRYSLER CHRONICLE

AN ILLUSTRATED HISTORY OF CHRYSLER
DeSOTO • DODGE • IMPERIAL • PLYMOUTH

BY JAMES M. FLAMMANG
AND THE AUTO EDITORS OF CONSUMER GUIDE®

PUBLICATIONS INTERNATIONAL, LTD.

Louis Weber, C.E.O.
Publications International, Ltd.
7373 North Cicero Avenue
Lincolnwood, Illinois 60646

Permission is never granted for commercial purposes.

Manufactured in U.S.A.

8 7 6 5 4 3 2 1

ISBN 0–7853–0779–6

Library of Congress Catalog Card Number 94–69612

ACKNOWLEDGMENTS

PHOTOGRAPHY

The editors gratefully acknowledge the cooperation of the following people, who supplied photography to help make this book possible. They are listed below, along with the page number(s) of their photos.

Special thanks: Steven J. Harris, Executive Director Chrysler Public Relations; Daniel F. Kirchner and Peggy Dusman, American Automobile Manufacturers Association; Leslie Lovett, National Hot Rod Association; Brandt Rosenbush and Barbara Fronczak, Chrysler Historical Collection; William B. Stewart, Senior Editorial Services Director, and Diana Budzinski, Editorial Services, FR Communications; Robert Young and Mal Foys, Chrysler Design Archives.

Lee Angle Photography: 216.
Bill Baile: 135.
Ken Beebee: 189, 199.
Les Bidrawn: 152.
Rich Blodgett: 122.
Joe Bohovic: 135, 143, 210, 216, 228, 241.
Terry Boyce: 185, 186, 187, 188, 189.
Arch Brown: 134.
Chan Bush: 61, 181, 218, 241, 245, 255, 267, 268, 270, 271, 283, 289, 290, 294, 296, 297, 311.
David Chobat: 242.
Jim Frenak: 78, 79, 80.
Chuck Giametta: 82.
Thomas Glatch: 143, 147, 152, 187, 197, 207, 220, 226, 229, 234.
Eddie Goldberger: 104.
Sam Griffith: 77, 80, 109, 115, 131, 166, 173, 196, 204, 224, 247, 380.
Jerry Heasley: 144, 182.
Bill Hill: 147.
Reed Hutchison: 95.
S. Scott Hutchinson: 172, 181.
Bud Juneau: 68, 70, 86, 109, 114, 127, 146, 151, 165, 180, 193, 196, 219.
Milton Gene Kieft: 47, 91, 106, 109, 112, 118, 122, 132, 144, 150, 165, 167, 182, 194, 206, 209, 215, 288.
Dan Lyons: 92, 112, 113, 116, 119, 172, 200, 207, 214, 215, 282.
Vince Manocchi: 42, 47, 49, 54, 60, 66, 67, 87, 90, 94, 102, 112, 124, 138, 139, 141, 142, 145, 150, 152, 153, 155, 156, 162, 164, 168, 172, 174, 178, 179, 184, 188, 190, 198, 204, 209, 216, 247, 278, 384.
Mark McMahon: 185.
Pete McNisholl: 143.
Doug Mitchel: 40, 44, 55, 63, 68, 69, 71, 75, 80, 84, 87, 89, 91, 103, 104, 107, 108, 114, 119, 125, 126, 133, 141, 149, 156, 160, 161, 162, 166, 174, 179, 184, 185, 193, 194, 196, 197, 218, 234, 246, 248.
Steve Momot: 133.
Mike Mueller: 116, 117, 118, 130, 139, 142, 144, 152, 161, 164, 187, 190, 220, 225, 227.
Rob Reaser: 115.
William J. Schintz: 131, 210.
Mike Slade: 228.
Robert C. Sorgatz: 226, 233.
Richard Spiegelman: 38, 43, 44, 45, 46, 50, 51, 105, 107, 173, 219.
Gerald Sutphin: 192.
David Talbott: 180.
Bob Tenney: 192, 206, 232.
Marvin Terrell: 134.
Ross Tse: 148.
Nicky Wright: 8, 9, 10, 46, 59, 86, 88, 106, 109, 112, 133, 134, 139, 145, 151, 157, 158, 159, 160, 161, 167, 173, 198, 208, 220, 224, 226, 233, 235, 239, 240, 241, 242, 263.

OWNERS

Special thanks to the owners of the vehicles featured in this book for their enthusiastic cooperation.

CHAPTER 2:
Ron Dehler; National Automobile Museum, Reno, Nevada; Len Soifert.

CHAPTER 3: Duke Davenport; Harry & Virginia DeMenge; Bob Erickson; Murray Hall; Maurice W. Ludwig; Sam & Emily Mann; Walter Muncaster; William L. Wilson.

CHAPTER 4: Palmer Carson; Dick & Nancy Harvey; Jim Kelso; Bruce Kennedy; S. Ray Miller Jr.; Jack Pufall; Sam H. Scoles; Ed Shumpert; Mr. & Mrs. Jack K. Tieche; Ron Yori.

CHAPTER 5: Farnum Alston; James K. Buffington; Harry & Virginia DeMenge; Sonny & Marie Glasbrenner; Harrah National Auto Museum; Robert R. Helfenstein; Joseph Leir Memorial Auto Collection; Bill Leonhardt; James Martin; Robert McAtee; Charlie Montano; Joe Moss; Ralph Neubauer; Ray Pfeiffer; Vito S. Ranks; Theodore J. Risch; Jerry Schlorff; Thomas P. Spencer; Bruce R. Thomas; Walter T. Thomas.

CHAPTER 7: Joe Abela; Ed Adams; Robert Bradley; Garfield Button; Robert Carlson; Vincent Daul; Blaine Jenkin; Wayne Kidd; Dr. Roger K. Leir; Ralph G. McQuoid; Robert H. Miller Jr.; Tom Morgan; Dick Pyle; Suburban Motors, Phoenix, Arizona.

CHAPTER 8: Merv Afflerbach; Tom Andrews; Behring Auto Museum; Bill Bost; James Bottger; Bob Brannon; Dwight Cervin; M. Crider; Myron Davis; Harry & Virgina DeMenge; Stanley & Phyllis Dumes; Rich & Norma Felschow; Robert Frumkin; Tim Graves; Bruce Kennedy; Bill Knudsen & John White; Brad & Reda Leasor; Paul A. Leinbohm; Russel A. Liechty; Andrew & Bonita MacFarland; Don Merz; Virgil & Dorthy Meyer; Cal & Lori Middleton; Charlie Montano; John G. Oliver; Monty Ostberg; Bob Porter; Bob Shapiro; James & John Sharp; Dr. John Spring; David L. Studer; Jerry Tranberger; Jeff Walther; Rex N. Yount; Mearl Zeigler.

CHAPTER 9: Mervin Afflerbach; Don Armstrong; Geoff Bonebrake; Richard Brinker; Richard Carpenter; Jim Crossen; Arthur & Suzanne Dalby; Harry & Myron Davis; Harry & Virgina DeMenge; Tom Devers; Alex Dow; Stuart Echols; Galen & Fay Erb; J. Franklin & S. Halloran; Roger & Connie Graeber; David L. Griebling; Stan & Betty Hankins; Ralph Hartsock; Maurice B. Hawa; Paul Hem; Bill Hill; Joe Holles; Art & Vicky Hoock; Marvin & Joan Hughes; Elmer & Shirley Hungate; Vern Hunt; Aaron Kahlenberg; Sherwood Kahlenberg; S. Kallaran & J. Alexander; Jim Kelso; William Lauer & R. McAtee; David Lawrence; Pete McNicholl; Dennis B. Miracky; Jack Moore; Bob & Janet Nitz; Monty Ostberg; Robert W. Paige; Charles Phoenix; Vito S. Ranks; Otto T. Rosenbusch; Dick Roynek; Jess Ruffalo; Jim Scarpitti; Bob Schmidt; Bob & Roni Sue Shapiro; Harold Stabe; Bob Strous; Neil W. Sugg; Joe Twainten; Dean Ullman; Charles Vickery; Jeff & Aleta Wells; Brian H. Williams; Bruce & Judy Wolfe.

CHAPTER 10: Bob Burroughs; Richard Carpenter; Donnie Carr; Bill Craffey; James R. Cunningham; George Dalinis; Myron Davis; J.B. Donaldson; Jack Driesenga; Ray & Lil Elias; Mike Elwood; Warren Emerson; Phil Fair; Paul Garlick; Ben Gipson/Speciality Sales; Ron & Kate Hanaway; Ralph Hartsock; Ward Hartsock; Roy Hawkins; Lloyd W. Hill; Al Houghton; Fred Emerson Huck; Ron Kendall; Guy Mabee; Greg & Rhonda Meredyk; Bob Mosher; Steve Nye/Ken Leighton; Amos Minter; Dr. Kenneth J. Patt; Donald Petty; Joseph Pieroni; Michael Porto; Larry Rohde; Jack Schrum; Ray Shinn; Roy Sklarin; Frank Spittle; Dick Tarnuter/Wisconsin Dells Museum; Keith Thompson; Bill Trnka; Alois Peter Warren.

CHAPTER 11: Jeffery Baker; Ray Banuls; Bill Barnes; Dale Bartholomew; Scott Brubaker; Richard Carpenter; Ed Catricala; Community Trading Center; Robert Costa; Harry & Virginia DeMenge; Tom Devers; Charles P. Geissler; Tony & Suzanne George; Robert Graves; David Griebling; Mike Guffey; Ralph Hartsock; Nick Juliano; Aaron Kahlenberg; Mark Kuykendall; Jim Labertew/R.P.M. Motors; Gregory Langston; Manny Montgomery; Allan S. Murray; Lawrence Pavia; Eric D. Rosynek; Joe L. Saunders; Walter Schenk; Lou Schultz; Duane & Carol Silvius; Nate Struder; Jeff Wentz; William E. Wetherholt.

CHAPTER 12: Larry Bell; Mary Lee Cipriano; Rick Cain; Glenn Cole; Jay Dykes; Joseph Eberle; Al Fraser; Wayne Hartye; Frank Kleptz; Tony Lengacher; Bryan McGilvray; Thom Moerman; David R. Mullett; Andrew Peterson; Richard Petty; Randall W. Renbarger; Odus West.

CHAPTER 13: William Korbel; Vince Manocchi; Doug Schliesser.

CHAPTER 14: Ann C. Coffin.

CONTENTS

Chapter 9
Flash and Substance; The Exner Era: 1955-59 . . . page 136

Chrysler Corporation sales plummet in 1954, but stylist Virgil Exner has the remedy for '55: the "Forward Look." In 1957, it's flash, fins, Torsion-Aire ride, TorqueFlite automatic—plus quality lapses and rust-prone bodies.

Chapter 10
From Compacts to Turbines: 1960-64 . . . page 170

Conflict of interest charges rock Chrysler's executive suite, and bizarre styling hurts sales. But Unibody construction, popular compact cars, a 5-year/50,000-mile warranty, and improved styling help reverse the decline.

Chapter 11
Big Cars & Muscle Cars Keep Chrysler Vibrant: 1965-68 . . . page 202

Pontiac starts the muscle-car war, but hot Hemi-powered intermediate Dodges and Plymouths take a back seat to no one. Elwood Engel works his styling magic on Chrysler's full-size fleet—and sales shoot upward.

Chapter 12
Best of the Breed; The Muscle Era Fades: 1969-73 . . . page 230

Muscle-car mania peaks, and quickly fades as the feds impose ever-stricter emissions and safety mandates. The ponycar market likewise sputters. No matter, Chrysler sales boom in 1973—until the OPEC oil embargo arrives.

Chapter 13
Downhill Skid in Perilous Times: 1974-78 . . . page 258

Chrysler enjoys a few successes, such as the Cordoba personal-luxury coupe, but competition and the cost of meeting federal standards erodes profits. Despite new front-drive subcompacts, Chrysler's future looks iffy.

Chapter 14
Iacocca to the Rescue: 1979-83 . . . page 286

With bankruptcy looming, Chrysler hires Lee Iacocca, recently fired by Henry Ford II. Government-guaranteed loans are sought—and granted in 1980. Chrysler stakes its future on fuel-efficient, front-wheel-drive cars.

Chapter 15
Minivans Help Create a New Chrysler: 1984-87 . . . page 322

With its loans paid off, a now-prospering Chrysler gambles on a K-car-based, garagable minivan—and hits pay dirt. Meanwhile, the firm spends much of its profits to diversify, at the expense of needed new-car programs.

Chapter 16
Searching for a Fresh Direction: 1988-92 . . . page 348

After taking over American Motors in 1987, and facing declining sales in 1988 (that would last into the '90s), Chrysler begins to shed off its earlier acquisitions to again concentrate on its core automotive business.

Chapter 17
Beyond Rebirth; Taking Aim at Tomorrow: 1993-96 . . . page 390

Having relied on the K-car too long, Chrysler moves into the Nineties with a focus on new products, led off by the high-profile Dodge Viper sports car, soon followed by the award-winning "LH" sedans—with much more to come.

Foreword

Change is a constant in life. It's certainly been true for my years in the automobile business. Yet one thing about Chrysler Corporation has remained the same throughout its distinguished 70-year history: a tradition of innovation and technical leadership for building better cars and trucks.

Walter P. Chrysler began that tradition with his very first car, the 1924 Chrysler Six. Boasting America's first affordable high-compression engine, it established the reputation for superior engineering that Chrysler still enjoys today. Many more innovations followed: "Floating Power" engine mounts, "Safety-Rim" wheels, the fabled hemi-head V-8 engine, torsion-bar suspension, and TorqueFlite automatic transmission, to name but a few. Today, that tradition of engineering excellence continues in our pioneering "Cab Forward" cars, as well as our new Dodge Ram trucks, the enormously popular Jeep Grand Cherokee, and our trail-blazing minivans.

But engineering alone, no matter how good, isn't always enough. To be successful, any new car or truck must offer superior value and unquestioned quality, especially these days. Here too, Chrysler Corporation has long shown the way, from the very first four-cylinder Plymouth—rugged, stylish, and priced right for "hard times"—to today's Neon, by any measure a world-class small car that's got the whole world talking because it represents such extraordinary value.

Of course, times *do* change, and with them, vehicle makers and their products. Nowhere is this more apparent than at Chrysler, which is now very different from the company it was even a few years ago. Neon provides a dramatic example. A key reason that Neon offers such high value is because of the rigorous efforts that have made Chrysler the most efficient vehicle producer in the world—which means we can deliver more car for less money than just about anyone else. That, in turn, reflects our development of platform teams, which not only enables us to respond to customer needs faster than ever, but assures that high quality is built into a vehicle even as it is being designed. We've also taken our commitment to quality directly to the public with efforts like our new Customer One program.

But let's not forget excitement—another Chrysler tradition, as you'll see in this book. From the legendary "Letter-Series" 300s of the Fifties through the awesome Chargers and Road Runners of the Sixties, and on to today's Viper—which has already become a legend in its own right—Chrysler history is full of cars with high performance and a style all their own.

This book chronicles Chrysler's past, but I'm happy to say that Chrysler's future has never looked brighter than it does right now. Reaching this point hasn't been easy, but it does make for a fascinating story I'm sure you'll enjoy.

Meanwhile, all of us at Chrysler will be working hard on vehicles that will write exciting new success stories for a future edition. Take it from me, the best part of the "Chrysler chronicle" is still to come.

Robert J. Eaton
Chairman and Chief Executive Officer
Chrysler Corporation

I'm often referred to as a "car guy," and it's true: I love cars. I also love the auto business, and as president of Chrysler Corporation, I think I've got one of the best jobs in the world.

But though I may be one of Chrysler's more visible car guys, I'm certainly not the only one. Today there are literally thousands of enthusiastic men and women, car lovers all, who are creating the vehicles that are driving this company toward a great future.

Yet such high enthusiasm is nothing new at Chrysler. In fact, this company's reputation for engineering leadership was forged by people with a passion for cars—starting with Walter P. Chrysler himself. Trained on the great Midwestern railroads, he recognized the importance of sound engineering and constant self-improvement. So it's really no surprise that he carried those passions with him into the automobile business, especially when he founded Chrysler Corporation some 70 years ago. His devotion to excellence is still part of everything we do.

That's not to say that Walter Chrysler didn't have a sense of style. Far from it. The magnificent custom-bodied Imperials of the early Thirties have long been bona fide Classics, and later Chrysler products like the handsome Town & Country models of the 1940s and the race-winning 300s of the 1950s and '60s have become highly valued collector's items.

But that's what a heritage of excellence can do, and it's reflected in products like our 1995 Chrysler Cirrus and Dodge Stratus with their world-class handling, performance, quality, and value, plus remarkable interior space and unmistakable "Cab Forward" design. In fact, these cars are so good that they started winning awards even before they went on sale. But lately that's become part of the Chrysler heritage, too, as witness the Chrysler LHS, Eagle Vision, Chrysler Concorde, Dodge Intrepid, Jeep Grand Cherokee, and Dodge Ram pickups—not to mention the car everyone's trying to beat these days, the Dodge and Plymouth Neon.

Of course, this book is mostly about Chrysler's past. I wish it could be about the future, for I believe this company's best years still lie ahead. We certainly have all the ingredients for continued high success, including one of the leanest, most efficient organizations in the business, state-of-the-art manufacturing facilities, and designers and engineers who are second to none. Then there are our multi-discipline "platform teams," which bring design, engineering, manufacturing, and marketing people together—and with our customers—to plan for success. And, do they achieve it. The latest examples are our new second-generation minivans, which raise the standard for a field we created over 10 years ago.

But then, innovations like the minivan, platform teams, and Cab Forward are also nothing new for Chrysler, as you'll see in this book. I'm sure you'll enjoy it, because reading about the past is always fun for "car people"—when we're not too busy building an even better future. That's what we've been doing at Chrysler, and we've only just begun.

Robert A. Lutz
President and Chief Operating Officer
Chrysler Corporation

Chapter 1

Walter P. Chrysler: Craftsman and Competitor

After beginning his career in railroad yards, Walter P. Chrysler became one of the giants of the emerging auto industry. As a spirited boy growing up in the Midwest, he learned the value of hard work—and the virtues of being tough.

In the latter part of the 19th century, America produced a small legion of uncommon men. Born to modest means, each of them rose to fame and power in the business world—mainly by dint of hard work and fortitude, ambition and aptitude.

Walter P. Chrysler may be seen as a virtual prototype of the breed. Emerging from a humble childhood on the plains, he nevertheless ascended to a lofty perch among home-brewed, all-American tycoons. Eventually, he would head one of the giants in the growing automotive field—one that proudly bore his own name. As Christy Borth later wrote, "Chrysler has been called a jack of all trades. What made him different was that he was also a master of them."

Born in 1875, son of an engineer for the Union Pacific Railroad, Walter Percy Chrysler grew up on a farm near Ellis, Kansas. As a boy, he sold surplus milk door-to-door, worked in a grocery store—even hawked calling cards and silverware. Curious and observant, he took an early interest in machinery. An avid reader of *Scientific American* magazine, he learned a great deal about the steam engines that were repaired in the shops near his home.

Following high-school graduation, Walter started worklife as a sweeper in those Union Pacific shops, where he could watch and learn. In 1892, he began an apprenticeship as a machinist, achieving journeyman status in 1895. Before long, Walter was honing his mechanical skills on railroads across the Midwest.

"Being a machinist," Walter Chrysler explained in his autobiography, "I have always wanted to know how things work." While working for the Chicago Great Western Railroad, he traveled to Chicago often, and in 1908 happened upon an auto show. "On the running board" of a Locomobile on display, he later wrote, "there was a handsome tool box that my fingers itched to open. . . . I spent four days hanging around the show, held by that automobile as by a siren's song."

Walter was determined to buy that white $5000 Locomobile. Lacking such a princely sum, he managed—with the aid of a co-signer—to secure a $4300 loan (without collateral) via Ralph Van Vechten, of Chicago's Continental Bank.

After shipping his acquisition home to Iowa (by rail), Walter tinkered with the new motorcar in his spare time. He yearned to study how its parts were manufactured: what its materials were, which methods were used to produce them, and how each component was machined. Chrysler disassembled the engine many times before taking his first ride in the car.

Chrysler foresaw that railroading had passed its peak, and would not continue to be a growth industry. Automobiles—that was the future, awash with limitless possibilities. As he said later, "The auto-

Chrysler's unassuming boyhood home at Ellis, Kansas (above), has been preserved—including the white picket fence. His father built this residence around 1889, when Walter was 14. In this rough railroad town, he had to be adept with his fists as well as his mind. Left: In addition to baseball exploits, Walter was "the local champion" marble shooter in his youth.

mobile provided flexible, economical, individual transportation . . . for either business or pleasure. . . . To me it was the transportation of the future."

Fiercely competitive, Walter was known for his short temper and rough-hewn persona. He'd learned to curse on the railroad, and carried that image for the rest of his days. Yet, he also loved some of the finer things in life,

notably music. In fact, he'd met his wife Della—with whom he was destined to spend a lifetime—at a music class, marrying in 1901.

Chrysler left the railroad in 1910 to become plant manager for the American Locomotive Company, in Pittsburgh. Around that time, he bought another automobile: a six-cylinder Stevens-Duryea.

One day, Walter got a call from a Boston banker named James J. Storrow. Not only did Storrow serve on American Locomotive's board, he also happened to be president of General Motors, which had been formed in 1909. Aware of Chrysler's capabilities, Storrow encouraged him to contact Charles W. Nash, then Buick's president, with an eye to a post in the automotive business.

American Locomotive, meanwhile, had raised Walter's salary to $12,000 a year. But he was tempted—and accepted Nash's invitation to visit the Buick factory at Flint, Michigan. Nash was impressed by Chrysler's record and ideas for production improvements, offering him a job as plant manager. Chrysler couldn't resist, and even agreed to a 50-percent pay cut from his current salary. After all, he'd been waiting patiently for just such an opportunity, and couldn't let dollars stand in the way.

Chrysler proved himself at Buick, where he started a program of cost estimation—an idea familiar in the locomotive field, but new to the auto industry. He also boosted efficiency, even setting up a track to serve as a crude—but effective—version of mass production.

Nash was named president of General Motors in November 1912. But since he also retained the same post at Buick, Chrysler was effectively blocked from rising to the top there.

Though never offered a raise from his initial salary, Walter knew he was a valuable man—and worth far more. One day in 1915, he tromped into Nash's office and demanded $25,000 a year. He

got it, too, and indicated that he'd expect twice that sum the next year.

Late in 1915, it became clear that William C. Durant—who'd founded General Motors, but then lost it—was a sure bet to regain control once again. Both Chrysler and Charles Nash wanted to leave the GM fold if that happened. Nash did depart, taking over the Thomas B. Jeffery Company.

Chrysler, meanwhile, chose to stick it out at General Motors. He became president of Buick (and in 1919, a GM vice-president), taking home some half-million dollars a year in cash and stocks. Among other forward-thinking moves, he recommended that GM obtain ample

interest in the Fisher Body company. With 60 percent of that firm's stock, they were assured of a continuous supply of bodies.

Chrysler ran Buick for three years, but fought with Durant much of the time—mainly because Durant refused to keep his hands off the Buick operation, despite Walter's threats to leave if he interfered. After boosting the company's output dramatically, Walter Chrysler left in March 1920, when his contract term ended.

For a brief period, Chrysler went without a job, although this was no great loss since he'd gained wealth as well as experience at Buick. Soon, James C. Brady and Ralph Van Vechten—the man responsible for loaning Walter money to buy that 1908 Locomobile—came calling. They asked Chrysler to take over as head of Willys-Overland. His reward: a $750,000 salary, plus extras that put total compensation over a million.

Formerly second only to Ford in production, Willys-Overland was by then one of several seemingly sinking ships in the auto industry, and $46 million in debt. Walter soon whittled that down to $18 million. His success in resuscitating Willys' fortunes, marked by rigorous cost-cutting, led to his reputation as a "company doctor" skilled at reviving sick corporations.

The Chalmers Motor Company in Detroit (above) boasted extensive facilities, some-what embellished here. "The Good Maxwell" of 1921 (below) wasn't all that different from its predecessor, but Walter P. knew he needed to improve the make's reputation.

Chalmers cars hadn't changed much since 1916. However, this '23 sedan (above) adopted four-wheel hydraulic brakes. Alas, Chalmers was about to expire, as the Chrysler badge moved to center stage. This $885 Model 25 Touring (right) was the most popular "Good Maxwell" in 1922. Maxwells came in six body styles, including a new Club Sedan and Club Coupe. They would soon be joined by a Sport Touring, Sport Roadster, and Travel Sedan. All rode the same 109-inch wheelbase. The windshield (below) opened on the four-passenger coupe. Regular and Sport Maxwell roadsters (below right) held just two passengers.

While at Willys, Walter Chrysler made one of those acquaintances that come only once in a lifetime. Three of them, actually: Fred M. Zeder, Owen Skelton, and Carl Breer. The threesome then toiled in New Jersey as consulting engineers for Willys-Overland's new-car projects, and were readying a concept for a new technically advanced, mid-priced six-cylinder automobile.

In the spring of 1921, Chrysler assumed the chairmanship of the faltering Maxwell and Chalmers organizations (in addition to his duties for Willys-Overland). Named for Jonathan Dixon Maxwell (who'd helped Elwood Haynes build his first motorcar in 1893) and Benjamin Briscoe, the Maxwell-Briscoe had entered production in 1904.

By 1908-09, after an ill-fated attempt to join Buick and create the United States Motor Company (shortly before Buick became part of the fledgling General Motors group), Maxwell-Briscoe ranked third in production. After gobbling up several small automakers, U.S. Motor appeared to be on the road to becoming an industry power, but Briscoe's empire collapsed during 1912. Walter E. Flanders, a well-known manufacturing man, was tapped to run the failed Maxwell company. By 1915, Maxwell reached sixth place in output, just behind Dodge and Studebaker.

Expansion came in 1917, as Flanders established a tie to the Chalmers Motor Car company. Both Maxwell and mid-priced Chalmers models were produced

on the same line, in Highland Park, Michigan—destined to become Chrysler's corporate headquarters. The six-cylinder Chalmers Model 6-30, introduced in 1916, ranks as the direct predecessor of the first Chrysler.

By late 1918, Flanders was gone and W. Ledyard Mitchell served as Maxwell's president. Before long, quality problems nearly killed the company. Bankers wanted Walter P. Chrysler to step in, but he was still busy bailing out Willys-Overland.

When Chrysler took the helm at Maxwell, he faced $26 million in debt and a stockpile of 26,000 unsold cars. Making a bold move, he ordered every car returned to the plant for axle reinforcements, then sold each one at a

small ($5) profit. The improved cars were promoted as "The Good Maxwell," a brash attempt to convince the buying public that quality woes—especially axle weaknesses—were behind them.

Late in 1922, following bankruptcy court battles by both companies, Maxwell and Chalmers finally merged. By then, Maxwell was selling well and making money. Chalmers was not, and faced liquidation in 1923. For its final season, the Chalmers carried four-wheel hydraulic brakes—adapted by Zeder, Skelton, and Breer from the system patented by Malcolm Loughead (known commercially as Lockheed) in 1919, first used on the 1922 Duesenberg.

Meanwhile, the Willys Corporation had slipped into receivership and liqui-

dation, but its Willys-Overland division continued to turn out cars—and soon earned a profit again. Zeder, Skelton, and Breer, newly incorporated as a group of consulting engineers, had continued work on a "light six" project. By a quirk of fate, that car wound up in the hands of William Durant, entering production as the Flint.

What Walter Chrysler truly wanted was an automobile under his own name. Zeder, Skelton, and Breer kept at their goal of designing a six-cylinder engine for such a car. In April 1923, they had one ready for dynamometer testing, and called Chrysler in to observe. Walter was ready, and insisted he had to have five experimental cars running by September.

With plenty of experience behind him— having helped save other automakers— Walter P. Chrysler (at home in 1924) was now ready to go it on his own.

Working in Detroit, the three engineers managed to finish one car by deadline. In November, the first "Chrysler" phaeton was driving east, ending up at Walter Chrysler's Long Island home. A month later, Chryslers were rolling off the assembly line at Highland Park.

Some men and women crave power. Others demand wealth, allegiance, veneration. Walter Chrysler wanted to build cars. At last, he was about to achieve the pinnacle of his dream.

13

Chapter 2

Start-Up and Expansion: 1924-29

When the first Chryslers rolled off the line in 1924, Ford still led the American automotive pack, capturing a whopping 55 percent of the market. The Model T Ford's days may have been numbered, but it was still running strong—though GM's Chevrolet, in second place, was beginning to nip at Ford's heels. Rounding out the top five in production were Dodge, Willys-Overland, and Buick.

Engineering was priority Number One for Walter Chrysler's new automobile. Prominence in that area would help his emerging company establish a laudable reputation, and rise rapidly to become the final member of America's "Big Three" automakers.

To guarantee top engineering from the outset, Chrysler employed the talents of the three experts he'd met during his stint at Willys-Overland: Fred Zeder, Owen Skelton, and Carl Breer. They had begun the project while still at work in New Jersey, but moved to Highland Park, Michigan, where the Chrysler would be built. Known fondly as the "Three Musketeers," the Z-S-B trio would dominate Chrysler industrial design through the Thirties.

Walter himself supplied the basic requirements for the first vehicle to bear his own name. Simply put, he wanted a car on a 110-inch wheelbase, weighing about 2600 pounds, and capable of at least 60-mph speeds. On July 31, 1923, barely 60 days after its design had been approved, a running prototype was ready. Shakedown tests over the next five weeks covered 25,000 miles, around the Allegheny Mountains.

If Walter Chrysler was ready for the marketplace, it wasn't quite prepared for him. Allegedly denied entry into the New York Automobile Show in January 1924—because his car wasn't yet in production—Chrysler set up a display at the nearby Hotel Commodore. (In fact, several other manufacturers also exhibited there.) For days, the hotel lobby was packed with visitors, some of whom just might be able to help with the $5 million needed to begin production. B.E. "Hutch" Hutchinson, Chrysler's esteemed financial advisor, managed to induce one of those guests—R. Edward Tinker, of Chase Security—to underwrite debenture bonds in the required sum.

Now Walter had the car *and* the money to get his own ball rolling. The touring car seen in New York carried a price tag just $40 above the popular Buick 24-45. That was the market Chrysler wanted to crack, a crowded but potentially rewarding segment that also included the Auburn Six, Hupmobile R-series, Nash Advanced Six, G-series Reo, and Studebaker Special Six.

Though attractive, the '24 Chrysler didn't look dramatically different from the competition. Oliver H. Clark, responsible for body design, later admitted that its "shape just sort of happened." Even so, Clark had based the design on eye-pleasing shapes, observing the principle of graduated panel

Introduced in mid-year 1928, the new Plymouth gave Chrysler an entrée into the low-price field, dominated for so long by Ford, and now Chevrolet.

widths (larger at the bottom).

Under the hood lay the new car's greatest goodies: namely, the new six-cylinder engine, designed and built with little regard to cost. Here, at least, Chrysler and the Z-S-B triumvirate permitted no compromises. A dependable, highly regarded powertrain was vital if Chrysler was to attain his goal of becoming a top player in the soon-to-shake-out automotive arena.

Walter told dealers that "the public has a definite idea of a real quality light car—one not extravagantly large and heavy for one or two people but adequately roomy for five, economical to own and operate." His Chrysler also would have "quick getaway, flashing pickup, power to conquer any hill." All that, plus "simplicity and accessibility throughout."

The high-compression, 201-cubic-inch L-head six, with its crankshaft running in seven main bearings, developed 68 horsepower. That translated to 0.3 horsepower per cubic inch—a phenomenal ratio in the Twenties. Hardly an exotic engine, it featured a detachable cylinder head, water pump, and vacuum fuel feed. In addition to cheaper production costs, the L-head configuration would result in quieter running than an overhead-valve design.

The top selling point wasn't the engine, but the four-wheel Lockheed hydraulic brakes. Though used on some Chalmers models in 1923, and first seen on the Duesenberg Model A in 1922, hydraulic halting was still a rarity. Hydraulic lines filled with fluid gave balanced braking force distribution—far beyond the capabilities of the usual mechanical systems, with their tangle of rods and wires.

George W. Mason, later to become head of Nash-Kelvinator, earned responsibility for overseeing production. Six body styles were authorized, ranging from the $1335 touring car up to a $2195 Crown Imperial. That Imperial badge would later draw distinction on its own.

Chrysler's goal of a 60-mph top speed proved conservative. The cars were actually capable of 70 mph, and proved their prowess at speed demonstrations around the country. In 1925, for instance, Ralph de Palma won the 1000-mile stock-car speed trials at Culver City, California. Another Chrysler even ran at the famed Le Mans track in France.

By the end of 1924, only 19,960 Chryslers had been registered to owners, but many more lurked in the pipeline. The company had produced a grand total of 79,144 automobiles this year, though the majority were Maxwells.

Walter Chrysler now had two choices: stay on as head of Maxwell and look forward to a comfortable retirement, or go all the way, turning it into a new Chrysler Corporation. Unable to take the "easy way," or to delay bold moves, he

opted for the latter, strongly supported by Hutch Hutchinson.

Even though 1924 profits were sufficient to pay off the indebtedness that made the first Chrysler possible, Walter lacked the funds to make the full commitment. Maxwell Motors Corporation, after all, was capitalized at some $40 million—well beyond his admittedly substantial personal wealth. To make the move, he sold his GM holdings, raised $15 million from bankers, and with the help of friend Harry Bronner bought out Maxwell's assets. The car, and the company, were now fully under Chrysler's control.

For 1926, Chrysler fielded a three-tier lineup, led by the six-cylinder G-70, but adding a four-cylinder "58" to replace the Maxwell. The Model 58 came in five body styles, and at $890 to $1095, was priced below the final Maxwells. A costly, more powerful Imperial also joined the line, giving Chrysler a response to Cadillac—and Packard and Peerless. Offering prestige, but not big profits, Imperials were the top-of-the-line Chryslers, but not a separate division (until much later). The Imperial E-80 came in six styles on a choice of three wheelbases (120, 127, and 133 inches), priced from $2645 to $3695.

Chrysler earned a healthy $17.4 million net profit in 1926, the year that General Motors acquired the Fisher Body coachworks. That meant Chrysler would have to turn to Hayes and Briggs for its bodies, but the company also was building its own now.

Production passed 182,000 units in 1927, again good enough for seventh place in industry rankings, as Chrysler offered a four-series lineup. A four-cylinder Series 50 starting at $750 served as predecessor to what would soon become Plymouth, while the new "60" carried a six-cylinder engine but a price tag more fitting for a four ($1075 to $1295).

Several automakers in the low-priced field had been flirting hard with fours—not always successfully. Others focused their attentions on six-cylinder engines. Walter P. would have both. Chrysler finished the year fifth in the sales race (seventh in production), though overall growth had slowed appreciably.

If you can't beat 'em, buy 'em. That could have been Walter Chrysler's attitude toward Dodge, a make that had been started in 1914 by brothers Horace and John (both of whom died in 1920). For all those years, the Dodge car had clung to traditional values of practicality and value, disdaining sportiness. That standard would continue under Chrysler rule. Dodge's reputation for dependability had been cemented back in 1916, when famed U.S. Army General John J. Pershing commanded a fleet of 250 touring cars during the Mexican border campaign against Pancho Villa.

A profitable concern with an impressive product, Dodge Brothers was in the

hands of bankers who would be pleased to sell—and Chrysler was the only logical buyer. Talks had begun in 1926. Dodges had been four-cylinder only, but the first six, a 241.5-cid L-head, was announced for 1928.

In June, the ink was dry on Chrysler's takeover. Chrysler gained not only the ample Dodge sales network, but also a foundry and forge, eliminating the need to go to outside suppliers for engine blocks and cylinder heads. Chrysler's assets, including the Dodge plant at Hamtramck, Michigan, now approached half a billion dollars.

Dodge was only the beginning of Walter Chrysler's expansion in 1928. At mid-year, he announced two brand-new makes, DeSoto and Plymouth. At last, he could offer a linear progression of models, from low-cost Plymouths to premium Chryslers.

DeSoto was initially the step-up from Plymouth in price, power, and size. Dodge ranked higher than DeSoto, but their positions would be reversed by the mid-Thirties.

Sales manager Joseph W. Frazer suggested the Plymouth name for Chrysler's low-priced make. Walter wasn't sure customers would make the connection to the Pilgrim settlement in Massachusetts, but Frazer insisted: "Every goddam farmer in America's heard of Plymouth Binder Twine." Either way, Plymouth soon would become the glue that held the Chrysler organization together.

To demonstrate his faith in Plymouth as a low-budget contender ($670 to $725 the first year), Chrysler drove the third car off the assembly line over to Ford headquarters in nearby Dearborn, Michigan. There, he presented the car to Henry Ford and son Edsel, who warned Walter of the perils in the low-priced arena.

Chrysler was now a full-fledged multi-make manufacturer, ready to attack the "Big Two" for sales. Many automakers now offered "companion" makes, including the new Marquette from Buick and Viking from Oldsmobile. Chrysler had a *trio* of companions, eager to attract customers at every price level. At the very top, semi-custom Imperial bodies were available on special order—cherished classics today.

More than 80,000 DeSotos went to customers by the end of its first full year of production, and Plymouth ranked 10th in output. Overall corporate sales rose a bit in 1929, though not as much as the industry in general. Then, in October, came the crash heard 'round the world. Wall Street had collapsed, and the Great Depression had begun—even if no one knew it quite yet. Optimistically, construction had begun on the 77-story Chrysler Building in New York City, but before long new automobiles would be the last things on most people's minds.

1924

Maxwell-Chalmers Corporation introduces the first Chrysler automobile

Features include Lockheed four-wheel hydraulic brakes and a high-compression (4.7:1) engine

The six-cylinder Chrysler draws praise from auto show visitors

An L-head engine features full-pressure lubrication, air cleaner/ silencer, replaceable-element oil filter

Maxwell continues in production; Chalmers fades into oblivion

More than 32,000 Chryslers are produced in 1924

19,960 Chryslers are registered during the calendar year, plus 44,006 Maxwells and 2003 Chalmers automobiles (for total of 65,969)

Ford's Model T retains its stranglehold on the market, with a 55-percent share; General Motors ranks second with 17 percent

Ralph de Palma wins July's Mount Wilson hill climb in a Chrysler, beating the former racing-car record. He also drives a Chrysler 1000 miles in 1007 minutes—averaging nearly 60 miles an hour

The first Chryslers are seen by the public in January

A full line of nine body styles goes on sale

Walter P. Chrysler shows off the first car (*top*) to bear his name, introduced to the public early in 1924. Note the winged radiator cap on this two-door Brougham. Powered by a high-compression, 201-cid, inline L-head six, B-Series Chryslers came in six body styles. Imperials served at the top end of the line. Walter Chrysler (*above*) poses with a prototype for the 1924 B-Series. The first prototype began road-testing in the summer of 1923. Production models switched to chrome radiator shells. First seen on 1924 models, the Chrysler badge (*right*) would soon become a familiar sight on American roads.

Could this early sedan (*above*) have set the stage for Chrysler's flamboyant three-tone paint jobs of the Fifties? Initially named B-Series, Chryslers soon adopted a B-70 designation to denote the car's top speed. Wood-spoke wheels were typical in the Twenties, and sun visors were popular on closed cars. The lowest-priced B-Series Chrysler was the $1335 touring car. This one (*left*) is identified as "Number One." Closed bodies cost considerably more. Four-wheel hydraulic brakes were a strong selling point, and shock absorbers were standard on all Chrysler models.

Chrysler's L-head six, "The Power Plant" (*above*), was considered the first high-compression engine to enter serious production. With a 3.00-inch bore and 4.75-inch stroke, the motor developed 68 horsepower at 3000 rpm. From the start, Chrysler engines (*right*) had full-pressure lubrication, air cleaner, and an oil filter. Note the horn at rear, the Ball & Ball carburetor, and high-mounted distributor.

Dressier and heavier than a touring car, the B-Series phaeton (*top*) sold for $1395, including courtesy lights and leather "paint-savers" atop each door. All Chryslers rode a 112.75-inch wheelbase, measuring 160 inches overall. Running-board step plates (*above*), standard on the phaeton, were a popular "luxury" in the Twenties. Production took place on the same assembly line that had previously turned out Chalmers models. *Right:* Zeder, Breer, and Skelton—Chrysler's "Three Musketeers" of engineering—earned credit for the B-Series engine, which utilized a detachable cylinder head. Its 4.7:1 compression ratio helped deliver a top speed past 70 mph. Note the large vacuum tank at the cowl. Like most American cars of its day (except Ford), Chryslers featured a three-speed gearbox and semi-elliptic leaf springs front and rear. The instrument panel held a speedometer, ammeter, gas and oil gauges, and a "radimeter."

Walter Chrysler in 1924 offered a near full-line of automobiles wearing his name, including this $1525 early B-Series roadster (*left*). Despite the emergence of Chrysler as a major player in the mid-price marketplace, Maxwell and Chalmers automobiles remained available for a time. In fact, the four-cylinder Maxwell line expanded for 1924. Chalmers cars, on the other hand, were leftovers from the prior year.

1924 Production

Total for all models	32,000 *
* Estimated	

1924 Engine Availability

No. Cyl.	Disp., cid	bhp	Availability
I-6	201.0	68	S-all

Walter P. Chrysler (*above*) and Fred Zeder are shown shaking hands in front of a $1795 Chrysler Brougham, a two-door coach. Closed sedans included shades for both the back and rear-quarter windows. Famed racing driver Joe Boyer (*right*) took the wheel of this early production Chrysler rumble-seat roadster, whose 29 x 4½-inch tires sat on five-lug wheels. Other body styles might have 30 x 5¾-inch rubber, on six-lug rims. Roadsters sold for $1515, plus the price of such extras as bumpers, wind wings, and running-board step plates. Two-tone paint schemes also were optional, even in the early years.

19

1925

The Maxwell-Chalmers firm is reorganized as Chrysler Corporation on June 6, 1925

Walter P. Chrysler is named president and chairman of Chrysler Corporation, with B.F. Hutchinson as vice-president/treasurer. Joe Fields is sales vice-president, Fred Zeder heads engineering

This is the last year for the Maxwell automobile

Chrysler Canada is organized

An expanded lineup includes the new Royal Coupe

Engines employ a new friction-driven vibration damper

A Chrysler competes in the renowned 24-hour Le Mans race

Some 68,793 Chryslers are registered during 1925, plus 36,236 Maxwells

A total of 132,343 Chrysler/Maxwell automobiles are produced

Chrysler earns more than $17 million for the year

Engines sit on a floating spring, to reduce vibration

By year's end, 3800 dealers are handling Chryslers

Walter Chrysler chooses to charge ahead, selling his GM holdings to raise cash

Chrysler's costliest regular-production sedan was the $2195 Crown Imperial (*top*). Note the oval opera window and landau bar at the rear quarter, which was covered by leather or fabric. Not only does this $1625 Chrysler roadster (*center*) wear two-tone paint, it sports such extras as wind wings and bumpers. All Chryslers now were known as Series B-70. The $1895 Royal coupe (*above*) included a rumble seat, golf bag door, and leather-covered rear quarters with landau bars.

Touring cars (*above*) didn't last long in Walter P. Chrysler's 1925 lineup, but the better-equipped phaeton continued to attract customers. Disc wheels were standard. Both open models now used a one-piece windshield. Walter P. Chrysler (*below*), K.T. Keller, and Fred Zeder stand with a Chrysler coupe.

In mid-1925, Chrysler introduced a four-cylinder Series 58 (*above*) to augment its six-cylinder models. Essentially an update of the former Maxwell, it retained that make's 109-inch wheelbase, but updated the engine. Series 58 prices began at $890 for the two-seat roadster and $895 for the touring car. Bumpers and wind wings cost extra. The upgraded four-cylinder engine (*right*) displaced 185.8 cubic inches and produced 38 horsepower. Early Series 58 cars had mechanical rear-wheel brakes, but hydraulically activated rear binders became standard after the end of 1925. Front wheels had no brakes at all. *Below:* Six-cylinder Chryslers enjoyed several mechanical improvements for 1925, including a friction-driven vibration damper on the engine, which rested on rubber mounts and a floating front platform. Chrysler purchased the Kercheval Body Company and began to produce its own bodies during 1925, forsaking the services of the Fisher organization.

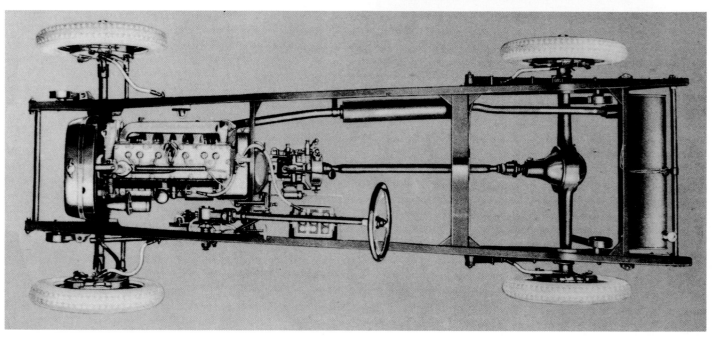

By 1925, Dodge had been in business for a decade, producing America's fifth best-selling car line. Formal bodies (*right*) went to a handful of customers. Three years hence, Dodge would be part of Chrysler. Like other models, the Dodge roadster (*center*) had a 24-horsepower four-cylinder engine. This Dodge seven-passenger sedan (*bottom*) sported slanted oval quarter windows.

1925 Production
Total for all models 76,600 *
* Estimated

1925 Engine Availability

No. Cyl.	Disp., cid	bhp	Availability
I-6	201.0	68	S-all

1925 DODGE

1926

1926 Imperial E-80
five-seat phaeton

The Maxwell nameplate is gone; the four-cylinder car is renamed Chrysler 58, marketed alongside the six-cylinder G-70

A new distinctively styled, higher-priced Imperial carries a more powerful 288-cid six-cylinder motor

An Imperial can top 80 mph in sustained driving

Floyd Clymer drives a stock Chrysler Imperial from Denver to Kansas City, averaging an amazing 51.8 mph for the day

An Imperial roadster paces the Indianapolis 500 race on Memorial Day

The regular six-cylinder engine grows to 218.6 cid and 68 horsepower

Eight bodies are offered for the G-70, priced from $1395 to $2095

Some 162,242 Chryslers are built during 1926—good enough for seventh place in the industry

Chrysler still ranks well behind Buick and Dodge

Kaufman Thuma "K.T." Keller resigns from GM to become vice-president of Chrysler manufacturing

The S.A. Chrysler plant opens in Antwerp, Belgium

Series 58 comes in five body styles, priced below the now-departed Maxwell

A new 92-horsepower, 288-cid six-cylinder engine let the Imperial E-80 phaeton (*top*) cruise at 74 mph. By 1926, the Maxwell-derived Chrysler Series 58 coupe (*center*) halted with hydraulic brakes. Two-tone paint, wire wheels, and bullet-shaped headlights helped give this Imperial roadster (*above*) a flashy look.

In Chrysler's G-70 series, priced half as high as Imperial, a two-door coach (*left*) cost $1445. For $420 more, the similarly structured Brougham had smaller rear quarter windows and landau bars. Most popular of the eight models in the G-70 line—which outsold the cheaper four-cylinder Chryslers—was the phaeton, which adopted adjustable front seats during the year. Just $895 bought a Chrysler 58 touring car (*below*). Closed cars wore "cadet" sun visors above a one-pane windshield, but open models used two-piece swing-out glass. Chryslers could be identified by their Viking hood ornament.

1926 Production

Series 58	81,089
Series G-70	72,039
Series E-80 Imperial	9,114
Total	162,242

1926 Engine Availability

No. Cyl.	Disp., cid	bhp	Availability
I-4	185.8	38	S-Series 58
I-6	218.6	68	S-Series G-70
I-6	288.0	92	S-Series E-80

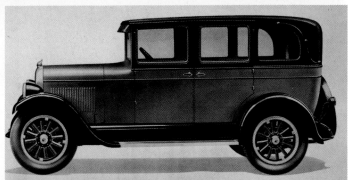

A true four-passenger model, the $3195 Imperial five-window coupe (*above*) seated all occupants inside. Chrysler's four-cylinder "58" evolved into the "52" (*above right*). The $1695 G-70 four-door (*below*) weighed 3060 pounds.

1927

Under K.T. Keller's guidance, Chrysler plants are turning out about 4000 cars per week

Four series are fielded for 1927: the four-cylinder 50, a "Finer 70," Imperial 80, plus a new budget-priced 60

Finer 70 bodies are modernized modestly; an attractive rumble-seat coupe is added to the line

A new five-passenger Imperial Town Car is available on special order, at a whopping $5495

Engineer Carl Breer begins to study auto-related aerodynamics, which will lead to the Airflow design

Chrysler builds 182,195 cars, compared to Dodge's 146,000; Buick is still well ahead with 255,160 units

An annual growth rate of 19 percent lags behind the prior year's 57 percent

Stockholders get $10 million in dividends

Dodge abandons four-cylinder models; it's poised for sale to Chrysler Corporation in 1928

Chrysler Motors Limited begins operations in Britain

Series 50, on a shortened wheelbase, foretells the soon-to-come Plymouth

Series 60 carries a smaller version of the 70's engine

Above: Regular, Sport, and Custom Sport phaetons were part of the "Finer 70" Chrysler lineup, which replaced the former Series 70. *Right:* An oval instrument panel in the 70 held a simple layout of gauges and controls. *Below:* Even rumble-seat riders had their own fold-down windshield, with wind wings, in this $1495 Series 70 roadster. Not many of these accessory items were sold.

Mrs. Walter P. Chrysler (*above*) enjoyed the use of a formal Imperial 80 five-seat Town Sedan, available to "ordinary" folk for $5495—on special-order only.

Imperial 80 roadsters (*right*) came only with a rumble seat. Wind wings and leather-topped doors were included in the $2595 price. Imperials rode a 120- or 127-inch wheelbase, but a 133-inch chassis could be ordered. Chrysler's Finer 70 two-door Brougham (*below*) sold for $1525. The Landau edition was similar, but was decorated with smaller quarter windows. Walter Chrysler (*below right*) and his colleagues were busy introducing new models, including this year's Series 60. On the same 109-inch wheelbase as the prior four-cylinder Series 58, it employed a new 54-horsepower, six-cylinder engine. This season's four-cylinder cars shrank to a 106-inch span. Chrysler executives already had begun talking with the Dodge folks about takeover prospects.

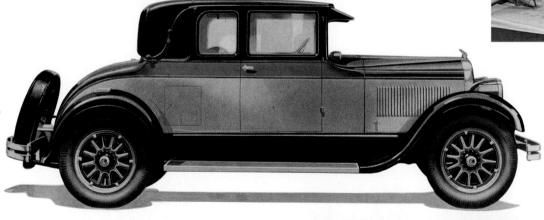

In addition to four- and five-seat coupes, Chrysler issued a $2895 Imperial 80 business coupe (*left*) that held only two. Its quarter windows were smaller, but storage space was immense. *Below:* Landau bars were popular on Imperials—and lesser Chryslers, too—even though they had no function.

1927 Production

Series 50	82,412
Series 60	NA
Series 70	48,254
Series 80 Imperial	NA
Total	182,195

1927 Engine Availability

No. Cyl.	Disp., cid	bhp	Availability
I-4	170.3	38	S-Series 50
I-6	180.2	54	S-Series 60
I-6	218.6	68	S-Series 70
I-6	288.6	92	S-Series 80

1928

Chrysler starts the year at a slow pace—but surprises are in store

Plymouth and DeSoto debut (as 1929 models) during the summer; they're new members of the Chrysler fold

Plymouth is the sole four-cylinder model from Chrysler, at first sold only through Chrysler dealers

Joe Fields heads DeSoto Motor Corporation; James C. Zeder (Fred's brother) is DeSoto/Plymouth's chief engineer

Chrysler Corporation takes over Dodge Brothers, Incorporated, on July 30; stock is exchanged, but the deal does not involve cash

Series 72 and Imperial six-cylinder engines grow in displacement to 248.9 and 309.3 cubic inches respectively

Imperials ride an all-new chassis on a massive 136-inch wheelbase

Headlight switches move to the steering column

Four Series 72 roadsters race at Le Mans, France, two of them finishing third and fourth overall

Imperial captures the second spot at a 24-hour endurance race in Belgium

Dodge drops its four-cylinder models

Chrysler is now a full multi-make manufacturer

Top and center: Imperial wheelbases grew to 136 inches, and hoods concealed a bigger, 309-cid "Silver Dome" or "Red Head" six-cylinder engine that yielded 100 or 112 horsepower. Semi-custom bodies for Chrysler's prestige line could be ordered from LeBaron, Dietrich, or Locke. Walter Chrysler (*above, at the left*) is joined by the "Three Musketeers": Carl Breer, Fred Zeder, and Owen Skelton.

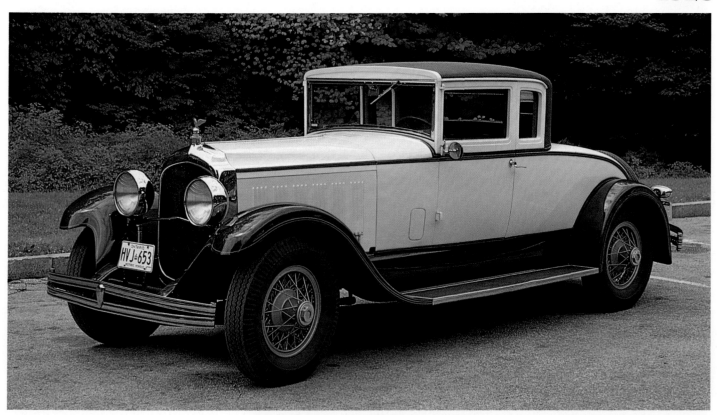

An Imperial Series 80 Club Coupe, bodied by LeBaron (*above and right*), cost $3995 in 1928. Only 25 were built. With the 112-horse Red Head six running on super-high 6.00:1 compression, this Imperial could top 100 mph. In fact, this model raced at Le Mans, finishing in third and fourth place. Note the extra-cost Buffalo wire wheels and the single windshield wiper. LeBaron also crafted open-bodied Imperials. In this enlarged form, Imperials were destined to achieve Classic status, enhancing Chrysler's image among the well-to-do as well as middle-class families. One step down from the Imperial was the Series 72, which evolved into the Series 75 in mid-1928. Both windshields of the $1835 Tonneau Phaeton (*below*) folded flat. Only 227 were produced.

Launched in July 1928, the new "Chrysler Plymouth" Model Q displaced the four-cylinder Chrysler Series 52. The rumble-seat coupe (*above*) was one of six body styles. Prices began at just $670. A luggage rack was standard (but a trunk was optional) on the $2995 Imperial 80 Town Sedan (*left*). Other Imperial sedans, for five or seven passengers, had rear-quarter windows. Close-coupled sedan styling, with blank rear quarters and dummy landau bars, was also offered on the less expensive Series 72 (*below*).

Purchasers of an Imperial formal sedan or limo enjoyed plush seating (*left*), with jump seats available for extra guests. Only 86 divider-window Limousines were built, with the same body as the seven-passenger sedan. Both took advantage of this year's longer 136-inch wheelbase. By June, Dodge (*bottom row*) was part of the burgeoning Chrysler empire. Standard Six Dodges, now powered by a 58-horsepower, 208-cid L-head six, began at $895, promising "smart appearance" in a "performance pacemaker." Victory Six Dodges used the same engine as Standard models, but the more costly Senior Six which started at $1495, held a 68-bhp, 224-cid motor. All three series used Midland steeldraulic four-wheel brakes.

1928 Production

Series 52	76,857
Series 62	64,136
Series 72	23,293
Series 80 L Imperial	2,123
Total	166,409

1928 Engine Availability

No. Cyl.	Disp., cid	bhp	Availability
I-4	170.3	38-45	S-Series 52
I-6	180.2	54/60	S-Series 62
I-6	248.9	75/85	S-Series 72
I-6	309.3	100/112	S-Series 80 L

1929

Chrysler's four-make lineup is arranged by price class

Plymouth rivals Chevrolet, but nonetheless lags far behind

DeSoto is officially on the market with a 55-bhp six-cylinder engine; it takes aim at Oakland/Pontiac

DeSoto's 174.9-cid six is no bigger in displacement than Plymouth's four-cylinder engine, but it delivers 10 more horsepower

DeSoto and Plymouth, riding a nearly identical chassis, differ noticeably in styling

Chrysler adopts a more efficient downdraft carburetor

K.T. Keller is named president of Dodge Division

Dodge launches the Series DA, a nicely updated version of the Victory Six

Chryslers get a new "slim-profile" radiator and longer fenders

Four-wheel hydraulic brakes gain larger drums and modern internal-expanding shoes

Lovejoy hydraulic shock absorbers become standard on Chryslers

Corporate output during 1929 totals 375,094 cars

Corporate car sales drop by 40.5 percent

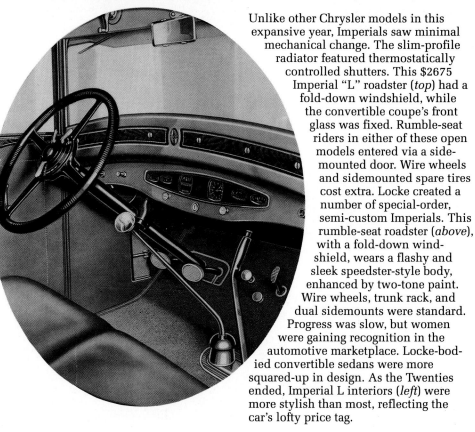

Unlike other Chrysler models in this expansive year, Imperials saw minimal mechanical change. The slim-profile radiator featured thermostatically controlled shutters. This $2675 Imperial "L" roadster (*top*) had a fold-down windshield, while the convertible coupe's front glass was fixed. Rumble-seat riders in either of these open models entered via a side-mounted door. Wire wheels and sidemounted spare tires cost extra. Locke created a number of special-order, semi-custom Imperials. This rumble-seat roadster (*above*), with a fold-down windshield, wears a flashy and sleek speedster-style body, enhanced by two-tone paint. Wire wheels, trunk rack, and dual sidemounts were standard. Progress was slow, but women were gaining recognition in the automotive marketplace. Locke-bodied convertible sedans were more squared-up in design. As the Twenties ended, Imperial L interiors (*left*) were more stylish than most, reflecting the car's lofty price tag.

Chrysler now had a full range of models, from low-budget Plymouth to mid-level Dodge and DeSoto, all the way to posh Chryslers and Imperials. Next in line (really for 1930) was a smaller Chrysler CJ Six, on a 109-inch chassis. Only a few CJ phaetons (*left*) were produced. A rumble seat came standard on the CJ Royal DeLuxe coupe (*below*).

Four centuries earlier, the Spanish explorer Hernando de Soto (*below*) had discovered the Mississippi River. Now, his image sat upon the radiator of the new DeSoto automobile. A 174.9-cid L-head six (*bottom left*), running 5.2:1 compression, powered all DeSoto Series K cars. DeSoto listed seven models, including an $885 phaeton (*below right and bottom right*), shown with accessory wind wings and a Moto-Meter. Note the twin taillights and tiny rear window.

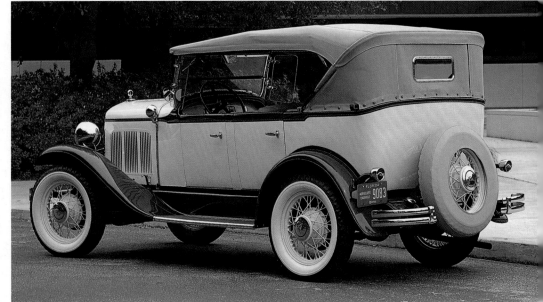

Above: Price-topper of the DeSoto line, at $955, the Model K Sedan de Lujo (DeLuxe) was also its heaviest model. Unless loaded with extra-cost gear, it looked similar to the regular five-passenger DeSoto sedan, but boasted a fancier interior. The fleet also included a Cupe de Lujo. DeSotos shared many body and chassis components with Plymouth, including their 109.75-inch wheelbase. Eager DeSoto dealers sold no other car makes. First named "Faeton" rather than phaeton, this open DeSoto (*right*) had a two-piece windshield and an $845 price tag. Further evidence of DeSoto's leaning toward model names of Spanish derivation was the Roadster Español (*below*), also selling for $845.

A 1929 Dodge Series DA standard four-door sedan weighed in at 2900 pounds.

The '29 Dodge Series DA two-door Brougham rode a 112-inch wheelbase.

A 1929 Dodge Series DA rumble-seat coupe was base-priced at $1025.

The 1929 Plymouth four-door sedan measured 169 inches long overall.

Dodge issued a bewildering array of models, starting with updates of the Standard and Victory Six. Then came a new DA-Series, borrowing its chassis and 208-cid engine from a 1928 model. The DA four-door sedan (*top*) sold for $995, or $1065 as a DeLuxe. A $995 DA Brougham (*second from top*) seated five. The DA coupe (*third from top*) came with or without a rumble seat. Even a $695 Plymouth sedan (*bottom*) could have an optional side-mounted spare tire.

1929 Production

Chrysler

Series 65	51,086
Series 75	48,850
Series 80 L Imperial	2,506 **
Total	102,442 *

* Approximate
** Includes identical 1930 models, but not custom-bodied versions.

DeSoto

Model K Six	Approx. 80,000

Dodge

Standard Series J (early)	NA
Victory Series M (early)	NA
Senior Series S	NA
Series DA (late)	NA
Total	124,557 *

* Calendar year

Plymouth

Model Q	66,097 *
Model U	108,345 **
Total	174,442

* Some early Model Qs were registered as 1928 models, but Chrysler always referred to them as 1929s.
** Model U production stretched into the 1930 model year, and this figure is a total for 1929-30 production.

1929 Engine Availability

Chrysler

No. Cyl.	Disp., cid	bhp	Availability
I-6	195.5	65/72	S-Series 65
I-6	248.9	75/84	S-Series 75
I-6	309.3	100/112	S-Series 80 L

DeSoto

No. Cyl.	Disp., cid	bhp	Availability
I-6	174.9	55	S-all

Dodge

No. Cyl.	Disp., cid	bhp	Availability
I-6	208.0	58	S-Series J
I-6	208.0	63	S-Series DA
I-6	224.0	68	S-Series M
I-6	241.6	78	S-Series S

Plymouth

No. Cyl.	Disp., cid	bhp	Availability
I-4	170.3	45	S-Model Q
I-4	175.4	45	S-Model U

Chapter 3

Technology Takes Hold: 1930-33

Despite lackluster 1929 sales, Chrysler should have been in sound shape with its new four-make lineup—even when pitted against Ford's Model A and a strengthening Chevrolet. Better yet, that quartet was arranged in a clear step-up pattern, to appeal to nearly every element of the market: economy-minded four-cylinder Plymouth, mid-range Dodge and DeSoto, with Chrysler (including Imperial) topping the line. Initially, DeSoto was the first step-up from Plymouth, with Dodge a notch higher, but their respective rankings would shift over the next few years.

All bets were off after the Crash of October 1929. As financiers and consumers alike began to realize that the boom of the Twenties had fizzled in an instant, new cars weren't likely to be a high priority.

Believing that economic conditions were likely to worsen, not improve, Walter Chrysler and B.E. "Hutch" Hutchinson knew that something had to be done immediately. Like most rival automakers, Chrysler quickly adopted tandem policies to weather the financial storm: slim down and cut prices. Unbridled expansion was out; "trimming the fat" was the only reasonable course to follow. That meant revising the company's overly broad selection of engines and model lineup.

Transformation couldn't happen instantly, so the first Chryslers to appear in January 1930 were largely carryovers. A second series followed in spring.

Engines earned the most attention.

Both Dodge sixes were deleted, shrinking the total to five six-cylinder powerplants. The smallest was new. That 195.6-cid version, with 62 horsepower and four main bearings (versus seven in other engines), drove a new low-priced Chrysler CJ-Series. Billed as the "lowest-priced six ever to bear the Chrysler name," the CJ came in six body styles, starting at $795. Like other powerplants, it came in two flavors: "Silver Dome" or higher-compression "Red Head."

More surprising was the emergence of an eight-cylinder engine. Or to be precise, a *pair* of eights. Why a straight-eight—which connoted affluence—at a moment when the economy was going down the drain? Because it was there, actually. Development had begun in 1927, under Fred Zeder's stewardship, as a reaction to the eights that had been launched by various rivals.

Stranger yet was the fact that the eights went into Dodge and DeSoto models, while Chryslers—and even the costly Imperial models—stuck with sixes. The decision made sense at the time. Because of its smaller displacement, the eight—207.7 cid for DeSoto, 220.7 cid for Dodge—just wouldn't have been a reasonable choice for the big Imperial, which ran with a 309.6-cid six.

Running in five main bearings, the eight was smoother and quieter than a six, but no powerhouse. Billed as the "lowest-priced eight in the world," DeSoto straight-eight models cost $965 to $1075, versus $810 to $945 for the sixes. After outselling the six at first, eight-cylinder models ultimately were

Pictured during the 1933 filming of *You're Right, Mr. Chrysler* are four of the corporation's top executives (*left to right*): Fred M. Zeder, Walter P. Chrysler, K.T. Keller, and A. van der Zee.

chosen by only about one-third of DeSoto buyers.

Upper-level Chryslers adopted a "multi-range" four-speed gearbox. Never a popular item, it would last only through 1932 (1933 in Imperials).

Styling for all four makes in 1930-32 retained the dead-upright profile of the late '20s, with Dodge the most conservative of the lot. Eight-cylinder Dodges began on a 114-inch wheelbase, then grew to 118.5 and 122 inches. Sixes rode the shorter chassis.

High demand made Plymouth a success from the start, and continued strong as the Depression deepened. Now sold by Dodge and DeSoto dealers, as well as Chrysler dealerships, the "entry-level" make was somewhat insulated from sales tumbles as the economy sank.

Success was well-deserved. Plymouths offered an appealing mix of low price and attractive styling—plus engineering that often put it ahead of Ford and Chevrolet. Plymouths featured all-steel construction, for instance, when most rivals still used wood-framed bodies. Four-wheel hydraulic brakes ranked a giant step ahead of the Ford/Chevrolet mechanical systems.

In spring 1930, a "New Finer Plymouth" was introduced. For this 30-U Series, the four-cylinder engine was enlarged for the third time in as many years: to 196.1 cid. Hydraulic shock absorbers and a fuel pump became standard. Frederick L. Rockelman left Ford to become Plymouth's president; Byron C. Foy took the helm at DeSoto.

Moving from the low-end market to the high end, the majestic Imperial hit

its peak in 1931, as a large eight-cylinder engine elbowed aside the six. The smooth, low-revving 384.8-cid L-head, running in nine main bearings, developed 125 horsepower. Even laden with nearly 5000 pounds, an Imperial could do 96 mph and accelerate from 0-60 in 20 seconds. Styled by Herb Weissinger, inspired by Alan Leamy's Cord L-29, the long, low '31 Imperial ranks as one of the loveliest Chryslers ever.

Smaller eights went into other Chrysler models, and continued in Dodge and DeSoto. All three makes also continued to offer six-cylinder engines, which grew larger through the early '30s. Another round of price cuts helped inspire sales.

Chrysler's reputation for practical, advanced engineering continued to flower. Ads, in fact, claimed that "Only Chrysler engineering gets Chrysler results."

Patented "Floating Power" debuted during 1931, first on Plymouth, but soon across the board. This was a two-point mounting system strategically placed so that the engine's natural rocking axis would intersect with its center of gravity to help keep the engine's natural vibration from reaching the frame and body. Rubber engine mounts provided flexibility and a cantilever leaf spring kept the engine properly aligned. Ads boasted that Plymouth had "The smoothness of an eight and the economy of a four."

Chryslers also featured automatic spark control and rustproofed (welded-steel) bodies. They also carried free-wheeling, a gadget that let the engine disengage from the gearbox when coasting, to enhance fuel economy. Pioneered by Studebaker, free-wheeling went into many American cars of the early Thirties—but was ruled illegal for safety reasons in some states. Optional automatic clutches let the driver shift gears without touching the clutch pedal.

Introduced in spring, the truly new Plymouth PA Series resulted from a $2.5 million development program, and its broader lineup included a dashing new rumble-seat sport phaeton and roadster. In a concession to the times, the line also included two "Thrift" sedans, helping Plymouth's model-year volume soar to nearly 107,000 units.

In fact, while most automakers were already faltering badly in 1930-31, total Chrysler output actually rose *above* pre-Depression figures. Then, in 1932, Plymouth rose to become the Number Three seller in the nation—a ranking it would hold for two decades.

February 1932 brought the last four-cylinder Plymouth (until 1978, that is). Horsepower rose to 65 (same as the '32 Ford V-8), and prices held the line. Even so, that wasn't quite enough to overtake the new Ford V-8, which captured the hearts of millions—and the pocketbooks of many. Ford notwithstanding, Plymouth made a reasonably good sales showing: nearly 84,000.

Rough times or not, styling sells cars, so the sheer vertical lines of 1930-32 were softening. In fact, Chrysler was evolving into a style leader for the industry, rather than a dowdy follower.

Turning the usual pattern upside-down, stylists had been involved from the start in the development of the Chrysler cars introduced during 1931. Now DeSoto, for one, showed a smoother (if chunky) profile in its 1932 SC Series, led by a barrel-like grille. Cars could also have "jumbo" 15-inch tires, for a more modern stance.

Dodge launched its largest model ever, and one of its best-looking. New double-drop frames with X-bracing lowered the passenger floors of all Chrysler products.

After a short life, eight-cylinder engines departed from the DeSoto line after 1931, but stayed with Dodge into '33. Eights would be strictly Chrysler choices for the next two decades, with Dodge and DeSoto offering a succession of flathead sixes.

In 1933, as America faced one of its worst economic years ever, Plymouth output shot forward. Sales pushed the 300,000-mark. A tempting mix of price and power was making a difference. The new six-cylinder Plymouth, fruit of a $9 million project, started as low as $445. Customers were encouraged to "Look At All Three," and lots of those lookers drove home the merchandise, billed as "A low-priced car without that 'low-priced look.'"

Though smaller in displacement than the prior four, Plymouth's 189.8-cid six pumped out a worthy 70 horsepower. The initial PC Series was sold through March 1933, followed by revised PCXX and PD DeLuxe lines on longer wheel-bases—deemed more fitting for a six-cylinder car. Streamlined styling hit Plymouth for the first time, led by fully skirted fenders and a rounder hood.

Chrysler products now turned to a model-year introduction, like most other makes, ending the confusing era of car-ryovers followed by half-year models.

Plymouth may have kept the corporation afloat through hard times, but other Chrysler products also fared well, with sales doubling in '33. DeSoto climbed from 15th place in 1930 to 10th in '33. Dodge reached fourth, courtesy mainly of its sixes. Its new DP Series sported a curved radiator and wire wheels. Dodge became the step-up model over Plymouth, as DeSoto moved upscale.

As always, the "Three Musketeers" (Zeder, Skelton, and Breer) and their hardy engineering team kept busy with advanced ideas. One such was a compact-car project. Striving mainly for a way to cut freight costs, Carl Breer designed a car on a 100-inch wheelbase, weighing just 1700 pounds, with a 130-horsepower V-8 engine. Unfortunately, interest in that concept faded away, but Chrysler had a bombshell ready for '34—a bomb that turned into a dud.

1930

The Great Depression is underway; automakers must cut back to survive

Carryovers again start the season, replaced by new models in the spring

The budget-priced Chrysler CJ Series Six debuts

Dodge and DeSoto offer eight-cylinder engines—but Chrysler doesn't

The K-Series DeSoto is displaced in May by the CK "Finer Six"

By March, Plymouth franchises go to all 7000 Chrysler, DeSoto, and Dodge dealers

Plymouths are restyled in the spring into a "New Finer" 30-U Series; prices are cut soon afterward

An exquisite dual-cowl phaeton is the costliest Imperial model

New "Steelweld" bodies use little wood

Engines again come in standard- and high-compression versions

Chrysler and Dodge cars are wired for radio installation, but few radios are sold

Organization and personnel changes begin, to ensure Chrysler's future

Price cuts are deemed essential if Plymouth is to challenge Ford and Chevrolet

Chryslers came in five series and 37 models for 1930, including Imperial. Prices started at $795. Seen here are the 1930½ CJ Six coupe (*above*) and a '30 custom limo (*left*). Standard bodies by Budd featured sturdy "Steel-weld" construction. Outside firms provided the custom coachwork.

Chryslers vied for attention at the 1930 Chicago Auto Show in the Congress Hotel.

If this Chrysler 70 coupe looks a little different than most, that's because it was produced for export. Note the unusual hood louver pattern, found on early 1930 models.

Topping Chrysler's non-Imperial lineup was the 124-inch-wheelbase Model 77 with its 268.4-cid L-head six. The Series 77 included the $1725 Royal four-door sedan (*left*). A view of the windshield on the Royal coupe (*above left*), also $1725, shows the sun visor, high-mounted parking lights, and dual wipers—a rarity in 1930. The sedan's interior (*above*) was typical of the times: floor-mounted gearshift, handbrake alongside, and instruments grouped at the center. All six-cylinder engines (except in the new CJ) were derived from the original 1924 design.

From the rear, a '30 DeSoto (*right*) looked much like any other contemporary auto. The rumble seat (*far right*) made this a four-passenger car. Convertibles (with wind-up windows) were beginning to replace roadsters. DeSoto ragtop output: 524 CF Eights and 184 CK Finer Sixes.

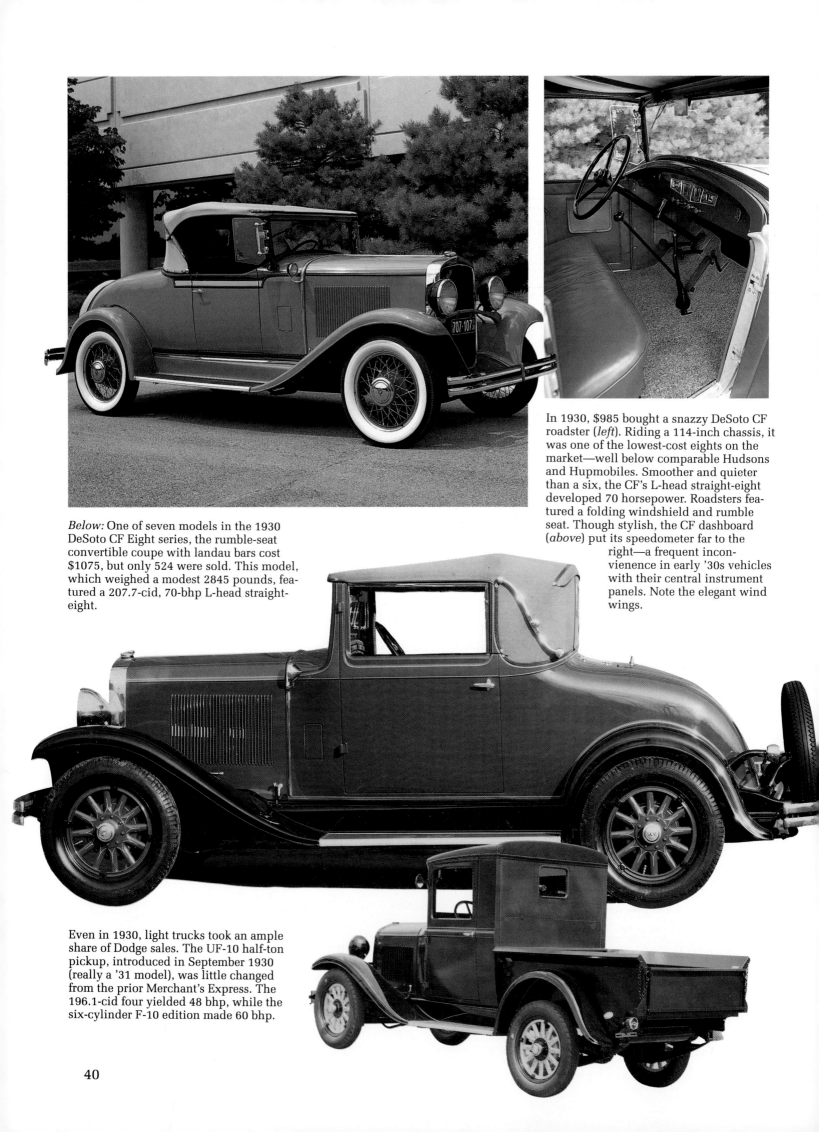

Below: One of seven models in the 1930 DeSoto CF Eight series, the rumble-seat convertible coupe with landau bars cost $1075, but only 524 were sold. This model, which weighed a modest 2845 pounds, featured a 207.7-cid, 70-bhp L-head straight-eight.

In 1930, $985 bought a snazzy DeSoto CF roadster (*left*). Riding a 114-inch chassis, it was one of the lowest-cost eights on the market—well below comparable Hudsons and Hupmobiles. Smoother and quieter than a six, the CF's L-head straight-eight developed 70 horsepower. Roadsters featured a folding windshield and rumble seat. Though stylish, the CF dashboard (*above*) put its speedometer far to the right—a frequent inconvienence in early '30s vehicles with their central instrument panels. Note the elegant wind wings.

Even in 1930, light trucks took an ample share of Dodge sales. The UF-10 half-ton pickup, introduced in September 1930 (really a '31 model), was little changed from the prior Merchant's Express. The 196.1-cid four yielded 48 bhp, while the six-cylinder F-10 edition made 60 bhp.

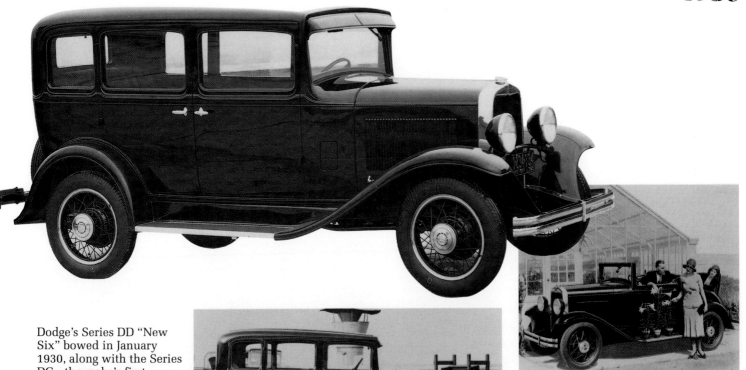

Dodge's Series DD "New Six" bowed in January 1930, along with the Series DC—the make's first straight-eight cars. Though plain and prim, the DD sedan (*above*) sold well, with 33,432 produced in 1930-32. It had a 189.8-cid six (smaller than the carry-over DA/DB sixes), while the new eight displaced 220.7 cid. Wheelbases measured 109 inches for the DD, 114 for the DC. Plymouth began the model year with a carryover Series U (*right*), then launched the "New Finer" 30-U (*above right*) in April 1930. Its four-cylinder engine grew to 196 cid and 48 bhp. Smaller wheels gave the 30-U a lower stance.

Above: The 2450-pound Plymouth 30-U two/four-passenger convertible sold for $695, and 1272 were built during the 30-U's late 1930-early 1931 model run. Buyers could choose between wood or wire wheels at no charge.

1930 Production

Chrysler

Model CJ6	29,239 *
Model 66	12,606 *
Model 70	18,733 *
Model 77	16,688
Imperial	2,506 **
Total	60,199 ***

* Totals represent 1930 and 1931 production combined for these models.
** Includes identical 1929 models, but not custom-bodied versions.
*** Calendar year

DeSoto*

Model K Six	30,000
Model CK Finer Six	7,500
Model CF Eight	19,500
Total	57,000

*Approximate

Dodge*

DA Six	15,000 **
DB Six Senior	7,000 **
DC Eight	20,000
DD New Six	30,000
Total	72,000

* Approximate
** Available 1930 figures combined with 1929 production.

Plymouth

Model U	108,345 *
Model 30-U	30,000 **
Total	NA

* Total Model U production includes 1929 and 1930 models.
** Approximate

1930 Engine Availability

Chrysler

No. Cyl.	Disp., cid	bhp	Availability
I-6	195.6	62	S-CJ6
I-6	195.6	65	S-66s built 1929
I-6	218.6	75	S-70s built 1929
I-6	218.6	68	S-66s built 1930
I-6	268.4	93	S-77, and 70s built 1930
I-6	309.3	100	S-Imperial

DeSoto

No. Cyl.	Disp., cid	bhp	Availability
I-6	174.9	57	S-K
I-6	189.8	60	S-CK
I-8	207.7	70	S-CF

Dodge

No. Cyl.	Disp., cid	bhp	Availability
I-6	189.8	61	S-DD
I-6	208.0	63	S-DA
I-6	241.5	78	S-DB
I-8	220.7	75	S-DC

Plymouth

No. Cyl.	Disp., cid	bhp	Availability
I-4	175.4	45	S-U
I-4	196.0	48	S-30-U

1931

As usual, carryovers start the season, followed later by the "real" '31s

A spectacular Imperial redesign is reminiscent of the L-29 Cord

Chryslers—including Imperials—now come with straight-eight engines

Free-wheeling is offered on all four Chrysler makes

"Floating Power" engine mounts debut in mid-season, initially on Plymouths

Carryover Plymouths are replaced in May by an all-new PA Series

Plymouth leaps from seventh place to fourth in production

Corporate market share grows appreciably, despite only a modest sales gain

The engine lineup includes only three sixes—but five straight-eights are offered

Imperials set 12 Class B stock-car records at Daytona Beach, Florida

Louie Miller drives a new Plymouth PA 6237 miles in just over 132 hours

Corporate cutbacks continue, but Chrysler's engineering staff adds members

In a Coney Island publicity stunt, an elephant stands on the roof of a Chrysler sedan

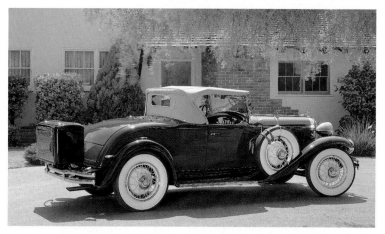

Imperials had panache in 1931. Witness this snazzy $3220 Series CG roadster (*above*), powered by a smooth 384.8-cid eight. No more puny sixes would fetter Imperial performance. An 88-bhp Chrysler CD-8 "New Eight" DeLuxe roadster (*left and below*) sold for half as much. Note the Trippe driving lights.

Like most '31s, the Chrysler CD-8 dash held central gauges (*left*). The "Redhead" version of the 260.8-cid straight-eight (*right*) is easy to spot. This rumble-seat Sport Roadster cost $1595.

Riding a 145-inch chassis, the $2845 Chrysler Imperial CG close-coupled sedan was massive, but only 1195 were sold. This model set several speed records at Daytona Beach.

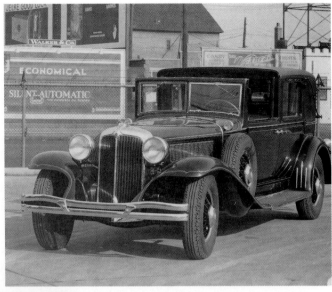

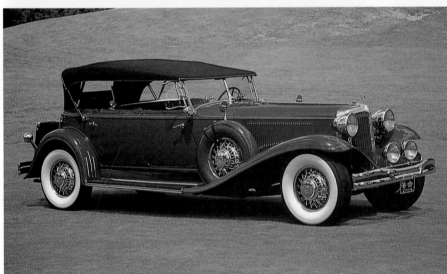

For the first time, styling was part of Chrysler's design process from the start. Despite tipping the scales at nearly 2½ tons, a glorious '31 Imperial (*left and above*) could reach 60 mph in 20 seconds, courtesy of its mighty new 125-horsepower straight-eight engine. Long, low, and unerringly distinctive, Imperials wore a rakish grille—not unlike Duesenberg's. And any resemblance to the graceful Cord L-29 was no mere coincidence. Custom bodies were available from Derham, Locke, Murphy, Waterhouse—and especially LeBaron. The dual-cowl phaeton (*above left*) shows a Canadian license, while the town car (*above right*) wears LeBaron coachwork with an open chauffeur's compartment. Note the split windshields. Four-speed gearboxes remained in Imperials and upper Chryslers, but not many owners needed its "emergency" low gear. Though far less imposing than the grand Chryslers, garden-variety DeSotos (*below*), Dodges, and Plymouths kept the corporation alive as the Depression worsened.

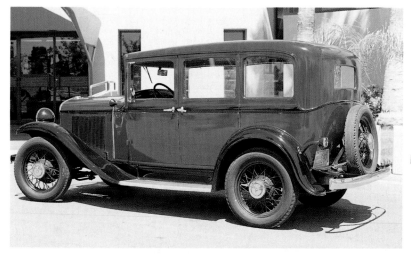

Below: Dodge continued to offer both six- and eight-cylinder models in 1931. Each engine grew in displacement when new DG and DH models arrived, replacing DC/DD.

DeSoto began the 1931 season with a carry-over CK Six, then launched a more curvaceous Series SA (*top left*) with a larger 205.3-cid mill and longer hood. The $775 four-door was the most popular SA model, with 17,866 built. A DeLuxe version went for $825. DeSoto coupes (*top right*) came with or without a rumble seat. A two-door SA sedan (*above*) debuted in May 1931, at $695—the cheapest DeSoto model. A second-series CF Eight gained a bigger 220.7-cid engine with 77 horses.

After starting the season with a carryover 30-U, Plymouth issued a new PA Series with "Floating Power." The PA rumble-seat coupe (*right*) went for $610, with 9696 produced. Four-door sedans (*second from bottom*) sold far better. A convertible coupe (*bottom*) cost $645. Cars could be ordered with either wood-spoke or wire wheels. A Dodge coupe (*below*) cost $835 with a six-cylinder engine, or $1095 with the eight. The boxy wagon is a Dodge DH Six Suburban commercial, with body by Cantrell.

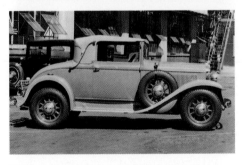

1931 Production

Chrysler

Model CJ	*
Model 66	*
Model 70	*
CM New Six	38,817
CD New Eight	14,355 **
CD DeLuxe Eight	9,100
CG Imperial	3,228 ***
Total	52,819 ****

* See 1930 production figures, which combine 1930 and 1931 totals.
** First series commenced July, 1930. Second series commenced January, 1931. Discontinued April, 1931 and replaced by DeLuxe Eight.
*** Includes early 1932 production.
**** Calendar year

DeSoto

Model CK Finer Six	4,757 *
Model SA Six	28,356 **
Model CF Eight	550 *
Model CF Eight Second Series	4,224 *
Total	NA

* Approximate
** 1931 and 1932 production figures combined.

Dodge*

DC Eight	4,300
DD New Six	12,900
DG Eight	9,500
DH Six	20,600
Total	47,300

* Approximate

Plymouth

Model 30-U	40,000 *

* Approximate

1931 Engine Availability

Chrysler

No. Cyl.	Disp., cid	bhp	Availability
I-6	195.6	62	S-CJ-6
I-6	217.8	78	S-CM-6
I-6	218.6	68	S-66
I-6	268.4	93	S-70
I-8	240.3	82	S-CD-8s built 1930
I-8	260.8	90	S-CD-8s built 1931
I-8	282.1	95	S-DeLuxe Eight
I-8	384.8	125	S-Imperial

DeSoto

No. Cyl.	Disp., cid	bhp	Availability
I-6	189.8	60	S-CK
I-6	205.3	67	S-SA
I-8	207.7	70	S-CF
I-8	220.7	77	S-CF Second Series

Dodge

No. Cyl.	Disp., cid	bhp	Availability
I-6	189.8	61	S-DD
I-6	211.5	68	S-DH
I-8	220.7	75	S-DC
I-8	240.3	84	S-DG

Plymouth

No. Cyl.	Disp., cid	bhp	Availability
I-4	196.0	48	S-all

Plymouth's Series PA bowed on July 11, 1931, although production had begun around May 1. Generally considered a 1932 model, it introduced "Floating Power," a method of mounting the engine that drastically reduced vibration. The $645 convertible coupe (*far right*) found 2783 buyers. Note the step to the rumble seat on the rear fender. A PA sedan (*near right*) set a San Francisco-New York-San Francisco record: 65 hours, 33 minutes, averaging 47.52 mph.

1932

Bodies receive a mild modernizing

Modified fans, air-intake, and exhaust systems deliver quieter running

Double-drop frames permit lowered floors

Vacuum-actuated automatic clutches appear as an option

General Tire "jumbo" 15-inchers are offered on DeSotos for a softer ride

Plymouth reaches the Number Three production spot for the first time, ahead of Buick and Pontiac

Chrysler Corporation sales decline—but far less than the industry average

The final four-cylinder Plymouths go on sale

A convertible sedan and seven-passenger sedan join the Plymouth lineup

Harold Hicks, designer of the tough Ford Model A engine, joins Chrysler's research team

Engine choices shrink, in a further attempt to slash production costs

All models have "Floating Power" this year

DeSotos now look different from Dodges and Plymouths

Imperials in 1932 rode on two wheelbases: 135-inch Series CH or 146-inch CL. Seen here is a CH Town Car by LeBaron.

The '32 Chrysler and Imperial Eights (*above*) were "Distinguished both in appearance and in performance." LeBaron bodied this Custom Imperial CL convertible coupe (*right*).

Stock-bodied Imperial CH sedans started at $1945 in 1932, and found just over a thousand customers. The CH line also included a coupe and convertible sedan.

The Second Series Chrysler CD New Eight Royal sedan (*left*) is really considered a 1931 model. At Coney Island, New York, a live elephant had climbed a platform atop a CD sedan to demonstrate the strength of its body, but this papier-mâché elephant traveled to dealers to promote the cars. The CD DeLuxe Eight (*right*) bowed in 1931 and continued into the '32 model year. This $1585 convertible coupe found just 501 buyers.

Few Chryslers approach the splendor of this plum-colored '32 Imperial CH Speedster (*left and above*). Imperial held a dozen American Automobile Association Contest Board stock-car speed records in its class. Free-wheeling and an automatic clutch eased shifting, but the Multi-Range four-speed gearbox would soon be gone. Note the covered sidemount spares on the Imperial Custom CL convertible sedan (*below left*). Only 474 CI Six roadsters (*below*) were built, part of the "Second Series." Closed models adopted a split windshield this season. DeSoto debuted a larger, more stylish model this year, the Series SC "New Six," sporting a barrel-shaped radiator. Shown (*bottom row*) is the $845 SC Custom convertible coupe.

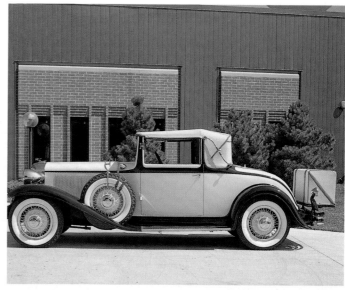

1932 Dodge DK Eight coupe

Dodge DG Eight roadster

"Suicide" doors gave access to some 1932 models, including the DeSoto SC convertible sedan (*top left*) and roadster (*above*), but others kept front-hinged doors. This roadster (*top right*) is one of 200 DeSotos made that year in Canada. Dodges (*right*) could have six or eight cylinders. Race legend Barney Oldfield poses (*below*) in an "official" AAA Plymouth.

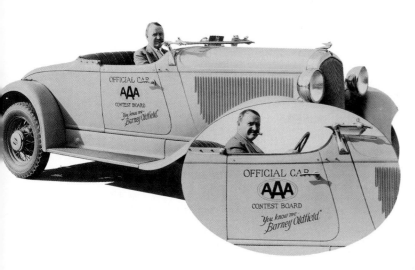

1932 Dodge phaeton

1932 Dodge Club Victoria

Below, left and right: Plymouth's 1932 Series PB listed two roadsters, (the make's last), as well as this $645 convertible coupe. Some 4853 were produced, compared to 325 Business and 2163 Sport Roadsters. They sold for $495 and $595.

Above: For an extra $40, Plymouth's 1932 PB Sport Roadster could be ordered in school colors as a "Collegiate Special." Sidemount spare cost extra.

Walter Chrysler (*left*) shows off the new '32 PB Plymouth. The PB (*above*) rode a wheelbase three inches longer than the PA, and squeezed 65 horses (up nine) from the 196.1-cid engine. Priced from $495 to $785, PBs were the final four-cylinder Plymouths.

1932 Engine Availability

Chrysler

No. Cyl.	Disp., cid	bhp	Availability
I-6	217.8	78	S-CM-6
I-6	224.0	82	S-CI-6
I-6	268.4	93	S-70
I-8	282.1	95	S-CD
I-8	298.6	100	S-CP-8
I-8	384.8	125	S-CG, CH, CL

DeSoto

No. Cyl.	Disp., cid	bhp	Availability
I-6	205.3	67	S-SA
I-6	211.5	75	S-SC
I-8	220.7	77	S-CF Second Series

Dodge

No. Cyl.	Disp., cid	bhp	Availability
I-6	189.8	61	S-DD
I-6	211.5	74	S-DH
I-6	217.8	79	S-DL
I-8	220.7	75	S-DC
I-8	240.3	84	S-DG
I-8	282.1	90	S-DK

Plymouth

No. Cyl.	Disp., cid	bhp	Availability
I-4	196.1	56	S-PA
I-4	196.1	65	S-PB

1932 Production

Chrysler

Model 70	*
Model CM6	**
Model CD DeLuxe Eight	***
CG Imperial	****
CI-6 "Second Series" Six	18,964
CP-8 Eight	5,113
CH Imperial	1,402
CL Imperial	220
Total	25,291 *****

* Listed by Chrysler for 1932, though production ceased in May of 1931. Production total included in 1930/31 figure.
** Production ran from July to December, 1931. Production total included in 1931 figure.
*** Production ran from July to November, 1931. Production total included in 1931 figure.
**** Production total included in 1931 figure.
***** Calendar year

DeSoto

Model SA Six	*
Model SC New Six	24,496
Model CF Eight Second Series	*
Total	NA

* Production total included in 1931 figure.

Dodge*

DD New Six	1,000
DH Six	20,000
DL Six	21,000
DC Eight	600
DG Eight	2,300
DK Eight	6,200
Total	50,100

* Approximate

Plymouth

Model PA	96,096
Model PB	83,910
Total	180,006

1933

Chrysler drops the unpopular four-speed gearbox

Engineering advances include a "silent running" transmission with helical gears—an industry first—along with a gas-pedal starter

The downdraft-carbureted engine adopts an automatic choke

Industry auto sales recover, but only modestly

Plymouth switches to a six-cylinder engine—and sales soar to nearly 300,000

Plymouth ranks a solid third in production, behind Chevrolet and Ford; Dodge jumps from ninth to fourth

The initial Plymouth six-cylinder models, produced only briefly, are replaced by longer-wheelbase versions

Dodge produces its final straight-eights

Carl Breer pens a compact car with a V-8, but the project is abandoned

Chrysler products finally adopt "normal" model-year debut dates

Plymouth's first six-cylinder cars are too small to attract customers

Dodge sales rise sharply, fueled by the new DP six-cylinder series

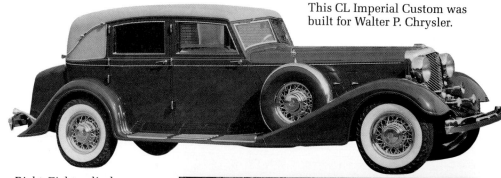

This CL Imperial Custom was built for Walter P. Chrysler.

Right: Eight-cylinder Chryslers were renamed CT Royal in 1933, on a 120-inch wheelbase with a 273.8-cid engine. Shown is a CT coupe, priced at $915 with rumble seat, or $20 less as a two-seater business coupe. Radiators now leaned rearward, magnified by fuller front fenders. Transmissions adopted helical-cut gears, and the gas pedal activated the starter motor. Nearly all Chrysler bodies had split windshields. The six-cylinder Series CO business coupe cost $745, while a noble Custom Imperial phaeton commanded $3395.

Imperial CL Customs rode a 146-inch wheelbase; CQ Eights, just 126 inches.

Walter P. Chrysler (*fourth from left*), once an apprentice himself, poses with a crew of auto workers.

The '33 Dodge DO Eight coupe looked much like a Victoria.

1933 Dodge panel delivery truck

Except for seven extra horsepower and a sharply raked radiator within new one-piece "air-flow" fenders, the 1933 DeSoto SD differed little from the prior SC. An SD business coupe (*top left*) sold for $665. DeSotos now ranked closer to Chryslers in trim and equipment. "Air-wheel" tires (*top right*), available on DeSotos, claimed to offer 50-percent greater traction. Switching to a six-cylinder engine, borrowed from the '30 DeSoto, helped send Plymouth (*left*) sales soaring—especially when a longer PD replaced the PC Series. Chrysler executives looking over the new engine are (*from left*): Carl Breer, Walter P. Chrysler, Fred Zeder, and Owen Skelton. Although Chrysler's L-head engines were state-of-the-art in the Thirties, they would become painfully dated by the Fifties.

1933 Production

Chrysler

CO Six	17,863
CT Royal Eight	10,389
CQ Imperial Eight	3,838
CL Imperial Custom	151
Total	32,241

DeSoto

Model SD	22,736

Dodge

DP Six	104,451
DO Eight	1,652
Total	106,103

Plymouth

PC Six	60,000
PCXX Standard Six	43,403
PD DeLuxe Six	195,154
Total	298,557

1933 Engine Availability

Chrysler

No. Cyl.	Disp., cid	bhp	Availability
I-6	224.0	83/89	S-CO
I-8	273.8	90/98	S-CT
I-8	298.7	108/100	S-CQ
I-8	384.8	135/125	S-CL

DeSoto

No. Cyl.	Disp., cid	bhp	Availability
I-6	217.8	82	S-all

Dodge

No. Cyl.	Disp., cid	bhp	Availability
I-6	201.3	75	S-DP
I-8	282.1	92	S-DO

Plymouth

No. Cyl.	Disp., cid	bhp	Availability
I-6	189.8	70	S-all

Chapter 4

Dream Into Nightmare: The Airflow Era: 1934-37

Had focus groups and rigorous consumer research existed in the early Thirties, there may never have been a Chrysler Airflow. What a shame that would have been for automotive history.

Critics at the time scoffed at the Airflow, branding it a profound, if not devastating, failure—a car too far ahead of its time to attract customers in the midst of the Great Depression. Even within the company, not everyone gave it their seal of approval, but Walter Chrysler himself did, and without great concern for public reaction.

No doubt about it, the Airflow qualified as the most radical mass-volume production car issued by an American company. And yes, the timing may have been unwise. Yet, just a few years later, it didn't look all that radical anymore. Today, while some still sneer at its shape, it's more often praised as a virtually *avant-garde* statement (for 1934) of what cars would be like in the years ahead—indeed, it was arguably the first

truly modern automobile.

The Airflow's origin is well-known. In 1927, the story goes, expert engineer Carl Breer spied a squadron of Army Air Corps planes flying overhead. That vision inspired the idea for a stream-lined car using aircraft-type design principles. Breer even talked it over with aviation pioneer Orville Wright before constructing a succession of scale models. Later on, wind-tunnel tests suggested a modified teardrop shape, and later yet, the Airflow name. Breer even managed to get a wind tunnel built at Chrysler's Highland Park, Michigan, headquarters. Learning aerodynamics as they went along, Breer and his staff created at least 10 full-size semi-streamliners, in addition to the models.

A running prototype, dubbed "Trifon Special," was finished late in 1932. Its engine sat 20 inches farther forward than normal, while the body sported a short, curved nose with faired-in head-lights—details that would be seen in the production version. The burly Walter

Chrysler's invaluable "Three Musketeers" of engineering (*from left*): Owen Skelton, Fred Zeder, and Carl Breer.

Chrysler enjoyed his first ride in the Airflow, especially the ample space front and rear, and the smooth ride. So, without considering the implications that an unconventional design might have in an era of non-prosperity, he gave an easy go-ahead.

An "engineer's" car, the Airflow was loaded with impressive innovations. For starters, its beam-and-truss body gave great strength, but weighed less than expected. Although not true unit construction, it was a tighter "interlocking" method of blending body and chassis. Body panels extended below the frame, attached to a cage-like superstructure. All passengers sat within the car's wheelbase, as the engine reached past the front axle, delivering a placid ride to rear-seat occupants. Seats stretched 50 inches across. Oliver Clark earns the credit (or blame) for the exterior styling.

Not only did retooling demand plenty of money and effort, it took too much time. Thus, the Airflow's debut had to be delayed until January 1934. Custom Imperials didn't arrive until June.

Jealous and uncertain of the Airflow's acceptance in the marketplace, General Motors and other rivals ran "smear" ads claiming that Airflows were unsafe. Analysts ridiculed the car's shape. By the time the cars hit dealer showrooms in serious numbers, rumors of flaws had helped to squelch what had initially been rather strong public interest—odd looks notwithstanding. Logically enough, plans for Airflow versions of Dodge and Plymouth were quickly nixed.

At the Chrysler end, marketers turned out to be lucky. They also insisted on a conventionally styled "Airstream" series. DeSoto, on the other hand, went whole hog with its lower-priced Airflows, submitting no alternate model as a backup. At year's end, it turned out that more DeSoto than Chrysler Airflows had been sold.

Airflows came on five different wheelbases, with any of five engines, all the way up to the long-stretching Custom Imperial on its massive 146-inch span. DeSoto Airflows were all sixes; Chrysler used straight-eights.

In 1933 and '34, Americans flocked to Chicago's Century of Progress, a massive exposition that showcased modern ideas and products. With so many people intrigued with modernity, it may seem strange that a "car of the future" was so rigorously shunned in the marketplace. Actually, it's not strange at all. People can gaze avidly upon what's new and different, but fail to translate that thought into a purchase—especially when one's pocketbook is nearly empty, and the immediate future looks uncertain. Even the most *avant-garde* thinker can turn staunchly conservative when the time comes to reach into his or her own pocket.

As Chrysler Corporation ended its first decade, its spectacular success could be credited mainly to the admirable engineering of its products. For the Airflow, engineering wasn't enough. Too many people considered the car ugly, though not everyone concurred in that appraisal.

Early on, Walter Chrysler had predicted that the Airflow would "bring about a whole new trend in personal transportation." In a way that was true, as Ford's also-radical Lincoln-Zephyr soon would demonstrate. Still, the Airflow's failure hurt Chrysler for the next two decades.

Looking backward, however, the Airflow ranks as one of the most significant industrial designs—ever! Not only did it launch streamlined, modern shaping into the automotive world, it signaled an end to traditional body construction and engine placement, plus other forward-thinking moves.

What saved the day for Chrysler was Plymouth, now planted firmly in the Ford/Chevrolet league. Like the "New Standard" Dodges, Plymouths displayed a tame version of streamlining—nothing that would turn anyone off. They also got a slightly larger six-cylinder engine. Plymouths now featured roll-down vent windows and "artillery" steel wheels (wires now looked old-fashioned on streamlined bodies). Both Dodge and Plymouth featured a new independent front suspension, but so did Chevrolet.

Despite the pending disaster, Chrysler turned a profit in 1934. Airflows lost money, true, but not a damaging sum. Most seriously, the Airflow debacle discouraged Chrysler from trying anything adventurous—not for many years, anyway. Retreat from the Airflow fiasco began in 1935, though the last examples wouldn't leave the factory until '37. In any case, Chrysler now focused attention on the more orthodox "Airstream" ("mainstream" might have been a better word!) Sixes and Eights. Pontoon fenders, raked radiators, and teardrop headlights gave some kinship to Airflows, but not enough to hurt sales. Synchromesh transmissions eased the pain of gear-clashing.

Even DeSoto now offered both the Airflow and Airstream. Production nearly doubled, but DeSoto's industry ranking was stuck at 13th, due in part to the debut of the successful Packard One-Twenty in the upper-medium-priced field. Sedans came two ways in '35: with an outside spare tire, or as a touring "trunkback" with the tire inside an integral luggage compartment. Dodge dropped its convertible sedan, but revived it for 1936-38.

Chrysler Corporation had another reasonably good year on the sales front, courtesy primarily of Plymouth, whose model-year output neared 327,500. Plymouth prices began at a moderate $510. Enjoying strong profits in 1935, Chrysler looked forward to soon overtaking Ford Motor Company as America's Number Two producer.

Meanwhile, Walter P. Chrysler turned the corporate presidency over to K.T. Keller that year. Fred Zeder was named vice-chairman, "Hutch" Hutchinson was chairman of the finance committee. Known for his devotion to machinery, Keller delegated authority well.

Each of the Big Three automakers had engineers working on compact-car projects in the mid-1930s, just in case continued economic turmoil might cause Americans to flirt seriously with smaller automobiles. At Chrysler, Carl Breer headed the "Star Car" project, named for the five-cylinder radial engine that was intended as a powerplant. The front-drive car rode a compact 100-inch wheelbase, but never really came close to production, even though prototypes scored well in extensive testing.

DeSoto produced its last Airflows in 1936, but Chrysler hung onto the concept for one more season. Following its pattern of catchy new ad themes each season, Dodge dubbed its '36 line "Beauty Winner." Not everyone agreed that Dodge would win many beauty contests, but like the Plymouth, it attracted an impressive number of practical-minded customers. New one-piece steel roofs eliminated the leak-prone fabric inserts, though Plymouth's would last another season.

By 1937, the "radical" Airflow didn't look so strange anymore—especially with this year's reworked front end, gently raked and rounded. Other '37s displayed transitional styling that some have dubbed a "potato" profile, with barrel-shaped grilles and pod headlights. Ornate dashboards planted gauges ahead of the driver, instead of in the center. Chrysler's revamped non-Airflow line included six-cylinder Royals and eight-cylinder standard and Custom Imperials. Volume passed 106,000 units, nearly triple the 1934 low. On the safety front, the '37s featured such items as non-snag door handles, rounded dashboard bottoms, and recessed knobs. On the other hand, a right-hand wiper still cost extra on cheaper models. Motorists didn't know it yet, but the crank-open windshields that let cool summer breezes flow through were in their final season. However, built-in windshield defroster vents added to driving convenience, while fully insulated rubber body mounts enhanced structural integrity.

Plymouth turned out more cars in 1937 than at any other time in the decade. For the first time, a Plymouth price tag topped $1000 (the new DeLuxe limousine), but a business coupe started at just $580.

Yes, Americans still suffered from the Depression in 1937. Recovery had arrived for some, but not for the masses who continued to face severe unemployment and deprivation. Yet, Chrysler Corporation looked forward to the late Thirties on an optimistic note. Things were looking up—or *were* they?

53

1934

Chrysler launches the daring Airflow—America's most radical production car

Chrysler also issues conventional models, but DeSoto offers only the Airflow

A delayed Airflow launch hurts the car's public image

Engineering excellence fails to lure customers, who scorn the shape

Airflow seats stretch 50 inches across—widest in the industry

Imperial Airflows get a new 323.5-cid straight-eight; it will last through 1950

An Imperial Airflow coupe does 95.7 mph in the flying mile at Bonneville, and sets 72 national speed records

Automatic overdrive is introduced during the model year for Chrysler/DeSoto Airflows

Plymouth's inline six is stroked to 201.3 cid

Dodges and Plymouths ride a new independent front suspension

An outside coachbuilder creates Westchester Suburban station wagons for Plymouth

The famed Raymond H. Dietrich joins Chrysler's styling staff

Negative reactions cause the scuttling of plans for Dodge and Plymouth Airflow models; conservative styling will reign at Chrysler for many years

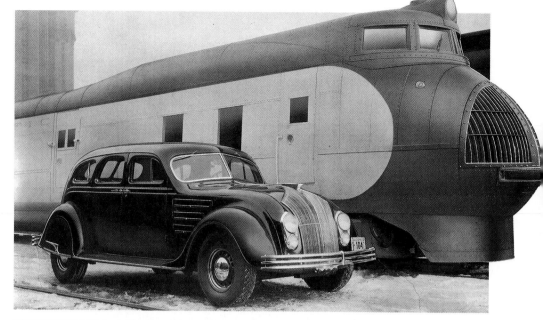

Radical design took many forms in the mid-Thirties. At Chicago's Century of Progress Exposition in 1934 (*above*), a Chrysler CV Airflow Imperial Eight sedan posed alongside the Union Pacific's M-1000 streamliner locomotive. Except for the six-passenger sedan's outside spare tire (*left*), Airflows were ultramodern in every dimension. The curved, stubby front end was its most controversial styling feature. Standard Airflows came on three wheelbases, priced from the $1345 CU to the $2345 CX Imperial.

Right: All Airflow passengers sat within the car's wheelbase, delivering an improved, remarkably smooth ride to rear occupants. A big man himself, Walter Chrysler appreciated the spacious interior with its immense 50-inch seats. Placing the Chrysler Airflow's eight-cylinder engine over the front axles helped boost passenger space. Note the tubular metal armrests and split back window.

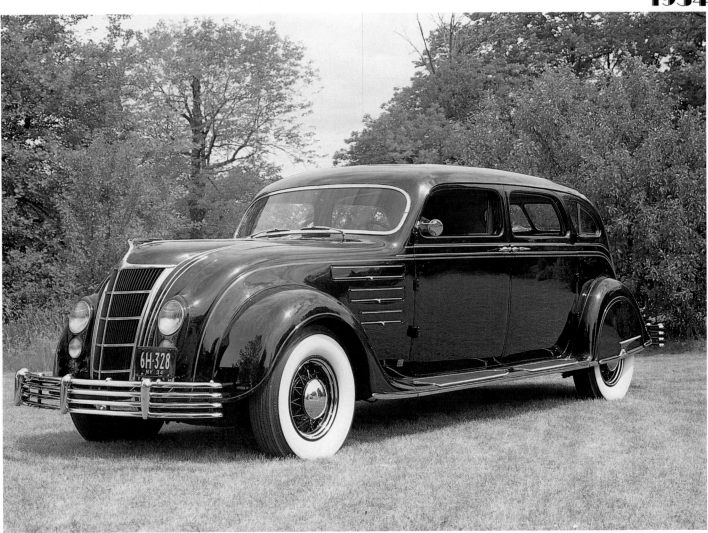

At $5000, the CW Custom Imperial was the biggest and costliest Chrysler Airflow (*above*). This sedan, with a 1935 grille, was first owned by A&P grocery-chain heir Huntington Hartford. CW bodies hailed from LeBaron, on a 146.5-inch wheelbase. Airflow vent wings (*below*) raised and lowered along with the door window.

Workmen prepare Airflow bodies at the Chrysler plant in Highland Park, Michigan, in 1934. Note the openings for the installation of fabric roof inserts.

A skeleton view (*below*) of the DeSoto Airflow reveals its cage-type inner structure. The beam-and-truss design combined great strength with light weight. In one test, a Chrysler Airflow was hurled off a 110-foot cliff. It landed wheels down and was driven away. Body contours were shaped to reduce wind resistance, boosting performance *and* economy. Airflows were lively performers and fine handlers. Ventilating air even circulated under the front seats (*below center*).

Chrysler Airflows looked especially sleek in five-passenger coupe form, available in CU (*above*) and CV series. The smallest of three straight-eight engines, 298.7 cid, went into the CU, rated at 122 bhp. Center-latched doors (*right*) exposed a vast interior with chair-height seats on chrome-tube frames—reminiscent of a 1930s dinette set. Passenger comfort beat that of any rival. The spare tire was easily accessible inside the coupe's trunk (*below*).

Chrysler's Series CA Six Brougham (*right*) cost $760—far below a '34 Airflow. It rode a 118-inch wheelbase and ran with a 93-bhp, 241.5-cid six. Output came to only 1575 units, but the CA four-door sedan, which cost $60 more, was far and away Chrysler's best seller—17,617 units.

56

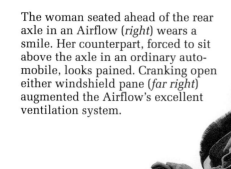

The woman seated ahead of the rear axle in an Airflow (*right*) wears a smile. Her counterpart, forced to sit above the axle in an ordinary automobile, looks pained. Cranking open either windshield pane (*far right*) augmented the Airflow's excellent ventilation system.

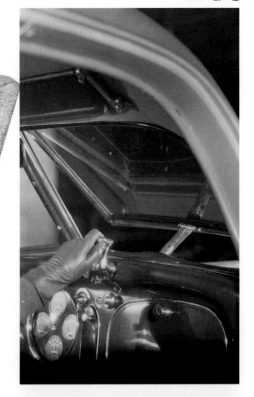

A radical profile wasn't the Airflow's only fresh idea. The cars had flush-mounted headlights, opening hood side doors, and a hidden radiator. Automatic overdrive arrived during '34. Later models added manual front seat adjustors.

Passenger ease and comfort were major selling points of the Airflow. Rear-quarter windows in the sedan (*far left*) opened for auxiliary ventilation. The woman operating the crank appears to have plenty of headroom, too. Trunks could be reached fairly easily from inside the car (*left*). Raising the rear seat back gave access for loading luggage into the rear compartment. Smokers weren't ignored, either. Even the rear-seat passengers had their own ashtrays (*above*) in an Airflow, mounted directly on the tubular chrome seat supports—not unlike the ashtrays used by train or bus passengers. Notably, the top-of-the-line Custom Imperial limousine sported the industry's first one-piece curved safety-glass windshield.

Curiously, all four '34 Chrysler Airflow Eight CU models were priced at $1345. The six-passenger four-door sedan (*right*) saw a production run of 7226 units, compared to only 732 five-passenger coupes, 306 Brougham coupes (with a different style rear seat), and 125 Town Sedans (with blanked rear-quarter windows). The wheelbase of the CUs measured a generous 123 inches. Note the elaborate engine cooling vents (*far right*).

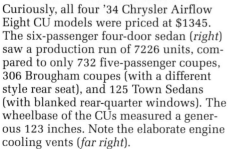

Even the appearance of Hollywood celebrities in promotional photos couldn't generate enough enthusiasm to trigger ample Airflow sales. Actress Ann Sothern (*above*) posed with a 1934 DeSoto Airflow SE six-passenger sedan. Riding a 115.5-inch wheelbase, the DeSoto carried a 241.5-cid, 100-horsepower six-cylinder engine, and rode 6.50 x 16 tires. At least Chrysler had a conventional series in 1934, to blunt the blow. DeSoto suffered through the first year with an Airflow alone, offered in four body styles. Each model sold for $995. Vaudeville entertainers Olsen and Johnson (*bottom right*) perch on the running board of a 1934 DeSoto Airflow sedan. Evidently, the Airflow roof had no trouble supporting half a dozen young women. *Below:* Couples in a pair of '34 DeSoto Airflows stop in front of a crossroads gas station in the Los Angeles area. Note the price of fuel in these Depression years: 10½ cents a gallon.

The '34 DeSoto Series SE Airflow Brougham seated six; only 522 were built.

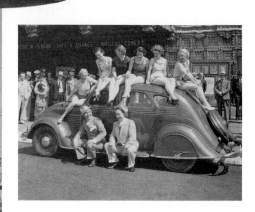

Dodge offered two drop-tops for 1934: a DS DeLuxe Six convertible sedan on a 121-inch wheelbase, and this DR DeLuxe Six convertible coupe on a 117-inch span. Priced at $765, it found 1239 buyers, versus just 350 for the $875 four-door. The year's best seller was the DR DeLuxe four-door sedan, also $765: 53,479 units. All '34 Dodges ran with a 217.8-cid, 87-bhp L-head six.

The best-selling Plymouth was the PE DeLuxe four-door. In spring 1934, a lower-priced Series PG replaced the PF Standard.

First Lady Eleanor Roosevelt sits at the wheel of a late '33 Plymouth PD DeLuxe convertible (*above*) with dual sidemounts and optional hood ornament. This open rumble-seat model started at $595. Plymouth ads encouraged shoppers to "Look at All Three." DeLuxe '34 Plymouth PGs (*right*) had standard free-wheeling, with an automatic clutch optional.

1934 Production

Chrysler		Dodge	
CA Six	23,802	DR DeLuxe Six	78,257
CB Custom Six	1,450	DS DeLuxe Six	1,750
CU Airflow Eight	8,389	DRXX New Standard Six	15,004
CV Airflow Imperial Eight	2,277	Total	95,011
CX Airflow Imperial Eight	106		
CW Airflow Imperial Custom Eight	67	**Plymouth**	
Total	36,091	PE DeLuxe	225,817
		PF Standard	39,544
		PFXX Special	35,298
DeSoto		PG Standard	20,512
Model SE Airflow	13,940	Total	321,171

1934 Engine Availability

Chrysler

No. Cyl.	Disp., cid	bhp	Availability
I-6	241.5	93	S-CA, CB
I-6	241.5	100	O-CA, CB
I-8	298.7	122	S-CU
I-8	323.5	130	S-CV, CX
I-8	384.8	150	S-CW

DeSoto

No. Cyl.	Disp., cid	bhp	Availability
I-6	241.5	100	S-all

Dodge

No. Cyl.	Disp., cid	bhp	Availability
I-6	217.8	87	S-all

Plymouth

No. Cyl.	Disp., cid	bhp	Availability
I-6	201.3	77	S-all

1935

Consultant Norman Bel Geddes touches up the Airflows with longer hood-lines and more conventional grilles, partially quashing the snub-nose look

A conventionally styled "Airstream" series joins Chrysler's slow-selling Airflow—it helps keep the company afloat

Airstreams share most body panels with the restyled Dodge and Plymouth, penned mainly by Ray Dietrich

Airstreams feature pontoon fenders and teardrop head-lights

Walter P. Chrysler turns the corporate presidency over to K.T. Keller

Dodge and Plymouth drop the short-lived independent front suspension

Drastic cost-cutting, initiated in 1934, pays off—Chrysler is now debt-free

Carl Breer sets to work on a small-car project, planning for a five-cylinder radial engine and front-wheel drive

Airflows account for only one-fifth of Chrysler/Desoto sales

Plymouth remains Number Three in model-year output; Dodge drops to fifth place

Imperials again come only with Airflow bodies; sales total less than 3000 units

For 1935, Chrysler grafted a more stylish grille onto the Airflow and added sturdier bumpers. The most popular model, the C-1 four-door sedan (*top*), saw only 4617 produced. A 323.5-cid straight-eight powered all Airflows except the huge CW. Series C-1 coupes (*above*) and sedans sold for the same price: $1245. Far more people picked an Airstream (*left*), with six or eight cylinders.

Series C-2 and C-3 Imperial Eight Airflows used 130/138-bhp versions of the 323.5-cid engine (*above*). Despite their differences, Airflow and Airstream Chryslers shared the same assembly line (*above center*). That's a Series C-1 Airflow in the foreground. On the Chrysler/DeSoto Airflow line (*right*), torch-wielding workmen prepare the roof.

Prototypes of the 1935 Chrysler Airstream and Airflow Imperial Series C-2 sedans (*top left*) show the vast differences between the two models—even though Airstreams adopted many Airflow-inspired streamlining touches this year. A Series CZ Airstream Eight DeLuxe convertible with rumble seat (*top right and center*) cost $1015, with only 101 produced. Airstream dashboards (*above*) featured two big round dials at the center. Chrysler offered fewer Airflow models in 1935, and sales again failed to take off. Airstream sedans came in regular and touring forms.

The '35 DeSoto Airflow Series SG Town Sedan featured
blanked quarter windows.

Both standard and business coupes were offered in the
1935 DeSoto Airflow line.

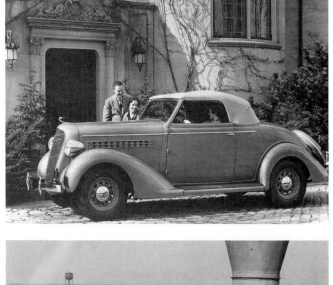

Taxi companies soon saw the merits of the 1935 DeSoto Series SF
Airstream sedans.

DeSoto launched a conventional Airstream series for 1935 to
join the Series SG Airflow (*top right*), again marketed in four
body styles. DeSoto's Series SF Airstream convertible coupe
(*above center*) sold for $835, but only 226 left the factory.
The fastback Series SF four-door sedan (*above*) was outsold
by the Touring Sedan, which featured a bustle trunk.

HISTORICAL

1935 Production

Chrysler
C-6 Airstream Six	24,458
CZ Airstream Eight	9,297
C-1 Airflow 8	4,996
C-2 Imperial Airflow 8	2,598
C-3 Custom Imperial Airflow 8	125
CW Custom Imperial Airflow 8	32
Total	41,506

DeSoto
Model SF Airstream	20,003
Model SG Airflow Six	6,797
Total	26,800

Dodge
DU New Value Six	158,999

Plymouth
PJ Six	76,342
PJ DeLuxe Six	251,106
Total	327,448

A 1935 Dodge Series DU five-window coupe (*above*) cost $645 as a two-seater, or $710 with a rumble seat. The latter sold only one-fourth as well. Dodge's "New Value Six" came in nine models, but just one series (down from three in 1934). Plymouths came in PJ and PJ DeLuxe trim, including the DeLuxe convertible coupe (*right top*) at $695. Its six gained five horsepower, to 82. Wheelbases measured 113 inches, except for long-chassis sedans at 128 inches. Prices began at $510. The heavily armored Plymouth "High-Speed Safety Car" (*right bottom*) aimed at police departments in the gangster era. Note the gun port in its bullet-resistant windshield, and the close-mesh screening that protected the radiator. A high-wheeled 1935 Plymouth PJ two-door sedan (*below*) with 20-inch wheels and special springs targeted rural doctors and farmers.

1935 Engine Availability

Chrysler
No. Cyl.	Disp., cid	bhp	Availability
I-6	241.5	93	S-C-6
I-6	241.5	100	O-C-6
I-8	273.8	105	S-CZ
I-8	273.8	110	O-CZ
I-8	323.5	115	S-C-1
I-8	323.5	120	O-C-1
I-8	323.5	130	S-C-2, C-3
I-8	323.5	138	O-C-2, C-3
I-8	384.8	150	S-CW

DeSoto
No. Cyl.	Disp., cid	bhp	Availability
I-6	241.5	100	S-all

Dodge
No. Cyl.	Disp., cid	bhp	Availability
I-6	217.8	87	S-all

Plymouth
No. Cyl.	Disp., cid	bhp	Availability
I-6	201.3	82	S-all

1936

Industry sales reach the highest total since 1929

Chrysler enjoys a stand-pat year, as Airstream models gain a modest facelift

Chevrolets get hydraulic brakes to rival Plymouth's; Ford sticks with mechanical binders

Plymouth breaks the half-million production mark for the first time, but is still well behind Ford and Chevrolet

The final DeSoto and Imperial Airflows are built; Chrysler's version will last one more season

Long-wheelbase sedans and limos join the DeSoto line

"Touring sedans" with integral trunks are gaining favor over "trunkless" body styles

The facelifted "Beauty Winner" Dodge line includes a revived convertible sedan

Chrysler posts an impressive $62.1 million profit, pays $2.3 million in year-end bonuses

Corporate output tops one million—well ahead of Ford Motor Company

Claiming more than 40 improvements, Plymouths look more like Dodges and DeSotos

Plymouth's standard line is renamed "Business," but the DeLuxe Series is far more popular

Imperial Airflows handily outsold their shorter-wheelbase Series C-9 companions in 1936. The Chrysler Imperial C-10 sedan (*above*) and equivalent coupe each cost $1475. The cheapest Chrysler, at $760, was the Series C-7 Airstream Six business coupe (*left*)—fender skirts cost extra. Airstream DeLuxe C-8 models rode a longer wheelbase.

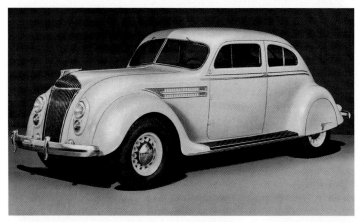

Only 110 Chrysler C-9 Airflow six-passenger coupes (*left*) were built in 1936, versus 1590 sedans in that series. Each rode a 123-inch wheelbase. In addition to the convertible coupe (*below left*), the C-7 Airstream Six series included a convertible sedan. Four-door sedans (*below*) outsold all other Airstream models.

A special 1936 Chrysler Imperial Airflow equipped with steel flanged wheels (*top left*) was purchased by the Missouri, Kansas, and Texas Railroad so its president and chairman of the board, Matthew Sloan, could inspect the rails. Town Car bodies (*above*) had to be ordered from outside coachbuilders. In fact, LeBaron crafted a half-dozen seven-passenger Town Sedans similar to this rendering (but with built-in trunk) on the Airstream DeLuxe Eight chassis. They sold for a towering $4995. DeSoto had built up a sizeable business selling cars to the taxi industry. Here (*left*), a fleet of Airstreams for Yellow Cab await delivery at the Dealers Drive Away Service Station. Tow bars were sold, rented, and serviced at this location. DeSoto Airstreams were offered in 12 DeLuxe and Custom models, Airflows in only two. A cutaway (*below*) reveals DeSoto Airflow construction as well as its commodious interior.

A 1936 DeSoto S-1 Airstream Custom Touring Sedan cost $865.

Like many automakers, Chrysler liked to use celebrities to publicize its products. At MGM Studios, actor Jimmy Stewart (*left*) posed alongside a 1936 DeSoto S-1 Custom Airstream convertible coupe. Just 350 were built, at $895. All DeSotos again had a 100-horsepower, 241.5-cid six—including the Airflow, issued for the last time. Only two S-2 Airflow models were released: the coupe (*above*) and four-door sedan.

Below and right: Even without the auxiliary trunk, one of the flashiest '36 Dodges was the Series D-2 convertible coupe, which rode a 116-inch wheelbase. *Bottom left:* Tan leather seats faced a central instrument panel. The L-head six (*bottom right*) again developed 87 horsepower.

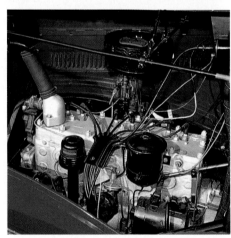

Despite minimal seating, the Dodge D-2 business coupe (*right*) was popular in 1936, trailing only trunkback sedans in sales. A total of 32,952 were built, priced at $640. Dodge offered nine models, including a long-wheelbase sedan.

Just $995 bought a Series D-2 convertible sedan (*right*) in 1936, but that was the highest-priced Dodge on the market. Only 750 left the factory. Dual sidemounts added to the car's panache. At 125 inches, the wheelbase of Plymouth's $895 Series P-2 DeLuxe 7-Passenger Sedan (*below*) measured a foot longer than regular five-passenger models.

Plymouth's P-1 Business Series had a seven-model lineup, including the two-door sedan (*left*) and coupe (*below*), priced $70 below the DeLuxe coupe. Note the contrasting-color fenders.

<table>
<tr><td colspan="2">1936 Production</td></tr>
<tr><td colspan="2">Chrysler</td></tr>
<tr><td>C-7 Airstream</td><td>43,471</td></tr>
<tr><td>C-8 Airstream DeLuxe</td><td>9,502</td></tr>
<tr><td>C-9 Airflow Eight</td><td>1,700</td></tr>
<tr><td>C-10 Airflow Imperial</td><td>4,500</td></tr>
<tr><td>C-11 Airflow Custom Imperial</td><td>85</td></tr>
<tr><td>Total</td><td>59,258</td></tr>
<tr><td colspan="2">DeSoto</td></tr>
<tr><td>S-1 DeLuxe Airstream</td><td>17,991</td></tr>
<tr><td>S-1 Custom Airstream</td><td>17,308</td></tr>
<tr><td>S-2 Airflow II</td><td>5,000</td></tr>
<tr><td>Total</td><td>40,299</td></tr>
<tr><td colspan="2">Dodge</td></tr>
<tr><td>D-2 Beauty Winner Six</td><td>263,647</td></tr>
<tr><td colspan="2">Plymouth</td></tr>
<tr><td>P-1 Business Series</td><td>92,835</td></tr>
<tr><td>P-2 DeLuxe Series</td><td>427,499</td></tr>
<tr><td>Total</td><td>520,334</td></tr>
</table>

1936 Engine Availability

Chrysler

No. Cyl.	Disp., cid	bhp	Availability
I-6	241.5	93	S-C-7
I-6	241.5	100	O-C-7
I-8	273.8	105	S-C-8
I-8	273.8	110	O-C-8
I-8	323.5	115	S-C-9
I-8	323.5	130	S-C-10, C-11

DeSoto

No. Cyl.	Disp., cid	bhp	Availability
I-6	241.5	100	S-all

Dodge

No. Cyl.	Disp., cid	bhp	Availability
I-6	217.8	87	S-all

Plymouth

No. Cyl.	Disp., cid	bhp	Availability
I-6	201.3	82	S-all

1937

Chrysler Airflows enter their final season, sporting better-looking front ends

Imperials are now conventionally styled

DeSoto fields a single (non-Airflow) series; model-year output more than doubles

All four Chrysler makes are restyled along a rounded-curve theme, sporting barrel-shaped grilles

The Airstream designation is dropped

New bodies are built mostly by Briggs

DeSotos and low-end Chryslers get a smaller 228.1-cid six

The revamped non-Airflow Chrysler line includes six-cylinder Royals, sharing their body/chassis with DeSoto

Plymouths adopt all-steel roofs, a year after Chevy

Crank-open windshields make their final appearance

Chrysler spends $22 million on plant improvements

Plymouth output hits the decade's high: 551,994 units

Plymouth promotes its "safety-styled" interior

Blower fans and hidden defroster vents are standard enhancing both safety and comfort

One of three final Airflow Custom Imperial leviathans, the "Major Bowes" edition (*top*) was dubbed "The World's Most Luxurious Motor Car." It weighed almost 7000 pounds, complete with lavish fittings. The 1937 Chrysler C-15 Custom Imperial Eight sedan (*above left*) used the same 323.5-cid engine as the final Airflows. The Series C-17 Airflow came as a four-door sedan (*above right*) or coupe.

The Chrysler C-14 Imperial rumble-seat coupe: $1070

Custom bodies for Chryslers continued into 1937. The Derham coachworks earned credit for the C-15 Custom Imperial Convertible Victoria coupe (*top left*), and also for the Custom Imperial with formal convertible Town Sedan body (*top right*). In addition to cab companies, some police forces turned to DeSotos (*above and right*). The DeSoto coupe's trunk had plenty of space for a two-way radio setup. By 1937, DeSotos were virtual duplicates of the Chrysler Royal Six, but priced a little lower: $770 to $1220, versus $810 to $1355. A closeup of three abreast in a DeSoto (*below*) demonstrates the breezy virtues of an open windshield, cowl vent, and wind wings. The $880 DeSoto S-3 Touring Sedan (*right*) was the most popular model: 51,889 units.

Like most convertible sedans in 1937, DeSoto's S-3 version (*above and right*), shown with and without fender skirts, failed to sell well. Only 426 were built, at $1300. DeSoto engines shrank in size and power, as wheelbases lost two inches, down to 116. Long-wheelbase sedans measured 133 inches. Not quite a thousand DeSoto S-3 convertible coupes (*below*) rolled out, with a $975 price tag. Dodge, too, continued to produce seven-passenger sedans as part of the 10-model D-5 Series. The extended four-door (*below right*) went for $1075, with 2207 built. Limos fetched $100 more, but only 216 were produced.

The Dodge D-5 fastback two-door sedan cost $780.

A 1937 Plymouth coupe (*left*) towed this miniature display of an auto factory— actually a $20,000 operating model of Plymouth's Lynch Road plant. Note the driving lights on the Plymouth P-4 DeLuxe coupe (*center*), far more popular as a two-passenger than with a rumble seat.

1937 Production

Chrysler	
C-16 Royal	86,000
C-14 Imperial	14,320
C-17 Airflow	4,600
C-15 Custom Imperial	1,200
Total	106,120
DeSoto	
S-3 Six	81,775
Dodge	
D-5	295,047
Plymouth	
P-3 Business Series	73,644
P-4 DeLuxe Series	478,350
Total	551,994

1937 Engine Availability

Chrysler

No. Cyl.	Disp., cid	bhp	Availability
I-6	228.1	93	S-C-16
I-6	228.1	100	O-C-16
I-8	273.8	110	S-C-14
I-8	273.8	115	O-C-14
I-8	323.5	130	S-C-17, C-15
I-8	323.5	138	O-C-17, C-15

DeSoto

No. Cyl.	Disp., cid	bhp	Availability
I-6	228.1	93	S-all

Dodge

No. Cyl.	Disp., cid	bhp	Availability
I-6	217.8	87	S-all

Plymouth

No. Cyl.	Disp., cid	bhp	Availability
I-6	201.3	82	S-all

Plymouth's $995 seven-passenger sedan (*above*), part of the P-4 DeLuxe Series, rode on a 132-inch wheelbase—seven inches longer than in 1936. Production totaled 1840 units. Plymouth interiors (*right*) focused on safety, with primary gauges ahead of the driver, recessed knobs, rounded dash bottom, and fold-away windshield crank.

Chapter 5

Easing Into Modern Design: 1938-42

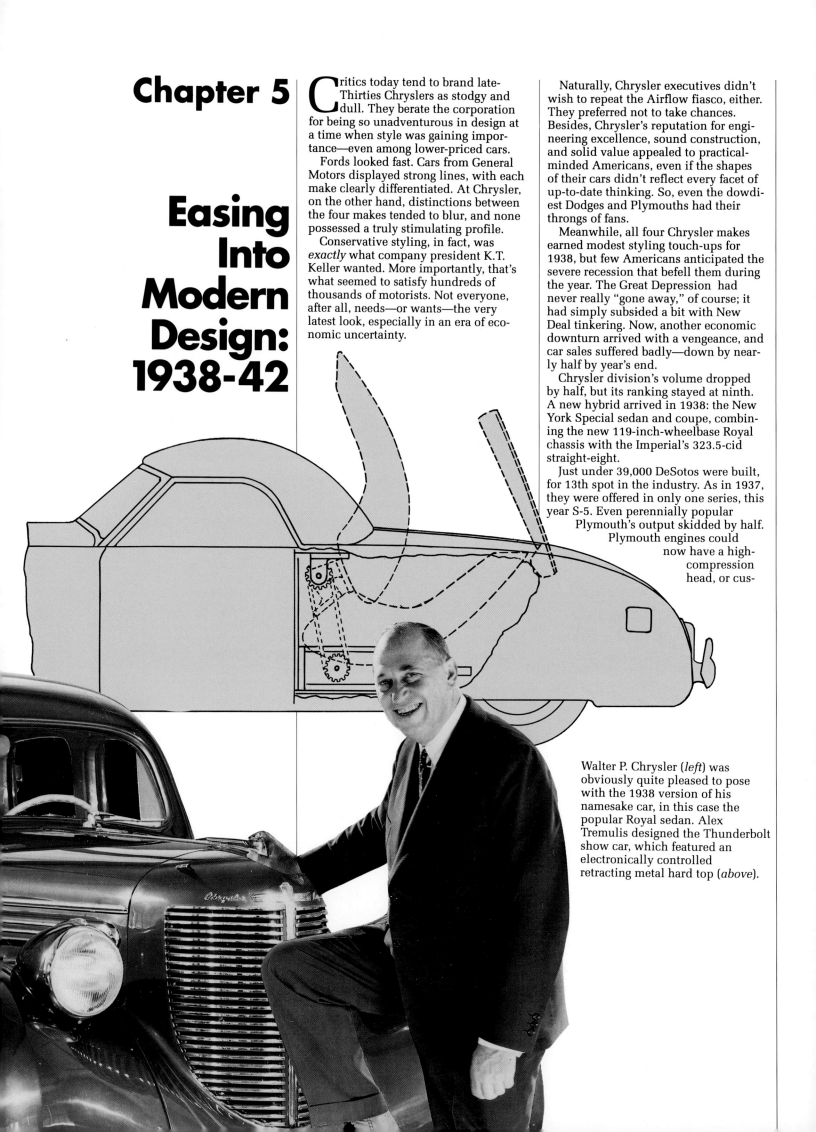

Critics today tend to brand late-Thirties Chryslers as stodgy and dull. They berate the corporation for being so unadventurous in design at a time when style was gaining importance—even among lower-priced cars.

Fords looked fast. Cars from General Motors displayed strong lines, with each make clearly differentiated. At Chrysler, on the other hand, distinctions between the four makes tended to blur, and none possessed a truly stimulating profile.

Conservative styling, in fact, was *exactly* what company president K.T. Keller wanted. More importantly, that's what seemed to satisfy hundreds of thousands of motorists. Not everyone, after all, needs—or wants—the very latest look, especially in an era of economic uncertainty.

Naturally, Chrysler executives didn't wish to repeat the Airflow fiasco, either. They preferred not to take chances. Besides, Chrysler's reputation for engineering excellence, sound construction, and solid value appealed to practical-minded Americans, even if the shapes of their cars didn't reflect every facet of up-to-date thinking. So, even the dowdiest Dodges and Plymouths had their throngs of fans.

Meanwhile, all four Chrysler makes earned modest styling touch-ups for 1938, but few Americans anticipated the severe recession that befell them during the year. The Great Depression had never really "gone away," of course; it had simply subsided a bit with New Deal tinkering. Now, another economic downturn arrived with a vengeance, and car sales suffered badly—down by nearly half by year's end.

Chrysler division's volume dropped by half, but its ranking stayed at ninth. A new hybrid arrived in 1938: the New York Special sedan and coupe, combining the new 119-inch-wheelbase Royal chassis with the Imperial's 323.5-cid straight-eight.

Just under 39,000 DeSotos were built, for 13th spot in the industry. As in 1937, they were offered in only one series, this year S-5. Even perennially popular Plymouth's output skidded by half. Plymouth engines could now have a high-compression head, or cus-

Walter P. Chrysler (*left*) was obviously quite pleased to pose with the 1938 version of his namesake car, in this case the popular Royal sedan. Alex Tremulis designed the Thunderbolt show car, which featured an electronically controlled retracting metal hard top (*above*).

tomers could order (since 1935) a lower-powered "economy" engine for no extra cost. The latter would last only into 1940. The "Business" line was renamed "Roadking" in March 1938, but remained no less spartan.

A four-door DeLuxe Suburban station wagon debuted as Plymouth's first "catalog" wagon. Bodywork was supplied by U.S. Body & Forge of Tell City, Indiana. It had done Plymouth wagons since 1934.

Handsomer styling by Ray Dietrich for 1939 put rectangular headlights into the fenders, which were lengthened and carried lower grilles. Each make featured a "prow" front, plus a vee'd two-piece windshield.

New model names for '39 Chryslers included Windsor (a Royal subseries), New Yorker, and Saratoga. Limited-edition, thin-pillared DeLuxe Town Coupes with Hayes bodywork wore Chrysler, DeSoto, and Dodge badges. Dodge fielded a two-series lineup for the first time since 1934, calling its cars Special or DeLuxe "Luxury Liners." DeSoto now also offered two series: DeLuxe and Custom.

On the engineering front, a new "Superfinish" process of mirror-finishing engine and chassis parts helped minimize friction. The improvement was especially welcome for engine bearings in cars that were shipped a long way before delivery. Gearshifts moved from the floor to the steering column, as they did on most American cars at this time. Plymouth convertible owners no longer had to lower the roof by hand; now vacuum did the job.

Nearly all automakers had been thinking about automatic transmissions, and plenty of engineers had come up with ideas. Reo had introduced a semi-automatic unit in 1933. Oldsmobile offered its own version in '37, and Buick launched a self-shifter for its Special series a year later.

Chrysler's Fluid Drive wasn't a direct reaction to GM's endeavors—including Hydra-Matic, which appeared on 1940 Oldsmobiles—but it stemmed from the same yen to eliminate bothersome gearshifting. The idea was simple enough: just mount a fluid coupling in tandem with the conventional clutch, so there would be slippage between the engine and transmission when the latter was "in gear." A driver could then start out in High (third) gear if he chose—though progress was painfully slow. Or, he could shift gears in the ordinary way, but enjoy super-smooth takeoffs.

Chrysler division dropped to 11th spot as the 1939 totals were tallied, despite a volume hike to nearly 72,500 units. DeSoto ranked 13th. No open DeSotos were issued, but certain closed models could be ordered with a sliding sunroof (that never actually went into production). Plymouth output recovered handily, past 417,000 units, despite new competition in the low-priced field from Studebaker's Champion.

New fastback-style bodies arrived for 1940, with separate fenders but smooth lines. All sedans now had a neatly integrated trunk, giving more luggage space than the old "trunkback" designs. Though better-looking each year, they still earned criticism for lagging behind Ford and Chevy. As one observer noted, the cars from Chrysler "wouldn't knock your eyes out, but wouldn't knock your hat off either."

Chrysler cars for 1940 ranged from the $895 Royal Six coupe to a $2445 Crown Imperial Limousine, as the division rose to 10th place. Chrysler offered Royal and Windsor Sixes; Eights included New Yorker, Saratoga, Crown Imperial, and the new Traveler. DeSoto reinstated its Custom convertible coupe, but soft-topped sedans were gone for good. With output up by 11,000 units, DeSoto held 13th place.

Dodge revived its long-wheelbase sedan and limo after a year's absence, and nearly two-thirds of Dodge's output was the upper DeLuxe series. Running boards and two-tone paint cost extra, but two-toning didn't become too popular. Chrysler's choice of spray patterns made its cars look too taxi-like. Dodge managed to rise from ninth to sixth place in the industry when the season's production totals were tallied.

Plymouth prices started at $645 (a bit above Ford), helping model-year output pass 420,000 units. Though mostly favored for practicality and economy, a Plymouth six could cruise at 65 mph.

Two striking LeBaron show cars emerged during 1940, wearing hidden headlights in flush-fendered bodies. Six of each were built. The Newport was an Imperial-based dual-cowl phaeton designed by Ralph Roberts. Alex Tremulis of Briggs penned the Thunderbolt, on a New Yorker chassis with a retracting hardtop.

An invalid for the previous two years, Walter P. Chrysler died in August. K.T. Keller remained in full charge, and engineers continued to run the company.

For 1941, Chrysler and Desoto could have something extra with Fluid Drive: semi-automatic shifting. Chrysler's "Vacamatic" and DeSoto's "Simplimatic" each incorporated a four-speed gearbox with two ranges. The driver used the clutch in the normal way, to select either Low (1-2) or High (3-4) range. Most driving could be done in High. The car started off in third gear, then the unit shifted automatically to fourth when the driver let up on the gas for a moment. Low range was mainly for hills and trailer-towing. Though not a true automatic, like Oldsmobile's (and now Cadillac's) Hydra-Matic, it worked simply and satisfied many Chrysler/DeSoto buyers in the Forties and early Fifties.

Considerably more Chryslers and DeSotos rolled out in 1941, awarding those upper makes eighth and 10th place, respectively. The most fascinating model was the Town & Country, Chrysler's first wagon. Unlike most station wagons, the T&C, designed by Dave Wallace, looked rather graceful. Sporting "clamshell" center-opening rear doors, it carried six or nine passengers beneath a steel roof. Only 997 Town & Country Chryslers were built for '41, plus 999 more for '42.

The Chrysler Traveler departed, but new Town Sedans had front-hinged back doors (other models were rear-hinged) and no rear-quarter side windows. Intriguing new upholstery choices included Highlander (Scots plaid and leatherette), Saran (woven plastic leatherette), and Navajo (resembling Indian blanket patterns).

DeSoto's heavy facelift brought a lower hood and the vertical grille "teeth" that would become the make's hallmark. Customers could order a host of extras, including an under-seat heater, pushbutton radio, and streamlined fender skirts. Dodge got a livelier look, courtesy of its clean facelift, but dropped from sixth to seventh spot in the industry. Dodges could have a three-speed Fluid Drive this year.

Manufacturers that could not yet offer automatic or semi-automatic shifting wanted to offer *something* to ease the burden. The answer? Vacuum. A vacuum-assisted unit allowed the driver to change gears with a fingertip's touch. Plymouth's version was called "Powermatic." Production of Plymouths grew modestly, enough to stay in third place, helped by a handsome facelift and the addition of cheaper, standard-trim base models.

Chrysler products looked even smoother for '42, as running boards hid behind flared door bottoms. Anybody could spot the slick new DeSoto, in particular, because of its "Airfoil" hidden headlights, billed as "out of sight, except at night." Six-cylinder engines grew in displacement, while hoods opened from the front, "alligator" style.

Not long after the 1942 model year had begun, on December 8, 1941, President Roosevelt declared war on Japan—a day after the bombing of Pearl Harbor in Hawaii. Automakers had been gearing up for war production for some time, but their efforts suddenly gained urgency.

Cars built after January 1, 1942, used painted metal instead of chrome trim. By early February, Chrysler—like other manufacturers—had halted civilian production of automobiles. America was at war, first with Japan and soon with Hitler's Germany. Soon, gasoline and rubber would be rationed, and pleasure driving curtailed. Industrial giants turned their full attention to products that would help the troops, as women entered the work force. On the "home front," as on the front lines, new cars were forgotten—except as fantasies for the future.

1938

A severe recession hurts the auto industry—car sales sink by nearly half

This is the last year for the "Dodge Brothers" insignia

Chrysler issues a New York Special sedan wearing a unique grille

The last Dodge convertible sedans are produced

Plymouth issues its first "factory" station wagon

Plymouth's "Business" line is renamed "Roadking" in an attempt to change its bottom-of-the-line image

This year marks the final use of non-independent front suspension in Plymouths

Walter P. Chrysler is stricken ill on May 26; he'll no longer be active in company management

Walter P.'s wife Della dies in the fall

Robert Cadwallader replaces Raymond Dietrich as Chrylser Corporation's top stylist

Plymouth maintains third place in output, while Dodge drops from fourth to fifth

Chrysler Corporation edges Ford Motor Company in model-year production

Plymouth Suburban DeLuxe station wagon bodies are still manufactured by an outside supplier

This '38 Chrysler Imperial C-19 New York Special sedan sported side-mounted tires.

This 1938 Chrysler Custom Imperial Eight Phaeton (*top*) wasn't a standard-issue model. Chrysler's New York Special sedan (*center*) rode a 119-inch wheelbase, as on the new Royal series, but power came from the big Imperial's 323.5-cid straight-eight engine. New York Special interiors (*above*) were color-keyed. Because many customers took to calling this model a New Yorker, that name came into use for '39.

With skirts and fog lights, a 1938 DeSoto S-5 coupe (*left*) sold for more than its $870 base price. DeSoto's instrument panel (*above*) looked quite ornate and symmetrical. Singer/actor Bing Crosby (*below left*) posed with a DeSoto, while Eddie Cantor (*below*) seems to be mimicking the hood ornament's shape.

DeSotos saw a variety of commercial applications in 1938, including ambulance duty (*above*). Note how the driver removed the B-post (*right*) to extract the stretcher. A new grille was part of the Raymond Dietrich facelift. DeSoto listed seven standard models, plus a pair of rare ones: a rumble-seat coupe and fastback Brougham. Except for seven-passenger sedans and a Custom Traveler, all models rode a 119-inch wheelbase. The four-door sedan, with 23,681 built, was the best seller.

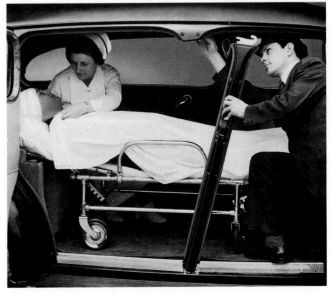

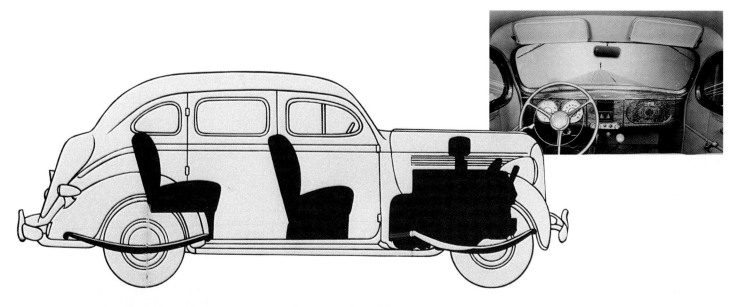

The '38 Dodge six developed 87 bhp.

The '38 Dodge displayed fender-mounted headlights and a new grille. The cutaway (*top left*) shows its basic layout. Dodge drivers faced two round dials (*top right*). The RC "woody" wagon (*center left*) used a 75-horsepower version of the Dodge six. Fastbacks (*center right*) no longer drew strong sales, but held ample luggage (*above left*). "Trunkback" sedans (*above*) were more popular by far.

During 1938, the Plymouth P-5 coupe (*above left*) changed its name from Business to Roadking. Only 338 of the coupes had a rumble seat, while 15,932 were strictly two-passenger models, priced $50 lower. An optional utility box could turn the two-seat coupe into a rudimentary pickup truck. Plymouth drivers still faced centrally mounted instruments (*above*). The 1938 Plymouth Westchester Suburban (*left*) rode a Series P-6 DeLuxe passenger-car chassis, yielding better handling and ride comfort than earlier wagons.

During the 1938 model run, Plymouth headlights (*below*) were lowered and moved rearward from the position shown, giving Plymouth front ends a closer kinship to other Chrysler Corporation cars.

1938 Production

Chrysler

C-18 Royal	43,300
C-19 Imperial	10,002
C-20 Custom Imperial	530
Total	53,832

DeSoto

S-5 Six	38,831

Dodge

D-8	114,529

Plymouth

P-5 Business/Roadking	74,785
P-6 DeLuxe	214,603
Total	289,388

1938 Engine Availability

Chrysler

No. Cyl.	Disp., cid	bhp	Availability
I-6	241.5	95	S-C-18
I-6	241.5	102	O-C-18
I-8	298.7	110	S-C-19
I-8	298.7	122	O-C-19
I-8	323.5	130	S-C-20
I-8	323.5	138	O-C-20

DeSoto

No. Cyl.	Disp., cid	bhp	Availability
I-6	228.1	93	S-all
I-6	228.1	100	O-all

Dodge

No. Cyl.	Disp., cid	bhp	Availability
I-6	217.8	87	S-all

Plymouth

No. Cyl.	Disp., cid	bhp	Availability
I-6	201.3	82	S-all

1939

Ford and GM cars look dramatically different for '39

Chrysler's fresh-looking revamps are less extensive under the skin

The restyling is Ray Dietrich's final effort at Chrysler, completed by the staff under Robert Cadwallader

Headlights move into the fenders, part of an industry-wide trend

Plymouth convertibles employ a vacuum-operated top—an industry first

Chrysler introduces semi-automatic Fluid Drive

The "Superfinish" method of mirror-finishing components sets a new standard for bearing smoothness

Chrysler launches the Windsor, New Yorker, and Saratoga series

Special Hayes-bodied coupes become available

Plymouth's convertible sedan is revived—only for this year

Chrysler delivers 25,000 trucks to the U.S. Army

Hitler's forces invade Poland in September; World War II is underway, but the U.S. officially remains "neutral"

Chrysler cars feature column gearshifts and "Safety Signal" speedometers

An outside firm supplied wood bodies for the '39 Chrysler Imperial station wagon (*top*), which boasted a 130-bhp version of the 323.5-cid eight. One style leader of the '39 lineup was the Royal Windsor Victoria Coupe (*center*), sporting Hayes coachwork. A sliding metal sunroof was announced for the '39 DeSoto (*above*), but never put into production. The column-mounted gearshift (*left*) was new for '39.

Like all 1939 models, the DeSoto Custom Touring Sedan (*above*) wore fender-mounted headlights. Hayes did the rakish bodywork for DeSoto's Custom Club Coupe (*right*).

Once again, Chrysler turned to Hollywood stars to help promote its products—in this case, the smoothly restyled DeSoto line. Praise for the cars came from actors Tyrone Power (*above left*) and Spencer Tracy (*above*), as well as from a relaxed Walt Disney (*left*). Each celebrity DeSoto wears "World's Fair" license plates. Billed as "America's smartest low-priced car," DeSotos rode a 119-inch wheelbase—or 136 inches for seven-passenger sedans. The limited-edition thin-pillared Hayes coupe was also offered by Dodge and Chrysler.

The '39 Dodge sported styling similar to other Chrysler products, but wore its own grille, headlights, taillights, and trim. It also rode on its own 117-inch wheelbase (three inches longer than Plymouth's), and received its own version of the corporate L-head six, a 217.8-cid unit developing 87 horsepower. This $1055 Hayes-bodied DeLuxe Town Coupe (*left*) found only 363 takers. Every '39 Dodge, Special or DeLuxe, was referred to as a "Luxury Liner."

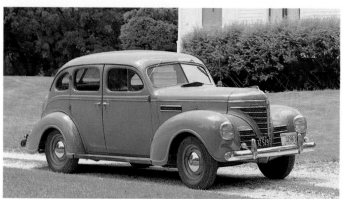

Plymouth's new 1939 look featured a peaked "prow" and vee'd windshield, plus fender-integrated square headlights. Both fastback and trunkback (*center left*) versions of the P-8 DeLuxe four-door sedan were still offered. Owners of the P-8 DeLuxe convertible coupe (*second row, right and right*) got a standard vacuum-powered top (a first), plus a rumble seat. The '39 ragtop cost $895; 5976 were built. Plymouth turned out 1680 Suburban wagons (*center right*) in the DeLuxe series, again wearing bodywork from U.S. Body & Forging Company. DeLuxe Plymouths adopted a column gearshift (*above*), while Roadkings stuck with a floor shift.

The last convertible sedan from Chrysler Corporation was the '39 Plymouth DeLuxe (*right*). Only 387 were built; at $1150, it was the costliest Plymouth of the year. Plymouth's coupe (*below*) could become a mini-pickup.

Plymouths saw police and educational duty (*above*). Driver training cars had dual controls for added safety.

For rough-road operation, 20-inch wheels were again available for all standard-wheelbase Plymouths (*above*). Panel delivery trucks (*below*) came only on the stiffer-sprung Series P-7 Roadking chassis. The Roadking line also included a Suburban wagon and utility sedan.

1939 Production

Chrysler	
C-22 Royal	60,001
C-23 Imperial/ New Yorker/Saratoga	12,135
C-24 Custom Imperial	307
Total	72,443
DeSoto	
S-6 DeLuxe	46,948
S-6 Custom	7,501
Total	54,449
Dodge	
D-11 Luxury Liner Special	71,000
D-11 Luxury Liner DeLuxe	112,046
Total	183,046
Plymouth	
P-7 Roadking	102,368
P-8 DeLuxe	315,238
Total	417,606

1939 Engine Availability

Chrysler

No. Cyl.	Disp., cid	bhp	Availability
I-6	241.5	100	S-C-22
I-6	241.5	107	O-C-22
I-8	323.5	130	S-C-23
I-8	323.5	132	S-C-24
I-8	323.5	138	O-C-24

DeSoto

No. Cyl.	Disp., cid	bhp	Availability
I-6	228.1	93	S-all
I-6	228.1	100	O-all

Dodge

No. Cyl.	Disp., cid	bhp	Availability
I-6	217.8	87	S-all

Plymouth

No. Cyl.	Disp., cid	bhp	Availability
I-6	201.3	82	S-all

1940

The '40 Chrysler Royal
Six sedan cost $995.

Walter P. Chrysler dies on August 18

Wheelbases grow on most Chrysler Corporation models; styling is totally new

Traveler coupes/sedans serve as a lower-cost alternative to Chrysler's New Yorker

DeSoto introduces a glitzier, two-tone Sportsman sedan

Long-wheelbase Dodges are revived, and still available on other Chrysler makes

Two-tone paint schemes become available on Chrysler, DeSoto, and Dodge

Running boards cost extra on some models—and soon will be history

Chrysler exhibits two stunning show cars: the Newport dual-cowl phaeton and Thunderbolt retracting hardtop

War in Europe forces the closing of Chrysler's Belgian plant; military truck orders arrive from France and Britain

After a sharp '39 drop, Dodge rises to sixth place in industry output; Plymouth again comes in third

Sealed-beam headlights become standard, as on most American automobiles

Highlander plaid upholstery debuts as an option on Windsors and New Yorkers

Each Chrysler make earned an all-new body for 1940. Three- and six-seater Chrysler Royal coupes (*above*) were sold. Lower floorpans and wider couch-like seats made interiors (*below*) roomier. Dashboards sported plenty of plastic—a new "wonder" material. Model makers (*right*) touch up full-sized mock-ups of the '40 models in Chrysler's Art Department.

For 1940, DeSoto bodies were prettier, wheelbases longer: 122.5 inches for standard models, 139.5-inches for seven-passenger sedans. The Series S-7S DeLuxe two-door (*top*) cost $905; a fancier S-7C Custom sedan brought $40 more. Both ran with a 228.1-cid, 100-bhp L-head six (106 bhp optional). Joining the line in March 1940 was the two-toned DeSoto S-7 Sportsman four-door sedan (*above left*), offered in three color combinations. Interior fabrics were two-toned to match. The least expensive model was the $845 S-7S DeLuxe business coupe (*left*). Despite its near-fastback profile, the trunk of a DeSoto sedan could swallow a lot of luggage (*above*).

New for 1940, featuring prominent fenders (note the "speedlines") and a lower roofline, the basic Dodge bodyshell was destined to last into early 1949. About 60 percent of output was the D-14 DeLuxe series, including the $860 two-door (*right*). As a sparser D-17 Special, it cost but $35 less. Running boards were now a $10 option. Two-tone paint was new, but not popular—viewed as taxi-like by many customers. After a year's absence, long sedans and limos were revived, on the 139.5-inch chassis. Mohair was popular in Dodge interiors (*below*). Among other extras, DeLuxe models got a full horn ring (*below right*).

The '40 Dodge four-door (*above*) came in Special or DeLuxe guise. Grillework (*left*) was fussy, but attractive.

1940 Production

Chrysler

Series C-25 Royal/Windsor	73,998
Series C-26 Traveler/ New Yorker/Saratoga	17,571
Series C-27 Crown Imperial	850
Total	92,419

DeSoto

S-7S DeLuxe	31,628
S-7C Custom	33,839
Total	65,467

Dodge

D-17 Special	66,504
D-14 DeLuxe	129,001
Total	195,505

Plymouth

P-9 Roadking	103,849
P-10 DeLuxe	316,416
Total	420,265

Plymouth wheelbases grew three inches for 1940, and rear passengers sat ahead of the axle. Bodies again came from an outside firm, but the P-10 DeLuxe Westchester station wagon (*above*), priced at $970, was gaining favor. The DeLuxe two-door sedan (*below left*), with front vent wings and extra bright trim, cost $775, versus $669 for the plainer Roadking. Business coupes (*below right*) had storage space behind the seat. The Plymouth PT-105 pickup (*bottom*) cost just $585, but only 6879 were built.

1940 Engine Availability

Chrysler

No. Cyl.	Disp., cid	bhp	Availability
I-6	241.5	108	S-Royal, Windsor
I-6	241.5	112	O-Royal, Windsor
I-8	323.5	132	S-Crown Imperial
I-8	323.5	135	S-Traveler, NY, Saratoga
I-8	323.5	143	O-Traveler, NY, Saratoga, Crown Imperial

DeSoto

No. Cyl.	Disp., cid	bhp	Availability
I-6	228.1	100	S-all
I-6	228.1	105	O-all

Dodge

No. Cyl.	Disp., cid	bhp	Availability
I-6	217.8	87	S-all

Plymouth

No. Cyl.	Disp., cid	bhp	Availability
I-6	201.3	84	S-all

1941

Chrysler and DeSoto offer a semi-automatic transmission that delivers a Lo-Hi shift

Town & Country is Chrysler's first station wagon; the woody fastback features "clamshell" rear doors

DeSoto's facelift includes prominent grille "teeth" that will identify the make well into the '50s

DeSoto ranks 10th in output—its best showing since its introduction

Plymouth keeps its third place ranking

Fluid Drive is now available on Dodges

Plymouths can have "Powermatic" vacuum-assisted gearshift

Chrysler, DeSoto, and Dodge offer Town Sedans with blank, more formal-looking rear quarters

The impressive Newport show car paces the Indianapolis 500 Memorial Day race

Chrysler Corporation earns a 24-percent market share, beating out Ford's 19-percent slice

Pearl Harbor is bombed on December 7, 1941; President Roosevelt declares war against Japan

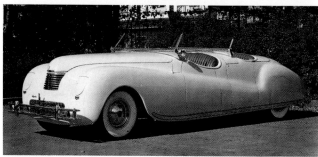

Left and below: Ralph Roberts penned the stunningly streamlined Chrysler Newport dual-cowl phaeton for 1941 show duty. LeBaron built six of them, based on the Imperial. Note the lack of door handles and the hidden headlights. This example once belonged to actress Lana Turner.

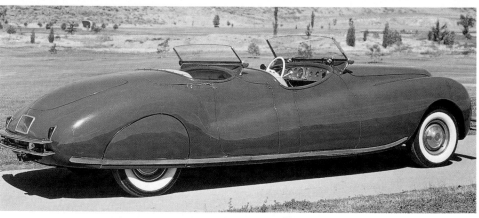

Each of the six Newport show phaetons (*above*) featured an integrated aluminum body and aircraft-style cockpit, with dual fold-down windshields. A yellow example paced the 1941 Indianapolis 500 race. Running gear was conventional. Chrysler's Saratoga line expanded for '41 to include club and business coupes (*left*). The brightest star was the new Windsor-based Town & Country (*bottom*), Chrysler's first "woody" wagon. Instead of the usual boxy shape, the T&C sported a rounded rear, with intriguing side-hinged "clamshell" doors that opened to a huge cargo bay. Unlike other woodies, T & C featured an all-steel roof.

Chrysler's other 1940-41 show car, the Thunderbolt (*right and below*), was designed by Alex Tremulis, then working at Briggs. Six were built, like the Newport, but this "Car of the Future" was an aluminum envelope-bodied, flush-fendered coupe with a fully retractable, electrically controlled hardtop. Pushbuttons operated the doors and hydraulic power windows. Note the enclosed front and rear wheelwells.

Chrysler Thunderbolt THE CAR OF THE FUTURE

Town Sedans with blanked rear quarters and front-hinged back doors were listed in each Chrysler series. The $1760 top-line Crown Imperial (*top row*), of which only 894 were built, rode the New Yorker's 127.5-inch wheelbase, 18 inches shorter than for other Crown models. Regular sedans, including the $1165 C-28 Windsor (*above*), got rear-hinged back doors. The New Yorker convertible (*above left*) cost $1548, but a Windsor Six went for $1315; either could have Highlander plaid upholstery (*second from top*).

DeSoto's heavy '41 facelift featured a lower hood and the grille "teeth" that would become the make's hallmark. Fashion leader was the S-8C Custom convertible (*above*); 2937 were built to sell at $1240. Note the optional spotlights and grille guards. Semi-automatic shift was available, working in concert with Fluid Drive. Custom DeSotos got spiffier interiors (*top right*), plus extra chrome trim. Only 2033 $982 Custom business coupes (*below*) were built; the $945 S-8S DeLuxe version sold 4449 copies. Sportsmen (*bottom left*) enjoyed the extra generous cargo space of the coupes. New DeSotos await water-borne delivery (*right*) to buyers who believed DeSoto's promise of "A dream of driving come true."

This '41 DeSoto Custom four-door is two-toned.

A clean facelift gave the 1941 "Luxury Liner" Dodges a livelier look, whether DeLuxe or Custom. New this year: a $1062 Custom Town Sedan (*above*) with blank rear quarters, priced $63 above the regular four-door. Running boards and skirts were optional. DeSoto also offered a Town Sedan. The Dodge convertible coupe (*left and below*) cost $1162; 3554 were produced. Popular extras included turn signals, skirts, and bumper guards. Though offered only as a DeLuxe, 22,318 buyers still chose the $862 business coupe (*below left*).

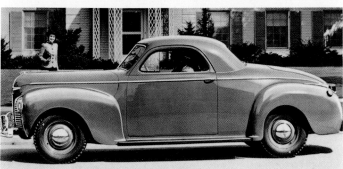

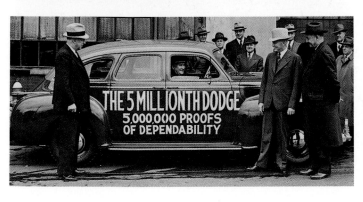

The 5,000,000th Dodge (*far left*) was a four-door sedan—always the most popular body. Rear-hinged doors (*left*) gave easy access to the roomy back seat. Custom Dodges boasted "Air-foam" seat cushions, twin wipers, and a passenger armrest. Higher compression boosted the six to 91 bhp.

The '41 Plymouth facelift featured a vaguely heart-shaped grille and triple "speedline" fenders. Engineering advances included an oil-bath air cleaner and "Safety-Rim" wheels. Top models took the Special DeLuxe badge. Already extinct on most makes, running boards could be omitted from Plymouths. The $1007 Special DeLuxe convertible coupe (*top row*) proved popular, with 10,545 built. Unlike other Chrysler Corporation ragtops, Plymouth's lacked rear quarter windows. Dashboards (*above*) could match the body color.

Youthful Hollywood favorites promoted "America's Low-Priced Luxury Car." Mickey Rooney shows off the 4,000,000th Plymouth (*above*), a Special DeLuxe convertible; as Andy Hardy, he's seen with Judy Garland (*left*). Though not terribly fast, some Plymouths saw police service (*right*).

90

The Plymouth PT-125 pickup cost $625.

Billed as "The One for '41," Plymouths again had a 201.3-cid six. Parking lights sat atop the headlights (*above left*). Center-mounted bumper guards and wing-tip extensions were optional. A Plymouth P-12 Special DeLuxe business coupe (*above right*) cost $795, versus $760 for the DeLuxe and $720 for a budget-priced no-name version. "Powermatic" vacuum-assisted shifting was offered this year. Well before Japan bombed Pearl Harbor on December 7, 1941, Plymouth was building vehicles for the military (*below*).

1941 Production

Chrysler

Series C-28S Royal	78,668
C-28W Windsor	58,031
C-30K/30N Saratoga/ New Yorker/T&C	23,408
C-33 Crown Imperial	1,596
Total	161,703

DeSoto

S-8S DeLuxe	45,798
S-8C Custom	51,699
Total	97,497

Dodge

D-19 DeLuxe	106,463
D-19 Custom	130,539
Total	237,002

Plymouth

P-11 DeLuxe	188,471
P-12 Special DeLuxe	354,139
Total	542,610

1941 Engine Availability

Chrysler

No. Cyl.	Disp., cid	bhp	Availability
I-6	241.5	108/112	S-Royal, Windsor
I-6	241.5	115	O-Royal, Windsor
I-8	323.5	137	S-Saratoga, NY
I-8	323.5	140	O-Saratoga, NY
I-8	323.5	143	S-Crown Imperial

DeSoto

No. Cyl.	Disp., cid	bhp	Availability
I-6	228.1	105	S-all

Dodge

No. Cyl.	Disp., cid	bhp	Availability
I-6	217.8	91	S-all

Plymouth

No. Cyl.	Disp., cid	bhp	Availability
I-6	201.3	87	S-all

1942

All four Chrysler makes are restyled; the basic look will resume when the war ends in 1945

Plymouth and Dodge get the most extensive revamp

"Alligator" hoods now open from the front

Running boards are concealed beneath flared door bottoms, an industry-wide trend

Hidden headlamps make DeSoto the easiest-to-spot '42 model

Dodge's engine is stroked to 230.2-cid; Plymouth's is bored out to 217.8-cid

Although Plymouth drops its slow-selling long sedans, the lineup now includes a blind-quarter Town Sedan

Automakers are already heavily involved in war production

U.S. civilian auto production ends in the last days of January 1942, or very early in February

Aluminum and other manufacturing materials are already in short supply

The final '42s go on sale without chrome trim; as elsewhere in the industry, they're called "blackout" models

Only senior Chryslers carry a 140-bhp straight-eight

Construction begins on a new aircraft-engine plant

Chryslers gained a smoother look for 1942, with grille bars wrapped around front fenders. Despite a short season, 999 shapely wood-bodied Town & Country sedan/wagons (*above and right*) found customers. Convertibles came in both the eight-cylinder New Yorker (*below*) and six-cylinder Windsor series. Initially named Navajo, the special southwestern-motif upholstery (*below right*) was called Thunderbird in 1942. A Chrysler C-36N New Yorker four-door sedan (*bottom*) exhibits "blackout" (painted or plastic-covered) trim.

Coachbuilding was a dying art in 1942, but the Derham company produced several custom models on Chrysler chassis. One Crown Imperial Town Car (*left*) had an open chauffeur's compartment and rounded rear roof. More severe was the formal Imperial Town Car (*below left*), with a squared-off rear roof. Fender skirts cost extra on the $1228 C-34W Windsor Club Coupe (*below*); 1713 were built.

No car since the Classic 1936-37 Cord had the concealed headlights now featured on all '42 DeSotos (*below*). They helped give DeSoto "Tomorrow's Style Today," plus a clean front-end look and a heap of publicity. The top seller, at $1152, was the S-10C Custom four-door sedan (*left*); 7974 were built. Convertibles came in both the DeLuxe and more costly Custom (*below left*) series. Total output: 568.

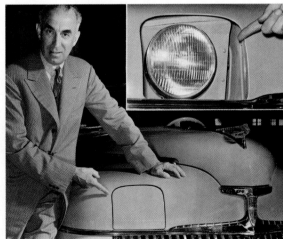

Though far less radical than DeSoto, the '42 Dodge line benefited from a heavy facelift featuring broader front fenders. Dodges came in DeLuxe or Custom trim, with a larger 230.2-cid engine delivering 105 horses, up 14. With 22,055 built, the most popular model by far was the $1048 Custom four-door sedan (*top*). The $995 Custom Club Coupe (*above left*) found 18,024 eager buyers. Fender skirts were optional on the Custom convertible coupe (*left and above*), which cost $1245. Only 1185 were built. Note the graceful swan-shaped mirror. A buzzer sounded if the parking brake was left engaged. The cheapest Dodge, the $862 long-deck DeLuxe business coupe (*below left*) saw 5257 copies. The $1008 two-door Custom sedan (*below*) was called Brougham.

A larger 217.8-cid six cranking out 95 bhp went under '42 Plymouth hoods. Standard-trim models were gone. The P-14C Special DeLuxe lineup expanded to include a Town Sedan with closed-in rear quarters (*above and left*). At $980, it cost $45 more than a regular four-door and found 5821 buyers. The '42 front end looked more massive.

Plymouth finally joined its siblings in ditching exposed running boards. The most expensive '42s were the Special DeLuxe convertible (*right*) and station wagon (*below*): $1078 and $1145. Output was 2806 and 1136, respectively. The rarest model was the $842 DeLuxe utility sedan—only 80 were called for.

1942 Production	
Chrysler	
C-34S Royal	9,564
C-34W Windsor	14,427
C-36K Saratoga	1,596
C-36N New Yorker	10,549
C-33 Crown Imperial	450
Total	36,586
DeSoto	
S-10S DeLuxe	11,100
S-10C Custom	12,915
Total	24,015
Dodge	
D-22 DeLuxe	31,681
D-22 Custom	36,841
Total	68,522
Plymouth	
P-14S DeLuxe	27,645
P-14C Special DeLuxe	124,782
Total	152,427

1942 Engine Availability

Chrysler

No. Cyl.	Disp., cid	bhp	Availability
I-6	250.6	120	S-Royal, Windsor
I-8	323.5	140	S-others

DeSoto

No. Cyl.	Disp., cid	bhp	Availability
I-6	236.6	115	S-all

Dodge

No. Cyl.	Disp., cid	bhp	Availability
I-6	230.2	105	S-all

Plymouth

No. Cyl.	Disp., cid	bhp	Availability
I-6	217.8	95	S-all

1943-45

Chapter 6 Planning for Tomorrow, as World War II Rages: 1943-45

Like all their industrial colleagues, automakers labored hard to produce as much war materiel as possible. Completed in 1941, Chrysler's Detroit Tank Arsenal had the potential of building five tanks per shift. In an unusual arrangement, the U.S. War Department gained title to the Arsenal, which Chrysler leased for a dollar a year. Chrysler also began work on an aircraft-engine plant in Chicago in '42. Chrysler factories turned out trucks, anti-aircraft guns, aero and marine engines, radar units, Corsair landing gear, rockets, and engines and fuselages for B-29 Superfortress bombers. Canadian plants turned out three-ton Dodge trucks; Plymouth manufactured munitions and military engines. Best-known of the Chrysler products were tanks—notably, Sherman tanks. Of some 25,000 tanks built during the war, 18,000 were the near-impervious Shermans. K.T. Keller was closely involved with military production during the period, and received several citations afterward for his efforts. By 1943, more than a thousand auto plants were cooperating in the war effort. In all, the auto industry delivered nearly $29 billion worth of equipment.

Women flocked to America's factories in World War II, here to assemble aircraft wings.

Among the better known of Chrysler's World War II products was the M-4 Sherman tank (*left*), which was built in several variations and by several companies. M-4s were 19.5 feet long and weighed 66,500 pounds. They could cruise at 24 miles per hour tops, but had a fuel range of only about 120 miles. Among other projects, Chrysler produced 7800 "Sea Mule" marine tugs (*below*) during the war. In addition, several hundred Harbor Utility Tugs (*bottom left*) were built for the Navy, for ship-to-shore service. They were designed to be hoisted on deck and accompany the host ship wherever it went. HUTs were of composite construction, built in five sections: three wooden pontoon hulls and two Model 2-A Sea Mule Tractors. The tugs were completely equipped with pushers, towing cleats, splash guard, chocks, and everything necessary for general tug service. These gas-powered Chrysler-Bell air raid sirens (*bottom right*) were mounted atop tall buildings in many larger American cities. They revolved in order to send the warning sound far and wide.

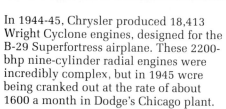

In 1944-45, Chrysler produced 18,413 Wright Cyclone engines, designed for the B-29 Superfortress airplane. These 2200-bhp nine-cylinder radial engines were incredibly complex, but in 1945 were being cranked out at the rate of about 1600 a month in Dodge's Chicago plant.

This Chrysler Historical Archives photo (*top*) depicts a flotilla of men and machines making its way to dangerous shores. The trucks, of course, were Dodges, which were built in vast numbers in a variety of configurations. Not every piece of war equipment was exotic. This smoke screen trailer (*above left*) looks like it was cobbled together from off-the-shelf parts. Note how it could be leveled. Chrysler built 253 units in 1942-43. Slogans (*above*) were a big part of the war effort, both to keep morale high and production strong. Note the Chrysler marine engine. Radar (*left*) was something new, providing vital guidance for aircraft entering battle areas. It wasn't until mid-war that radar production got underway, Chrysler earlier having turned out the less dependable searchlight-audio search units, also called satellite reflectors. Some 2098 radar units were produced; the searchlight reflectors were phased out after 1550 had been made.

It took nearly 100 operations and hundreds of machines (*above*) to produce .45- and .30-caliber ammunition. Tank engines (*below*) were tested before being released.

Chrysler Shipments of War

Products	Units
Air conditioning & refrigeration units	14,370
Bearings	238,109,000
Bofors guns, single	30,095
Pairs	14,442
Bomb chute assemblies, A20	300
Bomb shackles	364,871
Bomber, Boeing B-29 noses	568
Leading edges	559
Cowl sets	4,752
Bomber, Martin B26 nose & center sections	1,586
Bombs, E48 incendiary	101,232
Cartridges, .30-caliber carbine	485,463,000
Cartridges, .45-caliber	2,768,688,000
Cockpit enclosures, Douglas	4,100
Cores, .50-caliber	222,000,000
Engine assemblies, partial	12,214
Engines, industrial	119,814
Engines, marine	21,131
Engines, multi-bank	9,965
Engines, Wright B29	18,413
Field kitchen cabinets	62,192
Field kitchen conv. general units	233,118
Fire apparatus	20,404
Flight station cockpits, PV-2 Lockheed	688
Forgings, aluminum	8,307,549
Furnaces, gas & oil-fired	17,200
Gearboxes, 2-speed	2,100
Grouser kits	2,056
Gyro compasses	5,500
Heaters, misc.: water, domestic & export	29,589
Landing gears	10,202
Marine tractors	8,228
Nets, submarine	1,994
Nose cap assemblies, A20	907
Oerlikon magazine lever assemblies	156,585
Parts, tank (dollars)	$234,298,000
Parts: truck, marine, & industrial engines (dollars)	$173,128,000
Pontoons	9,002
Practice shells, 20-mm	3,000,000
Projectile balls, 20-mm	19,933,000
Propeller balancing stands	2,982
Radar units	2,098
Rockets, 4.5	328,367
Satellite reflectors	1,550
Shell forgings, 3-inch	671,446
Shells, practice, 20-mm	3,000,000
Shot, 20-mm armor piercing	1,989,801
Sirens, air raid	352
Ski pedestals	163,290
Smoke screens	253
Stoves, cook	37,932
Tanks	22,235
Tanks, modified	3,272
Trucks, modified	3,694
Trucks, ½-ton 4x2	1,542
Trucks, 1½-ton 4x2	6,216
Trucks, ½-ton 4x4	72,286
Trucks, ¾-ton 4x4	255,193
Trucks, 1½-ton 6x6	43,278
Trucks, 3-ton (China)	15,000
Wings, center section Curtiss	5,669
X-100, Type 1	406
X-100, Type 2	1,942
X-100, Type 3	1,418
X-100, Type 4	826

Chapter 7

Standing Pat in the Postwar Boom: 1946-48

In a "buyer's market" the consumer is king, and suppliers of products have to hustle for sales. What happened after the end of World War II was precisely the opposite. In the postwar "seller's market," automakers—and many other manufacturers—could sell just about anything they were able to deliver to a dealership.

Not only were car-deprived customers eager to throw dollars at automobiles as soon as they went on sale, some were willing to pay more than the asking prices. Under-the-table deals weren't uncommon as Americans with bulging wallets—Depression deprivations long since forgotten—wanted to be the first on their block to pull up in a brand-new automobile.

While some returning veterans and their families wound up living in hastily erected Quonset huts, courtesy of the postwar housing shortage, the first seeds of suburbia were about to be sown. And with it came a new hunger for automobiles as status symbols, not merely a means of mundane transportation.

Neither Chrysler nor any other automaker was in a position to unleash a totally new design in the early postwar months. But then, they didn't have to. Customers were more than happy to drive home in a warmed-over '42, whether it wore a Chrysler, Ford, or General Motors badge; or that of one of the independents: Hudson, Studebaker, Nash, Packard—even little Crosley.

Except for grille and trim revisions, none of the Chrysler models looked dramatically different from its '42 predecessor. Changes were of a bolt-on nature only, but did include front fenders that flowed smoothly into the front doors of all corporate makes except Plymouth. Chrysler's new so-called "harmonica" grille had the shiniest, most intricate pattern of the lot. Riding a longer wheelbase than Desoto, Dodge, or Plymouth, that make was the most alluring of the bunch, though the relationship among the four was easy to see. Credit for the mild updating goes to "Buzz" Grisinger, John Chika, and Herb Weissinger, a trio of Chrysler stylists who would soon go to the new Kaiser-Frazer Corporation.

Traditional distinctions between the four Chrysler-built makes continued. In addition to unique trim, each rode a different wheelbase and had its own engine specifications. Both club coupes and three-passenger business coupes were sold. The latter attracted salesmen and other business travelers, who needed extra storage space behind the front seat rather than room for passengers in the rear.

On a more frivolous note, some DeSoto/Plymouth hood ornaments even lit up at night. Chrysler engineers were not immune to gadgetry.

Appearances may not have changed much, but prices took a substantial hike, courtesy of postwar inflation. For example, a Chrysler Royal business coupe that cost $1075 before the war now passed the $1400 barrier. Plymouths stood nearly $300 higher than 1942 levels. Prices would continue to escalate throughout the late Forties, but most customers weren't distressed by spiraling inflation just yet.

Engine horsepower ratings dropped a bit, partly as a result of a revised rating system. Otherwise, basic drivetrains

were familiar to owners of prewar Chrysler products. Only Chrysler offered a straight-eight engine; the other three makes ran with six-cylinder power only. Fluid Drive continued as a popular option—even more so than before the war—but was still unavailable on Plymouths.

The intriguing prewar Town & Country wagon faded into history, but Chrysler took the wood-bodied notion into another realm, issuing a series of T&C four-door sedans and convertibles. Celebrities took kindly to the gracefully beautiful Town & Country convertibles, helping to spark interest in the full line. Chrysler actually had planned a full fleet of Town & Country body styles, but that idea got the axe. Though lovely, T&Cs demanded a heavy investment in upkeep. Just 8368 of the convertibles were produced from 1946-48, plus 7950 six-cylinder four-door sedans.

Derham built a custom Crown Imperial Town Limousine, plus many one-offs, including a dual-cowl Imperial phaeton and a New Yorker coupe styled like a Lincoln Continental. A.J. Miller of Ohio created a long-wheelbase limousine/hearse in this period. On the silly side, a promotional New Yorker took the shape of a giant Zippo lighter. No word whether that one "fired up" Chrysler sales.

DeSoto lost its long-wheelbase DeLuxe sedan, but kept the extended Custom models—including a new Suburban. Aimed at hotels and other commercial applications, the Suburban had a fold-down rear seat with no trunk partition, for huge cargo-carrying capacity. A roof rack let bellhops pack even more luggage aboard. DeSoto's flirtation with concealed headlights in '42 turned out to be short-lived. Postwar headlights were exposed in the usual manner, and hidden lamps wouldn't reappear on any American automobile until the Sixties. Between 1946 and '48, DeSoto produced a total of 11,600 taxis, making it the

division's fifth best-selling model.

Even less was new at Dodge, but that make managed fourth place in model-year output, with nearly 164,000 built. The old-fashioned foot-pedal starter was history, replaced by a modern dash-board pushbutton. Also on the technical side, Dodges had front brakes with dual wheel cylinders, an inline fuel filter, and a "Full-Flo" oil filter.

Scarcity of rubber for whitewall tires left automakers scurrying for a solution. The answer? Steel or plastic pseudo-whitewalls, snapped over the inner portion of the tire. Not until 1948 would true whitewalls be readily available once more.

Additional price boosts marked the 1947 season, but Chrysler's cars changed even less than they had for '46. Chrysler editions sported a handful of detail revisions: fender trim, instruments, wheels, and hubcaps. But you had to look closely to discern any difference in DeSoto, Dodge, or Plymouth.

The Traveler moniker returned, on a luxurious Windsor utility sedan with special paint and a wood luggage rack. Though related to DeSoto's Suburban, it had a separate, enclosed trunk instead of fold-down triple seats. Low-pressure Goodyear "Super Cushion" tires went on Chrysler wheels during the model year.

Despite production of more than 243,000 cars, Dodge dropped to fifth place in production (behind Buick) in the 1947 model year. Plymouth, however, hung on to third.

Only an expert could tell a 1948 Chrysler product from a '47 without checking the serial numbers—or noting the inevitable price hikes. The six-cylinder Chrysler Town & Country sedan faded away at mid-year, but the straight-eight convertible continued, billed as the "work or play convertible . . . magnificent in its utterly new styling." Deducing exactly what was new about the look for '48 would likely have exhausted the talents of Sherlock Holmes, but the pricey wood-paneled ragtop continued to draw plenty of attention.

Sixteen-inch tires began to be phased out in favor of 15-inchers that gave a slightly lower stance. A new protective oil coating for cylinder walls claimed to prevent scoring during the engine's break-in period. Dodge regained fourth place in production, slipping past Buick.

Chrysler buyers who shunned gearshifting could order the hydraulically operated transmission and fluid coupling combined as a single option this year. Some observers—then and now—considered Chrysler's semi-automatics a meager response to the "real thing." After all, GM had introduced the fully automatic Hydra-Matic before the war, and this year Buick put Dynaflow into its Roadmaster.

One writer called the Chrysler unit a

"full range of potential transmission trouble," but drivers got the benefit of mostly clutchless and shiftless motoring, in a comparatively trouble-free system. Fully automatic units, let's face it, were in their "teething" stage in the Forties, and hardly immune to serious breakdowns.

As installed in Chryslers and DeSotos, the semi-automatic had two gear positions: Low, governing first and second gears; High for third and fourth. Low was used mainly for fast starts or demanding conditions. Otherwise, all you did was shift into High (using the clutch) and press the accelerator. Then, let up on the gas at 14 mph or more, and a mild "thump" announced the shift from third to fourth. Until you needed to go into Reverse or Low, further stops and starts required no clutching or shifting at all. Chrysler claimed that Fluid Drive combined with the semi-automatic gearbox eliminated 95 percent of all shift motions.

Except for the Town & Country convertible, the '48 models were sold as late as March 1949, branded "first series" '49s. Prices stayed put (for a change), but the ruse didn't fool many customers. If it looked like a '48, most folks reasoned, it *was* a '48—at least after the "real" 1949 cars debuted (dubbed "second series"). Case closed. Not everyone quite understood the difference between model years and calendar years in the auto industry, but they knew two vastly different cars could not *both* be '49s.

Tailfins had already entered the automotive lexicon, introduced on the '48 Cadillac—part of GM's modernization program, portions of which debuted a year earlier than most competitors'. Nothing like Studebaker's all-new 1947 design had been seen before, while Hudson abandoned its prewar bodies after 1947, in favor of a modern, low-slung creation. Cars like those made everything older look sadly obsolete.

An experimental A-109 DeSoto/Dodge displayed such niceties as flow-through fenders, akin to those that graced the brand-new Kaiser and Frazer, issued as 1947 models. Would they appear on the actual 1949 Chrysler products?

Chrysler began to diversify after the war, adding plants in Delaware, Indianapolis, and New Orleans. Except for Dodge/Plymouth operations in California and Indiana, most assembly continued to be executed in Michigan factories—a stone's throw from the corporate headquarters at Highland Park.

Chrysler Corporation ended this first phase of the postwar era on a successful—and optimistic—note, helped by considerable plant expansion. As its real '49 models entered the marketplace, Chrysler had a strong foot in the Number Two spot, behind General Motors. Would it remain there? The answer depended on K.T. Keller's inclination to change with the times, or to stay on his present course.

Chrysler Corporation's 1946 cars, here a Plymouth Special DeLuxe ragtop, were mildly restyled and rushed to market.

1946

Chrysler's warmed-over '42 models, with new grilles and brightwork, sell strongly as postwar production gets underway

Inflation boosts car prices, and will continue to do so

In the postwar "seller's market," customers clamor for every car that the automakers can deliver

Chrysler offers six- and eight-cylinder models; all others are L-head sixes

Starter buttons go on the dashboard; foot-pedal starters are gone

Chrysler's Town & Country is now a wood-trimmed convertible and sedan, not a station wagon as before

DeSoto fields a new long-wheelbase Suburban sedan with a fold-down rear seat

DeSoto headlights now are exposed

Ford leads in model-year production; Chevrolet, Plymouth, Dodge, and Buick follow

Drivetrains are unchanged, but engines have slightly lower horsepower ratings

Early postwar cars wear fake whitewall tires—real ones are scarce for now

Chrysler's four makes continue to differ in engine displacements and wheelbases

Derham custom-built two identical 1946 Chrysler New Yorker Continental coupes (*above and left*) for the chairman of Schenley Distilleries. All-Chrysler ahead of the B-post, each displayed rear styling similar to the Classic Lincoln Continental, including a top-opening trunk. Price tag: $17,000 apiece.

1946-48 Chrysler New Yorker convertible coupe

Chrysler's A-109 experimental sedan (*below*), photographed in September 1946, suggests the box-on-a-box profile of the '49 models, but flow-through rear fenderlines wouldn't arrive until later. The A-109 engine (*left*) was a conventional flathead six.

DeSotos appeared to have changed more than most 1946 cars, due to their newly exposed headlights. Front fenders flowed into doors, matched by a wider grille and wraparound bumpers. An S-11C Custom convertible (*left*) cost $444 more than the '42. At $2093, the most costly model was the new eight-passenger Suburban (*below left*), with a metal-and-wood roof rack and fitted wood interior panels. With its rear seat folded (*below*), a vast cargo hold was revealed.

As usual, the four-door sedan (*left and above*) served as the mainstay of the DeSoto lineup. In 1946, four-doors came in S-11S DeLuxe trim for $1461, or S-11C Custom level for $50 more. Both rode a 121.5-inch wheelbase (same as in 1942), but seven-passenger sedans and limousines measured 139.5 inches between wheel centers. DeSoto also fielded a Club Coupe and two-door sedan in both series, plus a business coupe in DeLuxe trim only. Formal-look Town Sedans, offered in 1941-42, did not return after the war.

Even Dodge didn't attempt to differentiate between postwar models. Many publicity photos were identified as "1946-48," rather than for a specific year. Four-door sedans (*above*) came in either D-24S DeLuxe or D-24C Custom trim, with a $50 difference. Sun visors and spotlights were popular extras. A '46 Custom convertible (*top right*) cost $1649. The center brakelight on the DeLuxe business coupe (*right*) was a hallmark of 1940s Chrysler products.

Inside (*above*), as well as outside, changes were modest in the '46 Dodge Custom Club Coupe, with its roomy back seat. Price tag: $1384. A cheaper single-seat business coupe came only in the DeLuxe series. *Left:* The Dodge pickup truck—note the headlamps atop fenders.

Ads claimed that the '46 Plymouth was "Four Years Better," but revisions were modest—including a simpler grille. This Special DeLuxe two-door sedan (*left*), $1199 in 1946, has a load of extras: hood ornament light, turn signals, and back-up light. The P-15C Special DeLuxe four-door sedan (*below left*) was Plymouth's runaway best-seller.

Plymouth DeLuxe business coupe

Photographed in July '46, this experimental three-passenger Plymouth (*left*) had been proposed two years earlier. Had it been produced, it would have served as Plymouth's equivalent of the '49 Dodge Wayfarer, but with a removable fiberglass top and roll-down windows.

Even with its hardtop in place, the experimental Plymouth coupe (*right*) had a jaunty air. Note the prominent bumper guards.

1946 to 1949 First-Series Production

(Chrysler combined production figures for models built from 1946 through the first part of 1949. These cars bore no significant year-to-year changes, so they have been grouped together in the following charts.)

Chrysler

Royal	31,371
Windsor	214,903
Saratoga	5,605
New Yorker	67,019
Town & Country	12,526
Crown Imperial	1,400
Total	332,824

DeSoto

DeLuxe	55,494
Custom	185,901
Total	241,395

Dodge

DeLuxe	170,986
Custom	479,013
Total	649,999

Plymouth

DeLuxe	197,202
Special DeLuxe	862,287
Total	1,059,489

1946-1949 First-Series Engine Availability

Chrysler

No. Cyl.	Disp., cid	bhp	Availability
I-6	250.6	114	S-Royal, Windsor, T&C six
I-8	323.5	135	S-others

DeSoto

No. Cyl.	Disp., cid	bhp	Availability
I-6	236.6	109	S-all

Dodge

No. Cyl.	Disp., cid	bhp	Availability
I-6	230.2	102	S-all

Plymouth

No. Cyl.	Disp., cid	bhp	Availability
I-6	217.8	95	S-all

1947

Chrysler products show minimal change; Plymouth, Dodge, DeSoto, and Chrysler look almost exactly like the '46 models

A new Chrysler Traveler sedan, in the Windsor line, sports a roof rack; it rides an 18-inch-shorter wheelbase than the DeSoto Suburban

Starting in August, Chryslers ride Goodyear low-pressure "Super Cushion" tires

Chrysler and General Motors sign autoworkers' union contracts

The Taft-Hartley Labor Act brings a halt to strikes

Derham Bodyworks—one of the few remaining coach-builders—creates several intriguing conversions of Chrysler autos

Many DeSotos see use as city taxis—some even have a "moonroof"

Chrysler Corporation's model-year output rises from 580,000 to 832,000

Chevrolet regains the Number One spot in production; Ford is next, followed by Plymouth, Buick, and Dodge

Chrysler cars have revised fender trim, hubcaps, and carburetors

Plymouths still cannot have Fluid Drive, which is popular in the other makes

Chrysler launched the glamorous Town & Country convertible in 1946. At $2998, the '47 model (*above*) was the most costly Chrysler, apart from Crown Imperials. This year's T&C switched from real wood to Di-Noc decal inserts. A total of 7950 six-cylinder T&C sedans (*left*) were sold from 1946-48.

Comic actor Leo Carillo drove a mildly modified Town & Country convertible.

Long-wheelbase eight-passenger sedans (*left*) were available in three Chrysler series: Royal, Windsor, and a revived super-long Crown Imperial. In 1947, the Chrysler Series C-39K Saratoga eight four-door sedan (*below*) sold for $1973, while a Royal six equivalent cost just $1661. Except for a tiny instrument panel change, 1947 Chryslers looked identical to '46 models. Larger, low-pressure tires arrived during the year. The new Chrysler Traveler utility sedan was comparable to DeSoto's Suburban, but on a standard wheelbase. A DeSoto Custom Club Coupe (*below left*) sold for $1591, but the more spartan DeLuxe version brought $50 less.

DeSoto Suburbans (*left*) served well at airports. A Dodge convertible (*above*) cost $1871 in 1947. Plymouth's still lacked rear quarter windows (*below*). A Plymouth Special DeLuxe sedan (below *left*) cost $1289.

See page 105 for 1946-1949 production/engine data.

1948

Chrysler products are virtually identical to the '47s, but prices go higher

The seller's market is still booming; production rises past the '47 total

Chrysler's hydraulically operated transmission and fluid coupling combine into a single option

Real whitewall tires are finally readily available

Town & Country models now wear Di-Noc decals rather than genuine mahogany veneer

Chrysler continues the sale of '48 models into early 1949, until updated replacements are ready

Most owners consider the "first series" 1949 models to be '48s

A new Dodge assembly plant opens in San Leandro, California

Chevrolet again tops the model-year production race; Ford is second, then Plymouth and Dodge

Chrysler Corporation ranks second in car production, behind General Motors but ahead of Ford

Plant expansions help keep Chrysler sales strong

A new protective coating prevents cylinder scoring during engine break-in

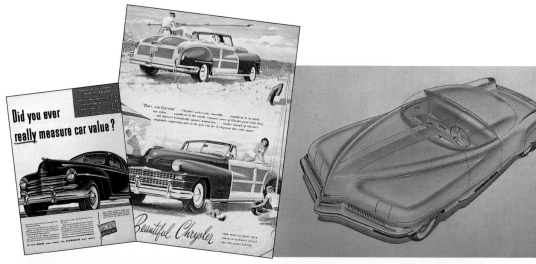

Chrysler and Plymouth ads (*top left*) promoted the glamour and value of the '48 production models, including the luscious Town & Country convertible. All-new cars wouldn't arrive until well after the start of the 1949 model year. Meanwhile, in the design studios, stylists kept busy with fanciful ideas for the future (*above and right*).

Peculiar promotions continued into the early postwar era—if not quite so numerous as in the Thirties, when people badly needed a laugh. One hapless Chrysler New Yorker (*left*) metamorphosed into a giant windproof Zippo lighter. The '48 Chrysler Windsor Traveler utility sedan (*below left*) featured an ash wood roof rack. Interiors (*below*) could have leather to complement body colors. This six-cylinder model carried a base price of $1846.

1948

The best-selling Chrysler New Yorker in 1948 was—no surprise—the $2411 four-door sedan (*left*), shown with the popular accessory sun visor. Chrysler offered 31 models in the 1946-early '49 era, so it's perhaps surprising that this single high-priced model was able to draw in 52,036 eager postwar customers. The eight-cylinder New Yorker lounged above a 127.5-inch wheelbase, a half-foot longer than the cheaper six-cylinder Royals and Windsors—and all of that extra length went into the hood. Car spotters in the Forties knew the difference, and that enhanced the big Chrysler's reputation.

Roof racks now were metal-and-wood, but the $2631 DeSoto Suburban (*above left*) still offered impressive cargo- and people-carrying capacity. Some 7500 were built in 1946-48. Spotlights cost extra on the $2296 DeSoto S-11C Custom convertible (*above right*).

In 1948, a long-wheelbase Dodge Custom sedan (*left*) commanded $2179, a 22-percent premium over the regular sedan. The Series B-1-PW Power Wagon (*right*) was a civilian spin-off of a four-wheel-drive wartime model. This version cost $2045 and weighed 5100 pounds. Low gearing helped the 102-bhp six move it along. Production was low: 8198 units in 1949, for example.

Plymouth's sportiest offering for 1948 was the Special DeLuxe convertible (*left*), seen here in Marine Blue. It cost $1857. Some 15,295 copies of this model were built from 1946 through early 1949. The $1529 Special DeLuxe four-door sedan (*above*) was far more popular, with 514,986 produced in the same period.

See page 105 for 1946-1949 production/engine information.

109

Chapter 8

Engineering Overpowers Fashion: 1949-54

The styling of Chrysler Corporation's 1949 "second-series" models was boxy and practical. For 1950, Plymouth (below) sported a new grille, but its shape remained as conservative as ever.

Fads didn't interest K.T. Keller, still occupying the driver's seat at Chrysler Corporation. Neither did streamlining. Practical transportation—that's what Chrysler's customers wanted, and that's what K.T. would give them. Stylists Buzz Grisinger and Herb Weissinger had left for Kaiser-Frazer, so Chrysler's new styling philosophy reflected the personal tastes of K.T. Keller. Disdaining low "torpedo" styling, Keller preferred the "three-box" theme, and insisted that function take precedence over form.

Oh yes, streamlined profiles with integral fenders had been considered for the "second-series" 1949 models. Considered, then vetoed. K.T. wanted tall, upright bodies with roomy interiors—the kind of car in which a person could sit comfortably with a hat on, and slip into without needing a chiropractor.

Chrysler executives judged the slab-sided '49s "stylish," and so did plenty of consumers, who shared Keller's view of the need for good-sense transportation. Convinced of Chrysler's reputation for engineering superiority, many drove home happy with their purchases—even if neighbors turned a jaundiced eye toward the car's less-than-luscious form.

In 1948, K.T. Keller had told the Stanford School of Business that a "buyer is proud of his car's symphony of line. . . . But he bought the car to ride in." For many buyers, that was indeed enough. But as suburbia and "white col-

lar" life took hold, Americans turned ever farther away from the strictly functional, falling in love with the tailfins and geegaws that Keller's competitors were eager to provide.

Customers soon would demonstrate that they savored the lush, low look of the products unleashed by General Motors in 1948-49. Not to mention the hot overhead-valve V-8 engines that now powered Oldsmobiles and Cadillacs, while Chrysler fielded old-fashioned inline powerplants. Ford's restyle for 1949, though also on the boxy side, at least leaned tentatively into the future.

For truly forward thinking, some of the independents had taken charge. Studebaker had issued its dramatically shaped new models for 1947, severing all ties with prewar design. Some loved the "coming-or-going" Studes, others hated them—but they definitely drew notice. Hudson launched its fabulous "Step-downs" for 1948; Packard and Nash adopted the curvy "upside-down-bathtub" look. Closest to Chrysler in appearance, perhaps, were the Kaiser and Frazer sedans, the only new makes to enter full production, introduced as 1947 models.

Chrysler's '49s were comfortable and

roomy, with good visibility. They sold reasonably well, if not quite in droves. But other makes did better yet, so while Plymouth retained its Number Three spot in production, its costlier mates dropped a few rungs. The postwar seller's market wasn't yet saturated, but manufacturers who dwelled in the past a little too long could easily be lulled into a false sense of security about the future. As one small portent for that future, Custom DeSotos outsold DeLuxe models by a 3-to-1 ratio. Shoppers wanted luxury, it seemed, and were willing to pay extra dollars for a few comforts.

Chryslers wore the most ornate '49 grilles, just as they had in 1946-48, but all four makes displayed similar shaping. All but the Crown Imperials wore stand-up, tacked-on taillights. Wheelbases were longer, with the exception of stubby low-end two-doors from Dodge and Plymouth. Front fenders were fully flush-styled for the first time. Beneath the hoods: familiar L-head sixes and a straight-eight.

DeSoto launched a new four-door Carry-All, similar to the roomy Custom Suburban but on a standard wheelbase. As part of its inexpensive Wayfarer series, Dodge offered a novel three-passenger roadster with side curtains, harking back to Thirties thinking. Meadowbrook and Coronet Dodges were bigger and better-trimmed. Plymouth claimed its Suburban was the first "modern" station wagon, but Chevrolet, Oldsmobile, and Pontiac also issued all-steel wagons during 1949. Plymouth's was cheaper, though, and sold well.

Chrysler's version of the still-popular semi-automatic transmission was called "Prestomatic" this year; DeSoto's took the "Tip-Toe" designation. Each again eliminated gearchanges, except when backing up or shifting to Low range. Dodge called its semi-shifter "Gyro-Matic." Chryslers now began using the ignition key instead of a pushbutton for starting the engine—a small but significant bit of progress, soon to become the norm. More important for safety were "Cycle-Bonded" brake linings, lacking the customary rivets that had an unfortunate tendency to eat into brake drums after the linings wore down.

Detail changes for 1950 included faired-in taillights. Hardtop coupes joined the body-style list, available as the Chrysler Newport, Dodge Diplomat, and DeSoto Sportsman. A Town & Country hardtop edged aside Chrysler's wood-trimmed convertible, and all Imperials halted with something unique: four-wheel disc brakes.

As the U.S. became involved in Korea, many Americans feared that auto production might again be curtailed or halted. Sales thus soared in the 1950 model year for all four Chrysler makes—and for their competitors as well. As a result, Plymouth dropped temporarily into fourth place. A three-month strike against Chrysler by the United Auto

Workers hadn't helped.

K.T. Keller's successor, Lester Lum "Tex" Colbert, took over the presidency of the company in the autumn of 1950 (K.T. moved up to board chairman). Colbert aimed toward decentralized division management and a total redesign of all makes as quickly as possible, plus an ambitious program of plant expansion.

The biggest news of 1951—indeed, of the decade—was the announcement of the new hemispherical-head V-8 engine. Installed initially in Chrysler Saratogas, New Yorkers, and Imperials, the "Hemi" operated with exceptional volumetric efficiency, and could deliver truly thrilling performance (for its day). In the lighter-weight Saratoga, that meant 0-60 times near 10 seconds, quicker than an Oldsmobile 88. Lower compression let the Hemi run on lower-octane fuel than most V-8s, but it had potential for far more power. Not all was perfect, of course. Hemi engines cost more to build, requiring twice as many rocker shafts and pushrods, for example.

DeSoto made do with an enlargement of its L-head six, but would get a smaller edition of the Hemi, named FireDome, for '52. All four makes earned mild 1951 restyling on the same basic bodies, mainly at the front end, then changed hardly a bit the next year. Plymouth edged back into third place in the 1951 production race (remaining there in '52), while Chrysler and DeSoto dropped a bit. Cutbacks for the growing Korean conflict were playing a role in production losses industry-wide.

Plymouth's lackluster sales performance could be attributed not only to drab looks—an opinion not universally shared—but to its relatively listless L-head engine and lack of any sort of automatic-shifting option. Chevrolet had issued Powerglide in 1950, Ford offered Ford-O-Matic in '51. Plymouth had nothing more than overdrive to tempt customers, and not until 1952.

Virgil Exner earns credit for much of the '53 reskinning. Though squared-off and upright, all four Chrysler makes exhibited a shapelier profile. The cars not only looked better, they seemed unrelated to their 1949-52 ancestors, even though Chrysler and DeSoto employed the same basic bodyshells. Plymouth and Dodge received new bodies on shorter wheelbases. All sported curved, one-piece windshields and mildly wrapped back windows, too—even Plymouth.

As a bonus, lighter weights boosted performance. Lightness was particularly good news at Dodge, where buyers could now order a 140-horsepower version of the Hemi V-8 engine. Dodge V-8s were quick and handled crisply, without sucking up too much fuel. A Red Ram got 23.4 mpg in the 1953 Mobilgas Economy Run, while other V-8 Dodges set speed records. Dodge sales boomed in '53, and one-fifth were hardtops or

ragtops, signaling a forthcoming role as Chrysler's "performance" make.

Production totals tell the 1953 model-year tale. Each of the four makes shot up the charts, even though their industry rankings didn't change much. At mid-year, Plymouth finally got a semi-automatic transmission, called "Hy-Drive," but clutch action was needed for first-gear starts.

Show cars also were beginning to boost Chrysler's image. Early examples, starting with the XX-500 in 1950, were styled in Italy by the Ghia company. Virgil Exner tried his hand at subsequent concepts, including the Dodge Firearrow roadster, completed in '53.

The next year, 1954, turned out to be Chrysler's worst season since World War II, as model-year sales fell below 800,000. Clearly, the public was finally shunning the "bigger on the inside, smaller on the outside" policy that had been used as an advertising theme. In fact, some models were slightly smaller than their '53 equivalents (albeit better-looking). "Downsizing" hadn't been invented yet, but the term applied to Chrysler's 1953-54 lineup.

Plymouth, sporting new model names and running an enlarged six-cylinder engine, hung onto third place in production, but not by much. Dodge slipped to eighth, despite its lively V-8.

At long last, Chrysler products could be ordered with a fully automatic transmission: two-speed PowerFlite. Introduced late in 1953 for Chryslers, it was even installed in Plymouths during the latter part of '54. In that year, a whopping 98 percent of Chryslers were ordered with it.

A Dodge Royal 500 convertible paced the Indy 500 race in '54 and 701 replicas went on sale, featuring Kelsey-Hayes chrome wire wheels, a rear-mounted spare tire, and a specially tuned 150-bhp Red Ram engine. Dodges overwhelmed the Medium Stock class at the 1954 Mexican Road Race, finishing 1-2-3-4-6-9.

Though little-publicized, Chrysler engineers led by George Huebner, Jr., were making their first stabs at a gas turbine engine—a task that would occupy them over the next decade. The first example, dubbed "CR1," went into a '54 Plymouth Belvedere hardtop.

This year saw the final use of the 1949 bodyshell. DeSoto advertised its '54 model as the "car with the forward look." That was nothing. Courtesy of Virgil Exner, Chrysler had a much farther-forward shape in mind for 1955. Something had to be done to get those sales figures back on track. Not just a little model-tweaking, but some stirrings akin to a rebirth.

Customers also had some surprises in store in the high-performance arena. Chrysler's new Proving Grounds could cope with cars at 140-mph velocities. Now, the company just might launch a vehicle that approached such limits.

1949

Carryover '48 models start the season; all-new designs debut at mid-year

All "Big Three" makes are modernized—Chrysler's are boxy, GM's sleek, Ford's in-between

Prices continue to increase

The wood-paneled Town & Country comes only as a convertible

Plymouth offers an all-steel station wagon—one of the first

DeSoto has a Carry-All four-door sedan with a fold-down back seat

Dodge issues a single-seat Wayfarer roadster with snap-in Plexiglas windows

An ignition key operates Chrysler starters

Industry production hits a record high: 6,253,651 units

Plymouth ranks third in output; Dodge drops to eighth

Sales are up in all divisions except DeSoto

Stylist Virgil Exner leaves Studebaker, signs on at Chrysler

Oldsmobile begins the "horsepower race" with its all-new overhead-valve V-8

Critics brand them dull, but Chrysler dubs '49s "stylish"

Chrysler drivers faced a big instrument cluster (*left*) and key-started the L-head eight. At $3206, the New Yorker convertible (*top*) was the costliest model—apart from Imperial and Town & Country.

Only one woody Town & Country model made the '49 Chrysler lineup, a $3970 ragtop (*above and below left*) with a 135-bhp eight and 131.5-inch wheelbase. An even 1000 were sold. Note the squarish decklid and unique taillights. The $2329 Windsor four-door sedan (*below*), with a 125.5-inch span and 116-bhp six, sold best: 55,879 copies.

A padded, Hartz cloth-covered roof distinguished several 1949 Chrysler New Yorker sedans (*above*), crafted by the Derham company. Slim, tacked-on Chrysler taillights looked almost like little fins. The top-selling New Yorker was the four-door sedan (*left*). For the last time, brake lights were center-mounted on the decklid.

Left: The '49 Chrysler New Yorker four-door cost $2726. *Below:* Underneath, the '49 Chryslers hadn't changed much—including the six- and eight-cylinder L-head engines.

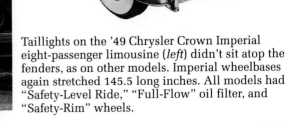

Taillights on the '49 Chrysler Crown Imperial eight-passenger limousine (*left*) didn't sit atop the fenders, as on other models. Imperial wheelbases again stretched 145.5 long inches. All models had "Safety-Level Ride," "Full-Flow" oil filter, and "Safety-Rim" wheels.

Like all 1949 DeSotos, the Custom convertible (*above*) had a 112-horsepower, L-head six-cylinder engine. Price tag: $2578, including a new full-vision plastic rear window. A total of 3385 were built. The ragtop shown has a special brown leatherette interior, as in Suburbans. More prosaic cloth went into the Custom Club Coupe (*below*), which captured 18,431 buyers. Fluid Drive with "Tip-Toe" hydraulic shifting was standard on Customs, $121 extra on DeLuxe models. Wheelbases grew four inches, and a bust of Hernando DeSoto replaced the former hood ornament.

"Woodies" soon would be extinct. In 1949, the $2191 DeSoto all-steel Carry-All sedan sold better than the $2959 wood-paneled station wagon (*below left*): 2690 versus 850. Note the unique taillights, how the wagon's spare-tire cover opened (*below*), and how the bumper center dropped.

Economy-oriented Dodge Wayfarers rode a short 115-inch wheelbase, while the Meadowbrook and top-line Coronet series measured 123.5 inches. A stubby Wayfarer semi-fastback two-door sedan (*left*) cost $1738, while a single-seat business coupe (*below*) went for just $1611. Turn signals cost extra. Only one Meadowbrook was issued: the $1848 four-door sedan (*second from bottom, left*). Four models made up the Coronet series, including a structural-wood station wagon (*second from bottom, right*).

Chrysler products could be found in countless commercial applications. This 1949 Dodge Meadowbrook (*left and above*) needed substantial modifications to be ready for ambulance duty. Note the siren and roof light. Fluid Drive was standard on all Dodge models, and Coronets could get an optional Gyro-Matic (semi-automatic) transmission for the first time, similar to that used in Chryslers and DeSotos.

Early examples of the unique Dodge Wayfarer roadster (*top, left and right*) had snap-in plexiglass side curtains. Later, conventional roll-up windows and vent wings arrived. Only three people could occupy the single bench seat. All Dodges used the same 230.2-cid L-head six, rated at 103 bhp. Coronet sedans could get an $85 "Town Sedan" option, with Bedford cloth upholstery. The best-selling '49 Plymouth was the $1629 Series P-18 Special DeLuxe four-door sedan (*bottom row*)—more than a quarter-million rolled off the line. This one has the accessory sun visor. Note the fluted bumpers, later popular with customizers. Plymouth wheelbases grew to 118.5 inches for DeLuxe and Special DeLuxe models, but were 111 inches for the DeLuxe two-door and business coupe (comparable to Dodge Wayfarers), and the new all-steel Suburban station wagon. Virgil M. Exner (*far right*) joined Chrysler in 1949, after stints at GM and Studebaker. Anyone who yearned to assemble a 1949 Dodge needed all these components (*right*).

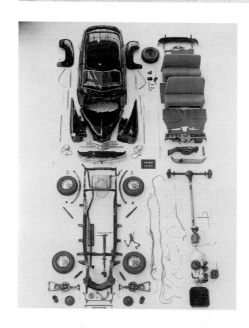

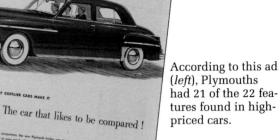

According to this ad (*left*), Plymouths had 21 of the 22 features found in high-priced cars.

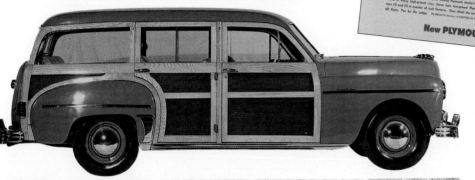

1949 Second-Series Production

Chrysler
Royal	19,076
Windsor	77,291
Saratoga	2,275
New Yorker	24,441
Town & Country	1,000
Imperial	50
Crown Imperial	85
Total	124,218

DeSoto
DeLuxe	23,495
Custom	70,876
Total	94,371

Dodge
D-29 Wayfarer	63,820
D-30 Meadowbrook/Coronet	193,037
Total	256,857

Plymouth
P-17 DeLuxe (wb 111.0)	61,455
P-18 DeLuxe (wb 118.5)	76,708
P-18 Special DeLuxe	372,222
Total	510,385

Chrysler claimed that its 1949 Plymouth P-18 DeLuxe Suburban (*top left*) was the industry's first all-steel station wagon, but a couple of rivals issued one around the same time. Billed as "The car with 101 uses," the $1840 two-door wagon carried its spare tire in a floor well. Folding down the rear seat created a 5 x 8-foot cargo area. The most expensive—and heaviest— Plymouth was the P-18 four-door woody station wagon (*second from top, left*): $2372 and 3341 pounds. Just 3443 were built, versus 19,220 Suburbans. The woody's spare tire rested in the tailgate, and the body now had a steel roof. Plymouth's $1982 Special DeLuxe convertible (*above and right*) contained rear quarter windows for the first time; 15,240 were produced.

1949 Second-Series Engine Availability

Chrysler
No. Cyl.	Disp., cid	bhp	Availability
I-6	250.6	116	S-Royal, Windsor
I-8	323.5	135	S-others

DeSoto
No. Cyl.	Disp., cid	bhp	Availability
I-6	236.6	112	S-all

Dodge
No. Cyl.	Disp., cid	bhp	Availability
I-6	230.2	103	S-all

Plymouth
No. Cyl.	Disp., cid	bhp	Availability
I-6	217.8	97	S-all

1950

Chrysler Corporation builds 1.27 million cars, an all-time record

President Harry S Truman orders troops to Korea for a "police action"

Chrysler endures a 104-day strike

Hardtop coupes debut from Chrysler, Dodge, and DeSoto

Chrysler products receive mild facelifts of their "three-box" shape

The center-mounted stop-lights are gone

Chrysler's Town & Country is a hardtop coupe only

All-disc brakes are available on Imperial

Closed Chryslers sport a three-piece rear window

Roll-down side glass is now standard for the Wayfarer roadster

The Chrysler Traveler sedan is revived, with a folding rear seat

The Ghia-styled XX-500 is the first of Chrysler's "idea cars"

K.T. Keller moves into the chairman's post; Lester Lum "Tex" Colbert is named president

Revised rear fenders display newly faired-in taillights

Apart from a broader grille, faired-in tail-lights, and a trim shuffle, the '50 Chrysler came in seven series. No longer a convertible, the wood-paneled Town & Country was now a hardtop coupe (*top*), priced at $4003. Only 700 were built. Standard equipment included four-wheel disc brakes! Twin spot-lights and driving lights cost extra. New Yorker Eight (*second from top*) and Windsor Six versions of the Newport hard-top coupe body style also went on sale, at $3133 and $2637.

The $2758 Chrysler New Yorker Eight four-door (*right*) was handily outsold by its $2329 Windsor Six counterpart, 78,199 to 22,633. This was the last year for the bottom-rung Royal series.

At $3179, the long-wheelbase, nine-seater DeSoto Custom Suburban sedan (*below*) appealed to only 623 practical-minded customers. Except for flush tail-lights and round parking lights, DeSotos changed lit-tle for 1950.

DeSoto's new hardtop coupe (*above*), named Sportsman, sold for $2489 as part of the Custom series. Despite a debut late in the model year, 4600 were produced. Note the huge three-piece wraparound rear window.

The $1927 Dodge Coronet four-door sedan (*top row*) differed from the $1848 Meadowbrook mainly in minor trim. Their output totaled 221,791 units. Sales of the $1727 Wayfarer Sportabout roadster (*left*) fell to 2903.

1950 Production	
Chrysler	
Royal	24,687
Windsor	112,213
Saratoga	1,300
New Yorker	29,335
Town & Country	700
Imperial	10,650
Crown Imperial	415
Total	179,300
DeSoto	
DeLuxe	33,329
Custom	100,525
Total	133,854
Dodge	
D-33 Wayfarer	75,403
D-34 Meadowbrook/Coronet	266,394
Total	341,797
Plymouth	
P-19 DeLuxe (wb 111.0)	119,903
P-20 DeLuxe (wb 118.5)	141,761
P-20 Special DeLuxe	350,290
Total	611,954

"The beautifully new Plymouth" wore flush taillights, smoother bumpers, and a simpler grille for 1950. The $1982 Special DeLuxe convertible (*above*) featured pleated upholstery; 12,697 were sold. Ghia built and designed the first of Chrysler's Italian-built concept cars, the Plymouth XX-500 (*left*).

1950 Engine Availability

Chrysler			
No. Cyl.	Disp., cid	bhp	Availability
I-6	250.6	116	S-Royal, Windsor
I-8	323.5	135	S-others

DeSoto			
No. Cyl.	Disp., cid	bhp	Availability
I-6	236.6	112	S-all

Dodge			
No. Cyl.	Disp., cid	bhp	Availability
I-6	230.2	103	S-all

Plymouth			
No. Cyl.	Disp., cid	bhp	Availability
I-6	217.8	97	S-all

1951

As the Korean War intensifies, production cutbacks are ordered

Mild facelifts are evident on each Chrysler make

Chrysler introduces its 180-bhp "Hemi" Firepower V-8 engine

The Town & Country nameplate now applies only to Chrysler's all-steel station wagon

"Hydraguide" power steering becomes available

Dodge introduces an all-steel Sierra station wagon

Plymouth series are renamed; they're now Concord, Cambridge, and Cranbrook

Plymouth debuts its first hardtop, the Belvedere

Dodge, DeSoto, and Chrysler offer "Tip-Toe" shifting

Bill Sterling places third in the *Carrera Panamericana* driving a Chrysler Saratoga; it takes first in the stock-car class

The Italian-built K-310 show car demonstrates some early ideas of designer Virgil Exner

The technically impressive "Hemi" is costly to build

Dodge issues its final Wayfarer roadsters

Chrysler New Yorker convertible: 1951 Indy "Official Pace Car"

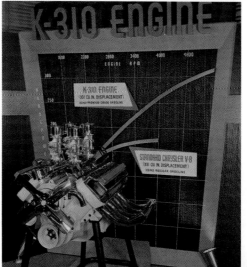

Chrysler's "Hemi" V-8 (*above*) ranked as the company's foremost feat of the decade. A four-carb V-8 (*left*) was developed for the K-310 show car. The chart compares its output to that of the standard 331-cubic-inch Hemi engine.

Though overshadowed by the Hemi V-8, Chrysler's new Hydraguide coaxial power steering (*right*) was an industry "first." Cadillac and Lincoln soon followed with their own systems. Fluid-Torque Drive was this year's designation for the semi-automatic four-speed transmission. Named for its more efficient hemispherical combustion chambers, the new V-8 was the most powerful engine in America. Hemi power took many victories in road racing and on NASCAR oval tracks.

Newport hardtops came in four of the five 1951 Chrysler series, including the New Yorker (*left*). A "V" on the hood (*above*) signaled the presence of the Hemi V-8.

Below: Secretly designed in Detroit, and built by Ghia on the Saratoga's 125.5-inch chassis, the Chrysler K-310 concept car was actually considered for production. Some features saw later use, including "gunsight" taillights, flush door handles, and a simulated decklid spare tire.

DeSotos received a styling facelift for 1951, displaying a more sloping nose, an abundance of chrome, and a lower, bolder version of the familiar toothy grille. Stroked to 250.6-cid, the L-head six gained four horses, to 116. Like all Series S-15-2 Custom DeSotos, the highly popular $2438 four-door sedan (*above and right*) had standard Prest-O-Matic (Fluid Drive with Tip-Toe shift). Customers snapped up 88,491 copies. DeLuxe DeSotos came with the regular three-speed manual, but the semi-automatic unit was optional.

For the last time, Dodge offered its Wayfarer Sportabout roadster (*above and right*). Barely more than a thousand went on sale, priced at $1924. Except for all-out sports cars, single-seat vehicles—even dapper ones—no longer seemed appropriate in the spreading suburbs of America. Buyers who liked the idea of a ragtop— but not the reality of water leaks and discomfort— increasingly turned to the "hardtop convertible." Dodge's Coronet Diplomat (*below*) looked best in two-tone paint. Note the large three-piece wraparound back window. Dodge built 21,600 Diplomats for 1951-52 combined.

In addition to the roadster, the 1951 Dodge Wayfarer lineup again included a business coupe and semi-fastback two-door sedan (*left*). The interior (*above*) looked a bit austere, but the dashboard contained full gauges.

1951 Production

(Chrysler combined model-year production for 1951 and 1952. Models that were available in only one of those two years will have production figures listed. In some cases, production figures for one-year-only body styles indicated what percentage of the total for other body styles was built in each year, and in those cases we've listed approximate 1951 and 1952 production figures.)

Chrysler*

Windsor	82,917
Saratoga	28,665
New Yorker	34,286
Imperial	17,303
Crown Imperial	442
Total	163,613

* Approximate

DeSoto

DeLuxe	See 1952
Custom	See 1952
Total	See 1952

Dodge

D-41 Wayfarer	See 1952
D-42 Meadowbrook/Coronet	See 1952
Total	See 1952

Plymouth

Concord	See 1952
Cambridge	See 1952
Cranbrook	See 1952

1951 Engine Availability

Chrysler

No. Cyl.	Disp., cid	bhp	Availability
I-6	250.6	116	S-Windsor
V-8	331.1	180	S-others

DeSoto

No. Cyl.	Disp., cid	bhp	Availability
I-6	250.6	116	S-all

Dodge

No. Cyl.	Disp., cid	bhp	Availability
I-6	230.2	103	S-all

Plymouth

No. Cyl.	Disp., cid	bhp	Availability
I-6	217.8	97	S-all

Plymouth's hardtop, the Belvedere, (*top*) came only in the Cranbrook series. The $1796 two-door sedan (*above*) was called Club Coupe.

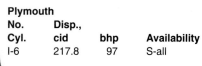

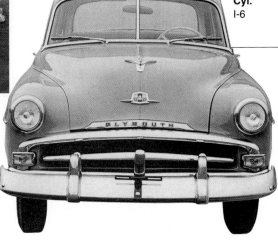

The cheapest and lightest Plymouth for 1951 was the Concord business coupe (*above*), with a single seat that held three people. Blackwall tires looked fitting on this no-frills model, whose $1537 base price attracted only 14,255 buyers in 1951 and '52 combined. Plymouth's fresh face (*right*) included a modified hood and lower grille.

1952

Chrysler and GM field mildly facelifted '51s, but Ford products enjoy a sleek restyle

Plymouth clings to the Number Three position, followed by Buick and Pontiac

A FireDome "Hemi" V-8 becomes available in DeSotos

Overdrive transmission is available for Plymouths and DeSotos

Chrysler still has no fully automatic transmission—or even a semi-automatic in Plymouths

Ford beats Chrysler to second place in corporate output—the first time since the Thirties

Ford/Chevrolet price wars begin; Chrysler and the independents will be hurt badly

Hemi-powered Saratogas tackle Oldsmobile 88s and Hudson Hornets on the NASCAR stock-car racing circuit

Three Hemi-powered C-4R Cunninghams compete at Le Mans

Chrysler exhibits the C-200 convertible

Automakers cut production as the Korean War rages on

The "seller's market" ends; shoppers become more choosy

Nearly unchanged for '52, the Chrysler New Yorker Newport hardtop (*above*) held a Hemi V-8. So did the Ghia Special show coupe (*right*). Later, Power-Flite replaced its semi-automatic gearbox. The Chrysler C-200 show convertible (*below*) evolved from the K-310 coupe.

Saratogas for '52 came in four models: coupe, sedan, wagon, and eight-seat sedan.

Left and right: Chrysler's "difference" was mainly the 180-bhp FirePower Hemi, billed as "the greatest engine achievement" by the company.

Ads dubbed Imperial (*above*) "the ultimate expression of taste and judgment [for] people who can afford any motor car in the world." A six powered most DeSotos, like the DeLuxe sedan (*above right*) and Custom Club Coupe (*right*). The new FireDomes got a 160-bhp V-8.

The '52 Dodge Coronet eight-passenger sedan cost $3064.

The 1952 Plymouth Cranbrook sedan (*left*) looked the same as the '51, but cost $21 less. New "saddleback" two-toning gave the $2216 Cranbrook Belvedere hardtop coupe (*below*) a unique appearance.

1952 Production

(See 1951 note)

Chrysler*

Windsor	42,683
Saratoga	16,835
New Yorker	17,914
Imperial	9,780
Crown Imperial	258
Total	87,470

* Approximate

DeSoto

DeLuxe	21,649 *
Custom	123,000 *
Firedome	45,800 **
Total	190,449 *

* Combined 1951 and 1952 production
** 1952 only

Dodge*

D-41 Wayfarer	78,404
D-42 Meadowbrook/Coronet	417,605
Total	496,009

* Combined 1951 and 1952 production

Plymouth*

Concord	139,914
Cambridge	281,201
Cranbrook	586,597
Total	1,007,712

* Combined 1951 and 1952 production

1952 Engine Availability

Chrysler

No. Cyl.	Disp., cid	bhp	Availability
I-6	264.5	119	S-Windsor
V-8	331.1	180	S-others

DeSoto

No. Cyl.	Disp., cid	bhp	Availability
I-6	250.6	116	S-DeLuxe, Custom
V-8	276.1	160	S-Firedome

Dodge

No. Cyl.	Disp., cid	bhp	Availability
I-6	230.2	103	S-all

Plymouth

No. Cyl.	Disp., cid	bhp	Availability
I-6	217.8	97	S-all

Plymouth Suburban station wagon: $2163

1953

The Korean War ends on July 26, 1953

Restyled, still-boxy Chrysler products wear curved windshields

PowerFlite automatic is available for Chryslers late in the model year

Dodge is one of the first production cars styled for Chrysler by Virgil Exner

A 140-horsepower "Red Ram" Hemi V-8 engine is available in the new-look Dodge

The Dodge V-8 breaks 196 AAA stock-car records at Bonneville

Plymouth's Hy-Drive option blends a manual shift with a torque converter

DeSoto sales are up sharply

Danny Eames drives a Red Ram Dodge to 102.62 mph

Briggs Cunningham drives a Chrysler-powered Cunningham to third place at Le Mans

There's hot competition for sales as the Ford "blitz" is underway; GM reacts with cutthroat sales techniques

A facelift of the basic 1949-52 body gave Chrysler a one-piece windshield and squared-up rear fenders. At $3945, only 950 Hemi-powered New Yorker DeLuxe convertibles (*above and left*) were built, on a shorter 125.5-inch chassis. Weight was 4295 pounds. Kelsey wire wheels cost $300.

Left: Every Chrysler except the six-cylinder Windsor carried the 331-cid FirePower Hemi V-8, still rated at 180 bhp. *Above:* In "America's first family of fine cars" for '53, the New Yorker DeLuxe ranked just below Imperial; New Yorker replaced the Saratoga series.

Chrysler's Custom Imperial designation was revived for 1953, consisting of a hardtop, sedan, and limo on a 133.5-inch wheelbase. The Custom Imperial Town Limousine (*above*) sold for $4762, complete with black leather upholstery in front, blue broadcloth in the rear, and a divider window. Power windows, brakes, and steering were included, as was the Hemi V-8 with Fluid-Torque Drive. Only 243 Town Limousines were produced, versus 7793 sedans. Crown Imperials, built in small numbers, rode a 145.5-inch chassis. Though still upright in overall profile, trailed by squared-off rear quarters, '53 Chrysler bodysides looked more rounded and showed more glass. At $3653, the Newport hardtop (*right*) was the second highest-priced New Yorker DeLuxe (behind the ragtop); 3715 were produced. Airtemp air conditioning joined the options list, as did PowerFlite later in the year.

Because the $4525 '53 Chrysler Imperial Newport rode a longer wheelbase than hardtops in other series, it had a distinct appearance. Wire wheels augmented its elegant demeanor.

The '53 long-wheelbase Crown Imperial Limousine (*above*) retained the separate-rear-fender design from the '52s. At $6994, just 111 were built. Could these models (*below*) be illustrating the virtues of Imperial's air conditioning?

Virgil Exner had yet another concept creation on tap for 1953, based on the New Yorker chassis. The Chrysler/Ghia D'Elegance show car (*top*) was a fastback coupe, featuring "gunsight" taillights that would appear on Imperials in 1955. Just one passenger fit in back, sitting sideways. Production never happened, but the basic shape later shrank to become VW's popular Karmann Ghia. The $3898 Town & Country wagon (*above*) was part of Chrysler's basic New Yorker series in '53; 1399 were sold.

The first Ghia-built concept car to carry a DeSoto badge was the Adventurer (*top*). Note the outside exhaust pipes. Inside (*above*), bucket seats seated four. Used as an ambulance and hearse, this '53 DeSoto FireDome long-wheelbase sedan (*above left*) kept the 1952-style body with separate rear fenders; 200 were sold. A "continental" spare tire highlights this $3114 FireDome S-16 convertible (*left*); 1700 were built. Its $2893 Sportsman hardtop counterpart (*below left*) found 4700 buyers. The $3078 Powermaster six-cylinder wagon (*below*) sold only 500 copies.

Virgil Exner-influenced restyling was only part of the '53 Dodge picture. Coronet Eights, like the $2494 soft top (*left and below*), had a real performance engine: the 241.3-cid Red Ram V-8. Rated at 140 bhp, this shrunken Hemi hid under a "Jet Air-Flow Hood." The functional Coronet dashboard (*below left*) held full gauges. An optional Gyro-Torque semi-automatic gearbox, priced at $233, added a torque converter to the familiar Gyro-Matic. Borg-Warner overdrive was also available. Dodge built 4100 ragtops for '53. Meanwhile, Chrysler stylists were fantasizing about future urban travel (*bottom left*), with a blend of rocket-like planes, monorails, and limited-access highways.

One ad (*right*) hyped Dodge as the "action car for active Americans," with "extra Power" from the new Red Ram V-8. The Hemi V-8 made a lightweight Dodge quite quick. An even dozen models were offered; four-doors and Club Coupes rode a 119-inch wheelbase, others a short 114-inch span.

1953 Production

Chrysler

Windsor	32,192
Windsor DeLuxe	52,277
New Yorker	49,313
New Yorker DeLuxe	27,205
Custom Imperial	8,859
Crown Imperial	160
Total	170,006

DeSoto

Powermaster	43,902
Firedome	86,502
Total	130,404

Dodge

D-46 Meadowbrook/Coronet	120,924
D-47 Meadowbrook Suburban	15,751
D-44 Coronet Eight (wb 119.0)	156,498
D-48 Coronet Eight (wb 114.0)	26,835
Total	320,008

Plymouth

Cambridge	201,955
Cranbrook	445,496
Total	647,451

1953 Engine Availability

Chrysler

No. Cyl.	Disp., cid	bhp	Availability
I-6	264.5	119	S-Windsor
V-8	331.1	180	S-others

DeSoto

No. Cyl.	Disp., cid	bhp	Availability
I-6	250.6	116	S-Powermaster
V-8	276.1	160	S-Firedome

Dodge

No. Cyl.	Disp., cid	bhp	Availability
I-6	230.2	103	S-D-46, D-47
V-8	241.3	140	S-D-44, D-48

Plymouth

No. Cyl.	Disp., cid	bhp	Availability
I-6	217.8	100	S-all

All-new styling with flow-through fenders, on a 114-inch wheelbase, gave '53 Plymouths a rather stubby profile. Not everybody responded avidly, even to the style-leading $2064 Cranbrook Belvedere hardtop (*top*), which captured 35,185 buyers. A Hy-Drive semi-automatic transmission was offered, but would be replaced in late 1954. The top-priced Plymouth was the $2220 Cranbrook convertible (*above and right*); 6301 were sold. Wire wheels were a factory option.

Plymouth Cranbrook Club Coupe: $1843

1954

Chrysler Corporation has its worst sales year since World War II

Market share skids to a dismal 13 percent

Plymouth barely beats Buick in model-year output

Chrysler and DeSoto sixes are in their final year

DeSotos and Dodges are available with PowerFlite, but a three-speed stick is still standard

Dodge launches a lush Royal V-8 series; the 500 convertible carries a "continental" spare tire and wire wheels, and paces the Indianapolis 500

Plymouth offers a renamed three-series lineup: Plaza, Savoy, and Belvedere

Plymouths gain a PowerFlite option during the year, and can also have power steering

Dodges finish in five of the top six places in the Medium Stock class at the *Carrera Panamericana*

Show cars include the DeSoto Adventurer II coupe, the road-ready Dodge Firearrow, and the Plymouth Belmont and Explorer

"Anything less," warned 1954 ads, was "Yesterday's Car." Chryslers added brightwork as part of a modest facelift. The New Yorker Club Coupe (*top*)—one of only 2079 built—ran a 195-bhp Hemi V-8, up 15. Imperials and New Yorker DeLuxes gained a four-barrel, dual-exhaust edition rated at 235 bhp. Windsor sixes, in their final season, kept a standard manual shift. Other models, including the $4560 Custom Imperial Newport hardtop (*second row*), had PowerFlite; 1249 were sold. Chrysler's *La Comtesse* show car (*right*) was a New Yorker with a plexiglass roof panel.

Chrysler built both a pink/white *La Comtesse* (*shown*) and a complementary bronze/black *Le Comte* show car.

Packing the high-performance Hemi V-8, the 1954 Chrysler Custom Imperial four-door sedan (*left*) cost $4260. Production of the 133.5-wheelbase sedans totaled an impressive 4324 units. The Derham Custom Body Company, one of the few remaining coachbuilders, created a Custom Imperial Landau (*below left*), with open driver's compartment and a Victoria-style half-roof. Imperials sported their own grille. With 26,907 built, the most popular '54 Chrysler was the New Yorker DeLuxe four-door (*below*).

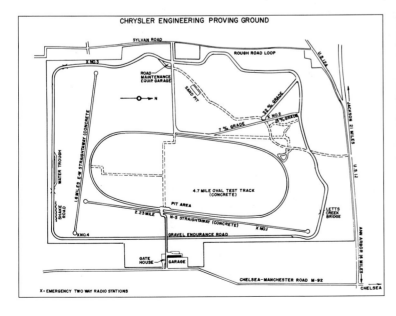

DeSoto added a high-fashion Coronado four-door sedan (*above left*) to its lineup during the 1954 model year, one of a series of "spring specials." The $2673 FireDome four-door (*above*), its Hemi V-8 now belting out 170 bhp, outsold its mates by far—45,095 units. This year, Chrysler opened its new 4000-acre Engineering Proving Ground (*left*), near Chelsea, Michigan. The oval track could handle vehicle speeds of 140 mph. The grand opening featured a demonstration of a turbine-powered Plymouth.

Inspired by the tube-framed Alfa-Cornero, DeSoto's dramatic two-seat Adventurer II show coupe (*left*) was built by Ghia, from a Chrysler design. It had a retracting rear window and matched luggage behind the seat. Ads (*above*) pushed DeSoto's PowerFlite automatic transmission.

A new Royal V-8 series deposed the Coronet as the top-line Dodge for '54, as the division marked its 40th Anniversary. The best-selling Dodge was the $2373 Royal four-door sedan (*right*), which garnered 50,050 orders. Dodge built limited-edition replicas (*below*) of the yellow Royal convertible that paced the Indianapolis 500 race, complete with continental kit and wire wheels. A few even packed a hot performance package with an Offenhauser manifold. Note the unusual Coral/White two-toning pattern, repeated inside, of the special-edition Royal hardtop (*below right*) that arrived at mid-year.

A "Pace Car" package with Kelsey-Hayes wire wheels added $201 to the price of a '54 Dodge Royal 500 soft top (*left*). Only 701 were built. In Dodge's show-car arena, the low-slung Firearrow (*right*) featured a bold black/white leather interior. A series of Firearrow "image" cars inspired the 1956 Dual-Ghia.

Plymouth issued a single-seat Belmont show convertible (*left*) in 1954. Standing barely 49 inches tall overall, its reinforced fiberglass body rode a 114-inch Dodge chassis with the 150-bhp V-8 and Plymouth's Hy-Drive transmission. A detachable fabric top stowed in the rear. Belvedere became Plymouth's top-line series; the $1953 four-door (*below left*) attracted 106,601 buyers. Exactly 6900 customers preferred the sportier $2301 Belvedere ragtop (*below*).

A man (*above*) works on the door panel of a Plymouth Belvedere Sport Coupe, one of 25,592 produced for '54. Chrysler's first experimental turbine car looked like the regular $2145 Plymouth Belvedere hardtop seen here (*second from bottom*).

1954 Production

Chrysler
Windsor DeLuxe	44,527
New Yorker	20,419
New Yorker DeLuxe	34,323
Custom Imperial	5,661
Crown Imperial	100
Total	105,030

DeSoto
Powermaster	19,184
Firedome	57,376
Total	76,560

Dodge
D51-1 Meadowbrook	11,395
D50-1 Meadowbrook	4,049
D51-2 Coronet I-6	19,401
D52 Coronet I-6 Wgns	6,701
D50-2 Coronet V-8 (wb 119.0)	44,061
D53-2 Coronet V-8 (wb 114.0, wgns)	4,238
D50-3 Royal V-8 (wb 119.0)	58,950
D53-3 Royal V-8 (wb 114.0)	5,853
Total	154,648

Plymouth
Plaza	113,266
Savoy	199,517
Belvedere	150,356
Total	463,139

1954 Engine Availability

Chrysler
No. Cyl.	Disp., cid	bhp	Availability
I-6	264.5	119	S-Windsor DeLuxe
V-8	331.1	195	S-NY
V-8	331.1	235	S-others

DeSoto
No. Cyl.	Disp., cid	bhp	Availability
I-6	250.6	116	S-Powermaster
V-8	276.1	170	S-Firedome

Dodge
No. Cyl.	Disp., cid	bhp	Availability
I-6	230.2	110	S-all I-6
V-8	241.3	140	S-Meadowbrook V-8
V-8	241.3	150	O-others (Offenhauser manifold available)

Plymouth
No. Cyl.	Disp., cid	bhp	Availability
I-6	217.8	100	S-all (early)
I-6	230.2	110	S-all (late)

Chapter 9

Flash *and* Substance; The Exner Era: 1955-59

Chief designer Virgil Exner's assertive first-generation "Forward Look" styling appeared for 1955, as seen here on (*bottom right and clockwise*) the Plymouth Belvedere, Dodge Custom Royal, Imperial, Chrysler Windsor DeLuxe, and DeSoto Fireflite.

Could these be Chryslers? Anyone accustomed to dismissing the fleet from Highland Park as frumpy, humdrum transportation got a big surprise in '55. Even those who'd consistently praised the company's engineering had to marvel at the audacious new packaging. Just a glance at a Chrysler or DeSoto demonstrated an irreversible split from the conservative past. Dodge and Plymouth seemed virtually unrelated to the square 1949-54 models.

For good reason, Chrysler Corporation posted record-setting sales and dollar volume in 1955. Confidence returned as its market share reached 17 percent, up from 13 percent in 1954. Although chairman L.L. "Tex" Colbert had been blamed by the media in 1954 for Chrysler's woes, he'd earlier initiated the improvements that took effect this year.

Credit for the phenomenal boost goes to Virgil M. Exner, and his first-generation "Forward Look" styling. With this fresh, assertive stance, Chrysler approached design leadership over General Motors for the first time since the early Thirties. The '55 program had begun under Henry King, before Exner took over. Senior makes—Chrysler, DeSoto, Imperial—were inspired by Exner's 1952 Imperial Parade Phaeton show cars. Dodge and Plymouth evolved separately, directed by Exner protégé Maury Baldwin.

Chrysler's Windsor DeLuxe got a new 301-cid V-8; New Yorkers and Imperials carried the 331-cid Hemi, boosted to 250 bhp. As decreed by Colbert, neither Chrysler nor DeSoto had a six-cylinder engine. Automatic-transmission levers now protruded from the dashboard.

Who could imagine Chrysler issuing a supercar? That's exactly what happened, as the Chrysler 300 made the scene. The sizzling hardtop contained a 300-horsepower Hemi V-8 with solid valve lifters and dual four-barrel carburetors—the most powerful full-size car in the world. A tight competition suspension made the big bruiser handle as well as it accelerated. Tom McCahill, the veteran car tester for *Mechanix Illustrated,* called the 300 "a hardboiled, magnificent piece of semi-competition transportation, built for the connoisseur."

DeSotos came in two series—Firedome and the new Fireflite—each packing a Hemi V-8 bored to 291 cubic inches. Setting a trend, spring brought gaudy specials, led by a limited-edition Coronado sedan with one of the industry's first three-tone paint jobs.

Imperial became a distinct make in 1955, handsome and elegantly trimmed. Nearly 11,500 were built in the model year—twice the 1954 total, though still far behind Cadillac and Lincoln.

"Flair Fashion" Dodge Coronets could have an L-head six-cylinder engine, or a 175-bhp "poly-head" V-8. Custom Royals carried a Red Ram Hemi, bored to 270-cid and rated at 183 horsepower, or 193 bhp in the power-pack D-500.

Ads called the '55 Plymouth "A great new car for the young in heart." In addition to an exciting new profile, featuring pointed fenders fore and aft, Plymouth finally offered a V-8 engine. The "Hy-Fire" polyspherical-head engine came with 241 or 260 cid. A "PowerPak" version with a four-barrel carb yielded 177 horsepower.

Customers seemed eager, and production jumped substantially, but Plymouth could manage no better than fourth in model-year output. On the other hand, its calendar-year total set a record, boding well for the future. Dodge managed an eighth-place finish. Dealers adopted a "conquest" theme for 1956. But not much conquest of Ford or GM sales transpired, as the total market fell almost two million units below record-breaking 1955. Still, DeSoto rose from 13th to 11th in the industry ranking. Plymouth held fourth, nosed out of third by Buick.

The '56 facelift brought true tailfins, destined to grow taller in succeeding seasons. Exner claimed they improved high-speed stability, but scoffers insisted they were mainly a novelty. Stylist Maury Baldwin later claimed that "Wind-tunnel tests proved conclusively that they aided stability at speeds over 60-70 mph." Either way, tailfins had a big impact.

Not only did Chryslers look even better than in '55, they gained power. Windsors now had a 331-cid poly-head engine; New Yorkers carried a bored-out 354-cid Hemi. That enlarged Hemi also found its way into the 300-B, but wielding 340 horsepower. Not potent enough? Dissatisfied customers could request the hopped-up version with 10.0:1 compression, good for 355 horses—the first Detroit V-8 to top the mystical "1 horsepower per cubic inch" barrier.

DeSoto's Hemi was stroked to 330 cid, developing 230 horsepower in the Firedome, 255 bhp in Fireflites. A glittery mesh grille replaced the traditional teeth. At mid-year came a lavish Adventurer hardtop with gold-anodized trim and a new 341-cid, 320-bhp Hemi. After DeSoto paced the Indy 500, about 100 "Pacesetter" replicas were built.

Dodge, meanwhile, stroked its "Super Red Ram" Hemi V-8 to 315 cubic inches and 218 horsepower. The potent D-500 option was available across the board, and standard in a new Golden Lancer hardtop.

Plymouth V-8s grew to 270 and 277 cid, delivering up to 200 horsepower. At mid-year, Plymouth launched its first Fury. Priced at $2866, the white hardtop wore gold anodized aluminum sweepspears and ran with a 240-horse, 303-cid version of the Hy-Fire V-8. A Fury could accelerate to 60 mph in 10 seconds flat.

Inside each model, pushbuttons controlled automatic transmissions. At mid-year, three-speed TorqueFlite became available—first in Imperials. It spread through the line for '57, though the two-speed PowerFlite remained available.

Chrysler violated an unwritten industry rule for 1957: never issue new styling *and* engineering in the same year. But infractions sometimes pay off, and Chrysler's gamble provided an impressive return. In essence, the corporation enjoyed a rebirth via vivid styling, technical achievement, and

more authoritative engines. "Torsion-Aire Ride" led the engineering advances. Front torsion bars turned once-clumsy Chrysler products into accomplished handlers, with no penalty in ride comfort.

Virgil Exner's Forward Look reached its zenith in 1957—longer, lower, wider, sleeker. Even critics of tailfins found it hard to fault Chrysler's tall and graceful versions, enhancing the cars' clean lines.

Chrysler Corporation captured a 19-percent share of the 1957 market, versus GM's 45 percent. Dodge rose from eighth to seventh place, while Chrysler and DeSoto again ran 10th and 11th. Plymouth output streaked past 762,000, for third.

Chrysler revived the Saratoga name, and the breathtaking 300-C—wearing a unique trapezoidal grille but little ornamentation—came in both coupe and convertible form. Beneath the 300-C hood sat a bigger 392-cid Hemi, cranking out 375 or 390 horsepower. Manual shift was now available, too. Tom McCahill urged his 300-C to 60 mph in 8.4 seconds, branding the car "motorized dynamite," a vehicle "not for the faint of heart."

Many buyers of Chrysler products got some bad news with their '57s, though it took a while to arrive. For the first time, the cars suffered serious rust problems—particularly around the front fenders. Plymouths deteriorated most. The problem lingered through 1958 and, to a lesser extent, in '59. Analysts cite the rushed development program for '57 models and declining quality control, now that Chrysler was producing its own bodies.

Imperials came in three series, including an elaborate Crown convertible. An optional round decklid hump suggested the presence of a spare tire—a "classic" theme favored by Exner. Output more than tripled. Long-wheelbase Crown Imperial limos now were built by Ghia, in Italy.

A lower-cost Firesweep series joined the '57 DeSoto lineup, riding Dodge's 122-inch platform. Adventurers carried a bigger engine, and added a convertible model.

Dodge's "Swept-Wing" styling perhaps lacked the graceful elegance of a Chrysler, but its performance potential drew raves again, as the Hemi got a rebore to 325 cubes. D-500 editions carried a 354-cid V-8 from junior Chryslers, rated at 340 bhp. *Motor Trend* praised the "close liaison with the road" due to Dodge's new suspension.

"Suddenly, It's 1960," the Plymouth ads promised. Not quite, maybe, but with the lowest beltline and tallest fins of the "Low-Priced Three," Plymouths looked particularly stunning. With five V-8s, including a new 301-cid version and a 318 for the Fury, Plymouth's 1957 output soared to more than half of Chevy's.

If 1957 was a great year, 1958 turned horrid—for the industry and for Chrysler Corporation. Each ChryCo make dropped sharply in sales, as a severe recession took hold and penurious customers took a new look at Ramblers and imports. Plymouth still ranked third, but Chrysler slipped to 11th, Dodge to ninth. Work stoppages also took a toll. The corporation suffered a $33.8 million loss, after turning in a $120 million profit a year earlier. Worse, corporate market share skidded from 19 to 15 percent.

Mild '58 retouching included standard quad headlights. Chrysler's Windsor moved down to Dodge's 122-inch wheelbase—priced closer to low-end DeSotos. A handful of 300-D stormers were ordered with Bendix Electrojector fuel injection. DeSoto's volume slipped to its lowest level in three decades, as the precarious make was squashed from above by Chrysler, from below by Dodge. At $4369, the Adventurer convertible was the priciest DeSoto ever.

The top engine at Dodge was a 361-cid wedge V-8. Plymouths used a trio of 318s, with a 350-cid "Golden Commando" V-8 optional. Hemis were quickly fading away.

"By 1959," recalled Virgil Exner of tailfins, "it was obvious that I'd given birth to a Frankenstein." GM, in particular, issued several monstrous rear ends this year. Facelifting proved more extensive in 1959, if less elegant. GM and Ford cars earned major restyling, and their sales rose by half. Chrysler's grew only modestly; market share slipped below 13 percent.

A new array of wedge-head V-8s edged aside the Hemis for good (well, for a few years anyway). A new 383-cid V-8 sat beneath Chrysler Windsor and senior DeSoto hoods, while New Yorkers and Imperials ran a 413-cid engine. Even the Chrysler 300-E lost its Hemi, in favor of a 380-bhp edition of the 413-cid V-8.

Plymouth's fins were more prominent and the budget-priced Plaza was gone, while Fury became a full-fledged series. Top choice was the Sport Fury hardtop and convertible, with a 318-cid V-8 or optional Golden Commando 361.

DeSoto endured a dismal year, unassisted by ornate front-end styling. Rumors of the make's imminent demise didn't help. Meanwhile, a celebration marked the production of the two-millionth DeSoto. Obviously, Chrysler executives wouldn't admit that the firm was preparing for DeSoto's departure.

Admit it or not, the mid-price market was shrinking. Ford's new Edsel was sinking fast. Rambler moved up to fourth in output, and the import invasion was underway. After unleashing a dramatic fleet of spectacular machines, complete with power packs and assertive model names, would Chrysler continue as a leader—or fall to the rear?

1955

Industry auto output leaps 44 percent in a boom year

Buick moves up to the third spot, followed by Plymouth, Oldsmobile, and Pontiac

Chrysler products flaunt "Forward Look" styling by Virgil Exner

A "Hundred Million Dollar Look" slogan reveals the cost of Chrysler's styling program

Plymouth finally offers a V-8 engine, as does Chevrolet

The PowerFlite gearshift lever pokes out from the dashboard

Wraparound windshields, suspended foot pedals, and tubeless tires are new

Three-tone paint schemes appear, led by the DeSoto Coronado

The New Chrysler 300 supercar dominates NASCAR racing

Imperial is now listed as a separate make

Dodge's "La Femme" hardtop features a pink/white exterior and interior, folding umbrella, and fitted purse

Chrysler Corporation posts its best sales total ever

Senior makes abandon six-cylinder engines; both "poly-head" and "Hemi-head" V-8s are produced

Lower and far sleeker, Chryslers rode a 126-inch wheelbase. Spring brought a pair of special editions to the Windsor DeLuxe line, including this "Blue Heron" variant of the Newport hardtop (*above and left*). Note its distinctive bodyside trim. Windsor DeLuxes got a new 188-bhp "Spitfire" 301-cid V-8, but the hot new Chrysler 300 hardtop (*below left*) packed an even 300 horses via its 331-cid Hemi V-8. Officially named C-300, it blended the Imperial's twin grilles with a New Yorker bodyshell and Windsor rear quarters. Increased spring rates gave the 300 great handling, but a stiffer ride. Standard gear included leather upholstery and a 150-mph speedometer.

1955 Imperial sedan

Shoppers flocked to Chrysler-Plymouth dealers on introduction day (*left*). Note the "Twin-Tower" taillights on the Windsor DeLuxe Newport hardtop in the foreground. The $4720 Imperial Newport behind it found 3418 buyers; this one riding on extra-cost Kelsey-Hayes wire wheels. To the right rear is a $3652 New Yorker DeLuxe Newport hardtop. With Club Coupes gone, Chrysler's least expensive two-door was the Windsor DeLuxe Nassau hardtop (*below left*), which at $2703 attracted 18,474 customers. All New Yorkers were DeLuxes for '55 and came with two-speed PowerFlite automatic transmission as standard. The Newport hardtop coupe (*below*) saw only 5777 built, compared to 11,096 copies of the $3690 St. Regis hardtop, which received different bodyside two-toning. New Yorkers sported different lower-grille styling than Windsors, as well as a 250-horsepower version of the 331-cid Hemi V-8, more sumptuous interiors, and added standard features.

The high-performance, limited-edition Chrysler C-300 (*left and below*) cost $4110, which included PowerFlite automatic. Some 1725 300s were built—not bad for an expensive niche model. Convertible sales were small for '55: 1395 copies of the $3090 Windsor DeLuxe (*bottom left*), plus 946 examples of the $3924 New Yorker DeLuxe.

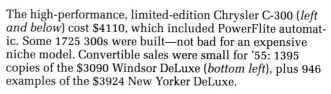

Not much time passed before Chrysler 300s began to flaunt their valor on the NASCAR circuit (*above*), under the auspices of the Kiekhaefer Mercury Outboard Racing Team and skilled pilots, such as Tim Flock. Ads promoted the coupe as "The Car That Swept Daytona." To reach the magic 300-horsepower mark, its Hemi V-8 (*left*) employed dual four-barrel carburetors, a hotter cam, and solid valve lifters. The $3690 New Yorker DeLuxe St. Regis (*below*) sported unique two-toning.

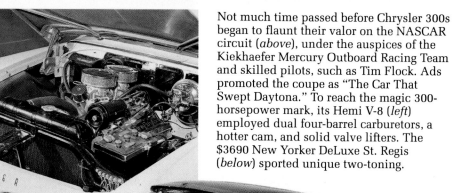

Workers (*above*) mate a Chrysler 300 front clip with its chassis. Two-toning on the St. Regis hardtop (*above right*) differed markedly from the Newport seen on page 139.

Three unit-bodied '55 Chrysler Falcon two-seaters were built and came close to production. Note the rakish side exhausts.

Tailfins and overall shape of the DeSoto Flight Sweep show convertible (*left*) and coupe (*above*) foretold '57 styling.

Riding Chrysler's 126-inch chassis, '55 DeSotos had a lower silhouette and the make's last multi-toothed grille. The plush Fireflite Coronado sedan (*left and above*) sported one of the industry's first three-tone paint jobs. Also-colorful two-toning was optional on the regular $2727 Fireflite sedan, $2939 Sportsman hardtop (*bottom left*), and $3151 convertible (*below*). The last saw only 775 built. Fireflites got a 200-bhp Hemi, now 291 cid.

Above: The PowerFlite gear selector protruded from the "gullwing" dashboard. *Above left:* Firedomes had a 185-bhp Hemi. They came in five models: sedan, wagon, two hardtops, and ragtop—priced from $2541 to $3170.

Though five inches longer in wheelbase than Plymouths, '55 Dodges used the same basic bodyshell. Bright color choices delivered a flashy, yet tasteful, appearance. Topping the line was the $2748 Custom Royal Lancer convertible (*left*), chosen by 3302 buyers. This one wears Heather Rose and Sapphire White paint and extra-cost wire wheels. Most Lancers had tiny chrome rear-fender trim suggesting fins, riding atop "Tandem-Jet" taillights. Bored to 270.1-cid, Dodge's Red Ram V-8 punched out 175 horsepower in a Coronet or Royal, 183 under a Custom Royal hood—or even 193 with the optional Power Package. Lancer two-door hardtops also embraced the mid-range Royal series (*below*), as well as the budget-priced Coronet V-8 line. Six-cylinder Coronets, meanwhile, were boosted to 123 bhp.

The '55 Dodge Royal Lancer hardtop cost $2395.

This Dodge was crashed at Chrysler's Proving Grounds to test new door locks. They remained locked when the car landed upside-down, skidding several hundred feet. "LifeGuard" latches became standard for '56.

The popular '55 Dodge V-8 Royal Lancer hardtop (*above*) sold 30,499 copies. *Left:* Two-toning extended to the interior.

1955 Production

Chrysler

Windsor DeLuxe	98,874
New Yorker DeLuxe	52,178
300	1,725
Total	152,777

DeSoto

Firedome	77,660
Fireflite	37,725
Total	115,385

Dodge

Coronet I-6	33,812
Coronet V-8	77,160
Royal V-8	76,660
Custom Royal V-8	89,304
Total	276,936

Imperial

C-69	11,260
Crown Imperial	172
Total	11,432

Plymouth

Plaza I-6	153,182
Plaza V-8	36,676
Savoy I-6	139,155
Savoy V-8	98,467
Belvedere I-6	108,738
Belvedere V-8	168,227
Total	704,445

Plymouth—the big new car with Glamour...Getaway...and Go!

SPECIFICATIONS Belvedere...Savoy...Plaza

The '55 Plymouth is 10 inches longer... lower and wider, too!

Plymouth promoted "Glamour . . . Getaway . . . and Go" (*left*), especially with a new "Hy-Fire" V-8 on tap. Ten inches longer for '55, Plymouths came in three series: Plaza, Savoy, and top-of-the-line Belvedere. A "Forward Look" Belvedere convertible (*above*) cost $2351; 6900 were sold. Its 260-cid V-8 (*below*) boasted 167 horses, 177 with "PowerPak." With freshly pointed fenders and two-tone paint, the $1953 Belvedere four-door sedan (*second from bottom*) was handsome enough to entice 106,601 buyers.

1955 Engine Availability

Chrysler

No. Cyl.	Disp., cid	bhp	Availability
V-8	301.0	188	S-Windsor DeLuxe
V-8	331.1	250	S-New Yorker DeLuxe
V-8	331.1	300	S-300

DeSoto

No. Cyl.	Disp., cid	bhp	Availability
V-8	291.0	185	S-Firedome
V-8	291.0	200	S-Fireflite

Dodge

No. Cyl.	Disp., cid	bhp	Availability
I-6	230.2	123	S-Coronet I-6
V-8	270.1	175	S-Coronet V-8, Royal V-8
V-8	270.1	183	S-Custom Royal V-8
V-8	270.1	193	O-Custom Royal V-8

Imperial

No. Cyl.	Disp., cid	bhp	Availability
V-8	331.1	280	S-all

Plymouth

No. Cyl.	Disp., cid	bhp	Availability
I-6	230.2	117	S-all I-6
V-8	241.0	157	S-all V-8
V-8	260.0	167	O-all V-8
V-8	260.0	177	O-all V-8

The $1837 Plymouth Savoy Club Coupe (*below*) ran with a 117-horsepower L-head six.

1956

All Chrysler makes sport modest tailfins—a hint of what is to come

Four-door hardtops are offered by each Chrysler nameplate

Pushbutton automatic-transmission selectors are new—and last through 1964

A "Highway Hi-Fi" record player is optional

The top Chrysler 300-B V-8 is rated at 355 bhp—one horsepower per cubic inch

A brash Plymouth Fury hardtop carries a 240-horsepower V-8

The corporation adopts 12-volt electrical systems

The limited-edition Adventurer is DeSoto's response to the hot Chrysler 300-B, Dodge D-500, and Plymouth Fury

An experimental gas-turbine Plymouth is driven from New York to Los Angeles

Plymouth's Plainsman show wagon hides the spare tire inside the rear fender; this feature will appear in production '57 wagons

The "Hemi" V-8 is bored to 354 cid, yielding 280 horsepower or more; "poly-head" V-8s grow to 331 cid

A DeSoto Adventurer paces the Indianapolis 500 race

Imperial wheelbases grew to 133 inches for '56 and fenders sprouted fins. "Gunsight" taillights returned. The Hemi V-8 gained 23 cubes and 30 bhp. The best seller was the $4832 sedan (*above*): 6821 units. Chrysler Windsors got a 225- or 250-bhp poly-head 331-cid V-8. With 53,119 built, the $2870 sedan (*below*) was the best seller. This $2905 Windsor Nassau two-door hardtop (*above left*) boasts a "Highway Hi-Fi" record player and a steering wheel clock. Bored to 354 cid, the New Yorker's Hemi yielded 280 bhp. An "Instant Heat" *gasoline* heater warmed passengers in this $4243 New Yorker convertible.

Chrysler New
Yorker sedan:
$3779

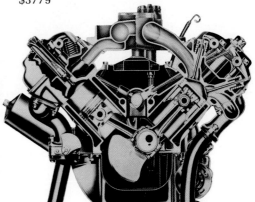

Hemispherical combustion chambers made
the Chrysler 300 engine (*above and below*)
amenable to big power hikes. Even with
one carb, the 354-cid V-8 had 340 bhp.

The 1956 Chrysler 300-B (*left, top and center*) sprouted modest
tailfins, and air conditioning could be ordered this year. More crucial to enthusiasts, the Hemi V-8—enlarged to 354 cubic inches—
could deliver as much as 355 horsepower (one horsepower per
cubic inch) with a dual-carburetor option. Veteran tester Tom
McCahill branded the 4145-pound 300-B a "mastodon of muscle."
At $4419, sales fell to 1102 units. At mid-year, Chrysler's dash-
mounted pushbutton controls (*above*) might not operate the usual
PowerFlite, but possibly the new three-speed TorqueFlite—one of
the best automatics ever. Virgil Exner designed the '56 Norseman
(*right*), not as a show car, but for test purposes. Rear pillars supported the cantilevered roof, as the car contained neither A- nor B-
pillars. En route to planned crash-testing to check out the strength
of the roof structure, the Norseman sank with the ill-fated *Andrea
Doria* in July 1956. Note the hidden headlights in the fastback's
pointed front fenders.

Stroked to 330.4 cid, DeSoto's Hemi V-8 made 230 horsepower in the Firedome series, 255 in Fireflites. A mesh design replaced the familiar grille teeth, while fins now topped the distinctive Tri-Tower taillights. Mid-year brought the limited-edition Adventurer hardtop (*right*), with gold-anodized aluminum trim and a new 341.4-cid, 320-bhp Hemi. Just 996 copies were built, at $3728, all painted gold, black, or white. With 8475 sold, the $3346 Fireflite Sportsman hardtop coupe (*below and below right*) was more popular. After DeSoto paced the Indy 500 race, about 100 "Pacesetter" Fireflite replicas were issued, at $3615 apiece.

In addition to the $2854 Firedome Sportsman hardtop, DeSoto offered a cheaper Seville (*above*). Firedome engines (*right*) used a two-barrel carb. A test driver at the Chrysler Proving Grounds garage (*left*) adjusts the "fifth wheel" on a '56 Dodge before entering the test track. Note the many vehicles on tap.

Dodge rear fenders grew tailfins for '56. A $2513 Royal sedan (*left and above*) came with a 315-cid Super Red Ram V-8 good for 218 bhp. Many Dodges wore three-tone paint, like this D-500 Royal hardtop (*below left*). The D-500 option boasted 230 horsepower with one four-barrel carb, 260 with dual quads. Mid-year brought a regional "Texan" edition of the Lancer two-door hardtop (*below*). Once again, Dodge tried (unsuccessfully) to attract female customers with a La Femme Custom Royal hardtop (*below center*), now two-tone lavender. Sierra wagons (*bottom right*) wore tacked-on tailfins. Prices ranged from $2716 to $2974.

Stock-car driver Lee Petty drove a '56 Dodge Coronet two-door.

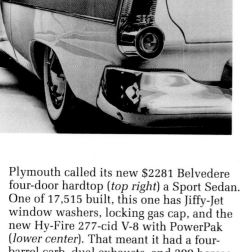

Plymouth called its new $2281 Belvedere four-door hardtop (*top right*) a Sport Sedan. One of 17,515 built, this one has Jiffy-Jet window washers, locking gas cap, and the new Hy-Fire 277-cid V-8 with PowerPak (*lower center*). That meant it had a four-barrel carb, dual exhausts, and 200 horses. Note the two gauges at the right of the dashboard (*upper center*) and the gear-selector pushbuttons on the left. Interior hues (*center right*) complemented body colors. Chief engineer Robert Anderson (*above*) showed off the new high-performance '56 Fury, an inch lower than other hardtops; it bowed at the Chicago Auto Show. These '56 Plymouths (*right*) are about to leave the assembly line.

The glassy '56 Plymouth Plainsman show car (*left*) placed its upright spare tire within the right rear fender—an idea earmarked for production '57 Suburban wagons. The rear-facing third seat also foretold future usage. Designed and built by Chrysler, the Plainsman wagon followed a Western motif, and it featured a padded, vinyl-covered roof as well.

Mid-year '56 brought the limited-edition Plymouth Fury hardtop, in white only, with gold-anodized aluminum sweep-spears. Its special 240-bhp, 303-cid V-8 boasted 9.25:1 compression, solid lifters, and dual exhausts. Now that a potent V-8 was available, Plymouths earned more respect on stock-car ovals. Herb Thomas took the wheel of a Plymouth at Bay Meadows (*second from top*). Not many pace cars looked as stylish as the new Fury (*second from bottom*), or held such potential for speed. Savoy was Plymouth's mid-level series, here (*above*) a $1982 Club Sedan with optional skirts. Some 57,927 were sold. The Savoy V-8 made 180 bhp.

1956 Production

Chrysler
Windsor	86,080
New Yorker	41,140
300-B	1,102
Total	128,322

DeSoto
Firedome	77,905
Fireflite	32,513
Total	110,418

Dodge
Coronet	142,613
Royal V-8	48,780
Custom Royal V-8	49,293
Total	240,686

Imperial
C-73	10,458
Crown Imperial	226
Total	10,684

Plymouth
Plaza	106,947
Savoy	226,162
Belvedere	152,248
Suburban	81,792
Fury	4,485
Total	571,634

1956 Engine Availability

Chrysler
No. Cyl.	Disp., cid	bhp	Availability
V-8	331.1	225	S-Windsor
V-8	331.1	250	O-Windsor
V-8	354.0	280	S-NY
V-8	354.0	340	S-300-B
V-8	354.0	355	O-300-B

DeSoto
No. Cyl.	Disp., cid	bhp	Availability
V-8	330.4	230	S-Firedome
V-8	330.4	255	S-Fireflite exc Adventurer
V-8	341.4	320	S-Adventurer

Dodge
No. Cyl.	Disp., cid	bhp	Availability
I-6	230.2	131	S-Coronet I-6
V-8	270.0	189	S-Coronet V-8
V-8	315.0	218	S-Royal V-8, Custom Royal V-8
V-8	315.0	230/260	O-all

Imperial
No. Cyl.	Disp., cid	bhp	Availability
V-8	354.0	280	S-all

Plymouth
No. Cyl.	Disp., cid	bhp	Availability
I-6	230.2	125	S-all exc Fury, Belvedere cvt
I-6	230.2	131	O-all exc Fury, Belvedere cvt
V-8	270.0	180	O-Plaza, Savoy, Belvedere
V-8	277.0	187	S-Belvedere cvt; O-Belvedere, Savoy, Plaza
V-8	277.0	200	O-all exc Fury
V-8	303.0	240	S-Fury

1957

Plymouth regains the Number Three ranking, ahead of Buick and Oldsmobile

The second-generation "Forward Look," called "Flite Sweep" styling, marks all Chrysler products

High-flying tailfins are featured across the board

"Torsion-Aire Ride" trades conventional front coil springs for torsion bars

Front ends may display either two or four headlamps—quad (or "dual") lights are not yet legal in all states

Chrysler offers the first compound-curve windshield in regular production

Imperials display curved side window glass, another first

Plymouth Suburban wagons carry the spare tire in the right rear fender; some DeSoto wagons get "Captive Air" tires

Chrysler makes prove frugal, winning in every category of the Mobilgas Economy Run

Plymouth and other Chrysler products show an unfortunate propensity to premature rust

Many owners complain of poor quality control on '57 Chrysler products

An early production 1957 Imperial hardtop

A 318-cid Hemi V-8 powered the stylish Dual-Ghia (*above and right*). Bodies were hand-formed in steel in Italy; drivetrains were installed at the Dual Motors plant in Detroit.

A '57 Chrysler New Yorker hardtop sedan (*above*) cost $4259—$86 more than the pillared sedan, and with 10,948 built was almost as popular. Upholstery matched body colors (*left*), and TorqueFlite automatic was standard. Chryslers stood longer, lower, and wider, with modest grilles and gracefully canted fins.

The all-new '57 Imperial (*left*) flaunted huge tailfins with vestigial "gunsight" taillights and curved side glass, an industry "first." This $4838 Southampton hardtop sedan attracted 7527 buyers. The elaborately trimmed Crown and LeBaron series joined the base pillared sedan and Southampton hardtops. A bigger Hemi V-8—392-cid and 325 horsepower—went into Imperials and New Yorkers. A Chrysler New Yorker convertible (*below*) cost $4638, but only 1049 were built. "Torsion-Aire Ride" improved handling on all models.

A lavish '57 Imperial Crown Southampton hardtop sedan (*above*) sold for $5406. The Crown lineup included a $5598 soft top (*right*); only 1167 were sold. Chrysler Windsors and New Yorkers could be had with a "Professional" option (*above right*). This dual-purpose Town & Country wagon converted from ambulance to family use in five minutes according to the company.

A Chrysler 300-C at Daytona Performance Trials

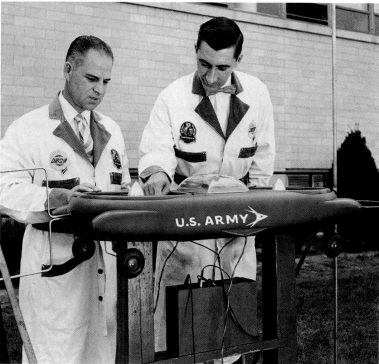

Chrysler Defense Operation engineers developed a working three-foot scale model of an aerial utility vehicle, under a contract from the Army Transportation Corps. A full-size version was supposed to "move like a hummingbird in the air and over land or water." Pictured are assistant chief engineer, M.S. Stuart (*left*), and supervisor of research and development, J.V. Gorton.

Chrysler's experimental retracting-hardtop Dart (*above*) makes its first high-speed oval run at the Engineering Proving Grounds. The sleek four-seater's streamlined shape was determined by mathematical analysis of the effect of 200-mph winds as they spread ink blots along the surface of a plastic model. Chrysler called it a "hydroplane on wheels." Tall as they were, the tailfins of Chrysler's production cars never reached the magnitude of those on the Dart (*right*). An original factory color photo (*below*) displayed the Dart's dramatic profile.

Striking and dramatic, the '57 DeSoto came in four series, with Tri-Tower taillights integrated into soaring fins. DeSoto built 1650 Adventurer two-door hardtops priced at $3997. Later came 300 ragtops (*right*). This year's Adventurer coaxed 345 bhp out of its slightly bored, 345-cid Hemi. Firedomes and Fireflites got a 270/290-bhp 341-cid V-8. Single headlights were standard on DeSotos, like the $3671 Fireflite Sportsman hardtop sedan (*below*), but quad lights could now be fitted. A new lower-cost Firesweep series, $2777 for the sedan (*below right*), borrowed Dodge's 122-inch platform and front fenders.

Carrying a 325-cid "wedge" V-8, the Firesweep was actually a Dodge Royal with DeSoto trim. The line included a $3169 Shopper wagon (*above left*), also sold as a Fireflite. Shoppers seated six (*above*); Explorer wagons held nine. Top-selling Fireflite was the $3487 pillared sedan (*below*): 11,565 units.

The least-costly '57 Dodge hardtop coupe, and the most popular with 44,397 sold, was the $2580 Coronet (*above*), with a standard 245-bhp V-8. Any Dodge, like this Lancer hardtop (*above right*), could have the high-performance D-500 engine (*right*) whipping up 285 horses. The Super D-500 made 310 bhp. Interiors (*far right*), usually two-toned to complement the body, featured a "Scope-Signal Speedometer" above a full gauge bank.

Dodge offered a convertible in the budget-priced Coronet series (*left*), starting at $2842, and sold 3363 copies. This brightly two-toned ragtop has the optional D-500 Hemi V-8 with TorqueFlite. Coronet Club Sedans (*below left*) could have either a 138-bhp "Getaway" six or a V-8. Depending on compression and carbs, the 325-cid Hemi yielded 245 to 310 bhp. A handful of light-weight Coronets even got leftover 354-cid Chrysler 300-B engines packing 340 horses. In addition to the new torsion-bar front suspension, "Swept-Wing" Dodges switched to 14-inch tires for a softer ride. Two-speed PowerFlite remained available for buyers who didn't want to pay more for the three-speed TorqueFlite. Style leader of Dodge's "Power Giants" truck line was the Sweptside pickup (*below*), whose cargo box wore the same slabsided, finned panels as two-door station wagons.

This Plymouth Belvedere Sport Sedan (*below*), with a 301-cid V-8 (*above*), showed less than 1000 miles when photographed. The convertible, here without Sportone trim (*bottom*), listed at $2351. Ads (*top left*) hyped newness and the size of the wagons.

Plymouth's 1957 V-8 chassis (*left*) was typical of the time, with a heavy frame and big chromed bumpers. Wheelbases grew to 118 inches (122 for wagons). Five V-8s were available: 277-cid with 197 or 235 bhp; 301 cid, rated at 215/235 bhp; plus the Fury's new 318-cid wedge at 290 bhp. Both TorqueFlite and PowerFlite were optional. Plymouths handled beautifully, courtesy of the new torsion-bar front suspension. Savoy was still Plymouth's mid-range series, starting at $2147 for the two-door sedan (*below and below left*); 55,950 were built. This one has the 132-bhp, 230-cid six and three-speed stick. A $2317 Savoy Sport Sedan hardtop bowed at mid-year.

Sitting lower than its linemates, the '57 Plymouth Fury (*above*) again sported off-white paint with a golden spear. Under the hood sat the biggest V-8 in its field: the 318-cid "V-800," with dual quad carbs and 9.25:1 compression—unleashing 290 horses and 325 lbs/ft torque. A red roof helped this $2349 Belvedere Sport Coupe (*above left*) draw attention. The $2317 Savoy Sport Sedan (*left*) looked at home in the suburbs, but sold only 7601 copies.

Hot Rod magazine sponsored a Chrysler 300-powered Plymouth with a heavily modified front end at Daytona Beach (*left*). Envy was the theme of this Fury ad (*below left*), which noted that even "professional competition drivers" bowed to the new V-800 engine. The $2925 Fury (*bottom*) mixed style, luxury, and go-power; 7438 buyers approved. Side air cleaners were used on the hot V-8 (*second from bottom*).

ENVY OF THE PROS, AND OF THE NEIGHBORS, TOO!

New Plymouth with the 290-hp FURY V-800 mill!

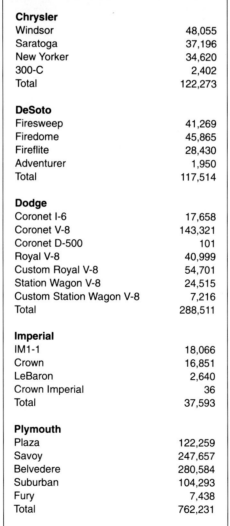

1957 Production

Chrysler
Windsor	48,055
Saratoga	37,196
New Yorker	34,620
300-C	2,402
Total	122,273

DeSoto
Firesweep	41,269
Firedome	45,865
Fireflite	28,430
Adventurer	1,950
Total	117,514

Dodge
Coronet I-6	17,658
Coronet V-8	143,321
Coronet D-500	101
Royal V-8	40,999
Custom Royal V-8	54,701
Station Wagon V-8	24,515
Custom Station Wagon V-8	7,216
Total	288,511

Imperial
IM1-1	18,066
Crown	16,851
LeBaron	2,640
Crown Imperial	36
Total	37,593

Plymouth
Plaza	122,259
Savoy	247,657
Belvedere	280,584
Suburban	104,293
Fury	7,438
Total	762,231

1957 Engine Availability

Chrysler
No. Cyl.	Disp., cid	bhp	Availability
V-8	354.0	285	S-Windsor
V-8	354.0	295	S-Saratoga
V-8	392.0	325	S-NY
V-8	392.0	375	S-300-C
V-8	392.0	390	O-300-C

DeSoto
No. Cyl.	Disp., cid	bhp	Availability
V-8	325.0	245	S-Firesweep
V-8	325.0	260	O-Firesweep
V-8	341.0	270	S-Firedome
V-8	341.0	290	S-Fireflite
V-8	345.0	345	S-Adventurer

Dodge
No. Cyl.	Disp., cid	bhp	Availability
I-6	230.2	138	S-Coronet I-6
V-8	325.0	245	S-Coronet V-8, Station Wagons
V-8	325.0	260	S-Custom Roya V-8
V-8	325.0	285/310	O-all (D-500)
V-8	354.0	340	O-all (D-500)

Imperial
No. Cyl.	Disp., cid	bhp	Availability
V-8	392.0	325	S-all

Plymouth
No. Cyl.	Disp., cid	bhp	Availability
I-6	230.2	132	S-all exc Fury, Belvedere cvt
V-8	277.0	197	S-Plaza
V-8	277.0	235	O-Plaza
V-8	301.0	215	S-Savoy, Belvedere V-8; O-Plaza
V-8	301.0	235	O-all exc Fury
V-8	318.0	290	S-Fury

1958

The worst recession of the postwar era takes hold—industry car sales drop 31 percent for the model year

Chrysler Corporation fares far worse; output plummets 46 percent

Chrysler products begin to abandon Hemi V-8s, turning to the simpler (and cheaper) wedge-head configuration

A handful of Hemis go on sale with fuel-injection

DeSoto output sinks below 50,000 units—the lowest since 1938

The hot Adventurer is the most costly DeSoto ever

Automatic speed control is offered on Chrysler and Imperial—an industry first

Imperial offers integrated electro-mechanical door-locking—the first such unit on an American car

A glassy Plymouth Cabana "dream wagon" show car foretells the four-door hard-top styling of the 1960-62 Chrysler wagons

Chrysler acquires a 25-per-cent interest in the French Simca auto firm

Chrysler products get a modest facelift, but few major changes

A Chrysler 300-D sets a Class E speed record at Bonneville: 156.387 mph

Chrysler New Yorker output fell sharply in 1958. The 392-cid Hemi put out 20 more horsepower than before, now 345, but this $4347 hardtop (*above and right*) snared only 3205 buyers.

Popular singer Fats Domino, known for *Blueberry Hill* and other hits, bought this New Yorker (*above*) that had been transformed into a multi-door, super-stretch Armbruster Club Car Limousine. Chrysler's mock-up of the Imperial D'Elegance II four-door hardtop show car (*right*) mixed basic Imperial ideas with such touches as flush door handles, hidden headlights, and a squarish steering wheel. A styling exercise only, it had no mechanical components. Virgil Exner reportedly disliked the design.

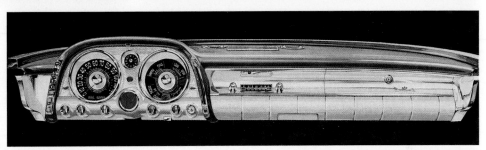

Above: Ads and brochures hyped "The Mighty Chrysler." Sales sagged. Save for the 300-D, Chryslers looked similar up front. Windsors/Saratogas had a 354 V-8.

Wearing a new grille, Imperials came in 10 models for 1958, including the $5388 Crown Southampton hardtop coupe (*top left and right*), of which 1939 were built. A row of pushbuttons on the dashboard (*second from top, right*) selected transmission gears. The rarely seen Crown Imperial Limousine (*above*), riding a stretched 145.5-inch chassis, was again produced by Ghia in Italy. Priced at a whopping $15,075, only 31 were built this year (36 in '57). Note the wrap-over rear roof band.

Even with "Flight-Sweep styling of the future," touted in this '58 Fireflite ad, DeSotos weren't selling. A Firesweep Explorer wagon (*right*) cost $3408.

Except for a fussier grille, new side trim, and quad headlights, DeSotos didn't change much for '58. A convertible joined the Adventurer line, $298 above the $4071 hardtop (*center left*). Just 350 hardtops and 82 ragtops were sold. Adventurers had a 361-cid V-8 (*above*) with dual quad carbs, good for 345 horsepower. A 305-bhp version of the wedge V-8 went into the $3972 Fireflite convertible (*center right*). Ragtops now came in all four series, even the low-end Firesweep, but sales totalled only 1775. In fact, the last '58 to roll off the line at the Detroit Wyoming Avenue Plant (*right*) on July 9, 1958, was a soft top.

Top: The '58 Dodge Regal Lancer "spring edition" hardtop had a 285-bhp 350 V-8.

Right: The six-cylinder Dodge Coronet Lancer "spring edition"

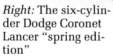

A new 350-cid Ram-Fire wedge V-8 engine went into the '58 Dodge Custom Royal Lancer convertible (*above left*), of which 1139 were sold. Dodges used four bodyside treatments during the year. A Sierra six-passenger wagon (*left*) cost $3035 in base trim, $3212 as a Custom; 18,896 Sierras were sold, plus 1300 Suburban two-doors. A fleet of Dodge police cars (*below*) joined the Missouri Highway Patrol.

Part of the '58 Dodge "Power Giants" line, the Sweptside D-100 pickup was the "handsomest truck on the road today!"

Plymouths entered 1958 with a mild facelift. A
Belvedere Sport Sedan (*above*) cost $2528. With twin
carbs, the 318-cid Fury V-8 (*right*) made 290 bhp.

AHEAD FOR KEEPS!

Here's your great new Plymouth...distinctive from its new *Silver Dart Styling* to new *Luxury Line Interiors*...with the custom-car comfort of *Torsion-Aire Ride*...the supreme ease of *Push-Button TorqueFlite**...and for you who really love fine cars, the response of the new *Golden Commando V-8**. See, ride, drive the leader of the low-price "3" today!

✴ Star of the Forward Look... *Plymouth*

Quad headlights, round taillights, and
reshuffled trim were the major changes for
'58 Plymouths. Ads (*above*) promoted
"Silver Dart Styling" and the "new Golden
Commando V-8," a 350-cid, 305-bhp wedge
V-8. At 36,043 units, the Belvedere Sport
Coupe (*above right*) sold twice as many
copies as the four-door Sport Sedan. Two-
tone "Sportone" bodyside treatment cost
extra. The Plymouth Cabana show wagon
(*right*), built by Ghia, had no engine. The
four-door hardtop body style featured center-opening doors. A sliding roof panel
made rear-seat entry easier.

A '58 Plymouth Savoy Sport Coupe (*left*) cost $2329 with a 132-bhp six and stick shift. Note the Sportone trim. Hardtops weren't offered in the low-priced Plaza series. A '58 Plymouth (*below*) undergoes inspection at the end of the assembly line.

1958 Engine Availability

Chrysler

No. Cyl.	Disp., cid	bhp	Availability
V-8	354.0	290	S-Windsor
V-8	354.0	310	S-Saratoga
V-8	392.0	345	S-NY
V-8	392.0	380	S-300-D
V-8	392.0	390	O-300-D

DeSoto

No. Cyl.	Disp., cid	bhp	Availability
V-8	350.0	280	S-Firesweep
V-8	350.0	295	O-Firesweep
V-8	361.0	295	S-Firedome
V-8	361.0	305	S-Fireflite; O-Firedome
V-8	361.0	345	S-Adventurer
V-8	361.0	355	O-Adventurer

Dodge

No. Cyl.	Disp., cid	bhp	Availability
I-6	230.2	138	S-Coronet I-6
V-8	325.0	252	S-Coronet V-8
V-8	325.0	265	S-Royal V-8
V-8	350.0	285	S-Custom Royal V-8, Station Wagons
V-8	361.0	305-333	O-all (D-500)

Imperial

No. Cyl.	Disp., cid	bhp	Availability
V-8	392.0	345	S-all exc Crown Imperial
V-8	392.0	325	S-Crown Imperial

Plymouth

No. Cyl.	Disp., cid	bhp	Availability
I-6	230.2	132	S-all exc Fury, Belvedere cvt
V-8	318.0	225	O-all exc Fury
V-8	318.0	250	O-all exc Fury
V-8	318.0	290	S-Fury
V-8	350.0	305	O-all
V-8	350.0	315	O-all (fuel injection)

Imports

No. Cyl.	Disp., cid	bhp	Availability
I-4	78.7	48	S-Aronde
I-4	78.7	57	O-Aronde
V-8	143.5	85	S-Vedette

1958 Production

Chrysler

Windsor	26,975
Saratoga	18,486
New Yorker	17,411
300-D	809
Total	63,681

DeSoto

Firesweep	19,414
Firedome	17,479
Fireflite	12,120
Adventurer	432
Total	49,445

Dodge

Coronet I-6	8,229
Coronet V-8	69,150
Royal V-8	15,165
Custom Royal V-8	25,202
Station Wagon V-8	20,196
Total	137,942

Imperial

LY1-L	7,063
Crown	8,000
LeBaron	1,039
Crown Imperial	31
Total	16,133

Plymouth

Plaza	94,728
Savoy	110,117
Belvedere	117,531
Suburban	116,120
Fury	5,303
Total	443,799

Imports

Simca Aronde	NA
Simca Vedette	NA

After a bleak 1958, Chrysler Corporation production grows modestly for '59

Tailfins continue to stretch skyward

Chryslers are powered by a 383-cid wedge V-8; Hemis are gone

Chrysler's 300-E gets 380 horses from a 413-cid V-8

Swivel semi-bucket seats become available on Chrysler products, but not many are ordered

This is the final year for the hoary Dodge/Plymouth L-head six

DeSoto sales continue gloomy—extinction is imminent

Chrysler offers an electronic control that changes the rear-view mirror to non-glare when headlamp beams hit its surface

The experimental DeSoto Cella converts liquid fuel into electrical energy

A second-generation gas turbine powers a Plymouth hardtop driven from Detroit to New York

Mild styling facelifts fail to match GM's major revamps

Despite a modest increase in sales, Chrysler's overall market share dwindles

Plymouth drops its budget-priced Plaza series

Only 140 Chrysler 300-E ragtops (*top*) were built in '59, plus 550 hardtops. Hemis vanished, replaced by a 413 "wedge" V-8. A 350-bhp version of the big wedge powered the $4533 New Yorker hardtop sedan (*above*).

Chrysler's restyling may have lacked grace, but output rose smartly. Still, only 286 New Yorker convertibles (*above and right*) went on sale. Note the unusual roof treatment on the $3353 Windsor hardtop sedan (*below*), which held a 383-cid wedge V-8; 6084 were sold.

The 1959 Chrysler Corporation lineup (*above*) included (*clockwise from lower left*) a Chrysler New Yorker, DeSoto Firedome convertible, Imperial LeBaron, Dodge Custom Royal Lancer, and Plymouth Fury Sport Sedan. The $5403 Imperial Crown Southampton hardtop coupe (*right*) gained a new grille, plus the 350-bhp, 413-cid V-8. It found only 1728 buyers. Chrysler's New Yorker Town & Country station wagon (*below*) seated six or nine, but appealed to just 1008 customers.

Virgil Exner's final show car was the bizarrely shaped, turbine-powered Chrysler Turboflite (*below right*). Note how the canopy roof raised (*below*) for entry. Massive fins (*right*) flanked a deceleration flap.

The "Golden Lion" 383 V-8 in a Chrysler Windsor hardtop coupe (*above*) delivered 305 horsepower. This one has the optional two-tone roof and swivel front seats. Prices started at $3289, but the four-door sedan sold better: 19,910 units versus 6775.

DeSoto Adventurer sales remained modest for '59: 590 hardtops (*left*), 97 ragtops. For $4427, a swiveling driver's seat was standard, but this hardtop has a six-way power version, plus automatic headlights and a Wonder Bar radio. The Adventurer's dual-carb 383-cid V-8 was now offered in other models. With 9171 built, the second most popular '59 DeSoto was the $3234 Firedome four-door sedan (*below left*), with a 305-bhp 383 engine. A Firedome Sportsman two-door hardtop (*below*) cost $3341; 2862 were sold. Mid-season Seville editions of the Firedome models helped celebrate DeSoto's Thirtieth Anniversary.

Quite a selection of accessories and care items (*right*) was available for a '59 Dodge Royal Sierra station wagon. A touch of a lever in a Dodge with $70.95 swivel front seats (*above*) rotated them 40 degrees outward.

Dodge endured a heavy-handed facelift for 1959, with limply hooded headlights and oddly shaped fins. Only 984 Custom Royal Lancer convertibles (*below*) were sold. Base price with the standard 361-cid V-8 came in at $3422. This Canary Diamond Yellow ragtop has the Super D-500 383-cid V-8 with high-lift cam and dual quads. Coral-and-white two-toning was a popular choice for the $3145 Dodge Custom Royal four-door sedan (*bottom*); 8925 were built. Coronets gained a Red Ram 326-cid V-8. New options included a Co-Pilot Speed Warning, self-dimming Mirror-Matic, and Level-Flite rear air suspension.

Above: Contrasting colors highlighted the fins of a $3201 Dodge Custom Royal Lancer hardtop, which attracted 6278 buyers. This one has the Super D-500 345-bhp V-8.

Not all of the 23,469 buyers of the $2561 Plymouth Belvedere Sport Coupe (*left*) appreciated the "elegance" of a simulated spare tire formed into the decklid. One of several new options, it came standard on the new top-line, high-performance Sport Fury hardtop and convertible. No longer a limited-edition wonder, Fury was now simply the name for the "second-best" Plymouth line. Plazas were gone, so the Savoy and Belvedere both moved down a notch. Heavy restyling gave Plymouths longer and higher fins, plus a garish grille and odd headlight eyelids.

The $2927 Plymouth Sport Fury hardtop coupe (*left and above*) sold rather well: 17,867 units. Soft top output reached 5990. A 260-bhp 318 V-8 came standard, but just $87 extra bought the new 305-bhp, 361-cid "Golden Commando" V-8.

The $2881/$2991 Plymouth Custom Suburban station wagon (*above*) was chosen by 32,017 buyers, many of them suburbanites. Six-passenger models came with a six or V-8. Stung by poor quality in 1957-58, '59 Plymouths (*right*) endured close scrutiny at the end of the assembly process.

A full line of Simcas, billed as "The world's most luxurious economy car," was "Imported from Paris by Chrysler." The larger $2298 Vedette promised "economy motoring plus 6-passenger comfort." Its "Aquilon" 143.5-cid (2351-cc) V-8 claimed 84 bhp. Vedette styling, echoing American tastes, embraced a wrapped windshield and tailfins. Smaller Simcas got a 78.7-cid (1290-cc) "Whispering Flash 4" with 45/48/57 horses and a finless rear end.

Simca Vedette four-door sedan

Simca Aronde Elysee four-door sedan

Simca Etoile Grand Large hardtop

Simca Etoile four-door sedan for '59

1959 Production

Chrysler
Windsor	35,443
Saratoga	17,470
New Yorker	16,329
300-E	690
Total	69,932

DeSoto
Firesweep	20,834
Firedome	15,076
Fireflite	9,127
Adventurer	687
Total	45,724

Dodge
Coronet I-6	15,686
Coronet V-8	81,096
Royal V-8	14,807
Custom Royal V-8	21,206
Sierra V-8	17,719
Custom V-8	5,871
Total	156,385

Imperial
MY1-L	7,798
Crown	8,332
LeBaron	1,132
Crown Imperial	7
Total	17,269

Plymouth
Savoy	132,302
Belvedere	116,041
Fury	65,257
Sport Fury	23,857
Suburban	120,802
Total	458,259

Imports
Simca Aronde	NA
Simca Ariane	NA
Simca Vedette	NA

1959 Engine Availability

Chrysler
No. Cyl.	Disp., cid	bhp	Availability
V-8	383.0	305	S-Windsor
V-8	383.0	325	S-Saratoga
V-8	413.0	350	S-NY
V-8	413.0	380	S-300-E

DeSoto
No. Cyl.	Disp., cid	bhp	Availability
V-8	361.0	295	S-Firesweep
V-8	383.0	305	S-Firedome
V-8	383.0	325	S-Fireflite
V-8	383.0	350	S-Adventurer; O-others

Dodge
No. Cyl.	Disp., cid	bhp	Availability
I-6	230.2	138	S-Coronet I-6
V-8	326.0	255	S-Coronet V-8
V-8	361.0	295/305	S-all exc Coronet
V-8	383.0	320/345	O-all (D-500, Super D-500)

Imperial
No. Cyl.	Disp., cid	bhp	Availability
V-8	413.0	350	S-all exc Crown Imperial
V-8	392.0	325	S-Crown Imperial

Plymouth
No. Cyl.	Disp., cid	bhp	Availability
I-6	230.2	132	S-Savoy, Belvedere, Suburban exc Custom 9P, Fury, Sport Fury
V-8	318.0	230	S-Fury; O-other exc Sport Fury
V-8	318.0	260	S-Sport Fury; O-others
V-8	361.0	305	O-all

Imports
No. Cyl.	Disp., cid	bhp	Availability
I-4	78.7	48	S-Aronde, Ariane
I-4	78.7	57	O-Aronde, Ariane
V-8	143.5	85	S-Vedette, O-Ariane

Chapter 10

From Compacts to Turbines: 1960-64

Not all was well in Chrysler's executive suite. Early in 1960, L.L. "Tex" Colbert turned the presidency over to William C. Newberg. Colbert assumed the chairmanship. Unfortunately, Newberg's reign lasted just 64 days—annulled by conflict of interest charges. Colbert then assumed a dual role, but more shakeups lay ahead.

At a nasty stockholders' meeting in April 1961, Colbert claimed "progress in cost reduction," but deplored the lack of sales improvement. Newberg, in a letter, decried Colbert's "czarist rule" and the firm's "frequent and unpredictable changes." Stockholders were angry, but Colbert prevailed—for a short while. On July 27, 1961, he resigned from Chrysler. Lynn A. Townsend became president; George H. Love was named chairman.

The early Sixties also brought the decline of Virgil Exner's leadership role. By 1964, he would be gone. Sooner than that—at the end of 1960—came the extinction of DeSoto, coupled with a consolidation into two divisions: Chrysler-Plymouth and Dodge.

In many analysts' eyes, Colbert's reign was the last interesting period for design and engineering, until the emergence of Lee Iacocca nearly two decades later. "After Colbert and Exner left," one executive explained later, "a sort of hibernation set in."

Chrysler made a bold move with the small-sized 1960 Valiant, and the similar '61 Dodge Lancer. Yet, the corporation was still best known for engineering—and for its recent leadership in styling. A small Chrysler in this era might have succeeded, but Townsend feared shrinkage might dilute the make's image. "Instead of risking the Chrysler image in any car-size contest,"

added division president Clare Briggs, "we have made capital of our car's tradition." So, Chryslers remained big and brawny.

All Chrysler products were "Unibodied" in 1960, except for Imperial. Unit construction made the cars tighter and more rattle-free (albeit more rust-prone). Otherwise, detail changes marked the 1960 season, including the first four-way flashers and an *automatic* swivel seat. Chryslers featured electro-luminescent "AstraDome" instrumentation, with bright dial markings. Imperials had a new high-back driver's seat, adjustable "spot" air conditioning, and an automatic headlight dimmer.

Chrysler trotted out what many consider the last true "Letter-Series" 300, before watering down the theme. The 300-F wore flamboyant canted fins, and ran with a "ram-induction" 413-cid V-8 with 375 or 400 bhp, and a new optional four-speed gearbox, Chrysler's first since the Thirties. A 375-bhp 300-F did a 16-second quarter-mile at 85 mph. Yet, *Motor Trend* suggested it had "traded a measure of its brute, racy feeling for that of a sporty, personal-type car."

DeSoto marked its last full season, fielding just two series. Unfortunately, only about 25,000 were sold, followed by just 3034 final '61s built in late 1960. Some DeSoto-Plymouth dealerships became Chrysler-Plymouth stores—intensifying already-existing rivalries.

After a feeble 1959, Dodge did better than other Chrysler makes. Flashy, sculptured styling helped. Dodge fielded a junior Plymouth-based Dart and senior Matador/Polara. Engines ran up to the 383-cid V-8 with ram-induction 330 horsepower. Sales soared

A 1960 Plymouth Fury hardtop sedan struts its soaring fins and lower-body brightwork.

to nearly 368,000 units, due mainly to the Dart, for a sixth-place ranking. During the Sixties, Dodge would strengthen its performance image, and move into the higher-price area left vacant by the loss of DeSoto. Chrysler would likewise move downward a bit.

Plymouth sales skidded in 1960, as the make barely hung onto third place. A grotesque front end and reach-for-the-sky fins probably didn't help. In Dodges and Plymouths, a 225-cid Slant Six (nicknamed for its canted block) finally put the old-fashioned L-head six out to pasture.

Ads promoted the Exner-styled Valiant as "Nobody's Kid Brother." The four-door sedan and wagon were considered the best-engineered of the Big Three compacts. They were also the quickest, the best handling—and the strangest looking, with a spare-tire outline on the rear deck that reminded some of a toilet seat. The 170-cid Slant Six made 101 bhp, 148 with "Hyper-Pak." Curiously, Valiant was listed as a separate make in 1960.

The big Plymouth's fins were shaved for 1961, but Dodge, Chrysler, and Imperial kept theirs. Valiant, now officially a Plymouth, added a hardtop and two-door sedan. They were duplicated in Dodge's new Lancer line. Imperial lost its pillared sedan, but added free-standing headlights—an Exner "classic" throwback idea. Putting Chrysler-Plymouth into one division meant Chrysler badging could adorn only big cars, yet dealers had several sizes to offer. Chrysler sales grew, but Plymouth's fell, to a position behind Rambler.

This was the last year for Chrysler's long-running Windsor series, and no four-speed gearbox was available for the 300-G. Chryslers wore an *inverted* trapezoidal grille between stacked, slanted headlights, while Plymouth tacked its taillights onto the sides of scalloped rear fenders. *Motor Trend* later suggested that the '61 Plymouth had "sparked a whole generation of Japanese sci-fi monsters." Senior Dodges weren't any better, with strange "reverse" fins.

Dodge Darts got a major facelift, copied for the most part by the bigger Polaras. The Matador series faded away. Dodge's D-500 option was now a 383-cid V-8 with twin carburetors and ram induction. A handful of Darts even got a costly 413-cid ram induction V-8. Dodge volume slumped 26 percent, due to an industry downtrend and little-liked styling. Lancers likewise failed to attract much attention.

In addition to bizarre styling on some models—but elegance on others—Chrysler was developing a reputation for indifferent workmanship. Engineering excellence wasn't enough if the actual cars that rolled off the line weren't properly assembled.

When design work on the '62 models began in 1958-59, stylists knew the fins had to go. Mid-priced cars hadn't sold well in the late Fifties, as underscored by the Edsel debacle. Economy imports were gaining. Chrysler pondered likely trends—and came close to catastrophe.

Thinking in smaller terms, Exner had a full fleet of new models in mind. Derived from a secret "theme car," they would exhibit classic styling cues, including a long hood and short deck. Though such a profile would be perfect a few years hence, it didn't fit 1962's thinking. Stylist Jeff Godshall later explained: "Exner's car looked like nothing Chrysler—or anyone else—had ever built." William Newberg had approved it, but Colbert, upon his return to power, vetoed the idea. Exner was ordered to issue an alternate, accomplished mainly by shaving the fins from the '61s.

Unfortunately for the sales department, "standard size" Dodges and Plymouths were smaller for '62, riding a new 116-inch wheelbase. This came about because Newberg had heard that Chevrolet was downsizing for '62, and instituted a crash program to do likewise for Plymouth and Dodge. Chevy didn't downsize, and Chrysler quickly learned that Americans didn't like shrunken "standard" cars. Not yet, anyway—and sales skidded badly. Valiant-like styling didn't help.

At mid-year, Dodge hurriedly issued the Custom 880, a *true* full-size model on Chrysler's wheelbase and not unlike the final DeSotos. It added badly needed sales to Dodge's total. Plymouth stuck with the smaller "full-size" cars until 1965 and suffered, dropping to eighth—its lowest position ever. The shrunken cars were roughly comparable to Ford's new mid-size Fairlane, but they fell far short of a Galaxie or Impala. But with big-block 413-cid V-8 power, the lightened Dodges tyrannized the nation's dragstrips.

Chryslers, meanwhile, looked luscious this season, retaining only the finest features of the recent past. The mid-range Windsor series now was marketed as a "non-letter" 300, available with many "real" 300 options. A total of 25,020 were sold, versus only 558 of the real thing.

Prior to his departure as styling chief, Exner had dubbed the '62s "plucked chickens." Elwood Engel, his replacement, was recruited from Ford. He would aim at more conventional styling for Chrysler. Exner's legacy consisted of originality and vivid imagination—commodities that turned out to be in short supply during many subsequent Chrysler seasons.

Looking over the early Sixties lineups, it was evident that the era of logical step-ups in price and size was over, sparking rivalries between Chrysler's two divisions. In a shrewd move to attract customers, Chrysler introduced a 5-year/50,000-mile warranty covering defects in materials and workmanship.

Promoted as the "Crisp, Clean, Custom Look," the 1963 Chryslers were the first to be styled under Engel. Even so, they wore a few Exner trademarks, including open wheelwells and sharp bodyside creases. The 300-J looked—and acted—even more like a regular Chrysler, promoted mainly for comfort. It carried a 390-horsepower version of the New Yorker's 413-cid V-8. Imperial, in the last year of its styling cycle, lost its "gunsight" taillights.

Unlike Plymouth, which stuck to downsized models, Dodge increased its wheelbase to 119 inches and pushed even harder on performance, with an engine proffered to racers: the 426-cid, 425-bhp wedge "Ramcharger." Dodge's new Dart compact (replacing Lancer) rode a longer wheelbase than the redesigned Valiant, and cost only a little more. Part of the trend toward bigger, posher compacts, the line even included a sporty GT hardtop and convertible. Darts easily outsold big Dodges. Meanwhile, Dodge's 880 series tried to take over DeSoto's role with a broader line, but fewer than 30,000 were sold. Nevertheless, the 880 was needed so Dodge dealers could have a two-tier offering like their Chrysler-Plymouth counterparts. Plymouth sales improved to nearly half a million; Dodge passed Rambler to rank seventh.

Chrysler Corporation earned a profit in 1963, and again in '64. Lynn Townsend credited the 5/50 warranty, plus broader market coverage and a stronger dealer organization. Total production ran second only to the superheated 1957 model year.

For 1964, Chrysler revived the Letter-Series convertible after a year's absence. Total 300-K output zoomed to 3647 units, still far behind non-letter 300s. Engel gave Imperials a clean new look, trading their Exner-created profile for a shape more akin to the square-edged '61 Lincoln Continental he had designed while at Ford.

Just two weeks before Ford introduced the Mustang, the Barracuda fastback coupe debuted. Nicknamed "glassback" because of its huge backlight, the sporty Valiant-based Plymouth compact came with a standard Slant Six, but a new 180-bhp, 273-cid V-8 was optional. That engine was also offered in the Valiants and Darts. Facelifting gave Dodge a more orthodox look, and the make returned to sixth rank for the first time since 1960. Dodge's 426-cid wedge engines continued to rule the nation's dragstrips, but now Dodge revived the half-forgotten Hemi. It was strictly for racing—mainly at NASCAR, where it soon dominated the pack. The 426-cid Hemi V-8 developed at least 425 horsepower. A second "horsepower race" was underway, and Chrysler Corporation was poised to take advantage of the action.

1960

The compact Valiant debuts as a separate make, marketed by Chrysler-Plymouth dealers

Dodge's new "junior" full-size series is the Plymouth-based Dart

Plymouth retains third place, but for the last time until the '70s; Rambler grabs fourth

All Chrysler Corporation cars except Imperial adopt "Unibody" construction

A Dodge/Plymouth overhead-valve "Slant Six" replaces the long-lived L-head six

"Ram-Induction" manifolding is available in the Chrysler 300-F and big Dodge/Plymouth V-8s

The Chrysler 300-F can have a French-built Pont-a-Mousson four-speed manual gearbox; this is the first 300 with four bucket seats

Chryslers add an electro-luminescent "AstraDome" instrument panel

Automatic swivel seats are optional

Valiant features an AC alternator, replacing the generator

A third-generation gas turbine is installed in a Plymouth, Dodge truck, and Turboflite show car

William Newberg lasts barely two months as Chrysler president, done in by conflict of interest charges

Newly Unibodied, '60 Chryslers sported large canted fins and a more sculpted shape. Wire wheels accent this $4875 New Yorker soft top (*top*), powered by a 350-bhp 413 V-8 (*above*). Note the swivel seats and center armrest in the brightly two-toned interior (*above right*). This model reached only 556 buyers. The $3989 mid-level Saratoga hardtop coupe (*right*) cost $3989; 2963 were built. Most popular, with 25,152 produced, was the $3194 Windsor four-door sedan (*below*).

Thirty-inch "Ram" tubing (*top left*) helped urge up to 400 horsepower from a Chrysler 300-F V-8. The $5411 300-F hardtop (*top right and above*) saw 943 copies built for 1960, plus 248 ragtops. Chrysler offered the Town & Country in the Windsor series, and also as a New Yorker (*right*). Six- and nine-passenger versions were available at $5022 and $5131. Only 1295 New Yorkers were sold, plus 2146 Windsors.

The Imperial LeBaron Southampton hardtop sedan (*left*) listed at $6318, a price that only 999 customers were willing to pay. Note the "gunsight" taillights perched in the tall "humpback" fins. Pillared sedans were also available (*bottom left*), offered in the Custom, Crown, and LeBaron series. Output for all three totaled 4621 units. The Crown Imperial Limousine (*below*) was a special-order model—at $16,500—but Ghia was asked to build only 16 copies. The limo weighed 5960 pounds.

DeSoto retreated to just three body styles in two series for 1960: Fireflite and Adventurer (*left*). High-performance models were history. Note the massive "V" bumper (*below left*). Built in Canada, this Adventurer (*below*) sports swivel seats. At $3579, the Adventurer four-door sedan (*center right*) found 5746 buyers.

Powerplants available in a Dodge Dart Phoenix convertible (*above*) ranged from the new, mild-mannered 225-cid "Slant Six" to the hot D-500 383-cid V-8. Newly Unibodied, Dodges came in almost twice as many models this year. With any one of the five V-8 engine choices underhood, a '60 Dart had little trouble scaling even a 32-percent grade (*left*).

A revitalized Dodge listed 35 models for 1960. The top-line Polara hardtop sedan (*above*) carried a base price of $3275. Polaras (and Monacos) rode a 122-inch wheelbase and wore taller fins than the lower-priced Darts.

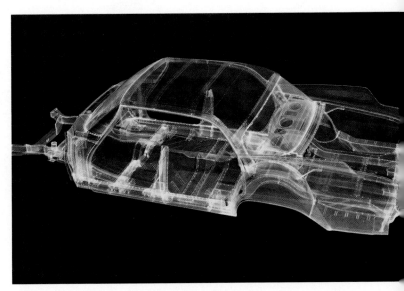

Highlights from the 1960 Dodge lineup: (*second row*) $3506 Polara hardtop wagon and $2278 Dart Seneca two-door sedan, (*third row*) $2695 Dart Seneca wagon and $2868 Dart Phoenix convertible, (*above two*) $2618 Dart Phoenix hardtop coupe, and (*above*) $2966 Matador hardtop coupe. The junior Darts, priced nose-to-nose with Chevy-Ford-Plymouth, captured 88 percent of Dodge sales.

"See-through testing" was made possible by this plastic model body (*above*), which "permitted the greatest step forward in body building since Dodge introduced steel bodies." Due to the modest weights of the new Unibody design, performance and economy didn't suffer. Darts rode a 118-inch chassis and measured 208.6 inches; "senior" models were 212.6 inches long (wagons 214.8).

Plymouth Fury convertible for 1960

"Some people own cars," declared one ad (*top right*). "Some cars own people. We built the Solid '60 Plymouth for those who want to be boss." Solid perhaps, but dubious restyling gave little claim to leadership. The $2599 Fury hardtop (*top left*) looks vastly long in this publicity shot; unique two-toning added sass to a $2656 Fury hardtop sedan (*below*). Priced between Falcon and Corvair—$2053 to $2566—the compact Valiant looked like nothing else on the American road—down to a simulated spare tire on the decklid of this V-200 sedan (*left*). Valiants also came in station wagon form, six or nine passenger. Here (*below left*), a V-100.

Lee Petty (*top*) waves from behind the wheel of a racing Valiant sedan, which competed in the compact stock-car class. Valiants won. Their new 170-cid Slant Six (*center*) delivered 101 bhp, 148 with "Hyper-Pak." Its slanted block and angled head permitted a lower hood. A stroked 225-cid version went into bigger Dodges and Plymouths. The $2130 Valiant V-200 sedan (*above*) pleased 106,515 customers.

1960 Production

Chrysler

Windsor	41,158
Saratoga	15,525
New Yorker	19,390
300-F	1,212
Total	77,285

DeSoto

Fireflite	14,484
Adventurer	11,597
Total	26,081

Dodge

Dart I-6	136,168
Dart V-8	187,000
Matador	27,908
Polara	16,728
Total	367,804

Imperial

Custom	7,786
Crown	8,226
LeBaron	1,691
Crown Imperial	16
Total	17,719

Plymouth

Valiant V-100	66,734
Valiant V-200	127,558
Savoy	78,204
Belvedere	62,744
Fury	55,487
Suburban	56,997
Total	447,724

Imports

Simca Aronde	NA
Simca Ariane	NA
Simca Vedette	NA

1960 Engine Availability

Chrysler

No. Cyl.	Disp., cid	bhp	Availability
V-8	383.0	305	S-Windsor
V-8	383.0	325	S-Saratoga
V-8	413.0	350	S-NY
V-8	413.0	375	S-300-F
V-8	413.0	400	O-300-F

DeSoto

No. Cyl.	Disp., cid	bhp	Availability
V-8	361.0	295	S-Fireflite
V-8	383.0	305	S-Adventurer

Dodge

No. Cyl.	Disp., cid	bhp	Availability
I-6	225.0	145	S-Dart I-6
V-8	318.0	230	S-Dart Seneca/Pioneer V-8
V-8	318.0	255	S-Dart Phoenix V-8
V-8	361.0	295	S-Matador; O-Dart Pioneer/Phoenix
V-8	383.0	325	S-Polara; O-Matador, Dart Phoenix
V-8	383.0	330	O-Polara, Matador, Dart Phoenix

Imperial

No. Cyl.	Disp., cid	bhp	Availability
V-8	413.0	350	S-all

Plymouth

No. Cyl.	Disp., cid	bhp	Availability
I-6	170.0	101	S-Valiant
I-6	170.0	148	O-Valiant
I-6	225.0	145	S-full-size I-6
V-8	318.0	230/260	S-full-size V-8
V-8	361.0	260-310	O-all full-size
V-8	383.0	330	O-full-size

Imports

No. Cyl.	Disp., cid	bhp	Availability
I-4	78.7	48	S-Aronde, Ariane
I-4	78.7	57	O-Aronde, Ariane
V-8	143.5	85	S-Vedette, O-Ariane

1961

178

One of just 337 built, this '61 Mardi Gras Red Chrysler 300-G convertible (*above*) sports the newly inverted trapezoidal grille flanked by diagonal quad headlights. This one has power swivel bucket seats. Its ram-inducted 413-cid V-8 (*left*) made 375 horse-power—or an optional 400. The long intake tubes stuffed fuel/air into the dual carbs. No manual shift was offered this year, as the 300-G switched from 14- to 15-inch tires and lost its simulated spare-tire trunk-lid. The 300-G hardtop (*below and bottom*) saw output increase to 1280 units. As before, the 300 series rode the New Yorker's longer 126-inch wheelbase.

Left: The 300-G badge told enthusiasts everything they needed to know. *Above*: Tall, pointed fins housed the back-up lights.

A "Golden Lion" 413-cid V-8 powered the $4175 Chrysler New Yorker hardtop coupe (*left*), shown in Sierra Sand and Tuscany Bronze. This loaded example, one of 2541, has all the options: power swivel seats (*below left*), power everything else, Mirrormatic, cruise control, air conditioning, Golden Touch radio, and "Flight Sweep" decklid. The $4592 New Yorker convertible (*below*) looked sharp in Capri Blue; only 576 were sold (plus 2135 Newport ragtops). With DeSoto doomed, its role in the corporate lineup was overtaken by the new Chrysler Newport—which actually cost slightly less. Unlike Plymouth and Dodge, both of which saw sales of their full-size models plummet, Chrysler managed to post a 25-percent gain for the model year. Base sticker prices for 1960 ranged from $2964 to $5841.

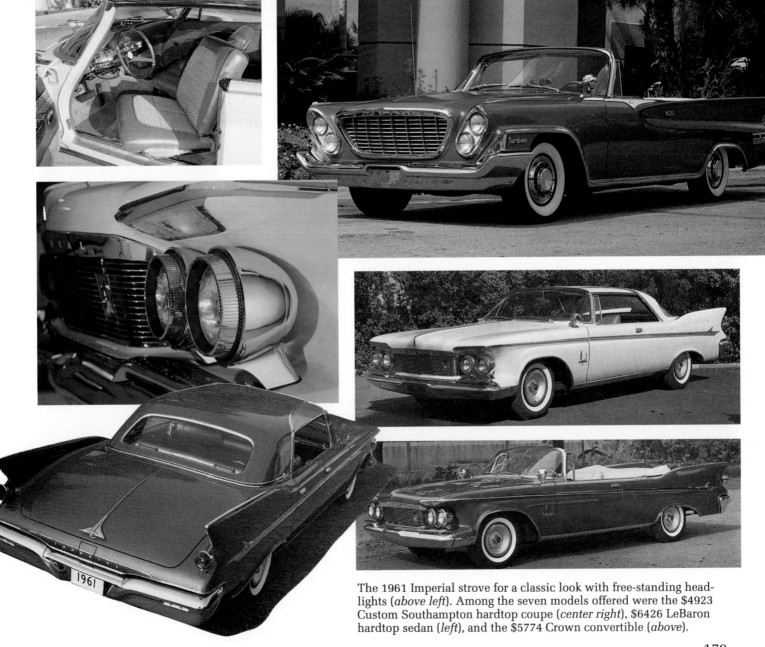

The 1961 Imperial strove for a classic look with free-standing headlights (*above left*). Among the seven models offered were the $4923 Custom Southampton hardtop coupe (*center right*), $6426 LeBaron hardtop sedan (*left*), and the $5774 Crown convertible (*above*).

A 265-bhp 361 V-8 was fitted to the final DeSotos (*above and left*), sold only as a hardtop coupe and sedan; 911 and 2123 were built. Upscale Dodges melded into a single "custom-size" Polara series (*below left*), here the $3110 hardtop sedan with its controversial reverse-slant fins. Darts wore another taillight treatment, as seen on the $2618 Dart Phoenix hardtop coupe (*below and bottom left*). In the spring, round taillights (*bottom right*) appeared on the Phoenix and Pioneer.

Polaras were called "the finest of everything Dodge," so a Polara D-500 convertible (*left*) had to be the finest of the finest. Its 383-cid V-8 yielded 325 horsepower and 425 lbs/ft torque. This red ragtop is loaded with options, including Auto Pilot speed control, Safe-T-Matic door locks, and Highway Hi-Fi. Six- and nine-passenger versions of the Dart Pioneer station wagon (*below left*) went on sale, with Slant Six or V-8 power. Dodge's new compact Lancer came in seven models and two series. Both the 170 and 770 series included a four-door sedan (*below*), at $2041 and $2137, but the $2164 hardtop coupe (*below center*) was a deluxe 770 only. Two-toning was optional.

Dodge Dart Phoenix sedan: $2595

Hoping for frugal operation, some taxi companies bypassed the usual big cars and turned to compacts, such as the Dodge Lancer, which shared its 106.5-inch-wheelbase chassis with Valiant. Lancers could have the 170- or 225-cid Slant Six.

Dodge's experimental FliteWing featured automatic flip-up side windows instead of the usual roll-down glass, intended to make entry/exit easier and eliminate the center pillar. Pushbuttons also operated windows in the ordinary manner.

Left: A $2137 Plymouth Valiant V-200 hardtop—new for '61—was sent out to pose with three Chrysler Corporation concept vehicles (*left to right*): Chrysler Imperial D'Elegance, Valiant-based Plymouth XNR, and Plymouth Cabana. The $2967 Plymouth Fury convertible (*below*) came with a 230-bhp, 318-cid V-8—but a large selection of big-block engines was optional. This ragtop stole the hearts of 6948 new-car buyers.

Plymouth labeled its '61 redesign "A harmony of motion." True, the oddly formed two-tone color combinations were gone, and views of the bullet-shaped taillights weren't distracted by tailfins. Still, the restyling of fenders, hood, and deck—with a strangely pinched grille up front and scalloped fenders aft—wasn't Plymouth's finest hour. With a 318-cid V-8, this Belvedere hardtop coupe (*above*) cost $2580. Taking a six saved $119. Belvederes had a bit less trim and fewer interior luxuries than the Fury, but more than the bottom-of-the-line Savoy. Mid-year brought a revived Sportone option, with more subtle two-toning than before.

1961 Production

Chrysler			
Newport	57,102	Crown	6,205
Windsor	17,336	LeBaron	1,026
New Yorker	20,399	Crown Imperial	9
300-G	1,617	Total	12,258
Total	96,454		
		Plymouth	
DeSoto		Valiant V100	54,642
Total	3,034	Valiant V200	88,436
		Savoy	63,642
		Belvedere	54,421
Dodge		Fury	53,765
Lancer 170	25,508	Suburban	34,929
Lancer 770	49,286	Total	349,835
Dart I-6	83,014		
Dart V-8	100,547	**Imports**	
Polara	14,032	Simca Aronde	NA
Total	272,387	Simca Ariane	NA
		Simca Vedette	NA
Imperial			
Custom	5,018		

Unibodied Plymouths began their assembly trek at the Detroit plant's main "gate line" (*above*), where bodysides were swung into position in their fixtures and clamped to the floor pan. Next, the roof and body were welded together. Production took 18 hours, requiring 737 operations. At the end of their journey, the cars reached the "O.K." lines (*top left*). Valiants earned a minor facelift for '61. With 84,751 V-100s and V-200s built, four-doors (*left*) were the mainstay of the compact line, joined for '61 with a V-100 two-door sedan and V-200 hardtop. At mid-year, V-200s could get the 145-bhp, 225-cid Slant Six.

1961 Engine Availability

Chrysler

No. Cyl.	Disp., cid	bhp	Availability
V-8	361.0	265	S-Newport
V-8	383.0	305	S-Windsor
V-8	413.0	350	S-NY
V-8	413.0	375	S-300-G
V-8	413.0	400	O-300-G

DeSoto

No. Cyl.	Disp., cid	bhp	Availability
V-8	361.0	265	S-all

Dodge

No. Cyl.	Disp., cid	bhp	Availability
I-6	170.0	101	S-Lancer
I-6	225.0	145	S-Dart I-6; O-Lancer
V-8	318.0	230	S-Dart V-8
V-8	318.0	260	O-Dart V-8

No. Cyl.	Disp., cid	bhp	Availability
V-8	361.0	265	S-Polara
V-8	361.0	305	O-Dart V-8 (D-500)
V-8	383.0	325	O-Polara (D-500), Dart V-8
V-8	383.0	330	O-Polara, Dart V-8 (ram induc)
V-8	413.0	350/375	O-Dart

Imperial

No. Cyl.	Disp., cid	bhp	Availability
V-8	413.0	350	S-all

Plymouth

No. Cyl.	Disp., cid	bhp	Availability
I-6	170.0	101	S-Valiant
I-6	170.0	148	O-Valiant
I-6	225.0	145	S-full-size I-6
V-8	318.0	230	S-full-size V-8

No. Cyl.	Disp., cid	bhp	Availability
V-8	318.0	260	S-full-size with TorqueFlite
V-8	361.0	305/310	O-full-size exc w/ PowerFlite or a/c
V-8	383.0	325-340	O-full-size exc w/ PowerFlite or a/c
V-8	413.0	350/375	O-full size

Imports

No. Cyl.	Disp., cid	bhp	Availability
I-4	78.7	48	S-Simca Aronde, Ariane
I-4	78.7	57	O-Simca Aronde, Ariane
V-8	143.5	84	S-Simca Vedette, O- Simca Ariane

1962

Dodge/Plymouth "standard" cars shrink to intermediate size, but sales suffer

"Downsizing" ranks as the major mistake of the decade—and years ahead of its time

Plymouth skids to eighth place in production; Pontiac grabs the Number Three slot

Mid-year brings a full-size, Chrysler Newport-based Dodge Custom 880

Chrysler fields a non-letter 300 series, as well as the 300-H; the Windsor Series is gone

A Plymouth Fury hits 190.073 mph at the Bonneville Salt Flats, the fastest ever for a stock-body production car

A CR2A gas turbine installed in a Dart is driven from New York to Los Angeles—and, in a Fury hardtop, delivers improved fuel mileage and response

Chrysler starts production of 50 turbine-powered cars, to be tested by selected motorists

Chryslers and Imperials display a cleaner rear end, as tailfins disappear

Plymouth revives the Sport Fury badge, on a bucket-seat coupe and convertible

Non-letter 300s can get a load of performance gear

Chrysler New Yorkers lost their fins and added a 300-style grille. A hardtop sedan (*above and left*) cost $4263, while a six-passenger Town & Country wagon (*below left*) went for $4766. *Below:* Joining the 300-H was a nearly identical, but less-potent, Sport 300 series.

Hot Rod magazine sponsored this Chrysler 300-H in the 1962 Winternationals drag races. "Letter-Series" 300-H output fell to a mere 435 hardtops and 123 ragtops.

The Chrysler 300 Sport and 300-H rode a 122-inch wheelbase in 1962. The $5090 300-H hardtop (*top left*) stickered at $5090, while the $4263 New Yorker hardtop sedan (*second from top, left*) pleased 6646 customers. Both had a 413 V-8. Buyers liked the finless Chryslers—output jumped 33.7 percent.

Only 554 '62 Imperial Crown ragtops (*top right*) were sold. Note the "space-age" dashboard (*second row, right*). Also offered: a $4920 Custom coupe (*third row, left*) and $6422 LeBaron sedan (*above*), both Southamptons. No Crown Imperial Ghia limos were built for '62, but 13 '63s (*above left*) were sold.

Photos dated February 1960 (*top row*) reveal what the '62 DeSoto Adventurer might have looked like—if the make hadn't expired. A $2257 bucket-seat Dodge Lancer GT (*above*) replaced the compact 770 hardtop coupe, and scored 13,683 sales. A sporty bucket-seat Polara 500 series topped the early '62 Dodge line. This is (*below*) the $2960 hardtop sedan.

Mildly restyled '62 Dodge and Plymouth hardtop coupes (*above*) served as Chrysler's "third-generation" turbine specials. Two of each were built. One Dodge ran coast-to-coast, getting 17 mpg. It accelerated from 0-60 mph in a quick 7.8 seconds. Darts (*below*) initially served as Dodge's full-size models, here the $2763 440 hardtop sedan. An experimental Lancer GT coupe seen at auto shows (*below right*) sported a sliding fabric sunroof.

A newly reduced, 116-inch wheelbase held the "standard-size" Dodge Dart series: Fleet, base, 330, and 440. Each was about six inches shorter and more than 300 pounds lighter than the '61. Only the top-rung 440 listed a convertible (*right*), priced at $2945 with a standard 318-cid, 230-bhp V-8. Other body styles came with the Slant Six. Either way, the public steered clear of the prematurely downsized Dodges, whose Lancer-like styling failed to overcome the bias against "smaller" big cars. Appearances could easily deceive when it came to Dodges in the '60s. This lightweight two-door Dart sedan (*below*) houses a 410-horsepower "Ramcharger" 413-cid "Max Wedge" V-8 (*third row, right*) with dual quad carbs. Such installations were rare.

Those who thought this $3019 Dodge Polara 500 hardtop (*above*) too small—6834 didn't—could get a big Custom 880 at mid-year. Few Dodge wagons (*left*) saw police duty. Hot rodders could order a wide variety of high-performance parts (*right*).

The facelifted '62 Plymouth Valiants, here a $2087 V-200 sedan (*right*), could have an optional 225-cid Slant Six rather than the 170-cid unit. A $2230 Signet 200 hardtop (*below*) bowed as a sporty bucket-seat cousin to workaday Valiants; 25,586 were sold. "Sleepers" were popular in '62. A black Plymouth Belvedere two-door sedan (*left center*) might look dull—but who knew what lurked under the hood? The $2742 Fury hardtop sedan (*bottom left*) looked sharper, and this one has the 335-horsepower "Golden Commando" 383 V-8.

Plymouth revived the Sport Fury badge at mid-year for its sportiest hardtop and (*above*) convertible. Engine choices reached 420 bhp, sales just 1516 units.

Paxton Products sponsored the "Andy Granatelli" Plymouth Fury (*left and below left*) with 413 cubes and floor shift.

1962 Engine Availability

Chrysler

No. Cyl.	Disp., cid	bhp	Availability
V-8	361.0	265	S-Newport
V-8	383.0	305	S-300
V-8	413.0	340	S-NY
V-8	413.0	380	S-300-H
V-8	413.0	405	O-300-H

Dodge

No. Cyl.	Disp., cid	bhp	Availability
I-6	170.0	101	S-Lancer
I-6	225.0	145	S-Dart I-6; O-Lancer
V-8	318.0	230	S-Dart V-8
V-8	318.0	260	O-Dart V-8
V-8	361.0	265	S-Polara
V-8	361.0	305	O-Dart V-8 (D-500)
V-8	383.0	325	O-Polara (D-500), Dart V-8
V-8	383.0	330	O-Polara, Dart V-8 (ram induc)
V-8	413.0	350/375	O-Dart

Imperial

No. Cyl.	Disp., cid	bhp	Availability
V-8	413.0	340	S-all

Plymouth

No. Cyl.	Disp., cid	bhp	Availability
I-6	170.0	101	S-Valiant
I-6	225.0	145	S-Savoy, Belvedere, Fury; O-Valiant
V-8	318.0	230	S-full-size V-8 exc Sport Fury
V-8	318.0	260	O-full-size exc Sport Fury
V-8	361.0	305	S-Sport Fury; O-full-size exc w/ PowerFlite or a/c
V-8	383.0	335	O-full-size exc w/ PowerFlite or a/c
V-8	413.0	410/420	O-Sport Fury

Imports

No. Cyl.	Disp., cid	bhp	Availability
I-4	57.6	50-52	S-Simca 1000
I-4	78.7	65	S-Simca 5

1962 Production

Chrysler

Newport	83,120
300	25,020
New Yorker	20,223
300-H	558
Total	128,921

Dodge

Lancer 170	19,780
Lancer 770	30,888
Lancer GT	13,683
Dart I-6	59,475
Dart V-8	86,885
Polara 500	12,268
Custom 880	17,505
Total	240,484

Imperial

Custom	4,413
Crown	8,475
LeBaron	1,449
Total	14,337

Plymouth

Valiant V100	59,380
Valiant V200	72,328
Valiant Signet	25,586
Savoy	68,602
Belvedere	39,477
Fury	37,464
Sport Fury	5,555
Suburban	31,422
Total	339,814

Imports

Simca 1000	NA
Simca 5	NA

Shrinking the full-size Plymouth turned out to be a major blunder. Sales sagged drastically—behind such ex-subordinate makes as Rambler and Pontiac. The $2924 Plymouth Fury convertible (*above*) weighed 3210 pounds, versus 3535 pounds in 1961, but only 4349 were sold. Demand for mid-size cars would soon escalate—but not quite yet. Valiant-like styling didn't help matters. Soon after start-up, Furys got full-length beltline moldings in a futile attempt to give it a longer look.

1963

Chryslers exhibit cleaned-up styling penned by Elwood Engel

Plymouth returns to fourth place in output, largely due to the Valiant's popularity

The corporation shows a record $161.6 million earnings; sales volume tops the billion-dollar mark

Chrysler stuns the industry with a 5-year/50,000-mile powertrain warranty—competitors scramble

The new '63 Chrysler models include a loaded New Yorker Salon

A "Pace Setter" 300 handles the Official Pace Car duties at the Indianapolis 500 race

The Chrysler 300-J comes as a hardtop only; the ragtop is gone

Dodge's and Plymouth's big-block V-8 grows to 426 cubic inches

A super-performance "Ramcharger" delivers up to 425 bhp

The Dart badge moves to a larger, all-new Dodge compact

New experimental vehicles include the Plymouth Satellite convertible

Chrysler launches a consumer evaluation program for its experimental turbine automobile

Chrysler acquires the British Cummins Diesel company

After a Chrysler 300 Sport paced the '63 Indy 500 (*top*), 2167 "Pace Setter" replicas were issued. Lacking a convertible, sales of the 300-J (*above and right*) sank to a record low. At $5860, the New Yorker Salon (*below*) was called "The world's most complete car."

By 1963, Chrysler's turbine cars had experimented with a series of seven different engines (*top left*). A fourth-generation engine went into 50 new turbine cars (*top and above*), slated for evaluation by "consumer representatives" all over the country. Styled by Elwood Engel, the Ghia-bodied hardtop borrowed a bit from the Thunderbird, but looked more radical.

Chrysler chief engineer Robert M. Rodger (*above*) shows off the 390-bhp V-8 for the 300-J. Lynn A. Townsend (*right*) served as president, 1961-66. Styling head Elwood P. Engel (*far right*), formerly from Ford, posed with an associate in the styling studio. At $6434, the LeBaron Southampton (*bottom right*) attracted 1535 buyers. The 149.5-inch-wheelbase Crown Imperial Limousine (*below*) listed at $18,500.

1963 Dodge Ramcharger 426-A engine

The former Dart was now called, simply, "Dodge." Front-end styling was new, as seen on this Polara 500 hardtop coupe (*top*). Bucket seats were standard (*top left*), and this one has the Stage II Max Wedge 426 Super Stock V-8 (*center left*). Rear-end styling was new, too (*above*). Note the unusual placement of the quad headlights (*right*) and the huge hood scoops on this 330 two-door sedan. It packs the Stage III Max Wedge, good for 425 horses.

Restyling for '63 gave full-size Dodge Custom 880s less of a Chrysler Newport look. New front-end styling featured more formal, squared-up lines. Three base 880 models expanded the 880 Custom lineup, for a total of nine, but the $3109 hardtop sedan (*left*) came only in Custom 880 trim. It found 2564 takers. A 361-cid V-8 was standard, but bigger-block engines could be ordered. The former Dart was now called "Dodge," and included the 330, 440, and Polara/Polara 500 series. Their wheelbase grew to 119 inches, only three inches less than the 880.

Recovering from the "downsizing" fiasco, Dodge turned to cleaner, more conventional lines for '63. Just $2983 bought a Polara ragtop, (*above*), which enticed 2962 people. The new Dart—a compact replacing Lancer—featured crisper styling and a longer wheelbase (111 inches) than sibling Valiant. An open Dart 270 (*below*) cost $2385; the bucket-seat GT, $2512. Four-door sedans came in base 170 or snazzier 270 trim (*below right*), but the $2289 hardtop coupe came only as a GT. Together with the ragtop, 34,227 GTs were produced for the model year.

1963 Dodge Polara hardtop

The Dodge 440 four-door sedan (*left*) could be had for $2438 with the 145-bhp Slant Six or $2546 with the base 230-bhp 318 V-8. Dodge's Sweptline pickup (*above*) came with a 140-bhp 225 Slant Six or optional V-8s.

193

Like Dodge, Plymouth displayed a more conservative, squared-up look for 1963. Likewise, Plymouth bored out the V-8 wedge to 426-cid, to create the sizzling "Super Stock" engine (*top right*). seen here in a $2538 Belvedere hardtop coupe (*top left*). The $3082 Sport Fury soft top (*second row*) came with a V-8 power and bucket-seats (*above*). Only 3836 were built. Plymouth offered only one hardtop sedan: the $2724 Fury (*above left*).

Valiant was completely restyled for '63. A $2454 convertible (*above*) joined the $2230 hardtop (*right*) in the Signet line. Sales: 9154 ragtops, 30,857 hardtops.

194

Hamilton Motors sponsored a series of Plymouth "Golden Commando" stock cars (*left*). This one packs a potent Super Stock 426 V-8 with automatic; the "Golden Commando" name ordinarily identified Plymouth's 383-cid V-8. A Sport Fury hardtop coupe (*below*) cost $2851; 11,483 were produced.

1963 Engine Availability

Chrysler

No. Cyl.	Disp., cid	bhp	Availability
V-8	361.0	265	S-Newport
V-8	383.0	305	S-300
V-8	413.0	340	S-NY
V-8	413.0	360	O-300
V-8	413.0	390	S-300-J

Dodge

No. Cyl.	Disp., cid	bhp	Availability
I-6	170.0	101	S-Dart
I-6	225.0	145	S-330/440/Polara I-6; O-Dart
V-8	318.0	230	S-330/440/Polara V-8
V-8	361.0	265	S-880
V-8	383.0	305	S-Polara 500; O-others exc Dart
V-8	383.0	330	O-all exc Dart
V-8	413.0	360	O-880
V-8	426.0	370/425	O-all exc Dart (ram induc)

Imperial

No. Cyl.	Disp., cid	bhp	Availability
V-8	413.0	340	S-all

Plymouth

No. Cyl.	Disp., cid	bhp	Availability
I-6	170.0	101	S-Valiant
I-6	225.0	145	S-Savoy, Belvedere, Fury; O-Valiant
V-8	318.0	230	S-full-size V-8
V-8	361.0	265	O-full-size
V-8	383.0	330	O-full-size
V-8	426.0	415/425	O-full-size

Imports

No. Cyl.	Disp., cid	bhp	Availability
I-4	57.6	50-52	S-Simca 1000
I-4	78.7	65	S-Simca 5

1963 Production

Chrysler

Newport	75,972
300	24,665
New Yorker	27,960
300-J	400
Total	128,997

Dodge

Dart 170	58,536
Dart 270	61,159
Dart GT	34,227
330 I-6	51,761
440 I-6	13,146
Polara I-6	68,262
330 V-8	33,602
440 V-8	49,491
Polara V-8	40,323
Polara 500	7,256
880	28,266
Total	446,029

Imperial

Custom	4,013
Crown	8,558
LeBaron	1,537
Crown Imperial	13
Total	14,121

Plymouth

Valiant V100	99,242
Valiant V200	85,903
Valiant Signet 200	40,011
Savoy	93,810
Belvedere	84,660
Fury	69,503
Sport Fury	15,319
Total	488,448

Imports

Simca 1000	NA
Simca 5	NA

1964

Dodge marks its 50th year in production; the Chrysler badge is four decades old

Chrysler's corporate output rises another 18 percent—the highest total since 1957

A convertible returns to the Chrysler 300-K line

Engel's all-new Imperial loses its free-standing headlamps, adopts more "formal" lines

The Dodge Dart and Plymouth Valiant add a 273-cid V-8 option

Dodge resurrects the Hemi V-8, but for pro racers only

Everyday performance-car zealots get a tamer 426 "Street Wedge"

Hemi-powered Chrysler products take first, second, and third at Daytona; the victorious Plymouth is piloted by a young Richard Petty

Plymouth's "glassback" Barracuda, a Valiant spin-off, debuts on April 1—just two weeks before Ford's Mustang

Chrysler acquires a controlling interest in Simca, a French automaker, then negotiates to take over the British Rootes Group

Chrysler earns a profit for the second year in a row, and the Letter-Series 300 sets a production record

The 1964½ Chrysler 300 "Silver Special" hardtop (*top*) came only in silver. Chrysler's "Letter-Series" was now the 300-K. The lower-cost 300 Sport saw 18,379 hardtops (*second from top*) and 1401 convertibles (*right*), priced at $3443 and $3803. The New Yorker Town & Country wagon (*above*), $4721 and $4828, sold 2793 copies.

Chryslers didn't change much for '64, but Imperials gained a clean, square-edged profile, not unlike the Lincoln Continental. All New Yorkers had a 413-cid V-8, including this $4131 hardtop sedan (*top*). New Yorker "post" sedans (*second row, right*) sold reasonably well, with 15,443 produced this season. This one has an adjustable steering wheel, Search-Tune AM radio, and optional roof trim. Anyone who wanted to "Move up to Chrysler" (*second row, left*), whether in a "crisp and hand-some" 300-K or a lesser model, now got a 5-year/50,000-mile warranty. Slow-selling Custom models were gone, but the Imperial lineup included a Crown convertible, hardtop sedan, and a $5739 hardtop coupe (*above and right*). The last found 5233 buyers. Also in the line: a $6455 LeBaron hardtop sedan (2949 built) and the rare Ghia Crown limo (10 built). This year, hardtops dropped the Southampton name.

A facelift highlighting a new grille and rear end gave Dodges a more orthodox appearance. As before, the 880 series rode a 122-inch chassis. At $2826, some 7356 base 880 sedans (*left*) were sold. This $2978 Polara 500 hardtop (*below*) boasts a 365-bhp, 426-cid wedge V-8 and a Hurst-shifted four-speed. Its dashboard is typical of the era, right down to the wide "strip" speedometer.

A fresh "barbell" grille decorated '64 Dodges, including the $2745 Polara hardtop coupe (*below*). Two-door Polaras came in base or 500 trim, the latter including brushed-finish body moldings as well as bucket seats and console gearshift, while the Polara had a front bench seat and slightly simpler exterior trim. With a $233 price advantage, the Polara was more popular than the Polara 500: 23,128 units built versus 15,163. The Polara 500 convertible (*below right*) was fairly rare, as output reached only 2624 (plus 4243 base Polara ragtops). A low windshield, long deck, twin headrests, and 426 Hemi marked the first Dodge Charger (*bottom*), a performance-oriented show car.

A handful of factory-built drag cars, including this lightweight Dodge 330 two-door (*above*), ran the new 426 Race Hemi. Dodge issued the Ramcharger Hemi (*below*), with 11.0:1 or 12.5:1 compression, for use on "sanctioned" dragstrips. This one has the new four-speed stick. A three-speed manual or automatic was also available. Jim Thornton (*below right*) won the '64 U.S. Nationals driving his "Candymatic" Ramcharger Dodge.

The compact '64 Dart sported a new convex grille. A 273-cid V-8 was a new option, and many of the $2318 GT hardtops (*above two*) got one. At the top of Dodge's size scale, the 880 series listed a $3264 Custom convertible (*above*) for only $37 more than a Polara 500 ragtop, and sold 1058 copies. The '64 Custom D-100 pickup (*left*) could have one of Dodge's hottest engines, the 365-bhp 426 wedge—although not many got one.

Facelifted Plymouths ran the gamut from mild to truly wild. Hardtops sported a new, sleeker roofline. This $2864 Sport Fury hardtop coupe (*right*), one of 23,695 sold, is girded for action with its 426 Stage III "Max Wedge" Super Stock V-8 and four-speed. Richard Petty won the 1964 NASCAR championship handily in a Fury hardtop with the new "slantback" roofline—but he used the 426 Hemi offered only to racers. Valiant sales grew, as a small-block 273-cid V-8 became available for Plymouth's compact, from the bottom-line $1921 V-100 coupe (*below right*) to the $2388 V-200 station wagon (*below*).

Left: A floor-mounted four-speed was the best choice to handle the Race Hemi's 425-plus horses. *Above:* Inspectors at the Dodge Assembly Plant checked '64 Valiants and Dodges at the final car conditioning area. Cars came down four lines.

200

Left: NASCAR drivers loved the new "King Kong" Hemi in a Dodge or Plymouth. *Below left:* Paul Goldsmith's Plymouth noses out Bobby Isaac's Dodge at the Charlotte, North Carolina, stock-car race track.

1964 Engine Availability

Chrysler

No. Cyl.	Disp., cid	bhp	Availability
V-8	361.0	265	S-Newport
V-8	383.0	305	S-300
V-8	413.0	340	S-NY; O-300
V-8	413.0	360	S-300-K; O-300
V-8	413.0	390	O-300-K

Dodge

No. Cyl.	Disp., cid	bhp	Availability
I-6	170.0	101	S-Dart
I-6	225.0	145	S-330/440/ Polara I-6; O-Dart
V-8	273.0	180	O-Dart
V-8	318.0	230	S-330/440/ Polara V-8
V-8	361.0	265	S-880
V-8	383.0	305/330	O-all exc Dart
V-8	426.0	365	O-all exc Dart
V-8	426.0	415/425	O-all exc Dart (ram induc)

Imperial

No. Cyl.	Disp., cid	bhp	Availability
V-8	413.0	340	S-all

Plymouth

No. Cyl.	Disp., cid	bhp	Availability
I-6	170.0	101	S-Valiant
I-6	225.0	145	S-Savoy, Belvedere, Fury; O-Valiant
V-8	273.0	180	O-Valiant
V-8	318.0	230	S-full-size V-8
V-8	361.0	265	O-full-size
V-8	383.0	305/330	O-full-size
V-8	426.0	365	O-full-size
V-8	426.0	400-425	O-full-size (Super Stock/Street)

Imports

No. Cyl.	Disp., cid	bhp	Availability
I-4	57.6	50-52	S-Simca 1000
I-4	78.7	65	S-Simca 5

1964 Production

Chrysler

Newport	85,183
300	33,318
New Yorker	31,044
300-K	3,647
Total	153,192

Dodge

Dart 170	77,134
Dart 270	66,069
Dart GT	49,830
330 I-6	57,957
440 I-6	15,147
Polara I-6	3,810
330 V-8	46,438
440 V-8	68,861
Polara V-8	66,988
Polara 500	17,787
880	31,796
Total	501,817

Imperial

Crown	20,336
LeBaron	2,949
Crown Imperial	10
Total	23,295

Plymouth

Valiant V100	90,370
Valiant V200	91,843
Valiant Signet 200	68,815
Savoy	87,993
Belvedere	93,529
Fury	88,218
Sport Fury	27,553
Total	548,321

Imports*

Simca 1000	NA
Simca 5	NA

* Estimated sales: 7,000

Chapter 11

Big Cars and Muscle Cars Keep Chrysler Vibrant: 1965-68

Former Chrysler chairman K.T. Keller died in 1965. He'd been inactive in the company for several years, but his legacy wasn't forgotten. Chrysler Corporation didn't seem to be trying quite so hard anymore, now that the giants—and their heroic ideas—had departed. Not that all was bad in Highland Park. Far from it. Chrysler division's output, for instance, soared past 206,000 cars in 1965—up 34 percent, for a new record by far. Plymouth, meanwhile, came close to its 1957 record-setting figure.

While other manufacturers were beginning to make hay with their mid-size cars, Chrysler had another idea: concentrate on the biggies. As a matter of fact, Dodge/Plymouth intermediates would gain favor in the latter half of the Sixties. Still, now that the premature-downsizing fiasco of 1962 was history, Chrysler's reputation could also be cemented by a fleet of completely redesigned full-size models.

Chryslers thus earned a full restyle under the direction of Elwood Engel: squarish but smooth, highlighted by his "trademark" bright-metal fender edging. Cleanly swept fenders ran in an unbroken front-to-rear line. Though a bit shorter than before, the big cars were no less roomy—a vital attribute for full-size American vehicles. Inside, a conventional column-mounted gearshift lever replaced the pushbuttons to control the TorqueFlite automatic transmission. Chrysler issued its last "Letter-Series" 300, the 300-L—not so super anymore, but still a pretty fair seller at 2845 copies.

Dodge Darts gained a mild facelift, with a partial vinyl roof optional for hardtops. Dodge also revived the Coronet name on a revamp of the 1962-64 "standard-size" models, marketing them now as "intermediates," taking aim at Ford's Fairlane and Chevrolet's Chevelle. Chrysler Corporation thus strode full-bore into the blossoming mid-size market, but without forgoing its big-car roots. The Hemi V-8 engine became a semi-production item for the Hemi-Charger, a lightweight, altered-wheelbase Coronet aimed strictly at drag-racing. Plymouth's equivalent version got a SuperStock designation. In the all-new standard-size Dodge line, a sporty personal-luxury Monaco hardtop coupe, somewhat akin to Pontiac's Grand Prix, joined the Polara and Custom 880. Big Dodges could have a 413-cid V-8, or even the 365-horsepower, 426-cid wedge engine.

At last, Plymouth got a full-sized model—its biggest ever, in fact—which helped sales considerably. The 116-inch 1962-64 platform that had failed to attract customers as a full-size model fared much better when promoted now as an intermediate, named Belvedere. The top model was the Satellite, a bucket-seat hardtop or convertible. Fury was the new biggie, a structural twin to Chryslers and large Dodges, though only Plymouth offered the pillared two-door body style. Engines ranged from the 225-cid Slant Six to a brawny Commando 426 wedge V-8. Meanwhile, the compact Valiant changed little, but the sporty Barracuda—introduced in mid-1964—could now get a "Formula S"

This '66 Dodge Coronet was part of the popular 500 series.

package that included a tightened suspension and a hotter 235-bhp version of the 273-cid V-8.

Strong sales in 1965 continued the next year, as Chrysler Corporation's market share rose a point, to 16.6 percent. Improvement was credited to a boost in Chrysler/Imperial sales, though Chrysler kept its 10th-place ranking. Full-size cars could get Chrysler's biggest V-8 ever: 440 cubic inches, developed mainly in anticipation of the emissions standards scheduled for 1968. As part of a mild facelift, Chrysler's overall length grew again, to 219 inches. Letter-Series 300s were gone, but production of the toned-down 300 nearly doubled. Evidently, customers still liked the numerical nameplate, even if it no longer stood for much. Also departed: the luxurious, but slow-selling, New Yorker Town & Country wagon.

The lightly facelifted Imperials were exquisite—the best looking in years—courtesy of Engel's work. The molded-in-the-deck spare-tire outline remained in its sensibly subdued form. Unfortunately, Imperials were still thought of as Chryslers in the public mind despite having been a separate nameplate for a decade. This was the final year for Imperials with a separate body and frame—and also the finale for the Ghia-built Crown Imperial limousine. Stageway, of Fort Smith, Arkansas, partially filled the gap by producing a few stretched Chrysler New Yorker limousines, and would do so for several years.

Dodge experienced an impressive resurgence, pushing its performance appeal even harder in an attempt to kill off any lingering image as a dowdy car for senior citizens. Ads implored presumably youthful shoppers to "Join the Dodge Rebellion" and see the "Dodge Boys." Despite minimal restyling, a total of 632,658 cars were built—one of the best Dodge years ever—for fifth place in the industry.

A Coronet-based Charger four-seat fastback debuted at mid-year, sporting hidden headlights and full-width taillights as previewed by the Charger II show car of 1965. Chargers came with a full range of V-8s, from the 318 to a new "Street Hemi." Dual folding rear backrests expanded cargo room.

Plymouth volume slipped, as sales veered over to Dodge and Pontiac. Little was new, though Belvedere and Satellite gained an extensive facelift. A luxurious new Fury VIP ranked as the prime full-size Plymouth, aiming—not too successfully—at Ford's LTD and Chevy's Caprice.

The "Street Hemi" V-8 was now a full production option for any Belvedere or Satellite (as for Coronet/Charger). It cost a hefty $1105 extra, but a Hemi Plymouth—though reasonably docile on the street—could deliver 14.5-second quarter-mile times and hit 60 mph in under seven seconds. Ordinary motorists might not have paid much attention to such figures, but the young fellows fascinated with muscular machinery quickly memorized every scrap of data issued by the manufacturer and "buff" magazines.

A competition Hemi was available on special order, as Richard Petty captured eight of Plymouth's 16 victories on the stock-car circuit (partly due to Ford's boycott this season). Lightweight Hemi-powered Dodge/Plymouth intermediates also shared drag-racing honors around the country. Already, however, the muscle-car era was nearing its peak, and the thrill soon would be gone. Strict government-mandated emissions and safety regulations were about to emerge, which, coupled with hefty insurance surcharges, helped spell the end for impassioned, intense automobiles.

Dodge sales fell badly, after a great '66—down to seventh in output, behind Buick and Oldsmobile. Restyling for 1967 followed a "delta" theme, including wedge-shaped taillights. Longer and lower, full-size Dodges (and Plymouths) again shared their structure with Chrysler. Charger added a new option: a 375-horse version of the 440 V-8, named Magnum. It was standard in the Coronet R/T ("road and track") hardtop coupe and convertible. Wagons departed as part of Dart's impressively curvaceous restyling, which also hit Valiant in a more squared-off form.

The Imperial was now Chrysler-based, thus Unibodied, though riding a three-inch-longer wheelbase and wearing much of its own sheetmetal. A Newport Custom series debuted at Chrysler, billed as "a giant step in luxury, a tiny step in price." So did a semi-fastback hardtop coupe roofline, with wide triangular C-pillars. Pillared four-door sedans were making a comeback against the four-door hardtop.

Ads warned that "Plymouth's out to win you over this year." Yet as the totals were tallied, sales slid again. Plymouth offered a GTX hardtop and convertible, topping the Belvedere line, with a 440-cid V-8. Big cars earned a modest, but imposing, facelift. Valiant and Barracuda restyling brought a separation to the two models, the latter losing its "glassback." Barracudas went against the new Camaro and Firebird, plus Mustang and Cougar. A sleek, gracefully curved convertible and notchback coupe joined the fastback.

A report on Chrysler's mid-Sixties gas-turbine project revealed that little maintenance had been needed. However, one-fourth of participants complained of fuel guzzling.

Domestic and international turmoil reigned in 1968, as the Vietnam War intensified and demonstrators took to the streets at the Democratic Convention in Chicago. For Chrysler Corporation, it was a very good year, as output set a record. Chrysler and Dodge matched their lofty '66 volumes, and Chrysler division edged up to ninth.

Imperials showed minimal change, but executives decreed that they would share more Chrysler sheetmetal, starting in 1969. Dual exhausts and a twin-snorkel air cleaner now were available, boosting output from 350 to 360 bhp. Chrysler Newports again carried the 383-cid V-8; the 300 and New Yorker ran with the 440.

Mid-size bodies earned a handsome reskinning. Dodge stomped mightily on high-performance with its "Scat Pack." Each Dart, Coronet, and Charger member had "bumblebee" racing stripes around their tails, hot engines, and wide rubber. The Charger's original fastback profile gave way to a "flying buttress" notchback roofline. Lean and muscular, the R/T version had a standard 375-bhp 440 V-8. The Hemi remained optional. More than 96,000 Chargers were produced for the model year—far more of them R/Ts than before. Despite its less-dramatic look, the latest edition actually was more aerodynamic than the 1966-67 fastback.

The performance king at Dodge was the no-frills Super Bee, kin to Plymouth's Road Runner, propelled by a special 335-bhp Magnum 383 V-8. Also new: the Dart GTSport (GTS) hardtop and convertible, with a 340- or 383-cid V-8 from the Barracuda "Formula S." A handful of Hemi Darts were built for competition.

Plymouth's Road Runner had one thing the Super Bee lacked: a connection with the Warner Brothers cartoon character, including colorful decals and a "beep-beep" horn. Sales far exceeded early projections. A pillared coupe arrived first, a hardtop at mid-year. A "Street Hemi" could be ordered if the 383 V-8 seemed too tame. Full-size Plymouths were forgettable—bulky and garish—yet accounted for nearly half of total sales. So, large Plymouths faced little risk of extinction. Barracudas could now have a 340-cid V-8, while the 383 returned (at 300 bhp) for the Formula S. A few Hemi-powered Barracudas aimed at dragstrip action.

Chrysler's vision of becoming an all-out multinational organization hit a snag or two in the Sixties. The Rootes Group, of which Chrysler had bought controlling interest earlier in the decade, was in serious trouble due to sagging sales. Chrysler-Plymouth dealers even sold its Sunbeam Tiger sports car (with a Ford V-8!) for a short time in 1967. Soon, they also began to market a Sunbeam fastback, followed in 1971 by the Plymouth Cricket—two forays best left forgotten. The latter was promoted as "the little car that can," but in fact it couldn't. It was gone after 1973.

No matter. Chrysler's reputation was built on big cars, not minis, and was recently amplified by its pulsating entry into the muscle-car arena. That would be enough to keep America's Number Three automaker alive and healthy—wouldn't it?

1965

American car production sets a model-year record at 8.8 million; Chrysler Corporation's total rises again

Automatic transmission pushbutton controls disappear

Chrysler's 300-L is the final Letter-Series model

The Coronet name returns on the revamped mid-size Dodge lineup

Dodge's hot Coronet Hemi-Charger and Plymouth's SuperStock aim at the nation's dragstrips—with impressive results

Monaco is launched by Dodge as a sport/luxury hardtop coupe

Full-size Plymouths return; Fury is its largest car ever

The mid-size Belvedere and bucket-seat Satellite join the Plymouth stable

New experimental vehicles include the Dodge Charger II, Plymouth XP-VIP, and the exotic LeBaron D'Or

Imperial Ghia Crown limousines make their last appearance

Chrysler volume sets a record, now outselling Cadillac; Dodge begins a long production rise

Mid-size Plymouths are based on the ill-starred 1962-64 "standard" line

Plymouth's sporty Barracuda offers a performance/handling "Formula S" package

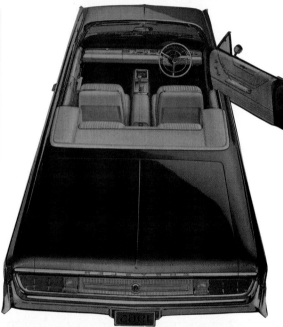

All '65 Chryslers got a new look, including the final "Letter-Series" 300. Riding a two-inch-longer wheelbase, the 300-L (*above and right*) could no longer be ordered with dual four-barrel carbs and ram-induction. Sole engine: the 360-bhp, 413-cid V-8. Only 440 convertibles (*top*) went on sale, at $4618, versus 2405 300-L hardtops, at $4153. Among New Yorker hardtops, the $4238 sedan outsold the $4161 coupe (*below*), 21,110 to 9357.

Save for badges and trim, it wasn't easy to distinguish a Chrysler 300 (*above*) from a 300-L. With a 383-cid V-8, the 300 hardtop cost $3551; 11,621 were built.

The $3070 '65 Newport hardtop coupe sold 23,665 copies.

Front-end revisions to the 1965 Imperial featured glass-covered headlights. All Imperials held a 340-bhp, 413-cid V-8. Top-of-the line was the LeBaron hardtop sedan (*above*), at $6596. Just 2146 were sold. Note the subtle spare-tire hump in the decklid of the $6194 Imperial Crown convertible (*above right*); 633 were built. At $18,500, Ghia constructed but 10 long-wheelbase Crown Imperial LeBaron Limousines (*right*).

Dodge's display at the 1965 Chicago Auto Show (*left*) included the predictive Charger II concept car, seen deep in the background. A closer view (*below center*) shows off the experimental hardtop's long fastback roofline, soon to appear on a production Charger. Marketers wanted to gauge public reaction to the fastback shape before turning it loose on a real-world car. Dodge also elected to attack Fairlane/Chevelle by reactivating the Coronet nameplate, for a square-cut, mid-size model on a 117-inch wheelbase. Line-leader was the bucket-seat Coronet 500 hardtop (*below*) and convertible, with an appetizing selection of hot engines.

Compact Dodge Darts, particularly the $2404 GT convertible (*left and above left*), looked more aggressive for '65. The 145-bhp, 225-cid Slant Six (*above*) cost extra even in the GT, but leadfoots could specify a new 235-bhp, 273-cid V-8.

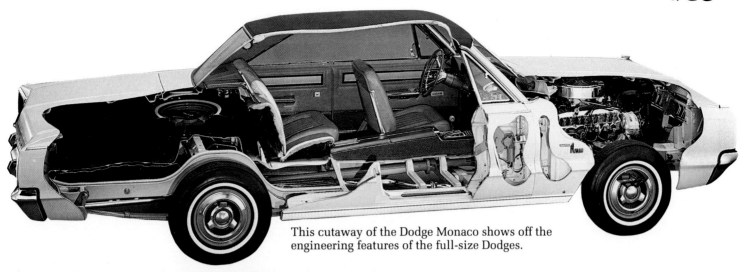

This cutaway of the Dodge Monaco shows off the engineering features of the full-size Dodges.

Conservatively restyled full-size Dodges displayed a "dumbbell" grille and "delta" taillights. Instead of mild-mannered family transport, the purchaser of this Custom 880 convertible (*left*) opted for a 426-cid "street wedge" V-8 with dealer-installed dual carbs and a four-speed gearbox. For the $3335 base price, a 270-bhp 383 was standard. Dodge offered half a dozen convertibles. Top of the mid-size models was the $2894 Coronet 500 (*below left*), this one with the step-up 318-cid V-8, rated at 230 bhp. Engine options reached all the way to the frenzied Hemi. Positioned between base Coronets and the 500, the $2770/$2868 Coronet 440 wagon (*below*) came in six- and nine-passenger guise.

The full-size Dodge Polara Police Pursuit (*above*) came with either a 383- or 413-cid V-8. Trying to cover all bases, Dodge also listed the lightweight Coronet-based Police Patroller (*right*).

Acrobatically piloted by Dick Landy, this Hemi-Charger Funny Car (*top left*) began life as a meek Dodge Coronet. Note the intake stacks on the car, pictured years after "Dandy" Mr. Landy menaced the nation's dragstrips (*top right and center*). Bud Faubel (*above left*) wielded this hot "Honker" Coronet (*left*). Rear wheels sat 15 inches forward, fronts 10 inches, to improve weight distribution. Roger Lindamood dragged with the "Color Me Gone" Hemi-Charger Coronet (*above*). Racers could order loads of light-weight body components (*center left*).

208

Truly full-size again, the big Plymouths were far roomier. A bolt-on subframe now held the engine and front suspension. The cheapest full-size hardtop was the $2691 Fury III (*below*), with 43,251 built. Fender skirts and a 383-cid "Commando" V-8 for this Fury III (*left*) cost an additional $172; 21,367 customers chose one. The lowest-priced big Plymouth was the $2376 Fury I two-door sedan (*below left*), with a standard 145-bhp Slant Six; 17,294 were sold. Just 2769 people bought the $2437 Valiant 200 convertible (*third from top, left*). The 101-bhp Slant Six was standard.

Plymouth's $3090 Fury III station wagon boasted a 128.9-inch load area with tailgate open. Including Fury I and II, full-size wagon sales totaled 51,135.

The Plymouth XP-VIP "idea car" (*left and above*) focused on comfort, convenience, communication, entertainment, and safety. A longitudinal roll bar helped guide the retractable photochromic glass top.

This altered-wheelbase Plymouth coupe (*left and below left*), propelled by the big 426-cid Max Wedge V-8, went drag-racing in the A/FX class as a "Golden Commando" team car. Note the enormous hood scoop and tremendous rear overhang.

The race-only "Super Commando" Hemi was conservatively rated at 425 horses.

Note the extra-size oil pan on the NASCAR version of Plymouth's Hemi V-8 engine.

Launched as a 1964½ model, the Valiant-based Plymouth Barracuda fastback added a "Formula S" edition (*bottom left*) for '65. Styling touches included a massive wrapped back window, ahead of a stubby trunklid (*above left*). A fold-down back seat gave a seven-foot cargo deck. The little 101-bhp, 170-cid Slant Six, initially standard, was succeeded by the 225-cid, 145-bhp version. The "Formula S" package included a firmer suspension, front anti-sway bar, bigger tires—plus a 235-bhp "Commando" 273-cid V-8 (*above*) with dual exhausts. Tamer Barracudas often had the 180-bhp 273-cid V-8. Fans of light cars with hot engines were likely to look twice when the Barracudas arrived (*center*)!

Barracudas shared sheetmetal—and the same assembly line—with Valiants. Though launched just a couple of weeks before Ford's Mustang, the Barracuda was more a reaction to the sporty Corvair Monza. Plymouth's imaginative fastback found a fair-size audience, with 64,596 built for the '65 model year. For vigorous performance, Barracuda's top 235-bhp engine featured a high-lift camshaft, solid valve lifters, unsilenced air cleaner, and a low-restriction dual-exhaust system.

1965 Production

Chrysler
Newport	125,795
300	27,678
New Yorker	49,871
300-L	2,845
Total	206,189

Dodge
Dart 170	86,013
Dart 270	78,245
Dart GT	45,118
Coronet	71,880
Coronet 440	104,767
Coronet 500	32,745
Polara	12,705
Custom 880	44,496
Monaco	13,096
Total	489,065

Imperial
Crown	16,235
LeBaron	2,164
Crown Imperial	10
Total	18,409

Plymouth
Valiant 100	94,113
Valiant 200	59,463
Valiant Signet	13,577
Barracuda	64,596
Belvedere I	56,842 *
Belvedere II	82,492
Satellite	25,201
Fury I	79,229
Fury II	66,757
Fury III	139,344
Sport Fury	44,620
Total	726,234 *

* Approximate

Imports*
Simca 1000	NA
Simca 5	NA

* Estimated sales : 12,000

1965 Engine Availability

Chrysler
No. Cyl.	Disp., cid	bhp	Availability
V-8	383.0	270	S-Newport; O-300
V-8	383.0	315	S-300; O-Newport
V-8	413.0	340	S-NY
V-8	413.0	360	S-300-L; O-300, NY

Dodge
No. Cyl.	Disp., cid	bhp	Availability
I-6	170.0	101	S-Dart
I-6	225.0	145	S-Coronet/440 I-6; O-Dart
V-8	273.5	180	S-Coronet/ 440/500 V-8; O-Dart
V-8	273.5	235	O-Coronet/ 440/500 V-8, Dart
V-8	318.0	230	O-Coronet/ 440/500 V-8
V-8	361.0	265	O-Coronet/ 440/500 V-8
V-8	383.0	315	S-Monaco; O-Coronets
V-8	383.0	270	S-Polara, Custom 880
V-8	383.0	330	O-Coronets
V-8	413.0	340	O-Polara, Custom 880, Monaco
V-8	426.0	365	S-Hemi-Charger Coronet; O-others exc Dart
V-8	426.0	425	S-Hemi-Charger 425 Coronet

Imperial
No. Cyl.	Disp., cid	bhp	Availability
V-8	413.0	340	S-all

Plymouth
No. Cyl.	Disp., cid	bhp	Availability
I-6	170.0	101	S-Valiant
I-6	225.0	145	S-Barracuda, Furys, Belvederes; O-Valiant
V-8	273.5	180	S-Satellite; O-Valiant, Barracuda, Belvederes
V-8	273.5	235	O-Valiant, Barracuda
V-8	318.0	230	S-Furys; O-Belvederes, Satellite
V-8	361.0	265	O-Belvedere, Satellite
V-8	383.0	270	O-Belvedere, Satellite, Furys
V-8	383.0	330	O-Belvedere, Satellite, Furys
V-8	426.0	365	S-Belvedere I SS; O-Belvedere, Satellite, Furys
V-8	426.0	425	O-Belvedere I SS

Imports
No. Cyl.	Disp., cid	bhp	Availability
I-4	57.6	50-52	S-Simca 1000
I-4	78.7	65	S-Simca 5

Chrysler Corporation enjoys another good selling season; market share grows

Dodge reaches fifth place in the production race, with a record number of cars built

Plymouth output sinks, despite a broad range of models

To counter Ford's LTD and Chevy's Caprice, Plymouth debuts the Fury VIP

Sales soar for Chrysler's non-letter 300 series

Dodge's new Charger is a fastback Coronet with hidden headlamps and bucket seats—both front and rear

Performance-oriented ads promote the "Dodge Rebellion"

A 440-cid V-8 is now standard in the New Yorker and Imperial, and optional in the big Dodge/Plymouth; it's the largest Chrysler-built engine ever

The 425-horsepower "Street Hemi" becomes available in mid-size Dodges and Plymouths

It's the final year for separate body-on-frame Imperials

Show cars include the 300X with lever steering and the "Mobile Executive" limo from Stageway

Arkansas-based Stageway produces a few long-wheel-base Chryslers

Led by Richard Petty, Plymouth cops 16 NASCAR Grand National victories

Chrysler's four series got new rooflines, plus individualized grilles, hoods, and trim. A new 350-bhp, 440-cid V-8 was standard in the $4233 New Yorker hardtop sedan (*top*), which found 26,599 buyers. Powered by a 383-cid V-8, the $3190 Newport hardtop sedan (*above*) sold 24,966 copies, but pillared sedans were far more popular. Options included a tilt/telescope steering wheel, new six-way power seat, rear-seat heater, and "Safeguard Sentinel" that turned lights on automatically at dusk and provided delayed shutoff.

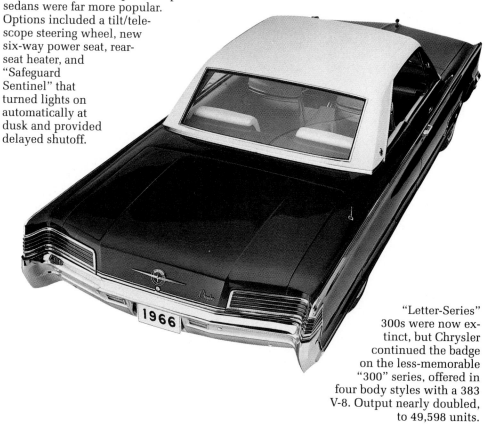

"Letter-Series" 300s were now extinct, but Chrysler continued the badge on the less-memorable "300" series, offered in four body styles with a 383 V-8. Output nearly doubled, to 49,598 units.

Except for revised eggcrate-style grille mesh, and an engine bored to 440 cubic inches, Imperials changed little for 1966. The big V-8 delivered 350 horsepower under the hood of a Crown hardtop coupe (*left*), available for $5887. Just 2373 customers took delivery of that model, but 8977 others chose a Crown hardtop sedan, while just 514 ordered a convertible. Owners of the immense six-window Crown Imperial LeBaron Limousine were likely to have a chauffeur hold the door open (*below*). A final batch of 10 Ghia Limousines was produced in Spain, using '66 Imperial grilles and decks. After that, the limos were produced in small numbers by Stageway, in Fort Smith, Arkansas, along with various Chrysler models.

Chrysler's 300X research car didn't look so extraordinary on the road (*above*), but the driver and passengers occupied a space-age interior (*above right*), complete with TV set. The driver inserted a keypunch card to start the engine and preset the seat adjustment. A handgrip unit replaced the steering wheel. Seats rode rubber-diaphragm suspensions, and the front passenger could rotate to the rear (*right*).

Exhibiting curvier rear fenders and wedge-shaped taillights, '66 Dodge Coronets came in four levels: base, Deluxe, 440, and sporty 500. The top-line 500 four-door sedan (*left*) cost $2586 with the 145-bhp Slant Six, $2680 with the base V-8. Bucket seats, center console, and padded dashboard were standard in the $2611/$2705 Coronet 500 hardtop coupe (*below and below left*). The Coronet 440's base 273-cid V-8 developed 180 horsepower, but this $2551 hardtop (*bottom left*) has the step-up 230-bhp, 318-cid V-8 mated to the popular TorqueFlite automatic. Inside, the 440 hardtop featured a flat, horizontal dashboard and a bench front seat with vinyl covering airfoam cushions. The 440 was the most popular Coronet series, accounting for just over half of total sales. All models, including station wagons, rode the same 117-inch wheelbase.

The compact Dodge Dart was now in the fourth—and final year—of its current styling generation. A modest facelift concentrated mainly on grille, taillights, and trim. The sportiest model was the GT convertible (*above*), which could be had with the 101- or 145-bhp Slant Sixes or the 180- or 235-bhp, 273.5-cid V-8. Base price with the small six was $2700. The GT also came as a hardtop coupe.

Mid-year brought the Charger (*top left and second row*), a fastback Coronet hardtop with hidden-headlamps, full-width taillights, front and rear bucket seats, full-length center console, and a 230-bhp 318 V-8. The red Charger has the optional 325-bhp, 383 V-8, the white one the "Street Hemi." That engine (*top right*), "intended for use in supervised acceleration trials" only, was sold "as is." It developed more than the rated 425 bhp. Sal Tovella sped this "Hemi-Hummer" (*left*) through the traps at Chicago-area drag strips. Two models from Dodge's full-size lineup: $2948 Polara hardtop sedan (*below left*) and $3604 top-line Monaco 500 hardtop coupe (*below*).

Plymouth reacted to the Chevrolet Caprice and Ford LTD with a posh VIP series. Sold as a $3133 hardtop sedan (*above*) or $3069 coupe (*left*), the upscale VIP had a vinyl roof, fender skirts, lush interior (*far left*), and a standard 318-cid V-8.

A Hemi V-8 (*above left*) came with a heavy-duty suspension. It transformed an otherwise sedate Plymouth Satellite hardtop (*above*) into a rowdy street machine—with four-speed or TorqueFlite. Mid-size Hemis won laurels at NASCAR as well as on drag strips. Barracuda, here with the Formula S package (*below*), got a square-front facelift. A regular $2556 Barracuda (*left*) could have "S" wheels and striping.

Above: The $3115/$3216 Fury III topped Plymouth's station wagon line—20,125 six- and nine-passenger versions were built. In the mid-size line, the $2986/$3087 Belvedere II wagon (*right*) appealed to 13,393 buyers.

1966 Production

Chrysler

Newport	167,671
300	49,598
New Yorker	47,579
Total	264,848

Dodge

Dart	75,990
Dart 270	69,996
Dart GT	30,041
Coronet	66,161
Coronet 440	128,998
Coronet 500	55,683
Charger	37,344
Polara	107,832
Monaco	49,773
Monaco 500	10,840
Total	632,658

Imperial

Crown	11,864
LeBaron	1,878
Total	13,742

Plymouth

Valiant 100	78,656
Valiant 200	43,929
Valiant Signet	15,552
Barracuda	38,029
Belvedere I	48,644
Belvedere II	102,480
Satellite	38,158
Fury I	61,926
Fury II	73,817
Fury III	146,747
Sport Fury	35,941
VIP	incl with Fury III
Total	683,879

Imports*

Simca 1000	NA
Simca 5	NA

* Estimated sales: 12,900

1966 Engine Availability

Chrysler

No. Cyl.	Disp., cid	bhp	Availability
V-8	383.0	270	S-Newport
V-8	383.0	325	S-300; O-Newport
V-8	440.0	350	S-NY

Dodge

No. Cyl.	Disp., cid	bhp	Availability
I-6	170.0	101	S-Dart I-6
I-6	225.0	145	S-Coronet I-6; O-Dart I-6
V-8	273.5	180	S-Coronet V-8, Dart V-8
V-8	273.5	235	O-Dart V-8
V-8	318.0	230	S-Charger, Polara 318 sdn; O-Coronet V-8
V-8	361.0	265	O-Charger, Coronet V-8
V-8	383.0	270	S-Polara/500, Monaco; O-Monaco 500
V-8	383.0	325	S-Monaco 500; O-all exc Dart
V-8	426.0	425	O-Charger (max perf cam avail)
V-8	440.0	350	O-Polara/500, Monaco/500

Imperial

No. Cyl.	Disp., cid	bhp	Availability
V-8	440.0	350	S-all

Plymouth

No. Cyl.	Disp., cid	bhp	Availability
I-6	170.0	101	S-Valiant
I-6	225.0	145	S-Barracuda, Fury sdns/wgns; O-Valiant
V-8	273.5	180	S-Satellite; O-Valiant, Barracuda, Belvederes
V-8	273.5	235	O-Valiant exc wgns, Barracuda
V-8	318.0	230	S-VIP, Spt Fury, Fury II wgns, Fury III cvt/htp/wgn; O-Belvederes, Fury
V-8	361.0	265	O-Belvedere, Satellite
V-8	383.0	325	O-VIP, Belvedere, Satellite, Furys
V-8	426.0	425	O-Belvedere, Satellite exc wgns
V-8	440.0	365	O-VIP, Furys

Imports

No. Cyl.	Disp., cid	bhp	Availability
I-4	57.6	50-52	S-Simca 1000
I-4	78.7	65	S-Simca 5

1967

218

Chrysler added a '67 Newport Custom series, in hardtop coupe (*above*), hardtop sedan, and pillared sedan body styles. The coupe cost $3407, versus $3219 for a base Newport. Deluxe interiors used cloth and textured vinyl. The $4264 New Yorker hardtop coupe (*top*) could get an optional 375-bhp 440 V-8.

Vertical taillights helped identify the four-model Chrysler 300 series (*second from bottom*), which now carried a standard 350-bhp 440 V-8. The new three-model Newport Custom series included this $3407 semi-fastback hardtop coupe (*above*); 14,193 were built for the model year. The $188 premium over the base Newport provided more deluxe trim.

The posh Imperial Crown hardtop sedan captured 9415 buyers.

Staunch and upright, the all-new Imperials now had Unibody coachwork, derived from Chrysler. Wheelbase shrank to 127 inches. The poshest Imperial was again the $6661 LeBaron hardtop sedan (*above*); 2194 were sold. A Crown hardtop sedan (*right*) fetched $5836, while the "basic" pillared four-door brought $5374.

Redesigned Imperials wore tall grilles and squarish fenders. Rear decks were longer, but bodysides remained flat, with full-length moldings above the rocker panels. All models had a 350-bhp engine, including the Crown hardtop sedan (*top and above*). With 9415 built, it accounted for more than 50 percent of total Imperial output. Only 577 Crown convertibles (*below*) were built, priced at $6244. This handsome Forest Green ragtop has climate-control air conditioning and a floor-button radio.

A $3199 Coronet R/T hardtop coupe (*left and below*) and $3438 convertible (*below left*) joined the "Dodge Boys" lineup, packing a brawny tuned 440 Magnum V-8 as standard fare. Rival to Pontiac's GTO, each R/T ("road and track") ran with a heavy-duty suspension and oversize brakes. If its 375 horses were too tame, the Hemi V-8 (with front-fender badges) could be had (*bottom right*). Fat redline tires were growing popular. A Hemi with four-speed went into this Dodge Charger fastback (*bottom left*), which has a 3.54:1 Dana 60 rear axle. A unique grille and wide lower-body stripes highlighted the freshened styling of the $2679 Coronet 500 hardtop coupe (*second from bottom, left*). This one also wears Hemi badges.

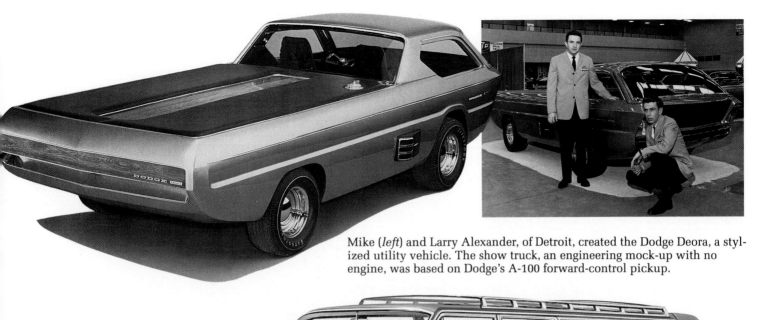

Mike (*left*) and Larry Alexander, of Detroit, created the Dodge Deora, a stylized utility vehicle. The show truck, an engineering mock-up with no engine, was based on Dodge's A-100 forward-control pickup.

Teens craved hot mid-sizes, but families found a $3265 Dodge Polara wagon (*second from top*)—with a 440-cid V-8 and roof rack—more practical. Longer and lower, the $3155 Polara 500 hardtop coupe (*above left*) sported a new semi-fastback roof and longer rear deck. Dodge claimed it "creates an image of sweep, power and motion unmatched in its field." The top-line Monaco hardtop sedan (*above*) listed at $3275. The Dodge Dart's sporty GT series again came only as a ragtop (*left*) and hardtop (*below*), with bucket seats and optional V-8s.

Featuring fresh straight-up '67 styling, base Plymouth Valiant 100s sold best. This brighter-trimmed $2308 Signet four-door sedan sold 26,395 units. Hardtops and wagons were gone.

Revised modestly, the mid-size Plymouth Satellite (*above left*) started at $2747. A "426 Hemi" badge gives an inkling of this coupe's prowess. VIP and Sport Fury (*above*) hardtops adopted new "Fast Top" rooflines, with vast C-pillars. Notchback Sport Fury coupes continued, but sagged in favor. Restyled Barracudas no longer displayed a close kinship to Valiant. In addition to a shapely $2639 fastback, here with the "S" option (*left*), a notchback and convertible were listed.

In Formula S form, a Barracuda convertible (*left*) strutted redline tires and hood ducts. A 280-bhp 383 V-8 was available. At $2449, notchback coupes (*above*) cost less than fastbacks.

NASCAR fans knew at a glance who sat behind the wheel of a car with Number 43 on the door—Richard Petty, who won the championship for Plymouth. The basic lines of his stock car weren't much different from a regular Plymouth, but the Hemi promised awesome performance.

1967 Production

Chrysler
Newport	107,369
Newport Custom	50,022
300	21,894
New Yorker	39,459
Total	218,744

Dodge
Dart	53,043
Dart 270	63,227
Dart GT	38,225
Coronet	4,933
Coronet Deluxe	29,022
Coronet 440	106,368
Coronet 500	39,260
Coronet R/T	incl in above
Charger	15,788
Polara	69,798
Polara 500	5,606
Monaco	35,225
Monaco 500	5,237
Total	465,732

Imperial
CY1-M	15,420
LeBaron	2,194
LeBaron Limo	6
Total	17,620

Plymouth
Valiant 100	75,731
Valiant Signet	33,238
Barracuda	62,534
Belvedere	5,477
Belvedere I	21,878
Belvedere II	88,347
Satellite	32,678
Belvedere GTX	incl in above
Fury I	42,068
Fury II	64,841
Fury III	160,078
Sport Fury	31,581
VIP	18,742
Total	637,193

Imports
Simca 1000	NA
Simca 5	NA

1967 Engine Availability

Chrysler
No. Cyl.	Disp., cid	bhp	Availability
V-8	383.0	270	S-Newport
V-8	383.0	325	O-Newport
V-8	440.0	350	S-300, NY; O-wgns
V-8	440.0	375	O-all exc wgns

Dodge
No. Cyl.	Disp., cid	bhp	Availability
I-6	170.0	115	S-Dart I-6
I-6	225.0	145	S-Coronet I-6; O-Dart I-6
V-8	273.5	180	S-Coronet V-8, Dart V-8
V-8	273.5	235	O-Dart V-8
V-8	318.0	230	S-Charger, Polara 318 sdn; O-Coronet V-8
V-8	383.0	270	S-Polara/500, Monaco; O-Monaco 500, Coronet
V-8	383.0	325	S-Monaco 500; O-all exc Dart, Coronet R/T
V-8	426.0	425	O-Charger, Coronet R/T
V-8	440.0	350	O-Polaras, Monacos
V-8	440.0	375	S-Coronet R/T; O-Charger, Polaras, Monacos

Imperial
No. Cyl.	Disp., cid	bhp	Availability
V-8	440.0	350	S-all

Plymouth
No. Cyl.	Disp., cid	bhp	Availability
I-6	170.0	115	S-Valiant
I-6	225.0	145	S-Barracuda, Fury sdns, Fury I wgn, Belvederes exc GTX; O-Valiant
V-8	273.5	180	S-Satellite; O-Valiant, Barracuda
V-8	273.5	235	O-Valiant, Barracuda
V-8	318.0	230	S-VIP, Furys; O-Belvederes exc GTX
V-8	383.0	270	O-Furys, Belvederes exc GTX
V-8	383.0	280	O-Barracuda
V-8	383.0	325	O-Barracuda, Furys, Belvederes exc GTX
V-8	426.0	425	O-Belvedere GTX
V-8	440.0	350	O-Fury wgns
V-8	440.0	375	S-GTX; O-Fury exc wgns

Imports
No. Cyl.	Disp., cid	bhp	Availability
I-4	57.6	50-52	S-Simca 1000
I-4	78.7	65	S-Simca 5

1968

The Big Three automakers restyle their mid-size models

Federal pollution regulations take effect—all makes must now have an exhaust-emission control system

A total of 9,403,862 new cars are registered this year, topping the record set in '65

Chrysler's output is up an encouraging 24 percent, after a '67 decline

Dodge moves up a notch in industry standings, to sixth place; Chrysler does likewise, to ninth

Dart adds a plush GTS with hot 340 or 383 V-8s

A no-frills Super Bee coupe joins the Coronet lineup

Road Runner is Plymouth's low-budget "muscle" offering

The final Imperial Crown convertibles go on sale; only 474 are built

Chrysler Corporation wagons can have a washer/wiper for the tailgate window

Chrysler and General Motors experiment with air-activated accessories

Chrysler markets the British-made Sunbeam fastback, but it fails to sell

Dodge's Charger is now a "semi-fastback" hardtop

For 1968, a $6115 Imperial Crown hardtop sedan (*top two*) could have a high-performance 440-cid V-8, with a twin-snorkel air cleaner coaxing out 10 extra horsepower. Dual exhausts joined the options list. A new grille wrapped around the fenders. With 8492 sold, this was by far the most popular Imperial. As before, the $4337 Chrysler 300 convertible (*above*) listed a 350- or 375-bhp version of the big-block V-8. Note the unusual seatbacks (*right*); the radio and Sun gauges are non-stock. Only 2161 buyers selected the 300 ragtop.

A '68 Chrysler 300 hardtop coupe (*right and below*) cost $4010, versus $4086 for the hardtop sedan, which sold almost as strongly: 16,953 versus 15,507. A PR blurb noted that "evolutionary styling changes follow Chrysler's successful pattern of the past several years," but that "high speed performance of the engines has been improved and several convenience items have been added." Meanwhile, turquoise-colored Newport Special hardtops gained popularity. That color scheme appeared later on 300s, too. A new spring option, "Sportsgrain" simulated-wood bodysides, bowed for Newport ragtops and hardtop coupes, but attracted only 175 and 965 buyers.

Left: Disappearing headlights enhanced the Chrysler 300 series for the first time. They sat behind movable doors that matched the rest of the 300's unique black-out grille. Cast-metal wheels became optional.

Part of only the Newport series, the Town & Country station wagon (*right*) featured a woodgrained side and rear treatment, plus an optional concealed tailgate window washer/wiper system. The Newport's base 383-cid V-8 added 20 horses, to 290. *Below:* Chrysler had been importing Simcas from France for a decade—and later, Sunbeams from Britain. The '68 Simca, with 14 structural and mechanical changes and 55 bhp, was offered as a Standard, Deluxe, or GLS. Prices started at $1655.

Above: The rear-drive Simca 1000 GLS four-door rode a short 87.3-inch wheelbase. This little French import weighed only 1608 pounds—a good thing, because the 944-cc (57.6-cid) four developed only 50 horsepower. *Right:* A larger front-drive, 1118/1204 series with full independent suspension, bowed in mid-1968. Sales were slow, so Simca departed the U.S. after 1971.

Dodge Coronets and Chargers earned a full redesign with "Coke-bottle" rear flanks. Blending youthful flair with big-block brawn, the $3613 Coronet R/T convertible (*left*) had a standard 440-cid Magnum V-8 (*below*), whipping out 375 horsepower.

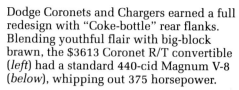

The newest member of Dodge's "Scat Pack" was the no-frills Coronet Super Bee (*left and below left*), packing a 335-bhp Magnum 383 engine (like Plymouth's Road Runner) and wearing "bumblebee" tape stripes. The price tag read just $3027 before options. The owner of this Super Bee (*left*) wasn't satisfied—it scats with a '69 440 Six-Pak V-8. The '68 Coronet R/T hardtop (*below*) cost a bit more, $3379, and came with the 375-bhp 440 V-8. Topping the mid-size hot-coupe lineup was the $3506 Charger R/T (*bottom*), now a semi-fastback hardtop with a "flying buttress" roof. It, too, came with the 375-bhp 440 and likewise wore similar racy striping at the rear.

Monster engines in bantam-weight bodies translated into dramatic dragstrip action. Note the immense hood scoop and wide tires on this SS/AA Dart Hemi.

The sporty $3189 Dart GTS hardtop (*above*) and companion $3383 ragtop held a 275-horsepower, 340-cubic-inch V-8 (*right*). Also featured were a louvered hood and bumblebee tail stripes.

Dodge's big Polara came in six body styles for '68, including this $3100 hardtop sedan.

The experimental Charger III was called "the most aero-dynamic car ever conceived and built by Dodge." Only 42 inches high, it had a swing-away steering wheel, elevating bucket seats, and spoiler air-brake flaps.

Full-size Dodges displayed a mild facelift. Once again, the Monaco 500 hardtop coupe served as the luxury leader of the Dodge line. Though its sticker was slightly reduced to $3869, sales slipped to 4568. Features included automatic temperature control, stereo tape-radio system, speed control, and foam-vinyl bucket seats with center folding armrests. A center console was optional, at no extra cost. Monaco buyers had a choice of three V-8s: a 290- or 330-bhp 383, or the biggest-block 440 with 375 horses. A hardtop coupe in the less-posh, standard Monaco line cost $500 less than the 500.

Shoppers for a '68 Plymouth Sport Fury could choose a sleek "Fast Top" (*above*) or regular hardtop. Introduced for '67, the lush Belvedere GTX hardtop coupe (*left*) and $3590 ragtop (*below*) wore a new blacked-out grille and simulated hood scoops. This one has the standard 375-bhp 440 V-8 (Street Hemi was optional); only 1026 were sold. Base V-8 for the Barracuda convertible (*below left*) was now the 318, but the Slant Six remained standard. A 340-cid V-8 was part of the Formula S package (*bottom left*). Hemi-powered mutants of the no-frills Road Runner soon saw dragstrip duty for the Sox & Martin team (*bottom right*) as "The Boss."

A double-hinged tailgate was standard on the $3131/$3239 (6/9-passenger) Plymouth Satellite Sport Wagon: Push the handle one way, the tailgate dropped down; push it the other way, it opened like a door.

1968 Production

Chrysler

Newport	143,989
Newport Custom	38,716
300	34,621
New Yorker	48,143
Total	265,469

Dodge

Dart	60,250
Dart 270	76,497
Dart GT	26,280
Dart GTS	8,745
Coronet Deluxe	46,299
Coronet 440	116,348
Coronet Super Bee	incl in above
Coronet 500	40,139
Coronet R/T	10,849
Charger	96,108
Polara	99,055
Polara 500	4,983
Monaco	37,412
Monaco 500	4,568
Total	627,533

Imperial

Crown	13,509
LeBaron	1,852
LeBaron Limo	6
Total	15,367

Plymouth

Valiant 100	80,624
Valiant Signet	30,171
Barracuda	45,412
Belvedere	41,898
Satellite	113,599
Sport Satellite	22,537
Road Runner	44,599
GTX	18,940
Fury I	28,996
Fury II	52,535
Fury III	168,001
Sport Fury	26,204
VIP	17,513
Suburban	56,208
Total	747,237

Imports

Simca 1000	NA
Simca 5	NA

1968 Engine Availability

Chrysler

No. Cyl.	Disp., cid	bhp	Availability
V-8	383.0	290	S-Newport, T&C
V-8	383.0	330	O-Newport, T&C
V-8	440.0	350	S-300, NY; O-T&C
V-8	440.0	375	O-all exc T&C

Dodge

No. Cyl.	Disp., cid	bhp	Availability
I-6	170.0	115	S-Dart I-6
I-6	225.0	145	S-Coronet I-6; O-Dart I-6
V-8	273.5	190	S-Coronet V-8, Dart V-8
V-8	318.0	230	S-Charger, Polara; O-Coronet V-8, Dart V-8
V-8	340.0	275	S-Dart GTS
V-8	383.0	300	O-Dart GTS
V-8	383.0	290	S-Monacos; O-Polaras, Charger, Coronet V-8
V-8	383.0	330	O-Coronet V-8, Charger, Monacos, Polaras
V-8	383.0	335	S-Coronet Super Bee
V-8	426.0	425	O-Charger, Coronet R/T
V-8	440.0	350	O-Polaras, Monacos
V-8	440.0	375	S-Coronet R/T; O-Charger, Polaras, Monacos

Imperial

No. Cyl.	Disp., cid	bhp	Availability
V-8	440.0	350	S-all
V-8	440.0	360	O-all

Plymouth

No. Cyl.	Disp., cid	bhp	Availability
I-6	170.0	115	S-Valiant
I-6	225.0	145	S-Barracuda, Belvedere, Satellite, Fury I/II, Fury III sdns and htp, Suburban; O-Valiant
V-8	273.5	190	O-Valiant, Belvedere, Satellite, Sport Satellite wgn
V-8	318.0	230	S-Sport Satellite, Fury III; O-Valiant, Barracuda, Belvedere, Satellite, Sport Satellite wgn
V-8	340.0	275	S-Barracuda Formula S
V-8	383.0	290	O-Belvedere, Satellite, Sport Satellite, Furys
V-8	383.0	300	O-Barracuda Formula S
V-8	383.0	330	O-Belvedere, Satellite, Furys, Suburban
V-8	383.0	335	S-Road Runner
V-8	426.0	425	O-Road Runner, GTX
V-8	440.0	350	O-Suburban
V-8	440.0	375	S-GTX; O-Fury

Imports

No. Cyl.	Disp., cid	bhp	Availability
I-4	57.6	50-52	S-Simca 1000
I-4	78.7	65	S-Simca 5

Chapter 12

Best of the Breed; The Muscle Era Fades: 1969-73

Performance wasn't a dirty word yet at Chrysler in 1970—witness (*clockwise from bottom*) the Dodge Charger RT, Dodge Challenger V-8, Plymouth Duster 340, Plymouth GTX, and Plymouth Barracuda convertible.

All told, Chrysler Corporation entered the Seventies in far better shape than it had the Sixties. Plymouth was reasonably strong, solidly in fourth place behind Pontiac, and ahead of Buick. Dodge dealers offered an entire fleet of great automobiles: mid-size, compact, full-size. In the luxury league, Chrysler ran neck-and-neck with Cadillac.

By 1969, chairman Lynn Townsend had recentralized the corporation, with major directives coming straight from Highland Park headquarters. At the same time, he'd strengthened divisional identities: Dodge versus Chrysler-Plymouth. More importantly for consumers, quality control was getting serious attention.

Ads declared that 1969 Chrysler products were "Your Next Car." All big cars exhibited new "fuselage" styling, devoid of creases and wrinkles, led by a combination bumper/grille. Chryslers measured 225 inches long and nearly 80 inches wide—among the most mammoth ever.

Imperial lost its slow-selling convertible, but gained its first pillared sedan since 1960. It wore hidden headlights (like the Chrysler 300) and employed sequential turn signals—a short-lived fad. Ventless side glass was installed in coupes with air conditioning. First seen on General Motors models, that styling revision was adopted industry-wide, but not appreciated by everyone. Imperial saw its third best year—even if the car was basically a Chrysler.

Coronets continued as the "sleepers" of the Dodge line—some of the smoothest, quickest mid-size cars to prowl American streets. The Super Bee augmented its pillared coupe with a new hardtop body. The base Coronet engine was the 273-cid V-8, with a 440 Magnum for R/T editions. A Swinger hardtop coupe joined the Dart stable, including a hot "340" boasting a 275-bhp, 340-cid V-8. Enjoying a mild restyle, Darts sold well, but Dodge slipped a notch, to seventh place.

The most exciting Dodge was the Charger Daytona, built to race at the Daytona 500 and other long-distance NASCAR events. Wearing a bullet nose and a flush-window fastback roof, the Daytona was instantly identified by its towering fins, which supported a huge airfoil/stabilizer. A 375-horse 440 V-8 was standard, the Hemi optional. This car was appropriately nicknamed the "Winged Warrior." At mid-year, a triple-carbureted 440 V-8 arrived, called "Six-Pak" by Dodge and "440 6 BBL" or "440+6" at Plymouth. Each breathed heavily through a scooped fiberglass hood.

Plymouth produced almost as many cars as in 1968, hanging onto its fourth-place spot. A 'Cuda option included a 340- or 383-cid V-8. Later came the 375-bhp 440 choice. Road Runner added a convertible. Plymouth scored only two NASCAR Grand National wins, now that Richard Petty was driving for Ford.

On January 9, 1970, John Riccardo took over Chrysler's presidency, promising continuity and progress. Both components for success would indeed be necessary, if the firm was to remain an eminent player in the industry.

Hurst Performance Products and Chrysler collaborated on the 300-H, a limited-production 300 with a Hurst floor shifter for the TorqueFlite, power-bulge hood, and special trim and paint. The final Chrysler convertibles went out the door in 1970, as Newports and 300s. Chrysler division sales dropped way down, Imperial plummeted by half, and the last Stageway-built LeBaron limousines were issued. At mid-year the first Cordoba arrived—a Newport hardtop trimmed in gold with an Aztec Eagle on the hood medallion and seat trim.

Dodge finally got a ponycar: the Challenger, galloping at the affluent end of the sporty compact market. Though different in appearance, it wore the same E-body as the latest Barracuda. Engines ranged from the Slant Six to the 440 V-8—or, for an extra $1277, a Hemi. Challengers sold well in their first season and lasted into 1974, but success ceased quickly as the ponycar craze evaporated. Elsewhere in Dodge's line-up, new "loop" bumper/grilles and detail changes were seen and Chargers could now have a Slant Six.

Plymouth—still a vibrant and distinct make—moved almost 685,000 cars, approaching Pontiac's third-place ranking. Captivation with performance was beginning to fade, but Plymouth still revved hard. Ads promoted the "Rapid Transit System," equivalent to Dodge's "Scat Pack." There was even a full-size performance car, the Sport Fury GT hardtop, though it sold poorly. New for 1970 was the winged Superbird, similar to Dodge's Daytona. A total of 1920 were built, intended mainly for competition.

A new—and very popular—Duster compact fastback coupe replaced the Valiant two-door sedan. It was available in Duster 340 trim. Barracuda entered its third generation lower, wider, and heavier, with convertible and notchback bodies, but no fastback. Hemi engines and the six-barrel 440 could have a "shaker" hood.

Chrysler's foray into Trans-American Challenge (Trans-Am) racing spawned two limited-production ponycars: the AAR 'Cuda and Challenger T/A. Each had the 340 V-8 with triple two-barrel carbs, "megaphone" side exhaust pipes, and much more—among the most blatant high-performance cars of all time.

Already, Chrysler's prospects for the future were beginning to dim. Shrinking sales produced a downward-spiraling effect, leaving less money available to develop new products and freshen old ones. Also, quality control and workmanship continued to deteriorate.

General Motors' engines dropped compression for no-lead/low-lead gas in 1971; Chrysler's waited. Muscle cars looked mean, but began a meltdown in prowess. Smaller, less powerful engines were becoming fashionable—and affordable—as performance fans opted for a blend of straight-line "go" and acrobatic handling. Still weighed down by a stable of thirsty, soft-suspended heavyweights, Chrysler seemed the least prepared of the Big Three for the future. Prices, meanwhile, began a steady escalation, the result of government requirements, inflation, and additional equipment. Consumers balked, but many of them savored the extra goodies.

The Imperial lost its Crown series for 1971, leaving only the LeBaron. Buyers could order a new Bendix anti-skid brake system for $250, and the unit would become available on the full Chrysler line for 1972. Chrysler revived the old Royal name at mid-year, for a trio of Newports.

Dart sales helped keep Dodge on a level keel. A fastback Demon coupe—equivalent to Plymouth's Duster—assumed the role of Dodge's performance compact. Engine choices ranged from the Slant Six to a 275-bhp 340 V-8 (in a sporty and spirited Demon 340). A new Scamp hardtop served as Valiant's version of Dodge's Swinger.

At the larger-size end, Coronet/Monaco grew more like Plymouth's Satellite/Fury as the years wore on: thirsty and humdrum. Mid-size models lost their squarish shape, adopting more radical sculpturing. Plymouth's Road Runner and GTX remained in the Satellite lineup, the latter in its last year. Barracuda added a fixed-pillar coupe. Alas, Challenger and Barracuda were the last convertibles offered by Chrysler—until 1983.

Dodge/Plymouth engine choices still reached all the way to the 440 V-8 and 426-cid Hemi. Plymouth rose to third in production, well ahead of Pontiac, but would reach that exalted standing only once more in the Seventies. In addition to dwindling consumer confidence and offering the wrong products for the times, Plymouths no longer delivered enough differences from Dodges. Chrysler got glamorous models, Dodge sporty ones. Plymouth soon would be reduced to a Dodge clone, providing budget-minded transportation—a role it had played before, but which no longer guaranteed success.

In 1971, Dodge dealers began marketing the Mitsubishi-built Colt—considerably more reliable than the British-built Cricket. As the decade wore on, "captive imports" from Japan would help Dodge establish a presence in the vital—and rapidly growing—subcompact field, spurred on by the new Chevy Vega and Ford Pinto.

Engine compression ratios dropped sharply in 1972, as part of detuning for low-lead gasoline. Switching from SAE "gross" to "net" horsepower ratings gave more realistic ratings of engine output.

Stylists began to back away from the "fuselage" look, but kept the 1969-71 full-size bodyshells. Squared-up fenderlines and reduced bodyside curvatures created a bulkier demeanor. Most Chryslers carried the new 400-cid V-8. Both the 300 series and the plain Newport were dropped, but a New Yorker Brougham joined up. Offering similar luxury for a far lower price, the Brougham captured almost twice as many customers as the fast-fading Imperial.

Dodge Polara/Monaco shoppers could get two versions of the 400 V-8, four variants of the 440. The Hemi disappeared as a production option. Challenger/Barracuda engine choices diminished, and their convertibles departed. A 240-bhp 340 was the top V-8—standard in Plymouth's 'Cuda, which could still zip to 60 mph in 8.5 seconds. Performance wasn't quite dead yet at Dodge/Plymouth. Even so, Dodge toned down its advertising, proclaiming: "The way things are today, maybe . . . what you need is a well-balanced, thoroughly instrumented road machine."

A Challenger Rallye replaced the departed Dodge R/T, carrying a rather tame 318-cid V-8. The Sport Fury badge left Plymouth's domain, edged aside by luxury-oriented "Gran" coupes and sedans. Road Runners dropped to a standard 340 V-8, while the GTX disappeared. Plymouth's compact Duster 340 outsold the bigger 'Cuda by better than two-to-one. The most popular Dodge model of all was the stylish—yet practical—Dart Swinger hardtop. Clearly, consumer tastes were shifting.

As 1973 emerged, Chrysler's New Yorker Brougham continued to steal sales from the Imperial. Chryslers carried only the 400 V-8 and a 215-bhp 440. Cars were longer thanks to the new federal five-mph front-bumper standard. New Yorkers adopted standard air conditioning.

Objection by some religious groups to the Demon name for some Dodge Dart coupes brought a badge change, to Sport. Equipped with a newly optional fold-down rear seatback and sliding sunroof, the Dart coupe was called "Convertriple" by Dodge, "Space Duster" by Plymouth. Scamps and Swingers also could get the sunroof. Duster and Dart Sport 340s kept their high-winding small-block V-8. Dodge Chargers could have a Rallye package with raucous striping, hood tie-downs, and "power bulge." Most Coronets could still get the big-block 440 V-8, tamed down in horsepower. Both the Dodge Challenger and Plymouth Barracuda abandoned six-cylinder engines.

Plymouth set a model-year production record, topping 882,000 units. Dodge tallied 665,000, and Chrysler turned out its best total since 1969. Not bad, but the oil-exporting nations of the world had a nasty surprise in store—one that would change the face of motoring in America.

231

1969

The new "fuselage styled" Chryslers are bigger (and heavier) than ever

A tall-winged Dodge Charger Daytona arrives, aimed specifically at NASCAR racing events

Chrysler and Ford products adopt concealed windshield wipers, *a la* GM

An optional "Super-Lite" driving lamp gives Dodges greatly improved visibility on the road, but is ruled illegal in some states

Station wagons have roof-mounted air spoilers

The Dodge Dart Swinger 340 replaces the GTS

A 440 V-8 with triple two-barrel carbs, or "Six Pak," is available in the Dodge Super Bee and Plymouth Road Runner

Imperials now share more of Chrysler's sheetmetal, but a successful restyle helps boost production a whopping 43.6 percent

A convertible joins the Plymouth Road Runner coupe and hardtop

Plymouth builds its last GTX ragtops, leaving only the hardtop

The Chrysler Historical Collection is established

Dodge wins 22 NASCAR Grand National races, trailing Ford's 26 victories

Chrysler's Town & Country station wagons become a separate series

Above and left: An optional high-performance 375-horsepower 440 TNT V-8 powers this Chrysler 300 convertible. Base priced at $4450, 1933 were built. *Below:* Billed as all-new, "bigger in every way," Chryslers stretched five inches—to nearly 225. Like its mates, this $3730 Newport Custom hardtop sedan rode a 124-inch wheelbase. It attracted 15,981 customers.

Rounded, low-roofed "fuselage styling" marked the '69 Imperial. Headlights now hid behind flip-up doors. Chrysler pitched the $6131 Imperial LeBaron hardtop sedan (*above*) for its "dramatically new blend of modern aerodynamic styling and the dignity of the luxury car tradition." At 229.7 inches, it measured five inches longer than before. LeBarons earned a major price cut, helping boost sales of this model to 14,821 units. An Imperial, it was said, "bespeaks trim, uncluttered formality."

Top, above, and above left: Dodge built just 505 Charger Daytonas, for stock-car racing. A protruding snout held hidden headlights. With a monstrous wing for high-speed stability, it was hard to miss. This Canadian Charger 500 (*bottom left*) looks tame enough, but packs the potent Hemi V-8 (*below*). In the U.S., this model weighed in at 3761 pounds, and listed at $3860. The Charger 500 was offered only as a two-door hardtop, but could be had in a luxury mode, with hidden headlights and a leather interior, or as a more performance-oriented edition with exposed headlights and flush grille.

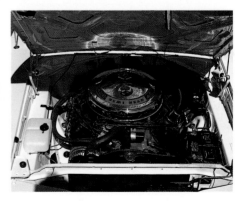

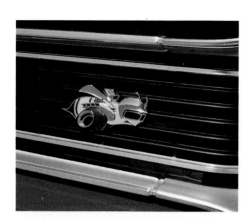

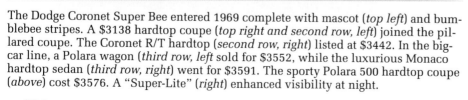

The Dodge Coronet Super Bee entered 1969 complete with mascot (*top left*) and bumblebee stripes. A $3138 hardtop coupe (*top right and second row, left*) joined the pillared coupe. The Coronet R/T hardtop (*second row, right*) listed at $3442. In the big-car line, a Polara wagon (*third row, left* sold for $3552, while the luxurious Monaco hardtop sedan (*third row, right*) went for $3591. The sporty Polara 500 hardtop coupe (*above*) cost $3576. A "Super-Lite" (*right*) enhanced visibility at night.

234

The '69 Dodge Dart GTS came as a ragtop or this $3226 hardtop (*top left*). It has a 275-bhp 340 V-8. Debuting at the '69 New York Auto Show, the Custom Swinger 340 show car (*top right*) featured Cibie lights, functional air scoop, and a rear spoiler. The fastback coupe was the best-selling Plymouth Barracuda body style, but this one (*second row*) is special because it's a 'Cuda 440 with, of course, the big-block 440 V-8. So is the green coupe (*third row*); its Super Commando engine is pictured. The yellow Barracuda ragtop (*left*) ran with a 340 V-8. For 1969, the Plymouth Road Runner changed only slightly. This one (*bottom right*) has the standard 383 V-8 and, of course, the famed road runner cartoon bird mascot (*bottom left*), as well as the standard "Beep, Beep" horn.

With the standard V-8, the new-for-'69 Road Runner convertible stickered at $3313, $230 more than the hardtop coupe. Despite its appeal, only 2128 were produced. High-performance fans wanted the biggest engines in the lightest bodies—and the ragtop weighed 340 pounds more than the hardtop, which captured 48,549 sales. The pillared coupe weighed only 15 pounds less than the hardtop, and found 33,743 customers.

Flowing lower-body contours coupled with squarish fenderlines gave full-size Plymouths a heavier look. Taller belt-lines helped make the windows appear shallower, and wipers were recessed. Fury I, II, and III served as the make's high-volume cars. The Fury III hardtop sedan (*left*) sold 68,818 copies, just edging out the formal and regular hardtop coupes combined (22,738 and 44,168 units, respectively). Engine choices ranged from a 318 V-8 to the big-block 440 V-8. Fury I and II models could have a Slant Six, but many thought them underpowered. The plusher Sport Fury hardtop coupe also came two ways, but the regular style (*above*) outsold the formal look, 14,120 to 2169 units.

1969 Production

Chrysler

Newport	111,499
Newport Custom	45,337
Town & Country	24,516
300	32,472
New Yorker	46,947
Total	260,771

Dodge

Dart	104,329
Dart Swinger 340	incl in above
Dart Custom	63,740
Dart GT	20,914
Dart GTS	6,702
Coronet Deluxe	23,988
Coronet 440	105,882
Coronet Super Bee	27,846
Coronet 500	32,050
Coronet R/T	7,238
Charger	89,904
Charger 500	incl in above
Polara	83,122
Polara 500	5,564
Monaco	38,566
Total	609,845

Imperial

Crown	2,664
LeBaron	19,413
LeBaron Limo	6 *
Total	22,083 *

* Approximate

Plymouth

Valiant	79,081
Valiant Signet	28,137
Barracuda	31,958
Belvedere	27,015
Satellite	85,323
Sport Satellite	28,834
Road Runner	84,420
GTX	15,602
Fury I	23,742
Fury II	44,315
Fury III	212,600
Sport Fury	17,868
VIP	13,781
Suburban	54,319
Total	746,995

Imports*

Simca 1118	**
Simca 1204	**

* Calendar year
** Combined sales: 7,776

Full-size Plymouths, including this $3155 Fury III hardtop sedan (*top*), were all-new this year. Compact Plymouth Valiants got new interior styling, but little other change. Valiants came in two series: 100 and Signet (*center left and left*), both in two- or four-door sedan form, starting at $2094. The Slant Six engine came in two sizes, with a 273.5-cid V-8 optional. Chrysler continued to import Simcas, but now front-drive models replaced the former rear-drives. The Simca 1204 hatchback (*above*) held a 73.4-cid, 62-bhp four.

1969 Engine Availability

Chrysler

No. Cyl.	Disp., cid	bhp	Availability
V-8	383.0	290	S-Newport, T&C
V-8	383.0	330	O-Newport, T&C
V-8	440.0	350	S-300, NY; O-T&C
V-8	440.0	375	O-all exc T&C

Dodge

No. Cyl.	Disp., cid	bhp	Availability
I-6	170.0	115	S-Dart
I-6	225.0	145	S-Coronet Deluxe/440; O-Dart
V-8	273.5	190	S-Dart V-8
V-8	318.0	230	S-Coronet 500, Charger, Polara; O-Coronet Deluxe/440, Dart
V-8	340.0	275	S-Dart GTS/Swinger 340
V-8	383.0	290	S-Monaco; O-Polara, Charger, Coronet
V-8	383.0	335	S-Coronet Super Bee
V-8	426.0	425	O-Coronet R/T, Charger R/T, Charger Daytona
V-8	440.0	350	O-Monaco and Polara wgns
V-8	440.0	375	S-Coronet R/T, Charger R/T, Charger Daytona; O-Monaco and Polara exc wgns
V-8	440.0	390	O-Coronet Super Bee

Imperial

No. Cyl.	Disp., cid	bhp	Availability
V-8	440.0	350	S-all

Plymouth

No. Cyl.	Disp., cid	bhp	Availability
I-6	170.0	115	S-Valiant
I-6	225.0	145	S-Barracuda, Belvedere, Satellite, Fury I/II; O-Valiant
V-8	273.5	190	O-Valiant
V-8	318.0	230	S-Barracuda, Sport Satellite, Fury III, Sport Fury, VIP, Suburban
V-8	340.0	275	O-Barracuda
V-8	383.0	290	O-Belvedere, Satellite, Sport Satellite, Furys, VIP
V-8	383.0	330	O-Barracuda, Belvedere, Satellite, Sport Satellite, Furys, VIP
V-8	383.0	335	S-Road Runner
V-8	426.0	425	O-Road Runner, GTX
V-8	440.0	350	O-Suburban
V-8	440.0	375	S-GTX; O-Furys

Imports

No. Cyl.	Disp., cid	bhp	Availability
I-4	68.2	56	S-Simca 1118
I-4	73.4	62	S-Simca 1204

1970

A national recession curtails new-car sales

Chrysler releases its last full-size convertibles

A Hurst-modified Chrysler 300-H reminds fans of the old "Letter-Series" models

Dodge responds to Camaro/Mustang ponycars with the Challenger; the redesigned Plymouth Barracuda is similar

This is the final year for high-performance Dodge Coronets

The last Imperial Crown models go on sale; the LeBaron series continues

Plymouth adds a compact Duster coupe and Road Runner Superbird "Winged Warrior"

Chrysler vehicles take 38 NASCAR Grand National wins (21 with the super-hot Superbird)

A headlight-delay system is optional on Chryslers

Chrysler begins to import the British-made Plymouth Cricket late in the year as a 1971 model

Dodge's Super-Lite option is dropped after only two years

New show cars include the Concept 70-X and Cordoba d'Oro

Chrysler fields two teams in Trans-American Challenge racing

Engineers continue work on the sixth-generation turbine engine

Chryslers revealed only detail changes for 1970. A 440-cid V-8 engine, rated at 350 horsepower, was standard in both the New Yorker and 300 series, with a 375-bhp variant optional. This year's Chrysler 300 came in hardtop coupe, hardtop sedan, and convertible (*top*) body styles, the last selling for $4580. Only 1077 were produced, and big Chrysler ragtops would be totally extinct in another year. A lower-priced Newport convertible was also available in 1970, selling for $3935, but it fared only slightly better: 1124 units. The New Yorker hardtop sedan (*center and above*) outsold both the pillared sedan and hardtop coupe—19,903 copies—despite a $4761 base sticker price. Chryslers rode a 124-inch wheelbase (Town and Country wagons, 122). With 39,285 built, the $3514 Newport four-door sedan was easily the most popular model.

Just 501 special Chrysler 300-H (for "Hurst") hardtop coupes (*left*) went on sale, with gold/white paint, heavy-duty suspension, and a tuned 440-cid TNT V-8. A floor shift controlled the automatic gearbox. Chrysler Newport Custom hardtop sedans (*below left*) went to 10,673 customers. Mid-year brought the first use of the Cordoba name, for a Newport special edition. Chrysler's Town & Country wagon (*below*) came with two or three seats.

Grille, taillight, and trim revisions marked the '70 Imperials. The hardtop coupe (*above left*) came in two levels, Crown and costlier LeBaron. The LeBaron coupe (*above*) commanded $6095, but sold far better than its Crown counterpart: 1803 versus just 254. Chrysler's Cordoba d'Oro show car (*left*) was a four-passenger luxury hardtop, promoted for its "smooth, pillarless monocoque design." Four rectangular openings on its sloped face contained experimental headlights, plus thermostatically controlled air intakes for the engine. Features included a road condition gauge, cantilever roof, and a spoiler that rose from the roof as the brakes were applied.

Dodge fielded its new Challenger as a rival to Mercury's Cougar. Offered in hardtop and convertible guise, it was kin to the third generation Barracuda. Base models started with the Slant Six, but R/T (road and track) was the hot number, with a standard Magnum 383 V-8. The R/T Special Edition (*left and above*) included a padded vinyl roof with "formal" backlight, leather seat facings, and woodgrain dash trim; 3979 were sold. This R/T SE hardtop has the 426-cid Hemi V-8 (*below left*) beneath its "shaker" hood. Sam Posey piloted a Dodge Challenger (*below*) in Trans-Am races. Note the wide hood scoop. A street version, named T/A, had a lift-off fiberglass hood and a toughened 340 V-8.

The $3785 Dodge Coronet R/T ragtop (*above, far left*) found only 296 buyers, and this rare example has a Hemi. At $3074, the Coronet Super Bee hardtop (*above left*) sold 11,540 copies, here in Plum Crazy paint. Less aggressive shoppers might choose a $3048 Coronet 500 hardtop (*above*). The $3743 Monaco hardtop sedan (*left*) was billed as the roomiest in its class. Polara wagons (*below*) came with a standard 318 V-8; 6620 were sold.

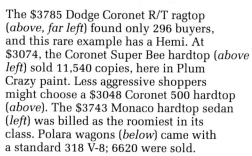

Bobby Isaac took the wheel of a Dodge-sponsored, Hemi-powered stocker (*top left*) at the Riverside 500 NASCAR race. A 375-bhp 440 Magnum V-8 powers this $3711 Dodge Charger R/T hardtop coupe (*above*). Nearly 10,000 were sold. For $1100 less, youthful buyers could still have a fast and sporty car—the Dodge Dart Swinger 340 hardtop (*left*). It was 415 pounds lighter than the Charger R/T, so the 340's 275 bhp was more than adequate. Plymouth's hot mid-size GTX (*below*), with a standard 375-bhp 440 V-8, came in several wild new colors; a Road Runner is to its right. Inspired by Trans-Am racing, the 'Cuda AAR (*bottom left*) featured menacing striping, hood tie-downs, and a triple-carb 340 V-8. Only 635 'Cuda ragtops (*bottom center*) rolled off the line, versus 18,880 hardtops. The ultimate 'Cuda (*bottom right*) had a Hemi.

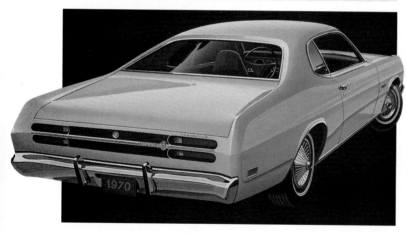

Now sold only as a hardtop, the $3535 Plymouth GTX (*top left*) could have an "Air Grabber" hood and triple carbs for its 440 V-8. *Top right:* The Superbird's towering rear wing and long hidden-headlight nose drove hordes of young car fanatics wild—especially in "Lemon Twist" and with a Hemi. Richard Petty piloted the Superbird (*center right*) to 21 NASCAR Grand National victories. Nearly 48,000 shoppers chose a $3246 Fury III hardtop sedan (*center left*), while Suburban wagons (*above right*)—base, Custom, and Sport—attracted 13,573 buyers. The well-equipped Fury Gran Coupe (*right*) cost $3833, and the Valiant Duster coupe (*above*), starting at $2172, enticed 217,192 buyers.

Chrysler had earlier purchased the Rootes group in England as part of its plan to go global. That plan didn't ultimately work out, but in 1970 Chrysler imported the Sunbeam Alpine (Rapier in England). Based on the Hillman Hunter sedan, the fastback body was supposedly inspired by the Barracuda. This GT cost $2475 (1969 price). Sunbeam was gone from America after 1970.

1970 Production

Chrysler
Newport	79,013
Newport Custom	31,279
Town & Country	15,269
300	21,007
New Yorker	34,209
Total	180,777

Dodge
Dart	155,382
Dart Swinger 340	13,785
Dart Custom	40,987
Challenger	63,094
Challenger R/T	19,938
Coronet Deluxe	14,566
Coronet 440	66,577
Coronet Super Bee	15,506
Coronet 500	15,497
Coronet R/T	2,615
Charger	39,431
Charger R/T	10,337
Polara	71,005
Monaco	24,692
Total	553,412

Imperial
Crown	1,587
LeBaron	10,229
LeBaron Limo	6 *
Total	11,822 *

* Approximate

Plymouth
Valiant	243,185
Valiant Duster 340	24,817
Barracuda	27,205
Barracuda Gran Coupe	8,779
'Cuda	19,515
Belvedere	24,246
Stellite	66,759
Sport Satellite	15,895
Road Runner	43,404
GTX	7,748
Fury I	17,166
Fury II	49,010
Fury III	134,447
Sport Fury	25,695
Fury Gran Coupe	incl with Fury II
Suburban	36,813
Total	744,684

Imports*
Simca 1118	**
Simca 1204	**
Sunbeam Alpine	NA

* Calendar year
** Combined sales: 6,035

1970 Engine Availability

Chrysler
No. Cyl.	Disp., cid	bhp	Availability
V-8	383.0	290	S-Newport, T&C
V-8	383.0	330	O-Newport auto, T&C
V-8	440.0	350	S-300, NY; O-T&C
V-8	440.0	375	O-all exc T&C

Dodge
No. Cyl.	Disp., cid	bhp	Availability
I-6	198.0	125	S-Dart
I-6	225.0	145	S-Challenger/ Coronet/ Charger/Coronet I-6; O-Dart
V-8	318.0	230	S-Dart/ Challenger/ Coronet/Charger Coronet/ Polara V-8
V-8	340.0	275	S-Dart Swinger 340; O-Challenger
V-8	383.0	290	S-Monaco, Polara Custom; O-Challenger/ Coronet/Charger Polara V-8
V-8	383.0	330	O-Challenger, Coronet, Polara, Plara Custom, Monaco
V-8	383.0	335	S-Coronet Super Bee, Challenger R/T; O-Challenger, Charger R/T
V-8	426.0	425	O-Super Bee, Challenger/ Coronet/Charger RTs
V-8	440.0	350	O-Monaco, Polara, Polara Custom
V-8	440.0	375	S-Challenger/ Coronet/Charger R/Ts

No. Cyl.	Disp., cid	bhp	Availability
V-8	440.0	390	O-Challenger/ Coronet/Charger R/Ts, Super Bee

Imperial
No. Cyl.	Disp., cid	bhp	Availability
V-8	440.0	350	S-all

Plymouth
No. Cyl.	Disp., cid	bhp	Availability
I-6	170.0	125	S-Valiant, Duster
I-6	225.0	145	S-Barracuda, Belvedere, Satellite, Fury I/II; O-Valiant, Duster
V-8	318.0	230	S-Barracuda Gran Coupe, Sport Satellite, Fury III, Sport Fury, Suburban
V-8	340.0	275	S-Duster 340; O-Barracuda
V-8	383.0	290	O-all except Valiant
V-8	383.0	330	O-all except Valiant
V-8	383.0	335	S-Road Runner, 'Cuda
V-8	426.0	425	O-Road Runner, 'Cuda, GTX
V-8	440.0	350	S-Sport Fury GT; O-other Furys
V-8	440.0	375	S-GTX; O-'Cuda
V-8	440.0	390	O-'Cuda, Road Runner, GTX, Sport Fury cpe

Imports
No. Cyl.	Disp., cid	bhp	Availability
I-4	68.2	56	S-Simca 1118
I-4	73.4	62	S-Simca 1204
I-4	105.0	73	S-Sunbeam Alpine
I-4	105.0	94	S-Sunbeam Alpine GT

1971

Horsepower ratings begin to fall, as emission-control standards tighten

Some engines run on regular or no-lead fuel

The "muscle car" era is ending—a victim of safety/emissions rules, rising insurance rates, and a trend toward cheaper cars

Plymouth and Dodge mid-size models are completely restyled

Plymouth finally regains third place in sales; Pontiac drops to fourth

Dodge moves up a notch to sixth place, Chrysler maintains 11th place

A Demon joins the Dodge line at mid-year; protests later lead to a name change

Plymouth adds a Scamp hardtop to the Valiant line

Imperial employs the first four-wheel anti-skid braking system, a $250 option

Dodge releases its last convertible and R/T models

The Plymouth GTX makes its final outing

Hemi engines are now available solely for competition

Chrysler buys a share of Mitsubishi Motors; Dodge dealers are marketing the Japanese-built Colt as the "captive-import" business continues to expand

Challenger and Barracuda are Chrysler's last ragtops—until the early '80s revival

Chrysler launched two Newport Royal models, with a standard 255-bhp 360 V-8. This $4153 hardtop (*top and above*) found 8500 customers. Chrysler Town & Country station wagons (*left*) started at $4951.

Only the Imperial's LeBaron series remained, its V-8 eased to 335 bhp. Despite a $6864 price, the hardtop sedan sold 10,116 copies. Bendix anti-skid braking added $250.

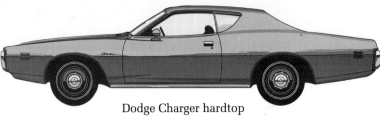

Dodge Charger hardtop

Dodge Charger hardtop

Charger Super Bee

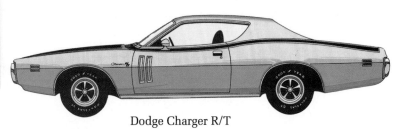

Dodge Charger R/T

Dodge's "Performance Corner" at the Chicago Auto Show (*top*) featured a yellow Dart Demon 340 coupe and a Charger SE. Nimble and spirited, the 275-bhp Demon 340 served as an update of the Dart GTS. Lesser Demons had a Slant Six or 318 V-8. Dodge Challenger sales skidded for '71, with the basic coupe the most popular: 23,088 copies. This well-optioned hardtop (*second from top, left*), started at $2848. Buddy Baker (*third from top, left*) drove Hemi Dodges at NASCAR. Dodge's Diammonte show car (*left*) was Daytona-inspired.

245

With Slant Six power, the Dodge Demon (*left*), on a 108-inch wheelbase, started at $2343. The sporty Demon 340 (*above*) looked hotter yet in Plum Purple, with a factory tach inside.

Some 102,480 Dodge Dart Swinger hardtops (*right*) came off the assembly line in 1971, starting at $2402. A top-line Dart Custom four-door (*below right*) listed at $2609. A 230-bhp 318-cid V-8 cost extra. New base-model Dodge Polaras joined the lineup. This $3497 hardtop sedan (*below*) went to only 24,187 buyers. Big Dodges rode a 122-inch wheelbase. In sedan form (*bottom left*), a Dodge Polara stickered at $3298; the Custom Polara commanded $3593. Topping Dodge's mid-size Coronet line was the $2682 woody-look Crestwood station wagon (*bottom right*)—just 3981 were sold, starting at $3404.

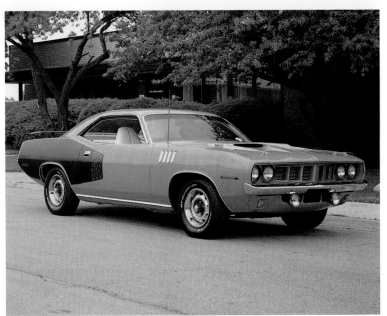

Clockwise, from top: Plymouth pushed performance at the 1971 Chicago Auto Show, led by a $3724 Sport Fury hardtop sedan. "Billboard striping" and a decklid wing emboldened a 'Cuda 383; 6228 'Cuda hardtops were produced. Don Prudhomme's 'Cuda race car showed off its garish paintwork. The 440+6 could be ordered in a GTX, but a four-speed could not. Richard Petty again campaigned a Plymouth, a Road Runner, at NASCAR Grand National races in 1971. Hemi aside, the 440+6 V-8 was the top choice in a Plymouth Road Runner hardtop; the pillared coupe and convertible were gone.

Sox & Martin's Hemi-powered Plymouth Duster (*right*) was often seen at this angle at the nation's dragstrips, with the front tires leaving the ground in a full-thrust takeoff. The super-hot Duster had a four-speed "Slick Shift," twin magnetos, and aluminum heads. Sox & Martin had won 17 major events in 1970. New to the Valiant lineup for '71 was the Scamp hardtop coupe (*second row*). Similar to Dodge's Swinger, it started at $2561 and found 48,253 buyers. *Third row:* In the mid-size Plymouth line, a Satellite Custom sedan (*left*) commanded $2908, while the Regent wagon started at $3,558. Their production came to 30,773 and 5146, respectively.

Full-size '71 Plymouths gained a restyle on the former "fuselage" body/chassis. They came in four series: Sport Fury (*above*), plus Fury I, II, and III. A power sunroof (*above right*) joined the Sport Fury options list—also available on Satellite and Fury hardtops.

Plymouth began to import the Cricket sedan (*top*) from Britain, billed as the "little car that can," and priced it at $1915. For the last time, the Simca 1204 hatchback (*above*) made its way to selected U.S. Chrysler dealers.

1971 Production

Chrysler

Newport	82,533
Town & Country	16,690
300	13,939
New Yorker	34,968
Total	148,130

Dodge

Dart	250,420
Challenger	29,883
Coronet	77,728
Charger	32,114
Polara	85,697
Monaco	25,544
Total	501,386

Imperial

LeBaron	11,558

Plymouth

Valiant	277,391
Barracuda	18,690
Satellite	147,027
Fury	225,003
Sport Fury	34,004
Total	702,115

Imports*

Dodge Colt	28,381
Plymouth Cricket	27,682
Simca 1118	**
Simca	**

* Calendar year
** Combined sales: 2,600

1971 Engine Availability

Chrysler

No. Cyl.	Disp., cid	bhp	Availability
V-8	360.0	255	S-Newport
V-8	383.0	275	S-Newport Custom, T&C; O-Newport
V-8	383.0	300	O-Newport Custom, T&C, Newport
V-8	440.0	335	S-300, NY; O-others
V-8	440.0	370	O-all

Dodge

No. Cyl.	Disp., cid	bhp	Availability
I-6	198.0	125	S-Dart, Challenger cpe
i-6	225.0	145	S-Challenger htp, cvt/ Coronet/ Charger/Polara I-6; O-Dart, Challenger cpe
V-8	318.0	230	S-Challenger/ Coronet/Charger/ Polara V-8; O-Dart
V-8	340.0	275	S-Demon 340; O-Challenger
V-8	360.0	255	O-Polara
V-8	383.0	275	S-Challenger R/T, Charger Super Bee, Polara Brougham, Monaco; O-Challenger, Coronet, Charger, Polara
V-8	383.0	300	O-Challenger, Coronet, Charger, Polara, Monaco
V-8	426.0	425	O-Challenger, Charger
V-8	440.0	335	O-Monaco, Polara
V-8	440.0	370	S-Charger R/T; O-Challenger

No. Cyl.	Disp., cid	bhp	Availability
V-8	440.0	385	O-Challenger, Charger

Imperial

No. Cyl.	Disp., cid	bhp	Availability
V-8	440.0	335	S-all

Plymouth

No. Cyl.	Disp., cid	bhp	Availability
I-6	170.0	125	S-Valiant, Barracuda cpe
I-6	225.0	145	S-Barracuda exc cpe, Satellite, Fury; O-Valiant, Barracuda cpe
V-8	318.0	230	S-Satellite, Fury; O-Valiant, Barracuda
V-8	340.0	275	S-Duster 340, 'Cuda; O-Barracuda
V-8	360.0	255	O-Fury
V-8	383.0	275	O-Barracuda, Road Runner, Fury
V-8	383.0	300	S-'Cuda, Road Runner; O-Barracuda, Fury
V-8	426.0	425	O-Barracuda
V-8	440.0	335	O-Fury
V-8	440.0	370	S-GTX, Fury GT; O-Fury
V-8	440.0	385	O-Barracuda

Imports

No. Cyl.	Disp., cid	bhp	Availability
I-4	68.2	56	S-Simca 1118
I-4	73.4	62	S-Simca 1204
I-4	91.4	57	S-Plymouth Cricket
I-4	91.4	70	O-Plymouth Cricket
I-4	91.5	100	S-Dodge Colt

1972

Plymouth drops to fourth place in production; Oldsmobile moves up to third

Horsepower and torque ratings are now given as "net" instead of "gross," causing published figures to drop sharply

Nearly all car engines run on low-lead regular gasoline

Chrysler offers solid-state ignition systems

A 400-cid V-8 replaces the 383 in Chryslers

The New Yorker Brougham joins the Chrysler lineup

A 400-cid V-8 is added, while the 440 carries on in full-size cars

Dodge deletes the Charger R/T and Super Bee performance models

The Dodge/Plymouth "Street Hemi" fades away; it's too costly to certify for emissions

Plymouth convertibles are history, along with the GTX and big-block Barracuda, but the Road Runner remains

Imperial's "Sure-Brake," four-wheel anti-skid system is available on Chryslers

A Chrysler Newport Royal hardtop coupe (*above*) listed at $4124. A new 400-cid V-8 became standard in the Newport Custom (*right*), but the Royal had the 360 V-8. The big 440 V-8, now rated at 225 *net* horsepower, was optional. A plusher Brougham series (*below*) joined the New Yorker line, here the $5350 hardtop sedan; 20,328 were built. All New Yorkers came with the 440 V-8.

At $6550, the Imperial LeBaron coupe cost $82 less for '72. Sales rose to 2332.

The Dodge Charger (*left*) was losing its performance potential, even if it still looked potent. The Hemi was gone, but the 440 V-8 could be ordered in conjunction with the Rallye package. Hardtop output reached 45,361 units. R/T and Super Bee editions were extinct. The Challenger ponycar (*below*) lost all its big-block engine options, as well as the convertible. With 22,505 built, the $3898 Polara Custom hardtop sedan (*below left*) was the second most popular model among the big Dodges.

Monaco continued as the top full-size Dodge, powered by a 360-cid V-8 (400 or 440 optional). The $4153 hardtop coupe (*left*) pleased 7786 buyers. The Demon coupe (*right*) faltered— output fell from 69,861 units in 1971 to 39,880 for '72. Priced at $2316 (down $27 from '71), this compact Dodge model weighed an even 2800 pounds.

A 1597-cid overhead-cam four-cylinder engine powered the Dodge Colt. Seen here are the four-door sedan (*right*) and the two-door hardtop (*far right*). Reclining seats were standard equipment.

Dodge's Colt wagon had four doors and a four-speed gearbox.

Dodge launched a new line of trucks, led by the D-100 series.

Plymouth's Satellite and Satellite Custom (*above*) four-door sedans were promoted as "ideal conveyances for the budget-minded family." Mid-size Plymouths rode a 117-inch wheelbase and carried a standard Slant Six or 318 V-8, but a new 400-cid V-8 was optional. Starting at $2678, the sedans appealed to 47,767 customers. A Satellite Sebring hardtop (*right*) came in regular and Plus guise, and 55,752 were sold. Only 7628 Road Runner hardtops (*top right*) made it out the door for '72. Fading fast, the RR listed at $3095 and came with a 240-bhp, 340-cid V-8. It was identified by its hood scoops, over-the-roof striping, and special wheels. The compact Valiant Duster 340 (*below*), powered by the same engine, cost only $2742. It found 15,681 buyers.

The Gran Coupe (*above*) was a high-price member of the big-Plymouth family. The $3941 hardtop appealed to 15,840 buyers, but only 9036 opted for the $3818 formal-roof Fury III hardtop (*right*).

The British-built '72 Plymouth Cricket came as a $2017 four-door (*above*) and a $2399 wagon (*top right*), but was plagued by quality ills. The Barracuda (*above right*) lost its ragtop and Gran Coupe, but still offered three engines.

1972 Production

Chrysler

Newport Royal	85,244
Newport Custom	45,061
Town & Country	20,589
New Yorker	22,876
New Yorker Brougham	30,934
Total	204,704

Dodge

Dart	263,418
Challenger	26,658
Coronet	66,348
Charger	75,594
Polara	108,839
Monaco	37,013
Total	577,870

Imperial

LeBaron	15,794

Plymouth

Valiant	330,393
Barracuda	18,450
Satellite	144,953
Fury	262,809
Total	756,605

Imports*

Dodge Colt	34,057
Plymouth Cricket	13,882

* Calendar year

1972 Engine Availability

Chrysler

No. Cyl.	Disp., cid	bhp	Availability
V-8	360.0	175	S-Newport Royal
V-8	400.0	190	S-Newport Custom, T&C; O-Newport Royal
V-8	440.0	225	S-New Yorker/Brougham; O-others

Dodge

No. Cyl.	Disp., cid	bhp	Availability
I-6	198.0	100	S-Dart
I-6	225.0	100	O-Dart
I-6	225.0	110	S-Challenger/Coronet/Charger I-6; O-Dart
V-8	318.0	150	S-Polara, Challenger/Coronet/Charger V-8; O-Dart
V-8	340.0	240	S-Demon 340; O-Dart, Challenger, Charger
V-8	360.0	175	S-Monaco; O-Polara
V-8	400.0	190	O-Charger, Polara, Monaco
V-8	400.0	250	O-Polara, Monaco
V-8	400.0	255	O-Charger
V-8	440.0	230	O-Monaco
V-8	440.0	235	O-Polara
V-8	440.0	280	O-Monaco
V-8	440.0	285	O-Polara, Monaco
V-8	440.0	330	O-Coronet, Charger

Imperial

No. Cyl.	Disp., cid	bhp	Availability
V-8	440.0	225	S-all

Plymouth

No. Cyl.	Disp., cid	bhp	Availability
I-6	198.0	100	S-Valiant
I-6	225.0	110	S-Barracuda, Satellite; O-Valiant
V-8	318.0	150	S-Satellite, Fury; O-Valiant, Barracuda
V-8	340.0	240	S-Duster 340, 'Cuda, Road Runner; O-Barracuda
V-8	360.0	170	O-Fury
V-8	400.0	190/250	O-Fury, Satellite
V-8	440.0	230/285	O-Fury

Imports

No. Cyl.	Disp., cid	bhp	Availability
I-4	91.4	55	S-Plymouth Cricket sdn
I-4	91.4	70	S-Plymouth Cricket wgn, O-sdn
I-4	97.5	83	S-Dodge Colt

1973

OPEC—Organization of Petroleum Exporting Countries—imposes an oil embargo in October, which soon leads to severe fuel shortages

Horsepower, torque, and compression ratios continue their downward trend

Industry model-year output shoots to 9.9 million cars, just before the oil embargo begins

Plymouth sags to a fifth-place production ranking, behind Oldsmobile and Pontiac

Dodge and Chrysler hold steady, keeping their hold on seventh and 11th places

All 1973 models must have five-mph front "crash" bumpers and 2½-mph rear bumpers

On June 26, Chrysler Corporation builds its one-millionth '73 model, a Chrysler Newport sedan

Subcompact and compact models enjoy record industry sales—but only briefly

Electronic ignition is now standard on all Chrysler engines

Anti-theft devices operate the horn and lights

Dodge's Demon is renamed the Dart Sport

Plymouth's "Space Duster," like Dodge's "Convertriple," blends a fold-down rear seat with a sliding steel sunroof

Above: Every Chrysler looked huge in 1973, enhanced by blockier lower-body, sheetmetal, and bigger federally mandated bumpers. Horsepower of the 440-cid V-8 dropped to 215 net, for both Chryslers and Imperials (*right front*). The latter featured hidden headlights. *Left:* Chrysler Newports displayed a new rectangular grille. Note the tiny port-hole in the rear pillar of the special-edition Chrysler "Mariner" hardtop.

A Newport was the millionth '73 car from Chrysler Corporation. Holding the marker: sales manager Francis Hazelroth (*left*) and plant manager Richard Cummins.

Dauntless muscle not long before, the Dodge Charger was more of a personal-luxury coupe by 1973—but it set a production record: 119,318 units. Hidden headlights were gone. Note the slim window slats in the rear pillar of this $3375 SE hardtop coupe (*left*). This year's Dodge Challenger (*below left*) exhibited "quiet good taste." The Rallye version was now an option. Base engine was the 318 V-8, with a 340 V-8 the sole option. Save for a fresh grille, the full-size Dodge Polara (*below*) showed little change for '73. Prices: $3729 to $4494.

A Dodge Monaco two-door hardtop (*left*) cost $4276 and weighed nearly two tons. Just $2578 bought a mini-size, Japanese-made Dodge Colt GT (*above*). A Dart Sport 340 (*below left*) could still burn rubber; the Swinger hardtop (*below*) started at $2617.

Sales of the Plymouth Road Runner recovered smartly in 1973, with 19,056 hardtops built. A 318-cid V-8 was standard now, but 340- and 440-cid engines could be installed instead. Plymouth Satellite's cheapest model was the Coupe (*below*), whose rear quarter windows were fixed. Base-priced at $2755, 13,570 were sold. A Satellite Custom four-door sedan (*below right*) cost $2974, versus $2824 for the base sedan. *Third row:* Plymouth again offered a long list of Fury models, including the posh top-line Gran Coupe (*left*), priced at $4064. With 18,127 sales, it outdid the $4110 Gran Sedan (*right*), which scored with 14,852 customers. The Valiant Duster fastback coupe (*bottom left*) was available with two Slant Six engines or the 318 V-8. Prices started at $2376. Note the prominent dual exhaust pipes on the Duster 340 (*bottom right*)—still looking like a hot number.

Skiers and snowbirds might have been tempted by Plymouth's special-edition "Aspen" four-door hardtop (*above and right*) in 1973. Painted white, with light blue striping, it could haul a great load of gear up to the slopes—especially with one of the big-block V-8 engines that remained available in the full-size Plymouth stable.

Hyped as "Easy to maneuver, easy to park," Plymouth Crickets came as a four-door sedan or wagon, the latter with 60 cubic feet of storage. Both rode a 98-inch wheelbase. Power front disc brakes were standard. The Cricket was dropped after '73.

1973 Production

Chrysler
Newport	101,778
Newport Custom	52,435
Town & Country	20,040
New Yorker	15,610
New Yorker Brougham	44,366
Total	234,229

Dodge
Dart	288,692
Challenger	32,596
Coronet	87,533
Charger	119,318
Polara	108,001
Monaco	29,396
Total	665,536

Imperial
LeBaron	16,729

Plymouth
Valiant	380,592
Barracuda	22,213
Satellite	218,204
Fury	261,187
Total	882,196

Imports*
Dodge Colt	35,523
Plymouth Cricket	NA

* Calendar year

1973 Engine Availability

Chrysler
No. Cyl.	Disp., cid	bhp	Availability
V-8	400.0	185	S-Newport/Custom
V-8	440.0	215	S-T&C, New Yorker/Brougham; O-Newport/Custom

Dodge
No. Cyl.	Disp., cid	bhp	Availability
I-6	198.0	95	S-Dart
I-6	225.0	105	S-Coronet, Charger; O-Dart
V-8	318.0	150	S-Challenger, Coronet/Charger V-8, Polara exc wgn; O-Dart
V-8	340.0	240	S-Dart Sport 340; O-Challenger, Coronet, Charger
V-8	360.0	170	S-Polara wgn, Monaco exc wgn; O-Polara
V-8	400.0	175	O-Charger, Coronet
V-8	400.0	185	S-Monaco wgn; O-Polara, Monaco
V-8	400.0	220	O-Polara, Monaco
V-8	400.0	260	O-Coronet, Charger
V-8	440.0	220	O-Polara, Monaco
V-8	440.0	280	O-Coronet, Charger

Imperial
No. Cyl.	Disp., cid	bhp	Availability
V-8	440.0	215	S-all

Plymouth
No. Cyl.	Disp., cid	bhp	Availability
I-6	198.0	100	S-Valiant
I-6	225.0	110	S-Barracuda, Satellite; O-Valiant
V-8	318.0	150	S-Satellite, Fury, Road Runner; O-Valiant, Barracuda
V-8	340.0	240	S-Duster 340, 'Cuda; O-Barracuda, Road Runner
V-8	360.0	175	O-Fury
V-8	400.0	190/250	O-Fury
V-8	440.0	230/285	O-Fury, RR

Imports
No. Cyl.	Disp., cid	bhp	Availability
I-4	91.4	55	S-Plymouth Cricket sdn
I-4	91.4	70	S-Plymouth Cricket wgn, O-sdn
I-4	97.5	83	S-Dodge Colt

Chapter 13

Downhill Skid in Perilous Times: 1974-78

In the auto industry, as in life, timing is everything. Chrysler's full-size cars earned a total redesign for 1974—just in time for the first energy crisis. Who wanted to sit for hours in gas lines to fill up a behemoth, when a subcompact sucked up just a fraction of the fuel?

Although Chrysler was criticized for its lack of foresight, the sudden action by the Organization of Petroleum Exporting Countries (OPEC) in the fall of 1973 came as a surprise to virtually everyone. Yes, a handful of critics had warned for years of America's reliance upon oversize automobiles guzzling imported oil, but their voices generally went unheeded.

Industry sales tumbled badly. Chrysler Corporation skidded slightly more than its competitors, though market share changed little. Dodge and Plymouth endured less pain than Chrysler and Imperial, mainly because compacts remained popular during the belt-tightening period. In fact, Plymouth rose from fifth place to third.

For years, Chrysler Corporation had been run largely by accountants, not "car guys." Spiraling prices hurt sales, too. Chrysler raised them in 1974, followed by Ford and GM, causing the Cost of Living Council to brand the automakers' price hikes "an act of consummate gall." Effectively thumbing his nose at the Nixon White House, Chrysler chairman Lynn Townsend then hiked prices another one-percent.

Full-size models were recognizably new for '74, slab-sided, and massive looking—though actually five inches shorter than the "fuselage" generation. Imperial dropped to Chrysler's wheelbase, thus hastening its demise. Both upper makes exhibited square pseudo-classic grilles, belatedly following an industry trend. All big Dodges wore Monaco badges in 1974, as the Polara nameplate disappeared. Even more than before, full-size Plymouths resembled their Dodge counterparts.

Dodge/Plymouth compacts showed little change, but continued to attract customers. More than a quarter-million Dusters were sold—cute and well-engineered, if conventional. Demonstrating that frugality didn't have to be spartan, two posher versions debuted: the Dart Special Edition and Valiant Brougham. On the other hand, Challenger/Barracuda production halted in March, mourned by few.

By the time the 1975 selling season began, the OPEC oil embargo—though lifted—had triggered a severe economic recession. Coupled with whirlwind inflation, this was not good news for either consumers or the auto industry. Instead of holding back, Detroit enacted another round of price hikes, heralding the dreaded "sticker shock" that soon became an inevitable element of the car-buying process. Even when a two-month inventory of unsold cars accumulated, Townsend refused to cut prices. Next came a frightful round of layoffs, in an attempt to slash costs. Townsend raised prices yet again, worsening the backlog. As a result, output fell 19 percent below

Chrysler scored a big hit with its 1975 personal-luxury Cordoba coupe, but the similar Dodge Charger—here a '77 with a T-bar roof—didn't sell nearly as well.

the feeble '74 total.

What could be done to stimulate sales? The answer, though familiar today, was an odd one in 1975: rebates. For the first time ever, an auto company decided to *pay* people to buy its products. Ford and GM soon followed along, firmly implanting this curious form of merchandising into the public awareness.

At the same time, Townsend set Chrysler on a condensed course. Only by cutting back sharply on production, he believed, could the corporation survive in this new, limited economy. If recovery occurred, Chrysler would be caught short, but it was a gamble worth taking.

Chrysler took yet another gamble, finally releasing the "small Chrysler" it had shunned for years. Though basically a luxurious variant of Plymouth's Satellite, the handsome Cordoba personal-luxury coupe captured the public imagination. Soft-selling TV commercials uttered by the suave actor, Ricardo Montalban, boosted sales. On a 115-inch platform, Cordoba rode the shortest wheelbase of any postwar Chrysler, and made an impressive showing against the Ford Thunderbird and Chevrolet Monte Carlo. It even shared a styling stroke or two with the Monte—blended with a taste of Jaguar. In its first season, 150,105 Cordobas were sold—almost three-fifths of Chrysler's total volume.

New Yorker Broughams topped the Chrysler line, loaded with lavish extras. But the Imperial nameplate faded away after only 8830 were built for '75. Luxury-car fans didn't know it, but the badge would be back—not once, but twice—in the next two decades.

Dodge got a Cordoba offshoot named Charger SE, borrowing its badge from the departed muscle coupes. This one failed to "charge" ahead, with just 30,812 produced. Both Dodge and Plymouth endured their worst years since 1962, as customers began to shun compacts. Shuffling of nameplates to offer a smaller Fury didn't help, especially as Ford introduced its new luxury compacts, the Granada and Monarch. Dodge dropped to eighth place; Plymouth could only reach sixth.

Not much was left of Chrysler performance, save for the Dart Sport and Plymouth Duster 360. Even the fabled Road Runner was reduced to an appearance package. Times were changing— only resolute leadfoots insisted on possessing the quickest car on the block.

Lynn Townsend retired as corporate chairman on October 1, succeeded by John Riccardo. Eugene A. Cafiero moved up the corporate ladder from Dodge production to become president. Riccardo promised that Chrysler would see no dramatic change in marketing strategy, but standing still was indefensible at this juncture.

Although the Imperial was gone, luxury-car buyers didn't have to fear—the New Yorker Brougham earned upgrades to fill the gap. Cordoba, meanwhile, out-sold every competitor except for Chevrolet's Monte Carlo. Chrysler stuck with 400- and 440-cid V-8s in 1976, but added an Electronic Lean Burn System. Foretelling future engine computerization, it used a "spark control computer" to sort out data received from sensors.

At mid-season, two new compacts began to edge aside the aging Dart and Valiant: the Dodge Aspen and Plymouth Volaré. Each came as a roomy fastback coupe, sedan, or station wagon. They looked pleasant enough and, with a choice of Slant Six or V-8 power, delivered a healthy balance of performance and economy. Even a four-speed manual gearbox was available, well-suited to the sportier Aspen R/T or Volaré Road Runner, running a 318- or 360-cid V-8. More than half a million rolled off the line in their first season.

A few years later, Aspen/Volaré earned the notorious distinction of suffering the most safety recalls of any model—until GM later wrestled that "honor" away with its infamous X-cars. Their unitized bodies also proved painfully rustprone, reminiscent of the quick-to-corrode 1957-58 models.

Chrysler's Operations Committee made two fundamental decisions in 1976: first, to abandon the slow-selling full-size cars; second, to concentrate on front-wheel drive subcompacts. Some executives fretted that a shift to small cars would harm the company; those in charge were convinced that the traditional behemoth, relic of a profligate era, deserved extinction.

General Motors "downsized" its full-size cars for 1977. Ford took longer to make the move. Chrysler's delay didn't help matters, but at least a "modern" subcompact would go to market.

In mid-1976, Chrysler-Plymouth dealers got a new captive import: the Mitsubishi-built Plymouth Arrow. This allowed dealers to offer a full-range line-up bearing the Plymouth badge.

Now that the Aspen/Volaré compacts were proving popular, Chrysler had a clever pair of spinoffs ready after the 1977 season began. The Chrysler LeBaron and Dodge Diplomat came as a fixed-pillar coupe or sedan, aiming at customers who craved a little luxury with their more modestly sized automobiles. LeBaron was the smallest Chrysler ever—a new mid-size breed—and brought back a revered old name. Nearly every creature comfort in the Chrysler catalog could be ordered for an already-well-equipped LeBaron or Diplomat, which came with the 318-cid V-8 (or for the frugal, a Slant Six). Despite their abbreviated opening season, both models sold well. In fact, Chrysler division now ranked as a high-volume make, issuing nearly 400,000 cars in the model year.

By now, cost pressures and declining profits helped blur the differences between Chrysler's three makes. In some cases, Dodge and Plymouth versions were even priced identically. Dealers didn't complain—and even encouraged the "cloning"—as each wanted to offer an example of every model in the Chrysler fold.

Confusion reigned throughout the Seventies, as customers said no to big cars in the wake of the OPEC oil embargo, flirted with intermediates, toyed with compacts—then didn't seem sure *what* they wanted. Even though Chrysler responded sluggishly, its executives were trying to adapt to the changing market. For evidence, it's necessary only to examine the '75 Cordoba/ Charger, '76 Aspen/Volaré, '77 LeBaron/ Diplomat—and, more daring yet, the Dodge Omni and Plymouth Horizon.

For the first time, an American automaker offered a front-drive subcompact. For once, Chrysler had a product that was *exactly right* for the times. Omni and the nearly identical Horizon four-door hatchback stood on a par with Volkswagen's trend-setting Rabbit. Actually, the pair were powered at first by an enlargement of Volkswagen's four-cylinder overhead-cam engine. Though less peppy than a Rabbit, Chrysler's '78 subcompact twins drew praise for their practicality, roominess, and softer ride. Consumers responded eagerly, snapping up nearly 189,000 in the first year. Chrysler suddenly stood in the lead among domestically built small cars. A rear-drive Pinto or Chevette seemed clumsy in comparison—and Ford was about to earn scads of unfavorable publicity for the alleged fire-propensity of its early Pintos.

Plymouth now fielded no full-size models at all, making the mid-size Fury the biggest car of the lot. Chrysler and Dodge stuck with biggies for one more season. Pillarless hardtop bodies, abandoned by other manufacturers, made one last stand.

Cordoba got a styling touch-up, while Charger continued with less change. Dodge added a sprightlier variant, the Magnum XE. Far more shoppers turned to Magnum than to Charger, but Cordoba beat both. Dodge's version of the latest import from Mitsubishi took a Challenger badge, abandoned at the end of the muscle-car era. Plymouth called its edition Sapporo. Most buyers skipped the standard engine and chose the bigger 2.6-liter four-cylinder unit with contra-rotating "Silent Shafts." In a few years, that engine would power a number of domestic Chrysler products.

Despite Omni/Horizon popularity, Plymouth finished a distant seventh in production. Dodge ranked eighth. Adding insult to injury, Ford had a good year, and Chevrolet slipped only a bit. Financial crisis loomed, but a potential savior rode to the rescue. Lee Iacocca grasped the sagging reins at the nation's Number Three automaker—trying to forestall disaster.

1974

The OPEC oil embargo is lifted on March 1

Athough the fuel crisis eases, the muscle-car era is dead

The Polara badge is dropped; all full-size Dodges are now Monacos

Dodge introduces rebates on the Monaco; full-size cars are not selling

Plymouth rises to third in output, followed by Oldsmobile and Pontiac

Chrysler Corporation's model-year production drops by 25 percent

All cars have front *and* rear energy-absorbing, five-mph bumpers—by government mandate, of course

A government-dictated interlock prevents engines from starting until seatbelts are fastened; buyers revolt

Four-wheel disc brakes become standard on Imperials

Dodge produces its final Challengers as the ponycar market fades

Plymouth builds its last Barracuda—another casualty of the sinking ponycar market

An all-new Plymouth Fury debuts, a kissing cousin to the the Dodge Monaco and Chrysler Newport

The "Sundance" name appears on a Plymouth for the first time—for now as a "spring special"

The $5686 Chrysler New Yorker hardtop sedan (*top and above*) boasted all-new styling, but still rode a 124-inch chassis. Output of this model tumbled to 3066 units, in part due to the OPEC oil embargo. A St. Regis package for the New Yorker Brougham two-door hardtop (*center*) featured "formal fixed-position rear quarter windows for greater privacy and styling elegance," plus a special vinyl roof. Individually adjustable bench seats came in white with gold or black accents.

A basic Chrysler New Yorker four-door hardtop (*left*) cost $5686; its Brougham sibling commanded $6063. Chrysler and Imperial adopted a faddishly square, pseudo-classic grille as part of their crisp, slab-sided restyling. The New Yorker's 440-cid V-8 made 230 or 275 bhp. Newports (*below left and below*) had a 400-cid V-8, with a tamed 440 optional. The hardtop coupe (*below center*) listed at $4752. *Third from top, left:* A half-century had passed since Walter Chrysler had issued his first automobile on January 5, 1924.

Topping the Dodge Charger line—and top seller of the series—was the SE (Special Edition) coupe (*left*), with a vinyl roof and slatted opera windows. Offered only with V-8 power, the SE sold for $3742. A base Charger coupe with a Slant Six engine cost $3412, while the pillarless hardtop started at $3412. Engine choices reached up to 205- and 245-horsepower versions of the 400-cid V-8, plus a 275-horse 440. *Above:* Like other Chrysler products in the mid-1970s, Dodge Charger hardtops came with several different rear-quarter window and roof styles.

Grille and taillight tweaks marked the '74 Dodge Charger (*above left*). A Rallye package added $100. Challenger Rallye models (*above*) wore a black grille and "strobe" stripes. A 360 V-8 replaced the 340 option. The 13-model, full-size Monaco line included this $4999 Brougham hardtop sedan (*left*). Polaras were gone for good.

A modular instrument panel (*left*) with a snap-in access plate went into the fully reworked Dodge Monaco. Glass area grew, too. *Above:* Monaco station wagons came in base, Custom, and Brougham dress.

All-new Dodge Colts, including the $3271 wagon (*right*), held single headlights. Colt hardtops came with a 1597-cc engine, but this sportier GT (*above*) has the optional two-liter four and Chrysler-built automatic transmission.

Dodge Dart Special Editions came in four-door sedan (*top left*) and hardtop coupe body styles. Note the distinctive upswept trim striping on this Dart Sport (*above*). The Dart Swinger, here with a sunroof (*left*), kept its traditional hardtop styling.

Center: Plymouth Barracuda prices started at $3067 with the standard 318-cid V-8. A more emissions-friendly 245-bhp 360 V-8 from the full-size models replaced the 340 in the $3252 'Cuda. Twin hood scoops and white-letter tires gave it a bolder look. Only 6745 base Barracudas were built in the model's final year, versus 4989 'Cudas. *Left and above:* Minor grille and trim touch-ups didn't help the $3545 Road Runner, which saw output drop to 11,555. Its optional 440-cid V-8 fell to 275 bhp.

Above: A mid-size Satellite Custom sedan cost $3329. *Left:* The $3621 Sebring Plus came only with a V-8.

Plymouth's Duster (*left*) could have a 360-cid V-8. The first '74 Valiant (*second from top*) leaves the assembly line; the $3794 Brougham (*above*) pushed luxury.

A '74 Fury Suburban wagon started at $5025; 7759 were built.

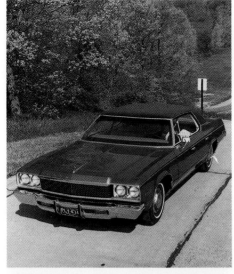

The $4675 Gran Fury hardtop sedan (*above*) looked bigger this year, but sales were slow: 8191 units. Plymouth also offered a Trail Duster sport-utility (*top right*) for the first time, with full-time four-wheel drive and a 318 V-8. Big-block V-8s added off-road zest. Note the roll bar.

1974 Production

Chrysler

Newport	49,696
Newport Custom	27,667
Town & Country	8,194
New Yorker	6,138
New Yorker Brougham	25,678
Total	117,373

Dodge

Dart	259,516
Challenger	16,437
Coronet	60,728
Charger	74,376
Monaco	66,671
Total	477,728

Imperial

LeBaron	14,426

Plymouth

Valiant	459,083
Barracuda	11,734
Satellite	150,963
Fury	118,283
Total	740,063

Imports

Dodge Colt	42,925

1974 Engine Availability

Chrysler

No. Cyl.	Disp., cid	bhp	Availability
V-8	400.0	185	S-Newport/Custom
V-8	400.0	205	O-Newport/Custom
V-8	440.0	230	S-T&C, New Yorker/Brougham; O-Newport/Custom
V-8	440.0	275	O-New Yorker/Brougham

Dodge

No. Cyl.	Disp., cid	bhp	Availability
I-6	198.0	95	S-Dart exc SE
I-6	225.0	105	S-Dart SE, Coronet; O-Dart
V-8	318.0	150	S-Challenger, Coronet, Charger; O-Dart
V-8	360.0	180	S-Monaco exc Brougham, wgns; O-Charger
V-8	360.0	200	O-Coronet, Charger, Monaco exc Brougham, wgns
V-8	360.0	245	S-Dart 360; O-Challenger, Charger
V-8	400.0	185	S-Monaco Brougham, wgns; O-Coronet, Charger
V-8	400.0	205	O-Coronet, Charger
V-8	400.0	245	O-Monaco exc wgns, Coronet, Charger
V-8	440.0	230	O-Monaco exc wgns
V-8	440.0	250	O-Monaco wgns
V-8	440.0	275	O-Coronet, Charger

Imperial

No. Cyl.	Disp., cid	bhp	Availability
V-8	440.0	230	S-all

Plymouth

No. Cyl.	Disp., cid	bhp	Availability
I-6	198.0	95	S-Valiant exc Brougham
I-6	225.0	105	S-Valiant Brougham, Satellite; O-Valiant
V-8	318.0	150	S-Barracuda, Satellite; O-Valiant
V-8	318.0	170	S-Road Runner
V-8	360.0	180	S-Fury exc wgn/Gran Fury
V-8	360.0	200	O-Satellite, Fury exc wgn/Gran Fury
V-8	360.0	245	S-Duster 360; O-Valiant
V-8	400.0	185	S-Gran Fury, Fury wgns; O-Fury
V-8	400.0	205	O-Satellite, Fury
V-8	400.0	240	O-Fury
V-8	400.0	250	O-Satellite
V-8	440.0	230/250	O-Fury
V-8	440.0	275	O-Satellite

Imports

No. Cyl.	Disp., cid	bhp	Availability
I-4	97.5	83	S-Dodge Colt
I-4	121.7	96	S-Dodge Colt GT; O-Dodge Colt

1975

Plymouth slips to sixth in production; Dodge drops one notch to eighth

All major automakers install catalytic converters

The new Chrysler Cordoba and Dodge Charger SE are built in Canada

Chrysler Corporation's model-year output skids another 19 percent, but industry auto sales are down just eight percent

GM's market share tops 53 percent; Ford's, 28 percent; Chrysler's, 14 percent

The new Cordoba personal-luxury coupe is the smallest postwar Chrysler yet, and similar to the revamped Dodge Charger

Cordoba is a success—Chrysler moves to tenth place in industry standings

The "final" Imperial is built on June 12, but the car itself continues as the Chrysler New Yorker Brougham

Plymouth's full-size car is now called Gran Fury; mid-size models adopt the Fury badge

A "Fuel Pacer" option warns when the driver hits the gas pedal too hard

John Riccardo becomes the corporate chairman; Eugene Cafiero is president

Hollywood actor Ricardo Montalban (*above*) took TV by storm in his role as pitchman for the all-new Chrysler Cordoba (*left*). His exotic pronunciation of the car's name helped capture quick public attention. Billed as "the new small Chrysler," it was the shortest model in decades—just 2.5 inches longer than a 1924 Chrysler Six.

A near-twin to the revamped Dodge Charger, the 115-inch-wheelbase Cordoba personal-luxury coupe (*above*) had styling touches reminiscent of a Jaguar XJ6 and Chevrolet Monte Carlo. Note the opera windows and half-vinyl roof. Upholstered in crushed velour or vinyl with brocade cloth, a Cordoba could instead have "fine Corinthian leather" (*left*).

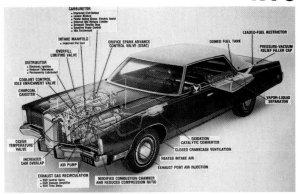

The opulent $6424 Chrysler New Yorker Brougham hardtop sedan (*above left*) had leather, velour, or brocade upholstery, as could the coupe and pillared sedan. Pulling a trailer (*left*) was a breeze for the $5254 Newport Custom four-door sedan. The 1975 Cleaner Air System (*above*) was designed to meet tightened federal emissions-control standards. All Chrysler and Plymouth engines had either an air pump or a catalytic converter, if not both, to cut pollution. Imperial was in its last year (for awhile); the $8698 LeBaron hardtop coupe (*below*) found only 2728 customers.

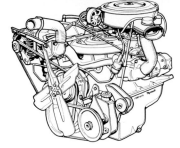

225-cid Slant Six

318-cid V-8

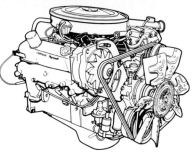

400-cid V-8

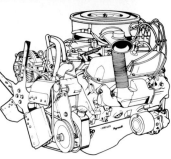

360-cid V-8

Fully restyled for '75, and upright in profile, the $4903 Dodge Charger Special Edition coupe (*top and left*) sold far more slowly than the Cordoba: 30,812 copies. The SE wore standard slatted opera windows. Mid-sized Dodges earned a major facelift. This $4154 Coronet Brougham hardtop coupe (*above*) captured 10,292 buyers. The $5460 Monaco Royal Brougham coupe (*below*)—with hidden headlights, vinyl roof, and cornering lights—topped the Dodge lineup, but together with the $5382 hardtop sedan accounted for only 5964 sales.

Upswept bodyside/roof striping was just one of the many appearance options for a Dodge Dart Sport (*left*). The semi-fastback Sport coupe (*above*) could have a Slant Six or 318 V-8, but the Sport 360 came with the bigger 230-horse engine as standard. Some 51,355 Sports were built for '75. Introduced in mid-1974, the well-equipped Dart Special Edition hardtop (*below*) cost $4232 (versus $3518 for a Swinger); only 5680 were built, plus 13,194 four-doors. Dart Sports rode a 108-inch wheelbase; other Darts, a 111-inch. A "Convertriple" option included a sunroof and a folding rear seat to expand luggage space making it a coupe/convertible/wagon.

Bumper revision hit the Mitsubishi-built Dodge Colt for '75. A new white-and-blue Carousel hardtop coupe (*left*) joined the line in mid-year. The Colt sedan (*above left*) shows off its new vinyl roof. Colts ran with a 1597-cc four (97.5 cid) that developed 83 horsepower at 5500 rpm and 89 lbs/ft torque at 3500 rpm. This was mated to a four-speed stick or optional automatic. A five-speed shift and two-liter "Silent Shaft" engine came later. A four-door wagon (*above*) was also offered.

Optional decklid graphics on a Plymouth Road Runner (*above*) let everyone know what you were driving. Despite a 235-bhp, 400-cid V-8 with dual exhausts as an option, sales skidded to 7183 units. The poshest Plymouth Valiant was the Brougham (*right*), while the compact Duster (*background*) might have a 230-bhp 360 V-8. A squared-up mid-size Fury replaced the Satellite line; the $4105 Sport hardtop (*top right*) attracted 17,782 buyers. Marketed as a "spring special," Plymouth's Silver Duster (*below*) appeared at the '75 Chicago Auto Show.

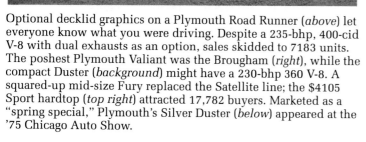

1975 Production	
Chrysler	
Cordoba	150,105
Newport	41,670
Newport Custom	27,080
Town & Country	6,655
New Yorker Brougham	26,039
Total	251,549
Dodge	
Dart	210,093
Coronet	84,498
Charger	30,812
Monaco	52,113
Total	377,516
Imperial	
LeBaron	8,830
Plymouth	
Valiant	267,525
Fury	113,779
Gran Fury	72,801
Total	454,105
Imports	
Dodge Colt	60,356

The '75 Gran Fury Custom hardtop sedan (*above*) was priced at $4837, and 11,292 were built. The upmarket Brougham sub-series wore a unique grille and single headlights flanking vertical parking lights. The $5146 coupe (*below*) was no longer a true hardtop; 6521 were sold.

Full-size '75 Plymouths adopted the Gran Fury nameplate to avoid confusion with the new mid-size line, renamed Fury. Riding a 122-inch chassis and weighing 4290 pounds, the Gran Fury Custom hardtop was equivalent to the nearly identical '74 Gran Fury shown here, save for a slight difference in the grille texture.

1975 Engine Availability

Chrysler

No. Cyl.	Disp., cid	bhp	Availability
V-8	318.0	150	O-Cordoba
V-8	360.0	180	S-Cordoba; O-Newport/Custom
V-8	360.0	190	O-Newport/Custom
V-8	400.0	165	O-Cordoba
V-8	400.0	175	S-Newport/Custom; O-New Yorker Brougham
V-8	400.0	190	O-Cordoba
V-8	400.0	195	O-Newport/Custom, New Yorker Brougham
V-8	400.0	235	O-Cordoba
V-8	440.0	215	S-T&C, New Yorker Brougham; O-others
V-8	440.0	260	O-T&C

Dodge

No. Cyl.	Disp., cid	bhp	Availability
I-6	225.0	95	S-Dart, Coronet
V-8	318.0	135	O-Charger
V-8	318.0	145	O-Dart
V-8	318.0	150	S-Coronet; O-Charger, Monaco
V-8	360.0	180	S-Charger, Monaco exc Brougham wgns; O-Coronet, Royal Monaco Brougham
V-8	360.0	190	O-Charger, Royal Monaco Brougham
V-8	360.0	230	S-Dart 360
V-8	400.0	165/190	O-Coronet, Charger
V-8	400.0	175	S-Royal Monaco Brougham; O-Monaco
V-8	400.0	185	O-Charger
V-8	440.0	195	O-Monaco exc Royal Brougham
V-8	440.0	215	O-all Monaco

Imperial

No. Cyl.	Disp., cid	bhp	Availability
V-8	440.0	215	S-all

Plymouth

No. Cyl.	Disp., cid	bhp	Availability
I-6	225.0	90	S-Valiant
I-6	225.0	95	S-Fury
V-8	318.0	135	O-Fury, Valiant
V-8	318.0	150	O-Dart
V-8	318.0	150	S-Coronet; O-Charger, Monaco
V-8	360.0	180	S-Charger, Monaco exc Brougham wgns; O-Coronet, Royal Monaco Brougham
V-8	360.0	190	O-Charger, Royal Monaco Brougham
V-8	360.0	230	S-Dart 360
V-8	400.0	165/190	O-Coronet, Charger
V-8	400.0	175	S-Royal Monaco Brougham; O-Monaco
V-8	400.0	190/235	O-Fury
V-8	400.0	195	O-Gran Fury
V-8	440.0	215	O-Gran Fury

Imports

No. Cyl.	Disp., cid	bhp	Availability
I-4	97.5	83	S-Dodge Colt
I-4	121.7	96	S-Dodge Colt GT; O-Dodge Colt

1976

Industry sales leap upward after a pair of bad years

Big and intermediate cars are selling best—to the surprise of many

Chrysler announces an agreement to purchase engines and transaxles from Volkswagen for its 1978 front-drive subcompacts

The compact Dodge Aspen and Plymouth Volaré debut, but the pair soon set a sad record for the number of safety recalls

Aspen is advertised as the "family car of the future"

Aspen/Volaré have cross-mounted torsion bars up front

After a long and successful run, the final Dusters and Darts are built

Plymouth issues its last full-size Furys

The New Yorker Brougham assumes Imperial's role—a good example of badge engineering

Plymouth Arrow hatchbacks are imported from Mitsubishi in Japan

An electronic Lean Burn System is fitted to the corporation's biggest V-8s for cleaner exhaust

The economy-tuned "Dart Lite" and "Feather Duster" are introduced by Dodge/Plymouth

Road Runner becomes a splashy package option on the Volaré

Top and above: Once again, Ricardo Montalban hawked the virtues of Cordoba, "the small Chrysler," which earned a mild facelift for '76. *Left:* "Inside," the brochure promised, Cordoba was "the essence of comfort." The instrument panel featured simulated Brazilian rosewood. Shag carpeting reached onto lower doors and seatbacks. "Cashmere-like" cloth/vinyl bench seating was standard, and velour 60/40 seating newly optional; buckets wore Corinthian leather.

A 175-bhp, 400-cid V-8 was standard in the Chrysler Cordoba coupe (*above*), which wore slim opera windows with matching side lamps. A Landau half-vinyl roof was optional. Smaller V-8s, 318 and 360 cid, were also available. Hiked in price to $5392 for '76, Cordoba offered the most engine choices of any Chrysler. "Engineering," the sales brochure insisted, "makes the beauty of Cordoba worth-while." Like other big Chryslers, the New Yorker Brougham (*below*) got engine modifications and low axle ratios to boost fuel economy. The $6737 hardtop sedan sold 28,327 copies. Not every customer knew that the '76 Brougham differed very little from the now-departed Imperial.

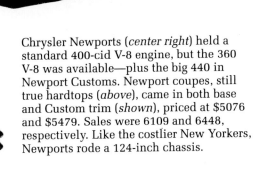

Chrysler Newports (*center right*) held a standard 400-cid V-8 engine, but the 360 V-8 was available—plus the big 440 in Newport Customs. Newport coupes, still true hardtops (*above*), came in both base and Custom trim (*shown*), priced at $5076 and $5479. Sales were 6109 and 6448, respectively. Like the costlier New Yorkers, Newports rode a 124-inch chassis.

Daytona (*above*) served as the sportiest model in the '76 Dodge Charger line, as evident by its distinctive two-tone paint scheme. For luxury, an SE (*right*) with louvered opera windows was the choice. Chargers might have a canopy or halo vinyl roof. A 150-bhp 318 V-8 was standard; 360 and 400 V-8s were optional.

Dodge's $5382 Royal Monaco Brougham coupe (*center*) wore opera windows, and stylish roof trim featured a wrapover band. Lesser Monaco coupes were true hardtops. Royal Monaco Broughams had hidden headlights, but the $5869 station wagon (*right*) rode a longer 124-inch wheelbase. These Broughams sold poorly: 4076 coupes and 2480 wagons. The $4763 Royal Monaco four-door sedan (*above*) was Dodge's most popular full-size car: 11,320 units. The base engine was a 170-bhp 360 V-8 (175-bhp 400 for wagons), with a 205-bhp 440 the top option. Overall length spanned 225.7 inches, 229.5 for wagons.

Little was new in the mid-size Dodge Coronet Custom coupe (*left*), which sported tri-section opera windows and wrapover roof styling. A Coronet Custom sedan (*below*) could have a Slant Six, or a broad choice of V-8s. Coronet prices ranged from $3770 to $5165.

Replacing the departing Dart, the Dodge Aspen got off to a good start. Base sedans began at $3371, but this Special Edition coupe (*above left*) stickered at $4413—with automatic, power steering, vinyl roof, 60/40 seats, and the 225-cid Slant Six. Buyers snapped up 21,564 copies of this model. Dodge promoted this Aspen (*left*) as a "comfortable wagon in a size all its own." An Aspen Special Edition wagon (*far left*) cost $330 more than the base model; 34,617 were sold.

Since 1975, Dodge dealers had been offering a Colt Carousel two-door coupe (*above*). Painted blue and white, it came with a vinyl roof. Colts rode a 95.3-inch wheelbase and came in coupe, hardtop, sedan, and wagon body styles. U.S. sales totaled 48,542 in 1976.

Above: Swinger and Swinger Special hardtops made the Dart's final lineup. Together, they attracted 14,801 buyers. Frugal shoppers could choose a Dart Lite (*right*). Its fuel-economy option featured an aluminum hood and aluminum intake manifold for the Slant Six. Dart four-door sedans garnered 34,864 sales; this one (*far right*) is a Special Edition.

The $5334 Plymouth Gran Fury Brougham coupe (*top and above*) found only 2619 buyers. Louvered opera windows graced this Fury Sport coupe (*above right*); 28,851 were sold. Compact Volaré wagons came in Standard and Premier levels, the latter (*below right*) with simulated woodgrain. The lightened Plymouth "Feather Duster" (*right*) focused on economy, with various aluminum components and a specially tuned 225-cid six. The posh Volaré Premier coupe (*below*) sold 31,475 copies.

Mean Mary Jean (*left*) hyped Plymouth in 1977, hoping to give it a youthful image. The "1" stood for the new Volaré's status in the lineup. Though Number 1 in Plymouth sales, weak workmanship cast a bad light on the new compact. The famed Road Runner badge continued, now as an option package for the Volaré (*above*). Included was a 318 V-8 (with a two-barrel 360 optional), three-speed floor-mounted transmission, heavy-duty suspension, exterior stripes, and sporty interior trim.

1976 Production

Chrysler
Cordoba	120,462
Newport	28,387
Newport Custom	27,928
Town & Country	5,539
New Yorker Brougham	39,837
Total	222,153

Dodge
Dart	68,538
Aspen	219,449
Coronet	41,163
Charger	65,900
Monaco	35,591
Total	430,641

Plymouth
Valiant	85,686
Volaré	291,619
Fury	102,847
Gran Fury	39,510
Total	519,662

Imports
Dodge Colt	48,542
Plymouth Arrow	30,430
Total	78,972

1976 Engine Availability

Chrysler
No. Cyl.	Disp., cid	bhp	Availability
V-8	318.0	150	O-Cordoba
V-8	360.0	170/175	O-Cordoba, Newport/Custom
V-8	400.0	175	S-Cordoba, Newport/Custom; O-New Yorker Brougham
V-8	400.0	210	O-all
V-8	400.0	240	O-Cordoba
V-8	440.0	205	S-T&C, New Yorker Brougham; O-Newport/Custom

No. Cyl.	Disp., cid	bhp	Availability
V-8	400.0	185/240	O-Coronet, Charger
V-8	400.0	210	O-Monaco
V-8	400.0	255	O-Coronet
V-8	440.0	205	O-Monaco

Dodge
No. Cyl.	Disp., cid	bhp	Availability
I-6	225.0	100	S-all sixes
V-8	318.0	150	S-Aspen, Coronet exc wgns, Charger, Monaco exc wgns/Royal; O-Dart
V-8	360.0	170	S-Coronet wgns, Royal Monaco; O-Aspen, Coronet, Charger, Royal Monaco Brougham
V-8	360.0	175	O-Coronet, Charger
V-8	360.0	220	O-Dart, Coronet
V-8	400.0	175	S-Monaco wgns/Royal Brougham; O-Coronet, Charger, Monaco

Plymouth
No. Cyl.	Disp., cid	bhp	Availability
I-6	225.0	100	S-Valiant, Volaré, Fury exc wgn
V-8	318.0	150	S-Volaré, Fury exc wgn, Gran Fury sdn; O-Valiant
V-8	360.0	170	S-Fury wgns, Gran Fury Custom; O-Valiant, Volaré, Fury, Gran Fury
V-8	360.0	220	O-Valiant
V-8	400.0	175	S-Gran Fury wgns/Brougham; O-Fury
V-8	400.0	200/240	O-Gran Fury
V-8	440.0	205	O-Gran Fury

Imports
No. Cyl.	Disp., cid	bhp	Availability
I-4	97.5	83	S-Dodge Colt, Plymouth Arrow
I-4	121.7	96	S-Dodge Colt GT; O-Dodge Colt, Plymouth Arrow

1977

The industry's model-year output tops 9.1 million cars; Chrysler Corporation production is up 25 percent

Imported-car sales hit the two-million mark

Plymouth is sixth in output—behind Oldsmobile, Pontiac, and Buick

Dodge moves to seventh in the production race; Chrysler takes over ninth

General Motors begins its downsizing wave, but Ford and Chrysler cling longer to their large cars

The LeBaron and Diplomat "senior" compacts arrive, built off the Aspen/Volaré platform

LeBaron and Diplomat exhibit a boxy Mercedes-like look, with square headlights

Dodge renames its mid-size models Monaco, displacing Coronet; the full-size Monaco becomes the "Royal Monaco"

Dodge and Plymouth get their last 440-cid V-8 engines

Volaré/Aspen-based LeBarons and Diplomats sell strongly from the start, as customers turn to smaller vehicles

Cordoba hardtops come with any of three vinyl roof treatments, each featuring small "opera lights"

T-bar roofs are available for Cordoba, Aspen, and Volaré coupes

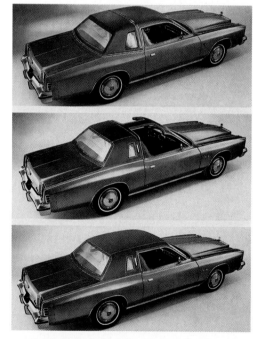

The Chrysler Cordoba, now in its third year, showed mildly revised front and rear styling, notably the grille (*above left*) and taillights (*top*). Also new was a "T-bar" hatch roof (*above*), with two removable smoked-glass panels, which Chrysler said provided a "convertible feeling." Two versions of the Cordoba were now offered, the base coupe and a new, slightly cheaper "S" edition. *Left:* In place of the T-bar roof (*center*), which cost $605, the Cordoba could be decked out with a "Crown" padded elk-grain landau vinyl roof (*top*), with an over-the-top illuminated lamp band, unique opera windows, and distinctive rear window treatment. This setup cost $579-$733. Also offered was a $116 "standard" Halo vinyl roof (*bottom*), a $112 Landau vinyl roof, and a $330 manual sunroof. Cordoba's base price this year was $5368. At $5433, the much larger Chrysler Newport hardtop sedan (*below*) appealed to 20,738 new-car buyers.

The "affordable" New Yorker Brougham hardtop sedan (*above*) listed at $7215. In the wake of Cordoba, Chrysler turned to an even smaller model: the mid-size LeBaron. Boxy in form, not unlike Mercedes, the coupe and sedan rode a 112.7-inch wheelbase and came in base or upscale Medallion trim, with new square headlights. Based on the Dodge Aspen/Plymouth Volaré, '77 LeBarons sold well: 54,851 units. A LeBaron Medallion sedan (*below left*) cost $5594. Note the large opera windows and wrapover roof band on the $5436 LeBaron Medallion (*below*).

Developed jointly by Calspan and Chrysler, this Research Safety Vehicle (*far left*) featured a reinforced body structure, soft elements, run-flat tires, and driver-side air bag. Chrysler's last turbine concept car was this LeBaron Turbine Special (*left*), with knife-edge-shaped front fenders and headlights hidden behind huge doors.

Sport-minded buyers of the compact Dodge Aspen coupe could order a $184-$207 R/T option (*above*), with blacked-out grille, E70x14 tires, and heavy-duty suspension. A $318 Super Pak option (*right*) added spoilers and louvered quarter windows, creating a car that begged to be noticed.

A Dodge Charger (*above left*) cost $5098; the Daytona package shown added $166 to the tab. The mid-size Coronet became Monaco for '77. At $4217, the deluxe-trim Brougham four-door (*above two*) attracted 17,224 buyers. The new Diplomat four-door (*above*), based on the Aspen, cost $5101, or $5313 in Medallion guise. Some 14,314 sedans were sold, compared to 23,238 coupes, offered in the same trim levels. The $4996 Royal Monaco Brougham sedan (*left*) saw 21,440 copies built.

Plymouth trimmed its full-size Gran Fury line to base and Brougham (*above left*) levels—plus Suburban wagons. Plymouth's highline mid-size Fury Salon (*left*) listed at $4185. Top mid-size seller was the $4132 Fury Sport coupe (*above*): 30,075 units. Note the plaid upholstery.

Like the Dodge Sportsman, Plymouth's Voyager Sport van (*top left*) came with ½-, ¾-, or 1-ton ratings. A ½-ton PB-100 van started at $5198, the long-wheelbase model, $5307. The boy-racer Road Runner (*above right*) could have a Super Pak with spoilers, wheel flares, and louvered side windows. The basic Volaré coupe (*background*) started at $3570. A Volaré wagon came in base trim, or as this $4271 Premier (*above*).

1977 Production

Chrysler

LeBaron	54,851
LeBaron Medallion	incl in above
Cordoba	183,146
Newport	76,389
Town & Country	8,569
New Yorker Brougham	76,342
Total	399,297

Dodge

Aspen	312,646
Charger	42,542
Monaco	94,080 *
Diplomat	37,552
Royal Monaco	53,434
Total	540,254 *

* Estimated

Plymouth

Volaré	382,418
Fury	116,162
Gran Fury	47,552
Total	546,132

Imports

Dodge Colt	70,876
Plymouth Arrow	47,599
Total	118,475

1977 Engine Availability

Chrysler

No. Cyl.	Disp., cid	bhp	Availability
V-8	318.0	135	O-Cordoba
V-8	318.0	145	S-LeBaron; O-Cordoba
V-8	360.0	155	O-Cordoba, Newport
V-8	360.0	170	O-Cordoba
V-8	400.0	190	S-Cordoba, Newport; O-New Yorker, T&C
V-8	440.0	195	S-T&C, New Yorker; O-Newport

Dodge

No. Cyl.	Disp., cid	bhp	Availability
I-6	225.0	100	S-Aspen exc wgns
I-6	225.0	110	S-Aspen wgns, Monaco; O-Aspen
V-8	318.0	135	O-Monaco, Charger
V-8	318.0	145	S-Aspen, Diplomat, Monaco exc wgns, Charger, Royal Monaco
V-8	360.0	155	S-Monaco wgns, Royal Monaco Brougham; O-Aspen, Monaco, Charger, Royal Monaco
V-8	360.0	170	O-Monaco, Charger
V-8	360.0	175	O-Aspen
V-8	400.0	190	S-Royal Monaco wgns; O-Charger, Monaco, Royal Monaco
V-8	440.0	195	O-Royal Monaco

Plymouth

No. Cyl.	Disp., cid	bhp	Availability
I-6	225.0	100	S-Volaré exc wgns
I-6	225.0	110	S-Volaré wgns, Fury exc wgns
V-8	318.0	145	S-Volaré, Fury exc wgns, Gran Fury exc Brougham wgns
V-8	360.0	155	S-Fury wgns, Gran Fury Brougham; O-Volaré, Fury, Gran Fury
V-8	360.0	170	O-Fury, Gran Fury
V-8	360.0	175	O-Volaré
V-8	400.0	190	S-Gran Fury wgns; O-Fury, Gran Fury
V-8	440.0	185/195	O-Gran Fury

Imports

No. Cyl.	Disp., cid	bhp	Availability
I-4	97.5	83	S-Dodge Colt, Plymouth Arrow
I-4	121.7	96	S-Dodge Colt GT; O-Dodge Colt, Plymouth Arrow

1978

The domestic auto industry enjoys its third-best year ever, but Chrysler Corporation's output sinks

Chrysler launches the first domestically built front-drive subcompacts: Dodge Omni and Plymouth Horizon

The initial Omnis and Horizons get an enlarged 1.7-liter Volkswagen engine

After only one year, Dodge Drops the Royal Monaco; Plymouth ditches the Gran Fury

It's also the final season for the mid-size Dodge Monaco and Plymouth Fury

The Corporate Average Fuel Economy (CAFE) standard takes effect, starting at 18 miles per gallon

A sign of the times: the 400/440-cid V-8s are available for the last time

Chrysler builds its last "big" Newports and New Yorkers on a 123.9-inch wheelbase

The mid-size Chrysler LeBaron has a standard Slant Six; two V-8s are optional

Dodge adds the sporty Magnum XE to sell alongside the Charger SE; a metal sunroof and T-top are newly optional

Chrysler sells all its European subsidiaries to Peugeot-Citroën

Lee Iacocca is fired from the Ford presidency by Henry Ford II, but is soon after hired to head Chrysler

Like most full-size Chryslers, this New Yorker Brougham St. Regis coupe (*top*) runs with the 190-bhp, 400-cid V-8; the big 195-bhp 440 V-8 was fading. The $493-$642 St. Regis package featured a padded canopy vinyl roof and opera windows. In this last year for truly massive Chryslers, New Yorker output fell to 11,469 coupes and 33,090 hardtop sedans. The $1898-cheaper Newport (*second from top*) was among the last true hardtops available, but only 8877 buyers cared. Cordoba (*above*) adopted vertically stacked rectangular headlights and a new grille mesh that dropped into the bumper. A $5724 Town & Country wagon (*right*) joined the LeBaron line ($5910 with a 318 V-8); 22,256 were built.

All Chrysler V-8s now used the Electronic Lean Burn System (*above*), which took data from sensors and adjusted ignition timing to deliver the leanest fuel mixture. Now Dodge's biggest cars, Monaco four-doors rode a 117.4-inch wheelbase. The $4568 Brougham sedan (*left*) found 8665 buyers. Two-door Monacos, like the $4507 Brougham coupe (*below left*), rode a 114.9-inch chassis; 6842 were sold. A new sporty Magnum XE coupe (*below center*) replaced the Charger Daytona. Its headlights sat behind a transparent panel (*below*).

The Dodge Diplomat coupe (*above left*) and sedan (*above center*) now listed three trim levels: budget "S," base, and top-line Medallion. A single base wagon was also added. The compact Aspen wore a restyled grille, and got a lock-up torque converter. This $4253 wagon (*above*) wears the $221 Special Edition woodgrain group. Aspen wagons sold well, 61,917 for '78. Dodge sprung a surprise with the hot "Li'l Red Truck" (*left*), sometimes called the Li'l Red Express. Costing about $5000, some 7306 examples were sold in 1978-79.

This Plymouth Horizon cutaway (*top right*) shows its transverse-mounted engine and Iso-Strut front suspension, which had an anti-sway bar. Even the Omni/Horizon engine (*above*) used Chrysler's Electronic Lean Burn system. A four-speed gearbox was standard; an automatic transaxle cost $303. Power steering listed at $148.

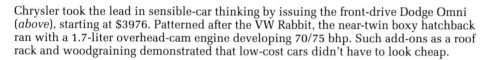

Chrysler took the lead in sensible-car thinking by issuing the front-drive Dodge Omni (*above*), starting at $3976. Patterned after the VW Rabbit, the near-twin boxy hatchback ran with a 1.7-liter overhead-cam engine developing 70/75 bhp. Such add-ons as a roof rack and woodgraining demonstrated that low-cost cars didn't have to look cheap.

Above: Plymouth's Super Coupe (*foreground*) exhibited bold add-ons, while the Road Runner, in red, looked plainer. Both were option packages for the compact Volaré. Full-size Plymouths were gone, making the $4568 Fury Salon (*far left*) the top-line sedan; 14,964 were produced. Formerly a separate series, Premier was now an option group for the $3899 Volaré sedan (*left*), of which 100,718 were built.

Plymouth Arrows came in base, GS, and GT guise. The GS hatchback (*above*) stickered at $4541. The MCA-Jet 1.6-liter four made 77 horsepower, but GS/GT editions could have a 93-bhp Silent Shaft 2.0 four. About 28,000 Arrows were sold in the U.S. in 1978. Mitsubishi-built Arrows were joined by a new sporty Sapporo coupe, which rode a 99-inch wheelbase, compared to the Arrow's 92.1 inches.

Restyled a year earlier, this season's Plymouth Trail Duster Sport (*above*) had a newly expanded options list. Extra-cost goodies included a Hurst transfer-case shifter, CB radio, and skylight sunroof. The base engine remained the 225-cid, 100-bhp Slant Six. Four V-8 choices were offered, from 318 to 440 cid. Prices for the two-wheel-drive PD-100 series started at $4647. With full-time four-wheel drive, a PW-100 stickered at $5684.

1978 Production

Chrysler

LeBaron	167,690 *
Cordoba	124,825
Newport	38,955
New Yorker Brougham	44,559
Total	376,029 *

* Estimated

Dodge

Omni	81,611
Aspen	197,707
Charger/Magnum	58,231
Monaco	54,851
Diplomat	78,642
Total	471,042

Plymouth

Horizon	106,772
Volaré	256,778
Fury	137,579
Total	501,129

Imports

Dodge Colt	42,909
Dodge Challenger	*
Plymouth Arrow	28,000 **
Plymouth Sapporo	*
Total	101,336 **

* Combined total: 30,427
** Approximate

1978 Engine Availability

Chrysler

No. Cyl.	Disp., cid	bhp	Availability
I-6	225.0	90	O-LeBaron
I-6	225.0	110	S-LeBaron
V-8	318.0	140	O-LeBaron, Cordoba
V-8	318.0	145	S-LeBaron; O-Cordoba
V-8	360.0	155	S-Cordoba S; O-others, LeBaron
V-8	360.0	170	O-all
V-8	400.0	190	S-Cordoba, Newport, New Yorker; O-Cordoba S
V-8	440.0	185/195	O-Newport, New Yorker

Dodge

No. Cyl.	Disp., cid	bhp	Availability
I-4	104.7	70/75	S-Omni
I-6	225.0	90	O-Aspen exc wgns, Diplomat
I-6	225.0	100	S-Aspen exc wgns
I-6	225.0	110	S-Aspen wgns; O-Aspen, Diplomat, Monaco
V-8	318.0	140	S-Aspen, Diplomat, Magnum, Monaco exc wgns
V-8	318.0	150	S-Charger
V-8	360.0	155	S-Monaco wgns; O-Aspen, Diplomat, Magnum, Monaco
V-8	360.0	165	O-Aspen
V-8	360.0	170	O-Diplomat, Magnum, Monaco, Charger
V-8	360.0	175	O-Aspen, Charger
V-8	400.0	190	O-Magnum, Monaco, Charger

Plymouth

No. Cyl.	Disp., cid	bhp	Availability
I-4	104.7	70/75	S-Horizon
I-6	225.0	90	O-Volaré exc wgn
I-6	225.0	100	S-Volaré exc wgn
I-6	225.0	110	S-Volaré wgn, Fury
V-8	318.0	140	S-Volaré, Fury exc wgns
V-8	318.0	155	O-Volaré, Fury exc wgns
V-8	360.0	155	S-Fury wgns; O-Volaré, Fury
V-8	360.0	165/175	O-Volaré
V-8	360.0	170	O-Fury
V-8	400.0	190	O-Fury

Imports

No. Cyl.	Disp., cid	bhp	Availability
I-4	97.5	77	S-Dodge Colt and Challenger, Plymouth Arrow and Sapporo
I-4	121.7	93	O-Plymouth Arrow
I-4	155.9	105	O-Dodge Colt wgn and Challenger, Plymouth Sapporo

Chapter 14

Iacocca to the Rescue: 1979-83

Chrysler Corporation had tried to stay competitive in the late Seventies by making reasonable, market-oriented product decisions. Yet, the decade ended with overwhelming financial woes. Although much of the pain was caused by outside factors (federal mandates, in particular), management had consistently displayed horrid timing. Even the laudable Omni/Horizon subcompacts would have sold more strongly had they been introduced in 1974, before shoppers returned to a short-lived big-car binge. More serious, the company had grown grossly inefficient—bloated, bedazzled, foundering.

Following up on strong Omni/Horizon first-year sales, Chrysler launched hatchback coupe variants for 1979. Named 024 at Dodge and TC3 at Plymouth, the nimble little 2+2s wooed import customers.

Dodge continued its Magnum XE for one more year, but dropped the Charger and Monacos. A new St. Regis shared its structure with the latest Chrysler Newport/New Yorker sedans—each drastically downsized. None sold powerfully. Chrysler's LeBaron added a Salon and woody-look Town & Country wagon, and a Cordoba option group harked back to the long-gone 300. Dodge fans had their last chance for a 360-cid V-8, in the Aspen. Having lost its Fury, Plymouth trailed Dodge in production. Tacking Plymouth badges onto captive

imports didn't fool the public. This year's entries were a new front-drive Champ from Mitsubishi, and a nearly identical Dodge Colt.

Long before his arrival, Lee Iacocca had acquired the status of a living legend. Heading Ford Division in the Sixties, he had fathered the Mustang. That dazzling feat provided a stepping-stone to the corporate presidency. During the Seventies, responsible for such quick-selling products as the Mustang II and Granada/Monarch, he grew *too* personally popular for chairman Henry Ford II. Fired on July 13, 1978, Iacocca faced a proliferation of job offers, but remained a "car guy." So, on November 2, 1978, he arrived at Chrysler Corporation as the new president, with an agreement that he was to succeed John Riccardo as chairman.

Chrysler not only stood near bankruptcy, but suggested "a state of anarchy," according to Iacocca's autobiography: "There was no real committee setup . . . no system of meetings to get people talking to each other." By February 1979, Chrysler was running out of cash. "Chrysler had no overall system of financial controls," Iacocca explained. "Nobody in the whole place seemed to fully understand what was going on. . . . I already knew about the lousy cars, the bad morale, and the deteriorating factories. But I simply had no idea that I wouldn't even be able to get

Chairman Lee Iacocca waits to shoot part of Chrysler's ad campaign, which pushed quality.

hold of the right numbers so that we could begin to attack some basic problems."

Over the next three years, Iacocca "had to fire 33 out of the 35 vice-presidents." For help, he turned to current and former Ford executives. Scads of workers got the axe. Costs were slashed by $500 million. The United Auto Workers Union even agreed to forego scheduled pay hikes. Adding to the obstacles, deposition of the Shah of Iran led to OPEC actions that sent gasoline prices skyward. Consumers who'd returned to big cars suddenly switched their tastes again. Even Chrysler's mid-sizers were too mammoth. A dismal drop in car sales sent Chrysler's cash-flow diagnosis from serious to critical. In August, the company's Supplemental Unemployment Benefit fund ran out—drained by 27,600 layoffs. Accountants tallied a staggering $1.1 billion annual loss. Market share dipped below 10 percent, as the inflation whirlwind pushed interest rates ever-higher. "Chrysler has no choice but to seek temporary assistance," warned chairman Riccardo. A "bailout" wasn't planned initially. Riccardo had first requested a freeze on government regulations, so the industry could concentrate on tooling for smaller models. Denied.

As an inveterate free-enterpriser, Iacocca was uneasy asking for government help, but it seemed the only recourse. Bankruptcy would have spelled disaster for dealers, suppliers, and employees. In August, G. William Miller, new Secretary of the Treasury, advised that the Carter Administration would consider loan guarantees.

Iacocca's ambitious five-year survival plan, presented to Congress in December 1979, called for $13.6 billion in spending cuts, and included a preview of proposed new models. "Here is the future of Chrysler," he proclaimed: the front-drive K-car and a revived Imperial for 1981; a luxury Chrysler-badged variant of the K-car for 1982; a restyled LeBaron/Diplomat and front-drive pickup for '83; then a K-based sports car; later, an Omni/Horizon replacement and possible V-6 engine. Many of his predictions arrived on schedule. Government aid (if any) would be limited to guarantees for loans made by private sources. Still, financiers had harsh words. "For most of them," Iacocca wrote, "federal help for Chrysler constituted a sacrilege, a heresy." Iacocca and Riccardo fought back in signed ads, asking: "Would America be better off without Chrysler?"

They also pointed to such precedents as guarantees to Lockheed and New York City.

Meanwhile, the 1980 season brought a smaller Cordoba—a crisp reskin of the LeBaron coupe—and closely related Dodge Mirada. Plymouth revived the Gran Fury nameplate, on a model similar to Chrysler's Newport. The Aspen/Volaré duo faced its final season.

In this appalling year, Chrysler's chance for survival looked particularly grim. Then, in mid-1980, a reluctant U.S. Congress issued the loan guarantees. Chrysler's survival package provided $3.5 billion in aid, including $1.5 billion in Federal loan guarantees. It also mandated $475 million in wage concessions from the UAW and $125 million from management.

The first salvo in the battle to save Chrysler was the K-car: the '81 Dodge Aries and near-twin Plymouth Reliant. Everyone knew that Chrysler had staked its near-term future on the front-drive, new-wave compacts. If they didn't sell, Chrysler was doomed. A widely circulated wire-service photo showed a smiling Iacocca next to the first K-car. "And if this one sells," read the impudent caption, "we're gonna build another one right away."

Sales took off, not with a bang, but a whimper. Then, after the first few months, K-cars were moving nicely. Plymouth output rose to sixth in the industry, due mainly to the Reliant. Even more important than K-car success was the fact that its platform could—and would—spawn a long series of front-drive spinoffs. Meanwhile, the traditional rear-drive Diplomat earned a touch-up, and would carry on into 1989. Chrysler's comparable New Yorker added a pricey Fifth Avenue option package.

In addition to the "bet-the-company" K-cars, Iacocca wanted a new flagship, to assure the public of Chrysler's future. Result: a revived Imperial—actually a reskin of the second-generation Cordoba, carrying a fuel-injected V-8. Its distinctive "bustleback" rear end was not unlike the recently restyled Cadillac Seville. Hailing from Canada, the $18,300 Imperial was to be built with quality uppermost, including a 5.5-mile road test. Yet, only 7225 went to customers in the first season.

Chrysler lost "only" $475 million in 1981, thanks largely to the K-car and drastic belt-tightening. The next year was a bad one for the industry as the American economy sagged, but actually brought Chrysler a $170 million profit. How? By selling the lucrative Chrysler Defense tank-making operation—a "last resort" step.

Two luxury K-car spinoffs arrived for 1982: an all-new Chrysler LeBaron, and similar Dodge 400. Slightly longer than K-cars, the two sold well. Heralding a confusion of names in the Eighties, the former LeBaron now wore a New Yorker

badge, while the prior version of that model evaporated. Dodge's Diplomat was cut to a four-door sedan, aiming mainly at taxi/police fleets. Plymouth's near-twin revived the Gran Fury badge. These two continued as Chrysler's "full-size" models, as the bigger rear-drive models faded away.

At mid-year, Chrysler added a woody-look LeBaron Town & Country wagon, plus a brace of convertibles: a LeBaron from Chrysler and a 400 from Dodge. Iacocca earns credit for the brilliant ragtop revival, a decade after the last open car to wear any Chrysler badge. Also in mid-season came an Omni-based Charger, available with the 2.2-liter K-car engine—a return to performance, if on a diminutive scale.

Imperial sales shrank, as its price rose. Seeking yet other markets, Dodge offered its first car/pickup, based on the 024 coupe and named Rampage; Plymouth's version was the Scamp. Chrysler then issued a handful of stretched-wheelbase front-drive limousines, based on the K-car. Chrysler was making versatile use of each platform. Yet another stretch of the K-car begat Chrysler's E Class of 1983. Sales failed to boom, but Dodge's similarly stretched 600 fared better. A sportier 600 ES sought the growing Eurosedan market.

Chrysler's available Electronic Voice Alert, delivering warnings in a synthesized voice, seemed to irritate as many drivers as it informed. Mid-year brought the first front-drive New Yorker, wearing a blind-quarter padded vinyl roof. Imperials rolled off their Canadian assembly line for the last time; Cordoba and Mirada confronted their final year. At mid-season, Dodge's mini-coupe added a racy—and swift—Shelby Charger edition. All of Plymouth's coupes adopted the Turismo badge, but Plymouth dropped to ninth place.

Due mainly to offshoots of the K-car, Chrysler Corporation's balance sheet went from red to black by 1983, when Iacocca proudly announced a $925 million profit—biggest in the company's long history. His personal appearances in TV commercials surely helped sales, too. In July, Iacocca announced that he was ready to pay back major creditors—seven years ahead of schedule. A week later, he presented bankers with a blown-up check for $813,487,500. His bold gamble had paid off, but was he really a wizard? Iacocca later insisted that he'd achieved nothing that another correct-thinking executive couldn't have accomplished. Perhaps, but most observers credit Iacocca's personality, his perseverance, his progressive ideas—not unlike the way in which Walter Chrysler had proven himself a corporate fix-it man six decades earlier.

Chrysler had been restored to health, lean and in fighting trim—eager to face the Eighties with its corporate head held high. Still, Iacocca's job was far from over.

1979

The second energy crisis begins in the spring, aggravated by a severe economic downturn and double-digit inflation

Auto sales start strong, but soon suffer from the fuel scare and soaring prices

Chrysler Corporation's model-year output tumbles 15 percent

Dodge finishes in the seventh spot, Plymouth ninth

Chrysler's market share dips below 10 percent

Omni/Horizon-based Dodge 024 and Plymouth TC3 coupes debut

The new Dodge St. Regis is kin to the downsized Chrysler Newport/New Yorker sedans

A 360-cid V-8 is the biggest corporate engine

The Dodge Charger is gone, leaving the Magnum XE coupe to carry on

Chrysler's financial woes worsen: sales are down 17.8 percent, and the corporation loses a record $1.1 billion

Chairman John Riccardo seeks advance tax credits, but this is denied by the government

Lee Iacocca is elected chairman, succeeding Riccardo; J. Paul Bergmoser is named president

Iacocca later writes in his autobiography that Chrysler Corporation in 1979 was in "a state of anarchy."

This Chrysler Cordoba (*top*) contains a 360-cid V-8, but a 135-horsepower, 318-cid V-8 came standard. Base price for the '79 model was $6337. More than 16,000 Chrysler New Yorker four-door sedans (*second from top*) carried a Fifth Avenue Edition option package, featuring edge-lit rear quarter windows and wire-wheel covers. Despite downsizing to a 118.5-inch wheelbase—on the same platform as prior mid-size cars— New Yorker/Newport sedans still looked impressively large. In a record year for Detroit, sales surged. Headlights were exposed on the Newport (*above and right*), while New Yorkers sported concealed lamps. Newport sedans could have either a 110-bhp Slant Six (not very popular), or a 318- or 360-cid V-8. Prices began at $6405 for the six-cylinder Newport, $6720 with a V-8. New Yorkers were all V-8-powered, and far more expensive, starting at $10,026. Output: 78,296 Newports, 54,640 New Yorkers.

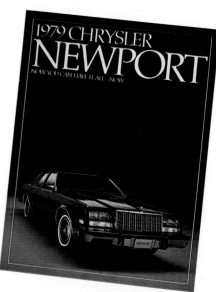

A unique cross-bar grille identified the Chrysler Cordoba "300" (*above*), added at mid-year. Harking back to the old 300-Series Chryslers, this specially trimmed coupe had bucket seats inside. With its 195-horsepower rendition of the 360-cid V-8, a "300" delivered fine performance for its time, despite its "road-hugging" 3880-pound curb weight. The $8034 sticker price topped that of the everyday Cordoba by $1697. Billed as "the most exclusive Chrysler you can own," the New Yorker Fifth Avenue Edition (*left*) wore a Laredo grain vinyl landau roof and a Champagne-colored interior. The option group cost as much as $1500 extra.

Chrysler's LeBaron Town & Country station wagon (*right*) displayed simulated teak/ash woodgraining; alternatively, the wagon could be ordered with plain bodysides. Two versions of the Slant Six engine were available, with 100 or 110 net horsepower, as well as the 135-bhp 318 V-8. T&C prices began at $6331, and sales totaled 19,932 units. A LeBaron Medallion four-door sedan (*below*) stickered at $6425 with the 225-cid Slant Six, or $6556 with the 318 V-8. All LeBarons rode a 112.7-inch wheelbase—2.2 inches shorter than Cordoba's. A power sunroof was optional (at $827) on the Medallion coupe (*bottom right*), which commanded $6017 with the base 100-bhp six, or $6328 with a V-8. Medallions sold better than base-model LeBarons, 46,803 versus 25,284, or the new mid-range Salon (36,480 built). The LeBaron nameplate harked back to the Thirties coachbuilt era, and survived into the Nineties on a front-drive Chrysler.

Dodge's Charger was gone, but the Magnum hung on for a second season, as a counterpart to Chrysler's Cordoba. A simple but bold slat-style grille gave the $6039 Magnum XE coupe (*left*) an assertive look. Headlights sat behind transparent covers, in a front end that drew considerable praise. Note the unusual two-toning on this Magnum XE (*below left*), with the optional T-bar glass roof. A total of 1670 Magnums were ordered with the GT package, which made the sporty coupe quite roadable. A St. Regis sedan (*below center*), kin to Chrysler's downsized Newport on a 118.5-inch chassis, joined the Dodge line-up with a $6532 base sticker.

Dodge Diplomats (*right*) offered a choice of five engines. The Slant Six had 100 or 110 horsepower, the 318-cid V-8 put out 135 bhp, and the 360 V-8 delivered 150 or 195. Coupes and sedans came in base, Salon, or Medallion trim. The $6127 station wagon, of which 9511 were built, came only as a mid-level Salon, with wood-look trim optional.

Sixties folk had a "Whole Earth Catalog." Car fans got a "Whole Dodge" book.

For the last time, a Dodge Aspen R/T coupe (*above*) could hold a 360-cid V-8, rated at 195 bhp. This year's R/T—a $651 package—flaunted "strobe" lower-body striping; sport mirrors were painted body color. Note the louvered quarter windows. Ambitious Aspen fans could even order a "finish-it-yourself" kit-car racer this year. Base-priced at $4516, an Aspen station wagon (*above right*) could be had with a Special Edition exterior package, which included simulated woodgraining. This Aspen four-door sedan (*below*) has the SE package, which cost as little as $100 extra. Aspens could have a Slant Six, or a 318 or 360 V-8. Sedans handily outsold coupes and wagons: 62,568, 42,833 and 38,183, respectively.

Engine options for a Dodge Aspen police car (*left and above*) ranged from a tame 225-cid Slant Six to a hotter 360 V-8 with dual exhausts. Aspens promised "efficiency and rugged . . . engineering."

No pickup on the market looked anything like a "Li'l Red Truck" (*right*), part of Dodge's "Adult Toy" line. Packed with panache, the short-wheelbase, Utiline D150-based pickup—sold only in Medium Canyon Red—sported lofty exhaust stacks reminiscent of an 18-wheeler, plus real oak wood panels along and inside the cargo bed. Note the running boards and slotted wheels on this example. A specially tuned variant of the police 360-cid V-8, with twin-snorkel induction into a Holley four-barrel carburetor but devoid of emissions gear, delivered 225 horsepower and 295 pounds/feet of torque. The Adventurer cab contained either bench or bucket seating. This truck is a collectible nowadays.

Dodge claimed that its new Omni-derived 024 (*left*) had captured "the crisp look of an expensive European sports car." A luggage rack was optional on the sporty 2+2 coupe. Priced at $4864, the 2195-pound hatchback rode a 96.7-inch wheelbase and carried a 70-bhp, 104.7-cid four. Plymouth's TC3 version differed little; both tempted buyers who ordinarily might have shopped for an import. Selling well in its second year was the plain-but-faithful $4469 Omni sedan (*below*). A rear defroster, AM radio, and whitewall tires came standard. Sedan sales reached 84,093 units.

Imported from Japan since 1978, the rear-drive Dodge Challenger coupe (*below*) wore minimal trim. The Mitsubishi-built sport coupe sold for $6487, with a standard 1.6-liter, 77-horsepower four-cylinder engine. A 2.6-liter (156-cid) four was optional, producing a more satisfying 105 horsepower. Note the slanted louvers to the rear of the quarter window. Even a Dodge Colt station wagon (*below right*) could have woodgraining on its bodysides. A new line of front-drive Colts, also from Mitsubishi, became available this year. Marketed alongside the rear-drive series, they ran with 1.4- or 1.6-liter engines.

A Plymouth Volaré sedan (*above*) promised "comfort and style," especially with the Premier option group. Less bold than a Road Runner, especially with whitewall tires, Plymouth's Duster package for the Volaré coupe (*right*) included louvered quarter windows for an extra $30, or could be ordered with plain panes. A Duster decor group added $90 more. A sunroof was optional on the subcompact Plymouth Horizon (*below*), which started at $4469. Horizon sedan production neared 100,000 units, but with only two series to sell (subcompact and compact), Plymouth's sales total sank below Dodge's.

Plymouth's Volaré Road Runner (*above*), shown with an optional T-bar roof, strutted "strobe" striping like the comparable Dodge R/T coupe. Engine options reached all the way to a 195-horsepower, 360-cid V-8. Volaré coupe prices started at $4387. Champ (*below*) was Plymouth's latest import, a front-drive hatchback minicar—nearly identical to Dodge's Colt—on a 90.6-inch wheelbase. A 1.4-liter, four-cylinder engine was standard, a 1.6-liter four optional. Plymouth dealers also sold the rear-drive Arrow sport coupe.

Weighing in at 2195 pounds, Plymouth's new Horizon-based TC3 hatchback 2+2 (*above*) could have an optional Sport Appearance package, including a rear spoiler, for as little as $278 extra. Starting at $4864, the "fasthatch" coupe rode a 96.7-inch wheelbase (2.5 inches shorter than Horizon), and differed little from Dodge's 024. A Rallye package was also offered, but proved to be less popular than the Sport option. TC3 sales totaled a solid 63,715 units.

Plymouth's sporty rear-drive Sapporo coupe (*above*) wore less trim in '79; the vinyl roof was dropped, and 12,322 were sold. Dodge's Challenger was similar.

The Mitsubishi-built Plymouth Arrow (*above*) wore rectangular headlights alongside a new grille, plus a bigger back window. The boldly trimmed "Fire Arrow" coupe was one of five rear-drive models. Fire Arrows featured wider tires on cast aluminum wheels and a 2.6-liter "Silent Shaft" engine. Others had a standard 1.6-liter four, with the 2.6 as an option. Developed for the U.S. Department of Energy by Chrysler and the General Electric Research & Development Center, the ETV-1 electric test vehicle (*right*) had a 75-100 mile range "under certain load conditions." According to Chrysler, the experimental car stressed "performance, driveability, comfort, and sleek, efficient design."

1979 Production

Chrysler

LeBaron	128,499
Cordoba	88,015
Newport	78,296
New Yorker	54,640
Total	349,450

Dodge

Omni	141,477
Aspen	143,584
Magnum	30,354
Diplomat	53,879
St. Regis	34,972
Total	404,266

Plymouth

Horizon	162,763
Volaré	209,686
Total	372,449

Imports*

Dodge Colt (FWD)	60,521
Dodge Colt (RWD)	29,215
Dodge Challenger	14,166
Plymouth Champ	27,031
Plymouth Arrow	21,829
Plymouth Sapporo	12,322

* Calendar year

1979 Engine Availability

Chrysler

No. Cyl.	Disp., cid	bhp	Availability	No. Cyl.	Disp., cid	bhp	Availability
I-6	225.0	100	S-LeBaron	I-6	225.0	100	S-Volaré
I-6	225.0	110	S-Newport; O-LeBaron	I-6	225.0	110	O-Volaré
V-8	318.0	135	S-LeBaron, Cordoba, Newport; O-NY	V-8	318.0	135	S-Volaré
				V-8	360.0	195	O-Volaré
V-8	360.0	150	S-NY; O-others				
V-8	360.0	195	S-"300"; O-others				

Imports

No. Cyl.	Disp., cid	bhp	Availability
I-4	86.0	70	S-Dodge Colt (FWD), Plymouth Champ
I-4	97.5	77	S-Dodge Colt (RWD) and Challenger, Plymouth Arrow and Sapporo; O-Dodge Colt (FWD), Plymouth Champ
I-4	121.7	93	O-Plymouth Arrow
I-4	155.9	105	S-Plymouth Fire Arrow; O-Dodge Colt (RWD) wgn and Challenger, Plymouth Sapporo

Dodge

No. Cyl.	Disp., cid	bhp	Availability
I-4	104.7	70	S-Omni
I-6	225.0	100	S-Aspen, Diplomat
I-6	225.0	110	S-St. Regis; O-Aspen, Diplomat
V-8	318.0	135	S-Aspen, Diplomat, St. Regis, Magnum
V-8	360.0	150	O-Diplomat, St. Regis, Magnum
V-8	360.0	195	O-Aspen, Diplomat, St. Regis, Magnum

Plymouth

No. Cyl.	Disp., cid	bhp	Availability
I-4	104.7	70	S-Horizon

1980

The recession deepens; domestic car sales suffer more than imports

All four major domestic automakers finish the year "in the red"

U.S. automakers lose $2.4 billion, as car sales fall below nine million

Chrysler Corporation's model-year output sinks 32 percent, to fewer than 765,000 cars

Chairman Lee Iacocca secures the needed federal loan guarantees to survive

Chrysler workers relinquish $622 million in salary and benefits, a requirement for the company to qualify for loan guarantees

The second-generation Chrysler Cordoba debuts

This is the final year for the 360-cid V-8

Mirada displaces Magnum in the Dodge lineup

De Tomaso and Turismo options are available for the Dodge 024/Plymouth TC3 mini-coupes

The final Aspen/Volaré models are built

By the end of 1980, Chrysler has used $800 million of the loan guarantees

Chrysler loses more than $1.7 billion; federal loan guarantees begin at mid-year

Show cars for '82 include the Cordoba de Oro and a Stealth 2+2 hatchback

The fanciest second-generation Cordoba was the Crown (*above*), with a padded landau vinyl roof and wrapover band, plus opera lights and windows. Wire wheel covers cost extra, but "premier" covers were standard. Essentially a reskin of the LeBaron, the reworked Cordoba (*right*) rode a 112.7-inch wheelbase. Styling was crisper and more formal, with the familiar long-hood/short-deck profile featuring modestly smaller dimensions. Engines: a Slant Six or 318- and 360-cid V-8s.

Few spokesmen have ever been as tied to a single product as Ricardo Montalban (*left*) was to the Cordoba. The popular actor's promotional duties for Chrysler extended into the '80s, as the stylish coupe entered its second incarnation. A special gold Chrysler "Cordoba de Oro" (*below*) appeared at the Chicago Auto Show—along with a Crown Corinthian Edition. The show car sported a simulated convertible top and gold-line tires on wire wheels with medallion centers crafted by the Franklin Mint. Demonstrating "understated elegance," sprayed in pearlescent gold, the coupe also wore hand striping in a darker gold hue. "Cordoba," the company said, "brings old world tradition and quality to a new fuel efficient package."

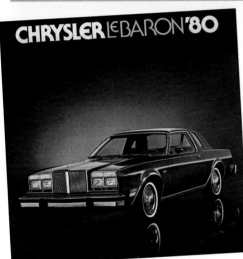

CHRYSLER LeBARON **'80**

The two-door Chrysler LeBaron (*above*) could have an LS "Limited" option group with distinctive two-toning. Coupes and sedans came in base, Salon, and Medallion dress, plus a cheaper Special sedan. Town & Country wagons again were bedecked with dimensional simulated wood. The LeBaron (*left*) came with a standard Slant Six and TorqueFlite, but a V-8 was available.

Right: Chrysler's sixth-generation turbine engine, dating from the 1960s, used a split accessory drive system. A seventh-generation turbine, unveiled in the late '70s, had split accessory drive, more efficient electronic fuel control, but less power. Chrysler's final turbine car was a nearly stock 1980 Mirada, with the 105-horsepower, seventh-generation engine. By then, the U.S. government had become heavily involved, awarding contracts to each Big Three automaker (the result of two OPEC fuel crises). Engineers managed to minimize throttle lag, boost fuel economy, and reduce hydrocarbon and carbon monoxide emissions to acceptable levels. Still, the turbines produced excessive oxides of nitrogen. With the company facing bankruptcy, and the new Reagan Administration vowing to slash the budget, the Department of Energy canceled Chrysler's contract. A truly promising eighth-generation turbine design was in the works when Chrysler abandoned the project in March 1981, having spent more than $100 million over a quarter of a century.

The St. Regis four-door sedan (*above*) continued as Dodge's largest model, promoted as "regular size" and again closely related to Chrysler's Newport and New Yorker. Sales of all three fell dramatically—causing additional distress to the corporation's anemic balance sheet. St. Regis power stemmed from an emissions-restricted 90-horsepower Slant Six, a 120-bhp 318 V-8 or, for the last time, the 360-cid engine, delivering either 130 or 185 horsepower. Base-priced at $7129, the St. Regis weighed 3608 pounds. A new Touring Edition commanded at least $1677 extra, but included a padded full vinyl roof, formal backlight, and special medallions on the rear pillars.

An "S" option for the $6372 Dodge Diplomat Salon coupe (*left and above*), of which 6849 were built, provided high-back bucket seats, fancy wheels, and bold bodyside trim. Restyled with squared-off fenders, bolder grille, and a more formal roofline, Diplomats came in four classes. Coupes rode the shorter (108.7-inch) wheelbase of the Cordoba/Mirada, acquiring a closer-coupled profile. Only the Slant Six was offered in the two-toned Special Sport coupe. Base, Salon, and Medallion Diplomats could get the 120-bhp 318 V-8; the 360 V-8 was reserved for the St. Regis and Mirada, both headed toward extinction.

Woodgraining was included only on the higher-priced Salon edition of the Diplomat station wagon (*right*), but only 2664 were built. They listed at $7041 with the Slant Six, but many got the optional 318 V-8. The base wagon brought $695 less. This year's facelift failed to spark Diplomat sales, or those of the related Chrysler LeBaron. Both ended the season with substantially reduced volume, as Chrysler Corporation struggled to survive. Like most cars in the inflationary late '70s and early '80s, Chrysler products endured steep price hikes not only when the model year began, but again during the season.

Heir to Magnum and Charger, Dodge's latest personal-luxury coupe was the Mirada, riding a Diplomat-sized, 112.7-inch platform. Closely related to the new-generation Cordoba, it wore a Magnum-style horizontal-slat grille. Standard and "S" editions went on sale, along with a CMX option package (*above and left*). Base engines were the modest 90-horsepower Slant Six and 120-bhp, 318-cid V-8, but a Mirada moved more quickly with the 185-bhp, 360-cid V-8. In its final year, a basic compact Dodge Aspen four-door sedan (*below*) started at $5162, and 26,239 were sold. They could have either the Slant Six or a 318 V-8. The 360-cid V-8 faded into Aspen history.

Though small in size, a rear-drive Plymouth Fire Arrow (*right and below*) looked tempestuous with its flamboyant trim and white-letter tires. Beneath the hood of this hottest version of the Mitsubishi-built coupe lurked a 2.6-liter "Silent Shaft" MCA-Jet four-cylinder engine, along with all-disc brakes. Note the flip-out quarter windows and rear-post louvers. In this final year for the Arrow line, 15,718 were sold in the U.S. On the domestic small-car front, neither the Plymouth Horizon sedan nor its TC3 coupe derivative changed much; output totaled 94,740 and 67,738, respectively. Each subcompact continued with a Volkswagen-based 1.7-liter engine, yielding 65 bhp. Coupes could get a new "De Tomaso" option with a sport suspension and wider tires.

Premier option groups tempted 12,644 Plymouth Volaré buyers, including fanciers of the station wagon (*above*). A Plymouth Volaré four-door sedan (*above right*) could have a Slant Six or V-8. A modestly trimmed Special held only the six, but included automatic transmission and power steering. After a year without a full-size sedan, Plymouth had one again—the $6741 Gran Fury (*right*), akin to Dodge's St. Regis. A 360-cid V-8 might go under the hood, for an extra $457. Base models outsold the costlier Salon: 15,469 units versus just 3255.

Plymouth sent a special Turismo/Spyder (*left*), based upon the subcompact TC3 coupe, to the 1980 Chicago Auto Show. Here, Chrysler's senior product planner/designer Bob Marcks (*left*) discusses the sportster with Chuck Gunderson, the company's director of product planning. Painted European Red, the "contemporary roadster" wore black body moldings. Note the car's louvered quarter windows and tunnel-roof rear end. Said Mr. Marcks: "This is a great car for singles and couples who travel." Chrysler insisted it was "looking for public reaction" to the sporty coupe, presumably with an eye toward possible production at some later date. But, as has usually been the case with concept vehicles, such production never came to pass.

Headlights weren't evident on Plymouth's prototype two-seat Turismo/Spyder show car (*right*), which featured a T-bar roof (not a fabric top), despite its official designation as a "roadster." A mid-engine-style hatch replaced the TC3's rear seat, for extra storage space. Designed "for the fuel conscious sportscar buff of the 1980s," the concept coupe featured dual exhausts, a lowered suspension, Recaro leather bucket seats, and (to clear the roadway), an Italian air horn.

1980 Production

Chrysler
LeBaron	86,465 *
Cordoba	53,471
Newport	15,061
New Yorker	13,513
Total	168,510 *

* Estimated

Dodge
Omni	138,155
Aspen	85,469
Diplomat	42,200 *
Mirada	32,746
St. Regis	17,068
Total	315,638 *

* Estimated

Plymouth
Horizon	162,478
Volaré	109,772
Gran Fury	18,724
Total	290,974

Imports*
Dodge Colt (FWD)	83,711
Dodge Colt (RWD)	6,734
Dodge Challenger	12,924
Plymouth Champ	39,756
Plymouth Arrow	15,718
Plymouth Sapporo	10,263

* Calendar year

1980 Engine Availability

Chrysler

No. Cyl.	Disp., cid	bhp	Availability
I-6	225.0	90	S-all sixes
V-8	318.0	120	S-all V-8s exc "300"
V-8	360.0	130	S-Newport, NY
V-8	360.0	185	S-"300"

Dodge

No. Cyl.	Disp., cid	bhp	Availability
I-4	104.7	65	S-Omni
I-6	225.0	90	S-Aspen, Diplomat, St. Regis, Mirada
V-8	318.0	120	S-Aspen exc Specials, Diplomat, St. Regis, Mirada
V-8	360.0	130/185	O-St. Regis, Mirada

Plymouth

No. Cyl.	Disp., cid	bhp	Availability
I-4	104.7	65	S-Horizon
I-6	225.0	90	S-Volaré, Gran Fury

No. Cyl.	Disp., cid	bhp	Availability
V-8	318.0	120	S-Volaré exc Specials, Gran Fury
V-8	360.0	130	O-Gran Fury

Imports

No. Cyl.	Disp., cid	bhp	Availability
I-4	86.0	70	S-Dodge Colt (FWD) Plymouth Champ
I-4	97.5	77	S-Dodge Colt (RWD) Plymouth Arrow; O-Dodge Colt (FWD), Plymouth Champ
I-4	121.7	93	O-Plymouth Arrow
I-4	155.9	105	S-Dodge Challenger, Plymouth Fire Arrow and Sapporo; O-Dodge Colt (RWD) wgn

1981

Industry sales drop sharply to 8.5 million cars as the recession continues

Chrysler Corporation's market share edges upward, past 10 percent; however, losses total $475 million

Ford's directors briefly ponder a merger with Chrysler

Dodge launches the Aries K-body compact; Plymouth's Reliant differs little

The K-cars mission is to help "rescue" the ailing Chrysler Corporation

The Imperial nameplate is revived on a short-lived personal-luxury coupe

Chrysler's biggest V-8 is now 318 cubic inches

Electronics and quality were touted for the new "bustleback" Imperial

The big Chrysler Newport and New Yorker make their last appearance; the New Yorker name will continue on a smaller model

Dodge produces its last St. Regis sedans

The corporation revives the 5-year/50,000-mile warranty

A Voluntary Restraint Agreement limits U.S. importation of Japanese autos, but not trucks

K-cars get heavy publicity, long before they arrive in showrooms; media reports stress their vital role

Aries/Reliant sales start slowly, then catch hold

"Our new Imperial is an electronic marvel."

Lee A. Iacocca
Chairman of the Board, Chrysler Corporation

Digital instruments were one of the "electronic marvels" touted by Lee Iacocca (*above*) for the reincarnated Imperial (*below*). Related to the Aspen/Volaré duo, by way of Cordoba/Mirada, Chrysler's latest flagship held a fuel-injected version of the familiar 318-cid (5.2-liter) V-8, yielding 140 horsepower. Compared to the previous Imperial, dropped during 1975, the new one was nearly a foot shorter in wheelbase, and 20 inches shorter overall, but because it weighed close to two tons, performance and fuel economy were less than astounding. Likewise sales: just 7225.

One of the most distinctive cars of the year, the $18,311 Imperial coupe (*above and left*) featured hidden headlights and knife-edge fenders to complement its easy-to-spot "bustleback" rear end. A $1044 electric sliding roof was the sole option. Sales fell far short of forecasts, despite Frank Sinatra crooning "It's time for Imperial." Each one was driven 5.5 miles and checked carefully after assembly in Windsor, Ontario.

Medallion sedans and coupes continued as the top-line Chrysler LeBarons (*top*). More than 57 percent of Chrysler New Yorkers (*above*) had the Fifth Avenue option. Fleet customers urged Chrysler to keep its full-size sedans in production. The $7324 LeBaron Town & Country wagon (*above right*) again wore woodgrained bodysides; 11,100 were sold.

Chrysler's $7247 Newport sedan (*above*) returned for the last time in the lineup. This would also be the final season for the similarly R-bodied but more costly $10,872 New Yorker, on a 118.5-inch wheelbase. Smaller New Yorkers would carry that long-lived badge further into the '80s. Newports again could have either a Slant Six or V-8; New Yorkers were V-8 only. Top powerplant for both models was a 165-horsepower version of the 318-cid (5.2-liter) V-8.

Crown editions were gone, but a simulated convertible top was installed on nearly a thousand Chrysler Cordobas (*above*). A 130-horsepower V-8 was now the strongest Cordoba engine. Cordobas might have an optional Special Edition padded vinyl landau roof (*right*). A new, cheaper $6745 Cordoba LS sported a 300-style cross-bar grille, but sales nonetheless failed to take off.

Capped by a simulated classic-inspired convertible top, the Dodge Mirada CMX (*right and below*) established a handsome presence, even if big engines were extinct. A total of 1683 CMX option packages were installed on Miradas. Otherwise, changes were minimal on this cousin to Chrysler's Cordoba, which started at $7700 and weighed 3350 pounds. The base Slant Six engine added hydraulic valve lifters, and the sole alternative was a 130-horsepower, 318-cid (5.2-liter) V-8. Sport Handling and Roadability option groups were available, but on the performance level Dodge's personal-luxury coupe seemed a pale shadow of its more muscular Charger ancestors—and sold in fewer numbers than the Cordoba.

Sales of Dodge's St. Regis four-door (*above*) dropped sharply, to 5388, and the short-lived Touring Edition was abandoned. The top St. Regis engine was a 165-bhp version of the 318-cid V-8, available in no other Dodges this year.

Virtually unchanged this season, the Dodge Diplomat four-door sedan (*above*) was destined to remain on sale through the Eighties—going mainly to fleet customers—while coupes and station wagons faced extinction. Only two engine choices were offered: the standard Slant Six, with new hydraulic valve lifters, or a 130-horsepower, 5.2-liter V-8. The least-expensive Diplomat two-door (*above right*) was called a Sport Coupe. Diplomat station wagons came in either base or step-up Salon (*right*) dress, while the costlier Medallion trim level comprised only a coupe and sedan. Prices were up this year, ranging from $6495 to $7777. Diplomats soon would be the largest Dodges on the market, sticking with traditional rear-drive and V-8 power into 1989.

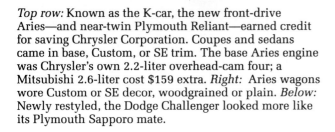

Top row: Known as the K-car, the new front-drive Aries—and near-twin Plymouth Reliant—earned credit for saving Chrysler Corporation. Coupes and sedans came in base, Custom, or SE trim. The base Aries engine was Chrysler's own 2.2-liter overhead-cam four; a Mitsubishi 2.6-liter cost $159 extra. *Right:* Aries wagons wore Custom or SE decor, woodgrained or plain. *Below:* Newly restyled, the Dodge Challenger looked more like its Plymouth Sapporo mate.

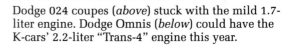

Dodge 024 coupes (*above*) stuck with the mild 1.7-liter engine. Dodge Omnis (*below*) could have the K-cars' 2.2-liter "Trans-4" engine this year.

Spotting a Dodge Charger 2.2 (*above*) from a distance wasn't difficult. At $399 extra, the 2.2-liter engine made the lightweight coupe a hot performer, without much sacrifice in fuel economy. Mileage-minded customers could now choose "Miser" editions of both the 024 coupe and Omni sedan. Mitsubishi-built Dodge Colts (*right*) ran with a 1.4- or 1.6-liter engine.

Four-wheel-drive gear is evident on this rendition of the Dodge Ram Royal SE Ramcharger sport-utility (*above*), which shared its front end and taillights with D-Series pickups, but rode a shorter 106-inch wheelbase. A 120-horsepower, 5.2-liter V-8 was standard. Base price was $9466, but $8257 bought a 2WD version. The Royal SE option group cost extra. Dodge claimed its imported Big Horn Ram 50 pickup (*left*) had the largest cargo area in its class. Base-model trucks used a 2.0-liter four, but the Royal and Sport got a 2.6-liter four with 105 bhp.

Airport limousine services, van pools—and big families—took a shine to the 127.6-inch-wheelbase Dodge Ram Royal SE 150 Maxi-Wagon (*right*), offered with either a Slant Six or 5.2-liter V-8. The Royal option package included extra trim and interior goodies. Few trucks looked more rugged than a four-wheel-drive Dodge Power Ram Custom SE W150 pickup (*below*), with a roll bar poking up from its cargo bed. Like other Dodge light trucks, the Power Ram Sweptline pickup (*below right*) displayed new aerodynamic styling with a bolder grille and fresh fenders, and offered more economical drivetrains. Both six and one-half- and eight-foot cargo beds were available.

Spiraling inflation remained, so Plymouth's Gran Fury sedan (*above and left*) endured a price hike for 1981, to $7387 with an 85-horsepower Slant Six. Packing a 318-cid V-8, the ante jumped to $7451. The Salon version was gone, leaving only a single model. Sales slumped dramatically, as just 7719 cars rolled off the line (only 468 with the six-cylinder engine). The Gran Fury badge would continue through the Eighties, but on a shorter wheelbase than this year's 118.5-inch span.

The new Chrysler-built 2.2-liter (135-cid) four-cylinder engine (*above*) featured a belt-driven overhead cam and hydraulic valve adjustment. Differing from Dodge Aries mainly in grille pattern, Plymouth's Reliant (*right and above right*) came as a coupe, sedan, or wagon, with a choice of two engines.

In TC3 form, Plymouth's Turismo (*above and left*) listed for $6149. A fuel-frugal "Miser" Turismo went for just $5299. Only a 63-horsepower engine was available at first, but an 84-horse 2.2-liter became available later. Plymouth Horizon four-door hatchbacks sold for $5690 in regular trim (*below*), or $5299 as a stripped-down Miser. Output totaled 58,547 units. As in the coupes, the base engine was a 1.7-liter four, but an 84-bhp 2.2-liter could be installed. Through the Eighties, Horizons generally outsold Dodge Omnis by a substantial margin.

Restyled for 1981, the Plymouth Sapporo (*top row*) more closely resembled Dodge's Challenger, with an eggcrate grille, taller deck, and wraparound back window. The 156-cid (2.6-liter) "Silent Shaft" four-cylinder engine made 105 horsepower. Sapporos rode a 99-inch wheelbase, with a standard five-speed manual gearbox or optional three-speed automatic. For $7588, power brakes and steering were included. Rectangular headlights and a new eggcrate-patterned grille marked this year's imported Plymouth Champ (*right*), which weighed about 1800 pounds, also produced by Mitsubishi in Japan, on a 90.6-inch wheelbase. The front-drive sub-compact hatchback held a transverse-mounted four-cylinder engine, of either 1.4- or 1.6-liter displacement, delivering 70 or 77 horsepower. A base-model Champ, which weighed in at about 1800 pounds, sold for $5263. An automatic transmission cost $286 extra, but only on Deluxe and Custom Champs with the larger engine.

1981 Production

Chrysler
LeBaron	43,133
Cordoba	20,293
Newport	3,622
New Yorker	6,548
Total	73,596

Dodge
Omni	77,039
Aries	155,781
Diplomat	24,170
Mirada	11,89
St. Regis	5,388
Total	274,277

Imperial
YS22	7,225

Plymouth
Horizon	94,859
Reliant	151,637
Gran Fury	15,739
Total	262,235

Imports*
Dodge Colt	42,796
Dodge Colt (RWD) wgn	**
Dodge Challenger	12,690
Plymouth Champ	42,128
Plymouth Sapporo	13,326

* Calendar year
** Included with Colt

1981 Engine Availability

Chrysler
No. Cyl.	Disp., cid	bhp	Availability
I-6	225.0	85	S-all sixes
V-8	318.0	130	S-all V-8s
V-8	318.0	165	O-Newport, NY

Dodge
No. Cyl.	Disp., cid	bhp	Availability
I-4	104.7	63	S-Omni
I-4	135.0	84	S-Aries; O-Omni
I-4	156.0	92	O-Aries
I-6	225.0	85	S-Diplomat, St. Regis, Mirada
V-8	318.0	130	O-Diplomat, St. Regis, Mirada
V-8	318.0	165	O-St. Regis

Imperial
No. Cyl.	Disp., cid	bhp	Availability
V-8	318.0	140	S-all

Plymouth
No. Cyl.	Disp., cid	bhp	Availability
I-4	104.7	63	S-Horizon
I-4	135.0	84	S-Reliant, late TC3; O-Horizon
I-4	156.0	92	O-Reliant
I-6	225.0	85	S-Gran Fury
V-8	318.0	130	O-Gran Fury
V-8	318.0	165	O-Gran Fury (Calif.)

Imports
No. Cyl.	Disp., cid	bhp	Availability
I-4	86.0	70	S-Dodge Colt (FWD) Plymouth Champ
I-4	97.5	77	S-Dodge Colt (RWD) wgn; O-Dodge Colt (FWD), Plymouth Champ
I-4	155.9	105	S-Dodge Challenger, Plymouth Sapporo; O-Dodge Colt (RWD) wgn

1982

"Engineering Excellence" was the principal reason for Chrysler's dramatic comeback, Lee A. Iacocca (*below*) explained on this brochure cover (*right*). Ever since 1924, in fact, engineering had been the propelling force at Chrysler Corporation. His claim that Chrysler's brand of change and hard work ultimately would "reshape" the entire domestic industry was typical of the outspoken chairman.

"When people ask me the reason for our resurgence, I answer in two words:

ENGINEERING EXCELLENCE.

Along with new personnel, new equipment and plenty of hard work, engineering excellence has enabled us to reshape the future of Chrysler Corporation and, in turn, the entire American automobile industry."

L. A. IACOCCA,
Chairman of the Board,
The New Chrysler Corporation

Hiked in price to nearly $21,000, the bustle-back Imperial (*below*) faltered badly on the sales front, despite heavy dealer discounts. Only 2329 were built for '82. Note the attractive wheels and hidden headlights. Just 279 buyers got an Imperial "Frank Sinatra Edition" (*bottom*), complete with unique emblems—plus tapes of the crooner's popular songs in a special console.

Priced lower than its Chrysler Cordoba mates, the LS edition (*above*) wore a crossbar grille. A simulated convertible top, at $554 extra, was installed on more than 1600 coupes. Cordoba's new landau vinyl roof (*right*) came in nine colors and with a wrapover molding. Lee Iacocca stunned the industry by authorizing production of a Chrysler LeBaron convertible (*below*). Based on the luxury compact, it arrived in base and Medallion trim.

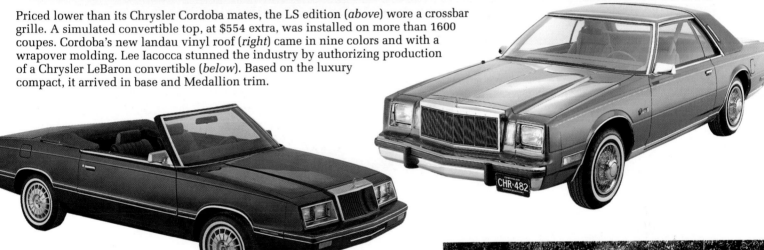

Chrysler New Yorkers (*above left and above*) rode a shorter 112.7-inch wheelbase, but kept rear-wheel drive. Like other models, the $10,781 sedan came in a choice of roof styles. Note the nearly vertical back window that accompanied the formal-look padded rear roof. Not only were LeBaron coupes transformed into convertibles, but Chrysler used the new front-drive LeBaron as a basis for extended-wheelbase limos (*left*), shown here in pre-production form.

309

This cutaway of a front-drive Chrysler LeBaron four-door sedan shows its transverse-mounted four-cylinder engine and suspension strut configuration.

Based on the K-cars introduced a year earlier, and replacing their rear-drive predecessors, Chrysler LeBaron sedans (*above*) came in two trim levels. Solid-section rear doors became a Chrysler hallmark. Two-door LeBarons (*above right*) held opera windows and had two engine choices. LeBaron Town & Country station wagons (*right*) were clad in dimensional imitation wood. Chrysler spent more than $75 million to equip the LeBaron's St. Louis assembly plant (*below*) with the latest technology, including 64 computerized robot welders.

A simulated convertible top was standard fare on a sleek Dodge Mirada coupe with the CMX option package (*above and left*). A total of 1474 CMX editions were sold, costing $935 more than a base Mirada. Note the premium turbine-style wheel covers, which held handsome P205/75R15 whitewalls. Mirada sales dipped sharply this year, as sharp (and economical) new front-drive Chryslers stole some of the thunder from mid-size, rear-drive models.

Dodge launched a sporty new 400 series (*above*), based on the K-car and closely related to Chrysler's fresh front-drive LeBaron. Two-doors arrived first, in base or premium LS trim, wearing opera windows in a part-vinyl roof. Four-door sedans came later, as did a convertible. *Above right:* Like LeBaron, the Dodge 400 held a transverse-mounted four-cylinder engine of 2.2- or 2.6-liter displacement, the latter produced by Mitsubishi. Though sharing basic dimensions with Aries, the 400 was slightly longer and far more plush.

Dodge issued a convertible at mid-year, shown here in prototype form (*left*). Both the Chrysler LeBaron and Dodge 400 ragtops were converted from coupes by Cars & Concepts, a Michigan specialty firm. Like all 400s, the convertible displayed a slat-style grille, similar to that installed on the Mirada coupes. Even the instrument panel hailed from the Aries/Reliant K-car, which served as a basis for the LeBaron and 400. Drivetrains and suspensions were identical, too. At $12,300, the convertible cost over $4000 more than a base 400 coupe. Now marketed only as a four-door, the Dodge Diplomat (*above*) sold fairly well to fleet customers. Prices started at $7750.

As before, Dodge Aries two-doors (*left*) came in base, Custom, and SE trim. Note the contrasting-color vinyl rear roof section. Some 19,787 two-doors were sold. More standard equipment this year made the compact Aries (and Plymouth Reliant) a better value because prices rose only moderately, now starting at $5990. Aries four-door sedans (*below left and below*) also came in three trim levels, wearing a plain or vinyl roof. The standard 2.2-liter four-cylinder engine got a new cooling fan. Options now included power front windows and 14-inch cast aluminum wheels. Four-door output totaled 52,268.

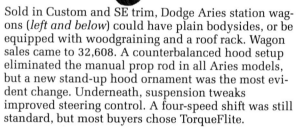

Sold in Custom and SE trim, Dodge Aries station wagons (*left and below*) could have plain bodysides, or be equipped with woodgraining and a roof rack. Wagon sales came to 32,608. A counterbalanced hood setup eliminated the manual prop rod in all Aries models, but a new stand-up hood ornament was the most evident change. Underneath, suspension tweaks improved steering control. A four-speed shift was still standard, but most buyers chose TorqueFlite.

Priced at $5799, the Dodge Omni 024 Miser (*top*) sold a bit better than the base coupe—or even the hot Charger 2.2, which started at $7115. Bodyside markings, two-toning, and a non-functional hood scoop made the Charger 2.2 (*above left*) easy to identify. In addition to basic, Custom (*above*), and Miser Omnis, Dodge offered a Euro-Sedan with blackout trim and Rallye gauges. Only 639 were built.

A Volkswagen-based, 104.7-cid (1.7-liter) four continued as the base powerplant for the Dodge 024 coupe (*above*), but the Charger 2.2's bigger engine signaled a return to performance at Dodge—albeit on a Lilliputian scale. Coupes were now marketed separately from Omni/Horizon sedans. Displaying the same front-end styling as the Charger, Dodge's Rampage (*right*) served as the first front-drive pickup truck from a Big Three automaker. Note the sloping hood and deep headlights. Sport versions had two-toning and other extras. An 84-horsepower, 2.2-liter engine handled performance chores. Sales reached 17,067 units in 1982.

Like Dodge equivalents, the Plymouth TC3 Miser (*above*) sold more strongly than the Custom or Turismo coupe. Its $5799 sticker price doubtless helped. A 2.2-liter engine under the TC3 Turismo hood (*left*) developed 84 horsepower. Performance got a big boost, but a Turismo cost $7115 and looked less aggressive than Dodge's Charger 2.2.

A Plymouth Reliant four-door sedan (*left*) exhibited quite a formal stance when fully dressed-up. The sedan had new roll-down rear windows, and all Reliants got a new no-link front anti-sway bar. Basic (*above*) and Miser Plymouth Horizons took the lion's share of sales, but 779 sedan customers got a costlier, blackout-trimmed Euro-Sedan.

Woodgraining and a roof rack helped give the Plymouth Reliant SE station wagon (*above*) a practical suburban personality. The 2.2-liter engine earned some improvements. Downsized to a 112.7-inch wheelbase, Plymouth's Gran Fury sedan (*right*) weighed 3345 pounds and cost $7750.

1982

Imported Plymouth Arrow pickups came in Royal (*left*), Custom, and Sport guise. Sports and Royals, which started at $6892, used the Mitsubishi 156-cid (2.6-liter) engine, packing 105 horsepower. Custom Arrow minitrucks carried a 122-cid four, good for 90 bhp. Neither the Plymouth Sapporo coupe (*center*) nor its Dodge Challenger counterpart changed much, following a restyling for '81. The Chrysler-Plymouth Stealth (*bottom*), a turbo 2.2 concept sports car, appeared at auto shows. Evolved from the TC3/024, the 2+2 hatchback featured flush window glass, full gauges, and Recaro leather seats. Production was not planned.

1982 Engine Availability

Chrysler

No. Cyl.	Disp., cid	bhp	Availability
I-4	135.0	84	S-LeBaron
I-4	156.0	92	S-LeBaron T&C; O-LeBaron
I-6	225.0	90	S-Cordoba, NY six
V-8	318.0	130	S-Cordoba, NY V-8s
V-8	318.0	165	S-Calif. Cordoba, NY V-8s

Dodge

No. Cyl.	Disp., cid	bhp	Availability
I-4	104.7	63	S-Omni
I-4	135.0	84	S-Aries, 400; O-Omni
I-4	156.0	92	O-Aries, 400
I-6	225.0	90	S-Diplomat, Mirada
V-8	318.0	130	O-Diplomat, Mirada

Imperial

No. Cyl.	Disp., cid	bhp	Availability
V-8	318.0	140	S-all

Plymouth

No. Cyl.	Disp., cid	bhp	Availability
I-4	104.7	63	S-TC3, Horizon
I-4	135.0	84	S-Reliant, TC3 Turismo; O-TC3, Horizon
I-4	156.0	92	O-Reliant
I-6	225.0	90	S-Gran Fury
V-8	318.0	130	O-Gran Fury
V-8	318.0	165	O-Gran Fury (Calif.)

Imports

No. Cyl.	Disp., cid	bhp	Availability
I-4	86.0	70	S-Dodge/ Plymouth Colt,
I-4	155.9	105	S-Dodge Challenger, Plymouth Sapporo

1982 Production

Chrysler

LeBaron	90,319
Cordoba	14,898
New Yorker	50,509
Total	155,726

Dodge

Omni	71,864
Aries	104,663
400	31,449
Diplomat	23,146
Mirada	6,818
Total	237,940

Imperial

YS22 Coupe	2,329

Plymouth

TC3	37,85
Horizon	37,196
Reliant	139,223
Gran Fury	18,111
Total	232,386

Imports*

Dodge/Plymouth Colt	75,031
Dodge Challenger	14,128
Plymouth Sapporo	13,326

* Calendar year

315

1983

Chrysler Corporation pays off $1.2 billion in federally guaranteed loans—seven years ahead of schedule

The corporation is earning money again: a $975 million profit for '83

Industry car sales grow to 9.1 million—up 14 percent

Some owners are annoyed by Chrysler's "talking" dashboard computer

A front-drive New Yorker joins the Chrysler lineup

The Chrysler E Class sedan is a stretch of the K-car

Dodge's stretched 400 sedan is called 600

The final Chrysler Cordobas and Dodge Miradas are built

A Charger nameplate replaces 024 on all subcompact Dodge coupes; Plymouth's near-clones wear a Turismo badge

A sporty Shelby Charger arrives at Dodge

The last "Slant Six" engines for cars are produced

Chrysler issues long-wheelbase Executive Limousines

A woody-look Town & Country convertible joins the LeBaron line at midyear; Mark Cross ragtops feature posh leather interiors, but plain bodysides

Lee Iacocca himself appears in Chrysler commercials

This is the last year (for now) for the slow-selling Imperial

After several years as a luxury option, the Chrysler New Yorker Fifth Avenue (*top and above center*) became a rear-drive model on its own—distinct from the new front-drive New Yorker, which was based on the K-car. Chrysler touted the Fifth Avenue's "aristocratic grille." Both the Slant Six and 318-cid V-8 engine were available, but this was the finale for the six. Except for a revised hood ornament, the last Chrysler Cordoba (*above*) looked about the same as before. Though Cordobas had helped enhance Chrysler's image in the late Seventies, sales had dwindled after the 1980 redesign, to just 13,471 for '83. The Imperial (*below*) was also in its final season, suffering the ignominy of a price cut. A mere 1427 coupes were produced.

This Chrysler two-seat convertible turbo prototype (*right*) appeared at selected auto shows in 1983, "to measure public interest in small specialty cars and evaluate production potential." In addition to a new 2.2-liter turbocharged engine, the open coupe had a five-speed manual gearbox, Euro-Sport suspension, and aerodynamically rounded front end. Its platform, spanning a shortened 90-inch wheelbase, stemmed from that used by the LeBaron line. Passengers could enjoy tunnel-style headrests in a handcrafted leather interior. A $15,595 Town & Country convertible (*below*) joined the LeBaron family in mid-year, displaying the same simulated wood on its body-sides as the familiar T&C station wagons. A total of 1520 were built, out of 9891 total ragtops. More than half of the plain-bodied ragtops came with the plush Mark Cross leather-trimmed interior.

Chrysler stretched the K-car wheelbase by three inches (to 103.3) to create the E Class sedan (*above*). Roomier in the back seat than the LeBaron, the new sedan featured revised rear-quarter styling. Chrysler's latest New Yorker was similar, but seated five instead of six and had a more formal roofline. A Mark Cross option with plush leather/vinyl upholstery added $696 to the $9341 E Class sticker. *Left:* The ever-versatile K-car's basic platform was stretched further yet to produce a Chrysler Executive Sedan and Limousine which sold for $18,900 and $21,900 respectively.

At $9731 each, 10,994 Chrysler LeBaron Town & Country station wagons (*above*) were produced for '83, all with attractive dimensional woodgraining and a roof rack. Standard on the T&C and optional on other models, a new Electronic Voice Alert system gave the driver aural warnings about 11 functions, via a synthesized human voice. Most owners soon grew tired of the voice, which tended to talk too much, and supplemented visual warnings on the dashboard. The rear compartment of the Executive Sedan (*left*) looked mighty inviting, with plush carpeting and separate seats. Legroom was vast in the sedan, as well as the seven-seat Limousine. Wheelbases were 124 and 131 inches, respectively, and curb weight came in at just under 3000 pounds.

Like Chrysler's Cordoba, the rear-drive Dodge Mirada (*above*) entered its final season, a vestige of the company's past. Base price was $9011. As usual, the CMX option (*left*) included a simulated convertible top. Dodge stretched the K-car's platform to get a new 600 series sedan (*below*), kin to Chrysler's E Class, led by the sporty ES. Base sedans had Torque-Flite, but the $9372 600 ES, of which 12,243 were built, got a new five-speed manual gearbox and sport handling gear.

With a wheelbase three inches longer than an Aries, and measuring 11 inches longer overall, the Dodge 600 four-door sedan (*above*) stickered at $8841. Both 2.2- and 2.6-liter four-cylinder engines were available. With 21,065 built, base models easily outsold the enthusiast-oriented ES.

Just one trim level of the Dodge 400 coupe (*above*) and sedan went on sale, as the short-lived LS edition disappeared. A two-door listed at $8014, and outsold the four-door, 11,504 to 9560. An intriguing idea—that unfortunately never turned into reality—was this Dodge 400 convertible with a rumble seat (*left*). The special ragtop appeared at auto shows "for evaluation as a possible future production model." By the time these cheerleaders from Farmington Hills, Michigan, were born, the rumble seat had long since gone the way of the dodo bird.

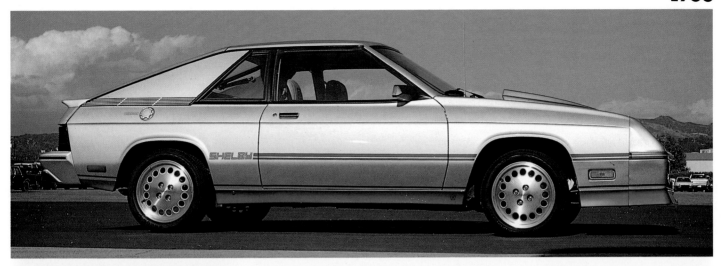

A high-performance variant of Chrysler's 2.2-liter engine powered the Dodge Shelby Charger (*top*), painted silver or blue and wearing single-section quarter windows. Even base coupes adopted the Charger nameplate. To squeeze 107 horses out of the 2.2-liter four (*above*), the Shelby folks boosted compression to 9.6:1 and revised the cam and exhaust. A five-speed was standard. A Dodge Rampage 2.2 mini pickup (*above right*) cost $7255 in base form, with an 84-bhp engine. Sales skidded to about 7500 units. Even Dodge Aries two-doors (*right*) displayed a rather formal roof treatment. A Peugeot-based 1.6-liter engine replaced the VW-derived 1.7 in the Dodge Omni (*below*). Few were sold, since the 2.2-liter four could be ordered.

Two- and four-wheel-drive versions of the Dodge Ramcharger sport-utility (*left*) had a 120-bhp V-8. This year only, Dodge Challengers (*below left*) could get a Technica performance package. Colts (*below*) were sold by Dodge and Plymouth dealers.

Plymouth added a Scamp GT pickup (*top*), kin to Dodge's Rampage. The TC3 was renamed Turismo (*above*); a larger engine powered the Turismo 2.2 (*right*).

Above left: Base-model Plymouth Horizons sold far better than the Custom series, though the price difference was only $230. The frugal Miser edition faded away, as did the slow selling Euro-Sedan. This Plymouth Voyager (*above*) would be the last traditional full-size van to bear that name, now that Chrysler was readying Dodge Caravan/Plymouth Voyager minivans with front-wheel-drive for 1984. Buyers could have a Slant Six or choice of two V-8s. The long-lived Slant Six engine went into the $8248 Plymouth Gran Fury Salon four-door sedan (*left*) for the last time. Optional this year, the 318-cid (5.2-liter) V-8 would soon be the sole engine offered.

Plymouth Reliant station wagons came in two trim levels, a $7636 Custom and this $8186 woody-look SE (*above*). The 2.2-liter base engine gained 10 bhp, to 94, mainly due to higher compression. With an EPA rating of 29-mpg city/41-mpg highway, Dodge/Plymouth compacts attracted economy-minded buyers. The base sedan sold best: 69,112 units.

A model adjustment hit the Plymouth Reliant lineup—neither the four-door sedan nor two-door coupe was available in the mid-range Custom series. Here (*above*), the $7417 SE sedan. A part-vinyl roof gave this two-door Reliant (*right*) a stately demeanor. A five-speed manual could now be ordered, but the four-speed remained standard and TorqueFlite was most often installed.

1983 Production

Chrysler

LeBaron	70,085
E Class	39,258
New Yorker	33,832
Cordoba	13,471
New Yorker Fifth Avenue	83,501
Executive	800 *
Total	240,947 *

* Estimated

Dodge

Omni	42,554
Charger	41,234
Aries	112,269
400	25,952
600	33,488
Diplomat	24,444
Mirada	5,597
Total	285,538

Imperial

YS22	1,427

Plymouth

Turismo	32,065
Horizon	46,471
Reliant	146,562
Gran Fury	15,739
Total	240,837

Imports

Dodge/Plymouth Colt	73,671
Dodge/Plymouth Colt Vista	4,303
Dodge/Plymouth Conquest	*
Dodge Challenger	*
Plymouth Sapporo	*

* Combined Total: 25,595

1983 Engine Availability

Chrysler

No. Cyl.	Disp., cid	bhp	Availability
I-4	135.0	94	S-LeBaron, E Class, NY
I-4	156.0	93	O-LeBaron, E Class, NY
I-6	225.0	90	S-Cordoba, Fifth Ave six
V-8	318.0	130	S-Cordoba, Fifth Ave V-8s

Dodge

No. Cyl.	Disp., cid	bhp	Availability
I-4	97.3	62	S-late Omni, Charger
I-4	104.7	63	S-early Omni, Charger
I-4	135.0	94	S-Charger 2.2, Aries, 400, 600; O-Omni, Charger
I-4	135.0	107	S-Shelby Charger
I-4	156.0	93	O-Aries, 400, 600
I-6	225.0	90	S-Diplomat, Mirada
V-8	318.0	130	O-Diplomat, Mirada

Imperial

No. Cyl.	Disp., cid	bhp	Availability
V-8	318.0	140	S-all

Plymouth

No. Cyl.	Disp., cid	bhp	Availability
I-4	97.3	62	S-late Turismo, Horizon
I-4	104.7	63	S-early Turismo, Horizon
I-4	135.0	94	S-Reliant, Turismo 2.2; Turismo, Horizon
I-4	156.0	93	O-Reliant
I-6	225.0	90	S-Gran Fury
V-8	318.0	130	O-Gran Fury

Imports

No. Cyl.	Disp., cid	bhp	Availability
I-4	86.0	70	S-Dodge/Plymouth Colt
I-4	97.5	77	O-Dodge/Plymouth Colt
I-4	155.9	105	S-Dodge Challenger, Plymouth Sapporo

Chapter 15

Minivans Help Create a New Chrysler: 1984-87

Some called it a miracle. Not only was Chrysler Corporation back in action, it was *prospering.* An accomplishment of this magnitude—difficult enough in good economic times—seemed astounding in an era of mounting inflation, soaring interest rates, and unprecedented competition from the ever-stronger imports.

Overhead had been slashed, operations streamlined, and favorable contracts with suppliers obtained. At the same time, funds were found to modernize Chrysler's aging factories and invest in advanced technology—an essential move to keep pace with the radically changing marketplace of the Eighties.

Starting with the K-cars, Chrysler had been issuing two new products a year. Each sold well, helped by competitive prices and improving workmanship—a vital component of the turnaround. Americans love a "comeback" story, whether in sports, entertainment, or business, and Chrysler gave them one to remember. Chairman Iacocca and his president, Harold K. Sperlich, had indeed transformed the company from a down-and-outer into a stunning success.

By 1984, the auto industry was finally beginning to recover, aided by declining gasoline prices, easing of interest rates—and a continuation of the Voluntary Restraint Agreement that limited Japanese auto imports. Chrysler's production more than doubled in the 1984 model year, and more good news was about to follow—though the end of the decade would see yet another downward slide.

This year's lineup barely resembled the selection of a few years earlier.

Chrysler stood far ahead of Ford in adopting front-wheel drive, and led GM in fuel-efficient models. The company further claimed to lead in robotics and computer-aided design/manufacturing. Chrysler also was the first Big Three company to establish a California design center—acknowledging the importance of that trend-setting market.

Now, the company had two spectacular front-drive products on tap: a hot coupe and a practical people-carrier. Their names: Daytona/Laser and Caravan/Voyager. Each was destined to make a major impact, earning raves along the way.

Yet another element of Iacocca's five-year plan, the Dodge Daytona and Chrysler Laser wore sleek, Porsche-like "fasthatch" bodies, on shortened renditions of the ever-versatile K-car platform. Though sales never approached those of the rear-wheel-drive Chevrolet Camaro and Ford Mustang, the Daytona symbolized a return to performance by the Dodge boys.

With optional turbocharger power, Lasers and Daytonas were particularly exciting—if somewhat crude—performers. The racy Daytona Turbo Z even sported ground-hugging lower-body extensions and a hatchlid spoiler. Not since the old Challengers and Barracudas of the early Seventies had Chrysler offered anything so tempting to sport/performance fans.

Also at Dodge, the 400 sedan departed, while "600" badges went on the coupe and stylish convertible—now available in ES trim, with a turbocharged engine. Turbos proved quite

The 1984 Plymouth Voyager minivan pioneered a new type of vehicle for active American families.

popular in several models, including LeBaron.

At Chrysler Division, what had been the New Yorker now took the Fifth Avenue badge. It captured more than 88,000 customers.

The foremost news of '84 wasn't a passenger car, but a minivan: the Dodge Caravan and nearly identical Plymouth Voyager, America's first front-drive compact vans. No longer than a K-car station wagon, these two set the pace for the phenomenal minivan boom. Roomy inside, Caravan/Voyager sat lower than rear-drive vans, for easy entry/exit and a car-like driving position. They were also billed as the first "garagable" vans. Through the mid-Eighties, they gave Chrysler its biggest infusion of profits.

Few realized that the design had first seen life back in 1973, scuttled because executives concluded that the marketplace wasn't ready for a minivan. A decade later, it was not only ready, but enthusiastic.

Dodge's Omni, meanwhile, added a short-lived GLH ("Goes Like Hell") edition—essentially, the Shelby Charger in an Omni body. Tap hard on the pedal, and this interpretation of the drab-but-popular subcompact turned into a small-scale stormer. If crude, it was also fun to drive, though torque steer in a turbocharged Omni was so horrid that one tester claimed the gas pedal worked as a "lane-change switch." Each year brought more standard Omni/Horizon features, as well as gradually improving workmanship.

With the demise of Cordoba/Mirada, the only rear-drive Chrysler products left were the Diplomat, Gran Fury, and Fifth Avenue, now powered only by the familiar 5.2-liter V-8. In addition to the Dodge/Plymouth Colt, dealers got new Mitsubishi-built wagons, named Colt Vista, plus a Conquest coupe evolved from the Mitsubishi Starion.

Chrysler next attacked the Euro-oriented premium sports sedan market, so favored by upscale "baby boomers." Chrysler LeBaron GTS and Dodge Lancer hatchback sedans debuted as 1985 models, produced at a new, highly automated plant in Sterling Heights, Michigan. Both normally aspirated and turbocharged versions of the 2.2-liter engine were offered, and their platform came from—what else?—the ever-versatile K-car.

The strong-selling Aries and Reliant earned an aero facelift, adding Luxury Editions. Chrysler's E Class, failing to find a niche in 1983-84, metamorphosed into the Plymouth Caravelle and managed to hang on through '88. Though similar to Dodge's 600 ES, Caravelle never came in a sporty edition.

In another name change, the last remaining rear-drive Chrysler became, simply, Fifth Avenue—still closely related to the fleet-targeted Diplomat and Gran Fury. Fifth Avenue sales jumped past 120,000, demonstrating that the traditional rear-drive luxury-car buyer hadn't yet become extinct.

Total car/truck sales hit a record 15.7 million in 1985. Passenger-car market share rose from 10.4 percent in 1984 to 11.3 percent in '85, versus 42.5 percent for GM and 18.9 percent for Ford. Chrysler acquired E.F. Hutton Credit in 1985, turning it into Chrysler Capital. In another move toward diversification, it purchased Gulfstream Aerospace Corporation. The company even announced that it might have half its assets in non-automotive operations by 1995. Late in the year, Chrysler announced plans for a joint venture with Mitsubishi in Illinois, which would become Diamond Star Motors. At the time, Chrysler held a 24-percent equity in Mitsubishi.

The last squared-off but good-looking Chrysler LeBaron and Dodge 600 coupes and convertibles rolled off the line in 1986—seemingly the finale for Dodge ragtops, to the sorrow of dealers. LeBaron/600 sedans and wagons (except for the 600 ES) carried on into 1988. Chrysler issued its own engine option: a 2.5-liter four, to replace the Mitsubishi 2.6-liter that had served well for several seasons. Base engine on most models remained the trusty 2.2-liter.

By now, Daytonas could have a T-top option and a "CS" handling package (named for Carroll Shelby). Shelby, an old friend of Iacocca's, agreed to apply his talents to hot Dodges, as he'd done with Mustangs back in the Sixties.

Two all-new LeBarons debuted for 1987, created by the staff of Chrysler's new design chief, Thomas Gale. Fully rounded, wearing hidden headlamps and a shapely tail, the J-bodied coupe and convertible stood far removed from their upright-stance predecessors. Because Chrysler wanted to reestablish that make's luxury image, no Dodge or Plymouth versions ever were produced.

Equally significant was the new P-body hatchback duo: Dodge Shadow and Plymouth Sundance. Though intended as replacements for the aging Omni/Horizon, the latter hung on through 1990, continuing to sell in respectable numbers. This year, Omni/Horizon dropped to a single "America" series, in an attempt to cut overhead and ensure quality—as the Europeans and Japanese were doing.

Shadow/Sundance exhibited rounded "aerosedan" styling, on a Daytona wheelbase. Once more, Chrysler borrowed from the multifaceted K-car platform. Dodge even got an enthusiast-oriented, turbo-powered ES edition, while Sundance helped Plymouth reach seventh place in industry output.

Daytonas, meanwhile, earned a hidden-headlight restyling, partly placating dealers who no longer had a Dodge convertible to offer. Not one, but two, turbocharged engines lured leadfooted customers to the Dodge fold. Top-of-the-line: the Shelby Z, packing a 174-horsepower "Turbo II" four.

Dodge Charger production halted in March, as sporty Daytonas and Shadows made the Omni-based coupe redundant. The Mitsubishi-built Conquest took a Chrysler badge, substituting for the departed Laser. After reintroducing 5-year/50,000-mile warranties earlier, Chrysler now launched 7-year/70,000-mile powertrain coverage.

During the year, Chrysler made major headlines by taking over the failed American Motors Corporation from Regie Nationale des Usines Renault (of France). With that acquisition came the highly popular Jeep—as well as the less-tempting Renault Alliance/Medallion. Chrysler also formed Acustar, a $2.9 billion parts manufacturing subsidiary.

For the first time since the eras of Virgil Exner and "Tex" Colbert, Chrysler was leading its Big Three rivals in crucial areas: fuel economy, front-drive platforms, four-cylinder engines, and computer-aided design/manufacturing. In fact, Chrysler was the only Big Three automaker to meet the government's 27.5-mpg fuel-mileage standard in 1985—even if Fifth Avenue buyers had to pay a gas guzzler tax. The CAFE requirement was rolled back to 26 mpg, but Chrysler topped the former figure through 1989.

Iacocca's gamble on the future appeared to be paying off. Yet, net profits had sunk for three straight seasons, as Chrysler's latest models failed to take off as anticipated, and new-car market share dipped to 10.7 percent. What, the analysts wondered, could be done to make the good news persist into the Nineties?

1984

Chrysler Corporation enjoys record earnings, a $2.38 billion profit; output more than doubles, passing 1.5 million cars and light trucks for the model year

Chrysler's North American market share for cars hits 11.6 percent

Domestic industry output passes 8.1 million cars for the model year—the recovery is finally arriving

Chrysler launches its instantly popular front-drive minivans: Dodge Caravan and Plymouth Voyager

Dodge's new Daytona sport coupe can have turbo power; Chrysler's Laser is nearly identical

Chrysler's cars meet CAFE requirements, but those from Ford and GM don't

Six models are available with a turbocharged four-cylinder engine; the turbo gives Chrysler an extra edge in technology—but what's needed is a V-6

Chrysler's rear-drive model drops the New Yorker designation; it's now called Fifth Avenue, and sells well

Dodge puts a "600" badge on a coupe and convertible

A 5.2-liter (318-cid) V-8 is the sole engine for Diplomat/Gran Fury

Chrysler marks its 60th anniversary in the auto business

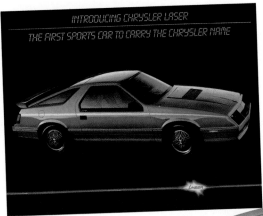

Broadening its lineup, Chrysler brought out the performance-oriented '84 Laser sport coupe (*above*). Purists might have scoffed at the description of the Laser as a "sports car" (*left*), but with turbo power it was a potent machine.

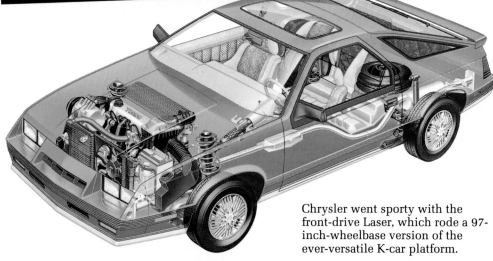

Chrysler went sporty with the front-drive Laser, which rode a 97-inch-wheelbase version of the ever-versatile K-car platform.

The four-door sedan formerly known as the New Yorker was now renamed Chrysler Fifth Avenue. In fact, it was really a continuation of the old rear-drive '81 LeBaron. Sales started strong, as the V-8 sedan appealed to "traditional" customers.

Despite its mild-mannered K-car powertrain, the $18,975 Chrysler Executive Sedan (*above*) and longer-wheelbase $21,975 Limousine drew 790 sales. Chrysler's $9565 E Class sedan (*below*) would soon be history, after only two years in the lineup. More upmarket, the $12,179 front-drive Chrysler New Yorker sedan (*below right*) wore a padded rear-roof section.

A turbocharged 2.2-liter four was available even in Chrysler LeBarons. Two-doors (*center left*), starting at $8763, got a padded rear roof and narrow quarter windows. Note the small rear side windows on the $9067 LeBaron four-door (*center right*). LeBaron convertibles (*above*) adopted power quarter windows and a roomier back seat. LeBaron's style leader was the $16,495 Mark Cross Town & Country ragtop (*above right*). Fake wood also decorated the $9856 Town & Country wagon (*right*).

Changes were modest through the '80s in the Dodge Diplomat sedan (*right*), which found a home mainly in police/taxi fleets—and among families who liked traditional rear-drive cars. Dodge's new Caravan (*below*) came in base, SE, and woody-look LE form, on a 112-inch wheelbase. Driving a minivan wasn't much different than piloting an Aries station wagon—just sitting a little taller and farther forward. Quick-release anchors allowed removal of the center and rear bench seats, to haul cargo. Even the windowless Dodge Mini Ram van (*below right*) sold well.

Wearing a new grille with the Pentastar emblem, the Dodge Aries four-door sedan (*above*) continued to attract budget-minded families, aided by a modest $6837 starting price. Dashboards gained temperature and voltage gauges. Slipping a 110-horsepower Shelby Charger powertrain into a tame Omni body created the hot-to-trot $7350 Dodge Omni GLH (*above right*). All Omnis sported a modernized dashboard this year.

The Dodge 600 four-door sedan (*above*) was joined by the shorter-wheelbase two-doors from what had been the 400 series. Sedans adopted a fuel-injected version of the 2.2-liter four-cylinder engine, but two-doors stuck with carburetors. All models got redesigned instrument panels, and the 600 ES sedan added a tach. Besides taking on the 600 badge, ragtops (*left*) gained a glass rear window, power-operated quarter panes, and a wider back seat. In addition to the $10,595 base model, a $12,895 Turbo version was offered. Ragtop 600 output totaled 10,960.

A Dodge Shelby Charger (*above*) wasn't hard to spot with its wide stripe down the hood and roof. This $8541 sporty coupe attracted some 7552 buyers.

Because of cost factors, Dodge's new Daytona (*top right*) looked little different from Chrysler's Laser—but would last longer. Both rode a modified K-car chassis, with a cut-down 97-inch wheelbase. Base-engine Daytonas ran with a fuel-injected 2.2-liter four, but turbos gained the most notoriety—both a $10,227 base version and a brash $11,494 Turbo Z, with ground-effects trim and a unique spoiler. Dodge gained a new turbocharged sports coupe under the Conquest badge (*above*)—similar to Mitsubishi's Starion, with pop-up headlights. Even the little Mitsubishi-built Dodge Colt (*left*) now had a turbocharged model.

Dodge's AD150 Ramcharger sport-utility (*above left*) had a two-wheel-drive powertrain with standard automatic transmission. The comparable AW150 was four-wheel drive, with four-speed manual shift. Both employed a 5.2-liter V-8. Prices started at $10,945 for the 4WD version. Priced as low as $7094, the ½-ton Dodge D150 pickup truck (*above center*) could have a 6½- or 8-foot cargo box, with Utiline or Sweptline styling. A new Sweptline D100 series had less cargo-hauling capacity. Standard engine was a 95-bhp, 3.7-liter six. Dodge also issued a ¾-ton D250 series, and one-ton D350, as well as a 4WD Power Ram option. A new grille gave the front-drive Dodge Rampage mini-sport pickup (*above right and right*) a sportier look. Prices began at $6786 ($7315 for the 2.2-liter edition).

Plymouth's Reliant coupe (*right*) started at $6837 ($7403 for the SE series). A new grille incorporated Chrysler's Pentastar badge. As before, a 2.2-liter four was standard, but the optional Mitsubishi 2.6-liter four gained eight horses, up to 101. Reliant station wagons (*below*) came in Custom and SE trim. A new instrument panel added several gauges. Plymouth Horizons (*below center*) were far more popular in $5830 base trim than as a $6148 SE. Instrument clusters were revised. This Plymouth Turismo hatchback coupe (*below right*) flaunted its 2.2-liter engine. The new front end adopted quad headlights, and the 2.2 version lost its fake hood scoop.

To create the Plymouth Conquest Turbo Sport Coupe (*above*), Chrysler rebadged the Mitsubishi Starion, with subtle touch-ups that included deleting the fake hood scoop. Dodge dealers also sold the Conquest. The 2.6-liter "Silent Shaft" four with dual-point throttle-body fuel injection developed 145 horsepower—plenty of punch for a 2822-pound car. A Technica package added digital instruments. Mitsubishi produced the new Colt Vista front-drive wagon (*right*), sold under both Dodge and Plymouth badges. The tall, aero-styled seven-seater featured all-independent suspension and an 88-bhp four. Gearbox choices embraced a five-speed or Twin Stick manual or three-speed automatic.

Nearly identical to Dodge's new Caravan, the Plymouth Voyager minivan (*left and below left*) featured a sliding passenger-side door and one-piece rear liftgate. Either a 2.2- or 2.6-liter ohc four delivered power through a five-speed overdrive manual or three-speed automatic transmission. Plymouth promoted the space-efficient van's walk-through capability and low step-up height. Called "Magic Wagon," it was intended for family transportation, recreation, or business. Marketed in base, SE, and LE trim, Voyagers provided seating for up to seven (*below*), and up to 125 cubic feet of cargo space.

1984 Production

Chrysler

Laser	59,858
LeBaron	100,413
E Class	32,237
New Yorker	60,501
Fifth Avenue	79,441
Executive	790
Total	333,240

Dodge

Omni	71,355
Charger	54,264
Daytona	53,635 *
Aries	120,032
600 cpe/cvt	34,689 *
600 sedan	37,381
Diplomat	22,163
Caravan	67,517
Total	461,036 *

* Estimated

Plymouth

Horizon	78,564
Turismo	49,716
Reliant	152,183
Caravelle	39,971
Gran Fury	14,516
Voyager	64,874
Total	399,824

Imports*

Dodge/Plymouth Colt	69,379
Dodge/Plymouth Colt Vista	15,270
Dodge/Plymouth Conquest	**
Dodge Challenger	**
Plymouth Sapporo	**

* Calendar year
** Combined total 7,069

1984 Engine Availability

Chrysler

No. Cyl.	Disp., cid	bhp	Availability
I-4	135.0	99	S-Laser, LeBaron, E Class, NY
I-4T	135.0	142	O-Laser, LeBaron, E Class, NY
I-4	156.0	101	S-Executive; O-LeBaron, E Class, NY
V-8	318.0	130	S-Fifth Avenue

Dodge

No. Cyl.	Disp., cid	bhp	Availability
I-4	97.3	64	S-Omni, Charger
I-4	135.0	96	S-Charger 2.2, Aries, 600 cpe/cvt; O-Omni, Charger
I-4	135.0	99	S-Daytona, 600 sdn
I-4	135.0	101	S-Caravan
I-4	135.0	110	S-Shelby; O-Omni, Charger
I-4T	135.0	142	S-Daytona Turbo; O-Daytona, 600
I-4	156.0	99	O-Caravan
I-4	156.0	101	O-Aries, 600
V-8	318.0	130	S-Diplomat

Plymouth

No. Cyl.	Disp., cid	bhp	Availability
I-4	97.3	64	S-Horizon, Turismo
I-4	135.0	96	S-Reliant, Turismo 2.2; O-Horizon, Turismo
I-4	135.0	101	S-Voyager
I-4	135.0	110	O-Horizon, Turismo
I-4	156.0	99	O-Voyager
I-4	156.0	101	O-Reliant
V-8	318.0	130	S-Gran Fury

Imports

No. Cyl.	Disp., cid	bhp	Availability
I-4	86.0	64	S-Dodge/Plymouth Colt
I-4	97.5	72	O-Dodge/Plymouth Colt
I-4T	97.5	102	S-Dodge Colt GTS Turbo
I-4	121.7	88	S-Dodge/Plymouth Colt Vista
I-4T	155.9	145	S-Dodge/Plymouth Conquest

1985

Dealers applaud record industry car sales—up six percent this year, to 11 million units

Chrysler Corporation sales grow 15 percent, though model-year output declines

Chrysler's passenger-car market share is 11.3 percent

The H-body Dodge Lancer and Chrysler LeBaron GTS hatchback sedans debut

Lancer takes the place of the 600 ES sport sedan; the GTS serves as Chrysler's answer to the "Eurosedan"

Plymouth introduces the Caravelle, a rebadged, lower-priced version of the departed Chrysler E Class

Aries/Reliant receive a much-needed facelift

Horsepower is going up industry-wide, continuing a trend that began in 1983

Chrysler announces a plan for a joint venture with Mitsubishi to build cars in Illinois; equity in the Japanese firm is 24 percent

Chrysler acquires E.F. Hutton Credit Corporation and Gulfstream Aerospace

NHTSA rolls back CAFE to 26 mpg—Chrysler is the only Big Three automaker meeting the 27.5-mpg rule

Chrysler sales total nearly $21.3 billion (up $1.7 billion); sales volume hits the highest level since '78

Chrysler jumps from ninth place in production to seventh, ahead of Plymouth

Above: Cast aluminum wheels were standard on the Chrysler Laser XE. *Left:* Note the distinctive two-toning of the popular rear-drive Chrysler Fifth Avenue. *Below:* A 2.6-liter, 101-bhp four became standard in New Yorkers.

Chrysler dropped the five-seat Executive Sedan, but sold 759 131.3-inch-wheelbase Limousines (*above*). At $26,318, they came with a power sliding glass divider window. Automatic shift was now standard in the $10,363 LeBaron Town & Country station wagon (*left*).

Chrysler blended a K-platform stretched to 103.1 inches and a new H-body to create the LeBaron GTS (Grand Touring Sedan) five-door hatchback (*above*), base-priced at $9024. A good performer with either the regular or turbocharged 2.2-liter four, the GTS got a firmer base suspension than other Chryslers, with gas-pressurized struts/shocks. A turbo engine could be ordered in any LeBaron body style, including the $9460 coupe (*right*). All LeBarons gained gas-pressurized rear shocks. *Below:* Stylish LeBaron convertibles came in base, Mark Cross, and woody-look Mark Cross Town & Country trim, priced from $11,889 to $16,994. Sales totaled 16,475 units.

Detroiters George and Melissa Mundar (*above*) got a preview of $1 million worth of robots at the Louisiana World Exposition. Chrysler's exhibit told how H-body sedans were computer-designed. Chrysler's fuel-injected turbo four (*right*) boasted higher peak boost pressure.

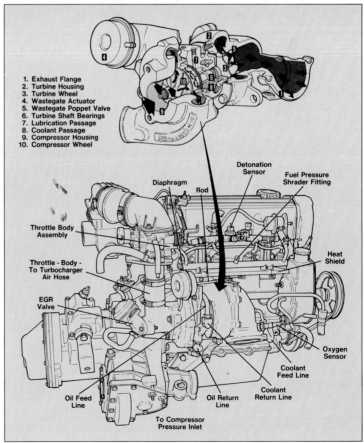

1. Exhaust Flange
2. Turbine Housing
3. Turbine Wheel
4. Wastegate Actuator
5. Wastegate Poppet Valve
6. Turbine Shaft Bearings
7. Lubrication Passage
8. Coolant Passage
9. Compressor Housing
10. Compressor Wheel

Detonation Sensor

Fuel Pressure Shrader Fitting

Diaphragm

Rod

Throttle Body Assembly

Heat Shield

Throttle - Body - To Turbocharger Air Hose

EGR Valve

Oxygen Sensor

Oil Feed Line

Oil Return Line

Coolant Feed Line

Coolant Return Line

To Compressor Pressure Inlet

Dodge Shelby Chargers (*left*) adopted turbo power. At $9553, 7709 Shelbys were ordered. The turbocharged Shelby engine (*above*) yielded 146 horses. Not many folks got to own the aggressively styled D150 Shelby high-performance, V-8-powered pickup truck (*below*).

Dodge Charger 2.2s (*above*) lost their wide bodyside moldings, but added a front air dam, fender extensions, and side spoilers. The high-output Charger 2.2 engine developed 110 bhp. The hot Dodge Daytona Turbo (*above center*) had bigger tires and higher engine boost pressure. A Dodge Ram B150 Value Wagon (*right*) rode a 109.6-inch wheelbase; other vans could have extended bodies.

Topping the Dodge Caravan line was the LE (*above and left*), wearing bodyside and liftgate woodgraining. An LE started at just over $10,000, versus $9147 for a base van. LE interiors (*above left*) featured plusher detailing than base or SE models.

Like its Chrysler LeBaron GTS sibling, the Dodge Lancer ES sport sedan (*right*) rode a 103.1-inch wheelbase. Listing at $9690, the ES came with a handling suspension and electronic instruments. Gas-charged shocks and struts gave Lancers a tauter ride than the GTS. Only two engines were offered: a 99-bhp, 2.2-liter four, or 146-horse turbo. A base-model Lancer started at $8713, and found 30,567 buyers (ES: 15,286). The step-up Dodge Diplomat SE (*below*) lured traditional rear-drive buyers, but most Diplomats went to fleet customers. At $10,418, the SE came with a full vinyl roof, and captured 13,767 buyers. Diplomat's 318-cid V-8 gained 10 horsepower via higher compression and new roller cam followers. Unlike the abandoned four-door 600 ES, this year's $8953 Dodge 600 sedan (*below right*) focused on comfort; 32,368 were sold.

In addition to attractive looks, the Dodge 600 ES Turbo convertible (*right*) delivered ample performance. Priced at $13,995 (versus $10,889 for the base 600 ragtop), the ES featured a sport/handling suspension, leather seating, console, Electronic Voice Alert System, electronic instruments, decklid luggage rack, Euro/sport steering wheel, and aluminum road wheels. Of the 13,809 ragtops produced this year, 5621 were ES Turbos, with the 146-horsepower, 2.2-liter four. All rode a 100.3-inch wheelbase.

Dodge's compact Aries (*above*) gained a rounded-edge facelift, with a new tapered grille. Coupes and sedans came in base, SE, and LE trim; wagons only in SE and LE dress. The sedans, priced from $7039 to $7792, were the most popular: 69,432 total. A 146-horse turbo four powered the Dodge Omni GLH (*above right*), which cost $7620. Some 6513 "Goes Like Hell" drivers bought one. Even the redesigned Dodge Colt (*right*) could have turbo power, in a GTS hatchback or Premier sedan.

The high-output, 110-bhp 2.2 four drove the Plymouth Turismo 2.2 (*left*), which wore new ground-effects lower-body moldings. Just 7785 were built, as opposed to 44,377 regular Turismos that listed at $6584, $931 less. The base engine remained the Peugeot-built, 64-bhp 1.6-liter. Equipment in the Turismo Duster package (*above*) included special striping, rear spoiler, rally wheels, and reclining bucket seats. Plymouth Reliant SE station wagons outsold their higher-priced LE mates (*below*) by far: 27,489 versus 8348. Body freshening included rounded corners, and interiors featured a soft-top instrument panel.

Formerly sold in Canada, the new Plymouth Caravelle SE (*above row*) was a mildly restyled version of the deleted Chrysler E Class. Like Dodge's 600, the $9007 sedan rode a 103.3-inch chassis. A 2.2-liter engine and TorqueFlite were standard, but most Caravelles got the Mitsubishi-built 2.6-liter "balancer" four, and some carried turbos. The Gran Fury came in only one model, the $9658 Salon sedan (*right*). Its 5.2-liter V-8 gained 10 horsepower for '85, to 140.

A Plymouth Horizon hatchback sedan (*right*) listed at $5977 in base form, or $6342 in SE trim. The base engine was the 1.6-liter four, the 2.2-liter motor an option. A "Fuel Pacer" upshift light could be installed to help improve gas mileage. A four-door sedan joined the Colt line (*below*), with the same independent rear suspension as the hatchback (*bottom left*). Colts earned a larger 1.5-liter four with higher compression, and sporty GTS three-doors could have a turbo. A front bench seat became available in the Plymouth Voyager (*bottom right*). A rear-seat convert-a-bed was a new option.

1985 Production

Chrysler

Laser	50,866
LeBaron	92,815
LeBaron GTS	60,783
New Yorker	60,700
Fifth Avenue	109,971
Limousine	759
Total	375,894

Dodge

Omni	74,127
Charger	56,557
Daytona	47,519
Aries	117,995
Lancer	45,853
600	58,847
Diplomat	39,165
Caravan	108,417
Total	548,480

Plymouth

Horizon	88,011
Turismo	52,162
Reliant	137,738
Caravelle	39,971
Gran Fury	19,102
Voyager	102,109
Total	439,093

Imports*

Dodge/Plymouth Colt	76,313
Dodge/Plymouth Colt Vista	23,593
Dodge/Plymouth Conquest	5,387

* Calendar year

1985 Engine Availability

Chrysler

No. Cyl.	Disp., cid	bhp	Availability
I-4	135.0	99	S-Laser, LeBaron/GTS
I-4T	135.0	146	O-Laser, LeBaron/GTS, NY
I-4	156.0	101	S-Limousine; O-LeBaron
V-8	318.0	140	S-Fifth Avenue

Dodge

No. Cyl.	Disp., cid	bhp	Availability
I-4	97.3	64	S-Omni, Charger
I-4	135.0	96	S-Aries; O-Omni, Charger
I-4	135.0	99	S-Daytona, Lancer, 600; O-Aries
I-4	135.0	101	S-Caravan
I-4	135.0	110	S-Omni GLH, Charger 2.2; O-Omni, Charger
I-4T	135.0	146	S-Charger Shelby; O-Omni GLH, Daytona, Lancer, 600
I-4	156.0	101	O-Aries, 600
I-4	156.0	104	O-Caravan
V-8	318.0	140	S-Diplomat

Plymouth

No. Cyl.	Disp., cid	bhp	Availability
I-4	97.3	64	S-Horizon, Turismo
I-4	135.0	96	S-Reliant; O-Horizon, Turismo
I-4	135.0	99	S-Caravelle
I-4	135.0	101	S-Voyager
I-4	135.0	110	S-Turismo 2.2
I-4T	135.0	146	O-Caravelle
I-4	156.0	101	O-Reliant, Caravelle
I-4	156.0	104	O-Voyager
V-8	318.0	140	S-Gran Fury

Imports

No. Cyl.	Disp., cid	bhp	Availability
I-4	90.0	68	S-Dodge/Plymouth Colt
I-4T	97.5	102	O-Dodge/Plymouth Colt
I-4	121.7	88	S-Dodge/Plymouth Colt Vista
I-4T	155.9	145	S-Dodge/Plymouth Conquest
I-4T	155.9	170	O-Dodge/Plymouth Conquest (intercooled)

1986

Car sales are up again in calendar 1986, for Chrysler and the industry

A record 11,453,705 cars are sold in America, 8,214,662 of them domestically built

Chrysler's market share edges upward, to 11.5 percent

Chrysler adds a 2.5-liter four-cylinder engine—the first domestic motor to use counter-balance shafts

The final Chrysler Laser coupes are built

Dodge Daytona carries on, with a T-top and C/S (Carroll Shelby) handling package now available

The last Dodge convertibles are produced—dealers are unhappy

Lee Iacocca receives more than $20.5 million: his basic salary is $727,972, most of balance comes from exercising stock options

Iacocca is the highest-paid auto executive of all time

A new proving ground opens in Arizona

Chrysler speculates that by 1995 half of its total assets might consist of non-automotive operations

Despite a gas-guzzler tax, the traditional rear-drive Chrysler Fifth Avenue still scores strong sales

In addition to base and XE editions, the Chrysler Laser now came as a sporty XT (*above*), boasting aero body elements and an upgraded suspension. The $11,854 XT, of which 6989 were sold, could have an optional T-roof. A 146-bhp turbo four (*left*) gave the Laser acceleration befitting its slick lines. A Chrysler 2.5-liter four replaced the Mitsubishi 2.6-liter as the mid-level option. Only 138 Chrysler Limousines (*below*) were built in its last year, all turbo-powered.

The rear-drive Chrysler Fifth Avenue sedan (*above*) grew more popular each year. Despite a $500 gas guzzler tax and $14,910 price tag, 104,744 were built for '86. The $11,370 LeBaron Town & Country wagon (*left*) added automatic rear load leveling.

Styling touch-ups for the Chrysler New Yorker sedan (*top left*) were apparent mainly at the rear. A 2.5-liter four was standard, the 2.2 turbo optional. A LeBaron GTS "Premium" (*top right*) cost $11,437. Some $10,127 LeBaron four-door sedans (*above*) strutted a new padded landau-style roof. This $9977 LeBaron two-door (*right*) showed revised front and rear styling; 24,761 were produced.

Only 501 Chrysler LeBaron Mark Cross Town & Country convertibles (*above*) were built for '86, listing at $17,595. Most had a decklid luggage rack; all wore the usual simulated wood panels. In base form, a LeBaron ragtop (*right*) started at $12,695, and sold 12,578 copies. The $16,595 Mark Cross edition—6905 built— featured such bonuses as leather trim, electronic gauges, and wire wheel covers (or aluminum wheels).

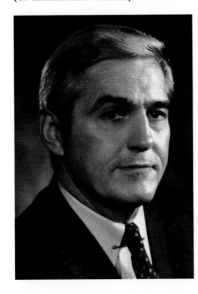

Robert A. Lutz (*far left*) joined the Chrysler organization on June 3, 1986, as executive vice-president of Chrysler Motors. Days later, he was elected to the corporate board of directors. Lutz's automotive career had begun at General Motors in Europe, followed by three years with BMW. Then he moved to Ford, serving as chairman of Ford of Europe, executive vice-president of international operations and, finally, executive vice-president of truck operations. Chairman Lee Iacocca (*left*) had another surprise waiting for the public, in the form of a fully restyled (but still K-car based) LeBaron for '87. By 1986, Iacocca ranked not only as the highest-paid auto executive ever, he was also the fourth-highest-compensated executive of *any* kind—and the best-known.

337

Automotive legend Carroll Shelby (*above*) lent his talents not only to the Dodge Shelby Charger, but to the modest Omni. An Omni GLH (*top right*) came with 110 bhp, but hot-car fans chose the 146-horse turbo. GLH sales reached only 3629 units. Ground-effects add-ons made the Shelby Charger (*above right*) look as hot as it ran; 7669 were built. The Daytona Turbo Z (*right*), chosen by 17,595 buyers, flaunted its own pavement-hugging body trim. A T-roof and "CS" handling package added to the fun.

Both engines for the Dodge Caravan (*left*) stuck with carburetors. As before, base, SE, and LE versions went on sale, with a new wraparound front air dam and newly optional cruise control. A Dodge B250 Ram Wagon (*below left*) could have a regular or Maxi body. An automatic transmission was standard. Appearance and interior extras accounted for the $924 price difference between a Dodge Ram 50 Sport pickup (*below*) and its non-Sport mate. Four-wheel-drive models were named Power Ram.

Base engine for the Dodge Aries (*top left*) was now a fuel-injected, 97-bhp, 2.2-liter four. Chrysler's new 100-bhp 2.5 four was optional. Wagons came in SE and LE trim—23,025 were built. Aries sedans (*top right*) offered three trim levels, with a five-speed gearbox now standard. Salon and SE (*above*) versions of the rear-drive Diplomat showed little change. The Dodge 600 and 600 ES sedan (*right*) displayed new front and rear styling and a revised grille; 31,544 were sold.

The new 2.5-liter engine was optional in the Dodge Lancer (*above left*). A crossbar grille instead of slats gave the Dodge 600 ragtop (*above*) a different look for its final year. Base models went for $11,695; an ES Turbo soft-top commanded $14,856. Five-door hatchbacks left the Colt line; a three-door with the GTS Turbo package (*left*) cost $7757.

Dodge and the PPG company sponsored this Pace Car for the Indy Car World Series. Sleek, swoopy, and extremely low to the ground, the car's front end looked like twin claws scraping the pavement. Described as "very slippery," the Pace Car had a drag coefficient of 0.236, and ran at speeds up to 194 mph. Its 2.2-liter Chrysler four was specially modified with twin turbochargers and 23-psi boost. Features included an integrated rear spoiler, big hood vents, and a single windshield wiper.

The biggest news in the '86 Plymouth Reliant line was the availability of a Chrysler-built 2.5-liter, 97-horsepower engine, to replace the optional Mitsubishi 2.6-liter unit. The new engine contained twin counter-rotating balancing shafts within the crankcase, to cut vibration. The base 2.2-liter four was now throttle-body fuel injected. Reliant station wagons, again in SE and LE (*above*) trim levels, found 27,255 buyers. Four-door sedans—in base, SE, and LE guise—were the most popular: 79,988 total units. The two-door sedan (*right*), also in three trim levels, captured only 15,762 customers.

Above: A lower-priced base model joined the Plymouth Caravelle SE sedan, which exhibited revised front/rear styling. Fuel-injected engine selections now included Chrysler's new 2.5-liter four, as well as the standard 2.2-liter four and optional 146-horsepower turbo. A Duster option package (*above right*) went on sale again for the Turismo coupe, base priced at $6787. No change was evident, except for the newly mandated center high-mounted stoplight. All engines were carbureted.

Mitsubishi-built Colt three-door hatchbacks came in base E or mid-level DL trim; this one (*left*) has the GTS Turbo package (total: $8072). Mitsubishi sold nearly the same car as the Mirage. The little-changed Plymouth Horizon (*above*) started at $6209.

The Plymouth Voyager (*left*) could now get cruise control. This specially equipped Voyager (*below left*), designed for emergency use by the Highland Park (Michigan) Public Safety Department, featured a "prisoner-proof" center compartment. Director Harold J. Johnson (*shown*) inspects the rear section, with its load of fire-fighting and medical emergency gear. A plexiglass/steel shield (*below*) separated the driver's compartment from the passenger seat.

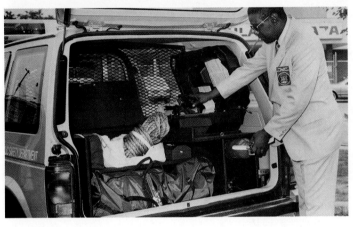

1986 Production

Chrysler

Laser	36,672
LeBaron	91,354
LeBaron GTS	73,557
New Yorker	51,099
Fifth Avenue	104,744
Limousine	138
Total	357,564

Dodge

Omni	73,580
Charger	50,655
Daytona	44,366
Aries	97,368
Lancer	51,897
600	59,695
Diplomat	26,953
Caravan	114,332
Total	518,846

Plymouth

Horizon	84,508
Turismo	46,387
Reliant	123,005
Caravelle	34,352
Gran Fury	14,761
Voyager	108,284
Total	411,297

Imports*

Dodge/Plymouth Colt	93,343
Dodge/Plymouth Colt Vista	35,096
Dodge/Plymouth Conquest	7,089

* Calendar year

1986 Engine Availability

Chrysler

No. Cyl.	Disp., cid	bhp	Availability
I-4	135.0	97	S-Laser, LeBaron/GTS
I-4T	135.0	146	S-Limousine; O-Laser, LeBaron/GTS, NY
I-4	153.0	100	S-Laser XE, LeBaron T&C wagon, NY; O-Laser, LeBaron/GTS
V-8	318.0	140	S-Fifth Avenue

Dodge

No. Cyl.	Disp., cid	bhp	Availability
I-4	97.3	64	S-Omni, Charger
I-4	135.0	96	O-Omni, Charger
I-4	135.0	97	S-Aries, Daytona, Lancer, 600
I-4	135.0	101	S-Caravan
I-4	135.0	110	S-Omni GLH, Charger 2.2; O-Omni, Charger
I-4T	135.0	146	S-Charger Shelby, Daytona Turbo; O-Omni GLH, Daytona, Lancer, 600
I-4	153.0	100	O-Aries, Daytona, Lancer, 600
I-4	156.0	104	O-Caravan
V-8	318.0	140	S-Diplomat

Plymouth

No. Cyl.	Disp., cid	bhp	Availability
I-4	97.3	64	S-Horizon, Turismo
I-4	135.0	96	O-Horizon, Turismo
I-4	135.0	97	S-Reliant, Caravelle
I-4	135.0	101	S-Voyager
I-4	135.0	110	S-Turismo 2.2
I-4T	135.0	146	O-Caravelle
I-4	153.0	100	O-Reliant, Caravelle
I-4	156.0	104	O-Voyager
V-8	318.0	140	S-Gran Fury

Imports

No. Cyl.	Disp., cid	bhp	Availability
I-4	90.0	68	S-Dodge/Plymouth Colt
I-4T	97.5	102	O-Dodge/Plymouth Colt
I-4	121.7	88	S-Dodge/Plymouth Colt Vista
I-4T	155.9	145	S-Dodge/Plymouth Conquest
I-4T	155.9	170	O-Dodge/Plymouth Conquest (intercooled)

1987

Chrysler takes over American Motors Corporation in August, lured by the Jeep line that becomes Jeep-Eagle division

The takeover gives Chrysler the Renault Alliance and Medallion, European-designed Premier—plus the new Bramalea, Ontario, assembly plant

Chrysler's model-year output increases after two declining years, but the improvement won't last

Car sales decline: the industry is down 11 percent for the calendar year, but Chrysler falls 16 percent

A sleek hidden-headlamp Chrysler LeBaron coupe and convertible debut

Shadow is Dodge's latest subcompact; Plymouth's Sundance differs little

Chrysler introduces a 7-year/70,000-mile limited powertrain warranty

Dodge's Daytona is restyled, including the Shelby Z

The Omni/Horizon subcompacts drop to single low-priced "America" models stickered at $5499

Chrysler buys the Italian Lamborghini company, maker of exotic cars

Chrysler pleads "no contest" to charges of disconnecting odometers from cars under test, pays a $16.4 million fine

The stock market crashes on October 19

The automatic transmission in the Chrysler New Yorker sedan (*top*) added an electronic lockup torque converter, to improve economy. New Yorkers, with a $14,193 sticker, sold nearly as well as the rear-drive Fifth Avenue: 68,279 units versus 70,579. Like other Chrysler products, the LeBaron GTS hatchback sedan (*above*) gained a stainless steel exhaust system. Highline and Premium editions were sold. Francois J. Castaing (*left*) joined Chrysler in August 1987 as vice-president of Jeep and truck engineering, following his early career at Renault and AMC. Born in France, Castaing had designed racing engines for Renault Gordini in the early Seventies. Early in 1991, he would be named vice-president of vehicle engineering and general manager of Jeep/truck operations.

Concealed headlights and long-hood/short-deck proportions, on a 100.3-inch platform, helped the $13,974 Chrysler LeBaron convertible (*above*) look completely different from the 1982-86 generation. Open LeBarons (*right*) served at the Indy 500 race. The actual pace car was red.

Designed by an international team that included the Lamborghini organization, Chrysler's Portofino concept vehicle (*above*) featured doors that pivoted upward. With a Lamborghini 3.5-liter V-8 engine mounted amidships, the show car claimed a 150-mph top speed. Note the high flush-mounted door handles and the oddly shaped, shelf-style rear spoiler. The Portofino served as the forerunner of "cab-forward" styling that emerged at Chrysler with much fanfare in the early Nineties. Formerly wearing Dodge and Plymouth badges, the rear-drive, Mitsubishi-built Conquest sport coupe (*right*) went on sale under the Chrysler banner. This gave dealers a replacement for the abandoned Laser. Two turbocharged engines were available, producing 145 or 175 bhp. Chrysler continued to offer the Town & Country station wagon (*below*), and a LeBaron four-door sedan, on the familiar K-car platform.

Dodge Aries (*above*) lost its mid-level SE series, but added standard front bucket seats. The four-door sedan came in base and upscale LE trim ($7655 and $8134). Only 4710 base four-doors were produced, versus 66,506 LE editions, which could be ordered with a front bench seat. Two-doors sold far more slowly: 7721 total. On a stretched K-platform, the Dodge 600 sedan (*left*) came in $9891 base and $10,553 SE dress, related to the Chrysler New Yorker and Plymouth Caravelle. New features included a stainless steel exhaust and a lockup torque converter with the 2.5-liter engine. Turbo power remained available, but the 600 coupe and ragtop were gone.

In addition to new front/rear styling with concealed headlights, Dodge's Daytona got a hotter engine for the $12,749 Shelby Z (*right*). The Z's Turbo II four produced 174 horsepower, versus 146 for the Turbo I that went into the mid-level Pacifica, and was optional in base Daytonas. Note the Shelby Z's ground-sniffing front end. Planning to replace the long-lived Omni, Dodge launched the P-body Shadow (*below*) in three- and five-door hatchback body styles, on a Daytona-sized front-drive wheelbase. Plain and turbocharged 2.2-liter engines were offered, as for the nearly identical Plymouth Sundance. A five-speed gearbox was standard. An enthusiast-oriented Shadow ES option included bigger (15-inch) tires. New front-end styling marked the imported Dodge Colt four-door sedan (*below right*), priced from $7290 to $8638.

Dodge Chargers had two personalities: base model with the same engine as the Omni sedan, or sizzling Shelby (*above*) with the 146-horse turbo four. Only 2011 Shelby Chargers were built this year, versus 24,275 regular Chargers. The Shelby stickered at $9840, or $2841 more than its tame companion. Charger output ground to a halt in March, deemed no longer necessary with lively Daytonas and Shadows in the lineup. A sporty Dodge Lancer ES (*left*) cost $10,428, $954 more than a base model, and sold more slowly: 9579 copies versus 17,040. A new overhead console was optional.

Changes to the Dodge Caravan (*top*) came at mid-season: a stretched Grand Caravan assembled in St. Louis and a new Mitsubishi-built V-6. Wheelbases of the extended minivans grew seven inches (to 119.1), weight jumped 300 pounds, and cargo volume grew to 155 cubic feet. Standard-size Caravans, produced in Windsor, Ontario, remained on the roster. The addition of the 3.0-liter V-6 brought total engine choices to four, starting with the 95-bhp, 2.2-liter four. The 2.5-liter four became the base engine for extended minivans. A fully equipped Dodge Omni America hatchback sedan (*above*) sold for just $5499 when launched as an early '87 model. The America program streamlined production, improved quality, and helped cut costs by trimming the Omni (and Plymouth Horizon) line to a single-price series with limited options. The new mid-size Dodge Dakota pickup (*above right*) bowed for '87 with a 6½- or 8-foot cargo box, $6590 base sticker, and a four or V-6. Dodge joined the compact sport-utility race with the Raider (*right*)—basically a Mitsubishi Montero with Dodge badges, $10,165 base price, and a 109-bhp, 2.6-liter four.

Both the Plymouth Turismo coupe (*above*) and Horizon sedan joined the America program, with each model limited to a single-price series. A Turismo was priced at $7199, with very few options available. Sales wouldn't begin until 1989, but the Plymouth X2S concept coupe (*left*), unveiled at the Chicago Auto Show in February 1987, clearly foretold the forthcoming Eclipse/Laser/Talon trio. All three would be built at the new Diamond-Star Motors plant in Normal, Illinois, a joint venture of Chrysler and Mitsubishi. The Plymouth Sundance (*below*) came in one trim level (with lots of options), its suspension tuned more for ride than handling.

Like Dodge's Aries, the Plymouth Reliant (*above*) got a stainless steel exhaust system and lost its mid-level SE series. The four-door (71,717 built) came in $7655 base and $8134 LE trim, with newly standard front bucket seats. Two-door Reliants (9331 built) also came in two levels, but wagons (22,905 built) were available only in the LE series. Plymouth Caravelles (*right*) gained stainless steel exhaust and an electronic lockup torque converter for the automatic gearbox when coupled to the 2.5-liter four. Electronic speed control was now optional. The base engine was the 97-bhp four, the 146-bhp turbo optional. Prices started at $9762.

A concept version of the new Plymouth Grand Voyager (*top row*) appeared at auto shows. The aero-styled, long-wheelbase wagon featured a "moon roof" windshield for greater headroom and visibility, plus dual tires on 17-inch alloy wheels. The concept minivan also included storage space in a bin with a slide-out tray. A center jump seat folded down for use as an armrest, or outward to become a child's seat. The versatile seat could also be altered into an entertainment area. A fold-out table even contained a vacuum cleaner. Mid-year brought a V-6 engine option to Plymouth minivans. The new extended-length Grand Voyager LE (*right*), riding a generous 119.1-inch chassis, wore woodgrained bodyside appliqués.

1987 Production

Chrysler

LeBaron	143,998
LeBaron GTS	39,050
New Yorker	68,279
Fifth Avenue	70,579
Total	321,906

Dodge

Omni	66,907
Charger	26,286
Daytona	33,104
Shadow	76,056
Aries	99,299
Lancer	26,619
600	40,391
Diplomat	20,627
Caravan	153,191 *
Total	542,480
* Calendar year	

Plymouth

Horizon	79,449
Turismo	24,104
Sundance	75,679
Reliant	103,953
Caravelle	42,465
Gran Fury	10,377
Voyager	140,799 *
Total	476,826
* Calendar year	

Imports*

Dodge/Plymouth Colt	79,367
Dodge/Plymouth Colt Vista	29,380
Chrysler Conquest	11,590
* Calendar year	

1987 Engine Availability

Chrysler

No. Cyl.	Disp., cid	bhp	Availability
I-4	135.0	97	S-LeBaron sedan, GTS
I-4T	135.0	146	O-LeBaron GTS, NY
I-4	153.0	100	S-LeBaron cpe/cvt/wgn, NY; O-LeBaron GTS
V-8	318.0	140	S-Fifth Avenue

Dodge

No. Cyl.	Disp., cid	bhp	Availability
I-4	135.0	96	S-Omni, Charger
I-4	135.0	97	S-Aries, Daytona, Lancer, 600
I-4	135.0	95	S-Caravan
I-4T	135.0	146	S-Charger Shelby, Daytona Pacifica; O-Daytona, Shadow, Lancer, 600
I-4T	135.0	174	S-Daytona Shelby Z
I-4	153.0	100	S-Daytona; O-Aries, Lancer, 600
I-4	153.0	102	S-Grand Caravan; O-Caravan
I-4	156.0	104	O-Caravan
V-6	187.0	144	O-Caravan
V-8	318.0	140	S-Diplomat

Plymouth

No. Cyl.	Disp., cid	bhp	Availability
I-4	135.0	95	S-Voyager
I-4	135.0	96	S-Horizon, Turismo
I-4	135.0	97	S-Sundance, Reliant, Caravelle
I-4T	135.0	146	O-Sundance, Caravelle
I-4	153.0	100	O-Reliant, Caravelle
I-4	153.0	102	S-Grand Voyager; O-Voyager
I-4	156.0	104	O-Voyager
V-6	187.0	144	O-Voyager
V-8	318.0	140	S-Gran Fury

Imports

No. Cyl.	Disp., cid	bhp	Availability
I-4	90.0	68	S-Dodge/ Plymouth Colt
I-4T	97.5	105	O-Dodge/ Plymouth Colt
I-4	121.7	88	S-Dodge/ Plymouth Colt Vista
I-4T	155.9	145	S-Chrysler Conquest
I-4T	155.9	175	O-Chrysler Conquest (intercooled)

Chapter 16

Searching for a Fresh Direction: 1988-92

During the mid-Eighties, in the opinion of *Ward's Automotive Yearbook,* Chrysler "had spent huge sums on stock buybacks and acquisitions when it should have spent more on long-term capital investment." For instance, more cash should have been diverted toward the development of Chrysler's own V-6 engine. What the corporation "needed was a global strategy for the 1990s, and a platform to replace its K-car."

Chrysler's attempts to forge ahead faced stiff and sundry obstacles. In January 1988, the company announced a plan to sell off its recently created Acustar parts-manufacturing subsidiary, and use the cash to develop cars and engines. The United Auto Workers union quickly stepped into the fray, and by March the proposal was scuttled. On the other hand, a new Electronics Group plant in the Acustar family opened in Alabama—the first new components facility in two decades—signaling the intention of boosting sales to *non-Chrysler* customers, including Ford and General Motors.

Late in 1987, Chrysler Corporation had pleaded "no contest" to a charge of odometer-tampering. Now, it would have to set up a $20 million trust fund for workers laid off from the soon-to-be-defunct Kenosha, Wisconsin, plant––a facility that had been expected to remain in use after the AMC acquisition. The Diamond-Star

plant opened in Illinois, preparing for its joint venture with Mitsubishi. By the Nineties, much of Chrysler's ambitiously planned diversification—with the exception of financial services—would be aborted.

In the new-product battle, extended minivans earned the most attention for 1988. The Dodge Grand Caravan and Plymouth Grand Voyager measured 14 inches longer overall than conventional-size mates, which remained on sale. To help pull the extra weight and boost towing capacity, a Mitsubishi 3.0-liter V-6 engine became optional.

Chrysler's New Yorker nameplate moved to a new platform, related to the all-new Dodge Dynasty. All New Yorkers carried the Mitsubishi V-6 engine, which was optional in Dynasty. Like nearly all Chrysler engines by 1988, the V-6 had port fuel injection. For the first time, anti-lock braking could be ordered, at $956 extra on the New Yorker. Billed as a "contemporary family sedan," Dynasty became the most popular model from any Chrysler division (though many went to rental agencies rather than private owners).

Anti-lock brakes began a phase-in for Dynasty during '88. A Shelby option for the Dodge Lancer debuted, with a 174-horsepower turbo engine.

The French-made Renault Medallion now wore an Eagle badge, as did a new

The acquisition of AMC gave Iacocca the popular Jeep line.

Premier. Styled by Giugiaro of Italy, prior to Chrysler's takeover of AMC, the Premier sedan was built in Canada. Some critics said ho-hum, but *Ward's Auto World* called it "one of the surprise goodies in today's product-cluttered marketplace." Production of the four-wheel-drive AMC Eagle station wagon ceased early in the '88 model year, burying the last vestige of AMC's 34-year automotive history.

Automobile output from U.S. plants slid sharply in the 1988 model year, foretelling further declines as the decade ended. Net profit skidded for the fourth year in a row. By 1990, in fact, production stood on a par with the bad old days of the early Eighties. Because overall earnings remained high in '88, however, Chrysler employees got profit-sharing payments for the first time.

New Yorkers for 1989 boasted a new four-speed automatic transaxle with adaptive electronic control. Options included an anti-theft alarm system. Only the turbo LeBaron GTS remained; base and mid-range versions were named, simply, LeBaron. Sales of that hatchback sedan had been declining of late, after a strong start in 1985.

Meanwhile, the Aries/Reliant duo entered its final year, well-deserving of retirement after helping Chrysler survive. Taking their place as family Dodges and Plymouths: the new Spirit and Acclaim sedans, with 2.5-liter four-cylinder engines. Spirits could get sporty ES trim; Plymouth offered a luxury LX instead, each with available V-6 power. Both were promoted for their value-for-dollar pricing.

Daytona coupes could get a C/S (Caroll Shelby) competition package. Turbocharged engines even went into some minivans, while the new "Ultradrive" electronically controlled automatic transmission became optional. Publicity resulting from early flaws hurt Ultradrive (also installed in New Yorker and Dynasty), and Chrysler—to its discredit—stonewalled critics while working out the kinks.

In its final year, Dodge's Lancer added a Shelby edition. Imported Dodge/Plymouth Colts got a next-generation restyle. That subcompact also wore an Eagle Summit badge.

Back in mid-1986, a two-seat "Q-coupe" had made the auto-show rounds, as a Chrysler/Maserati joint venture. Finally, Chrysler's TC by Maserati arrived at showrooms—the first production two-seater marketed by the company since its very earliest days. Though Italian-built, the design was Chrysler's—yet another variant of the K-car, wearing a wedgy convertible body, not too dissimilar from LeBaron. Sold as "one-price" models, the convertibles failed to attract many customers. *Automotive News* magazine branded the TC "Flop of the Year," and production halted late in 1989. However, at 1989 auto shows, performance fans "oohed" and "aahed"

over the Viper RT/10 roadster, whose styling aped the long-gone Shelby Cobra.

LeBarons could have a V-6 in 1990, while the GTC coupe and convertible got a new VNT "Turbo IV" engine—plus an electronically variable suspension. The LeBaron name also went on a four-door sedan, a Spirit/Acclaim clone.

All Chrysler products now were front-drive. After half a dozen years out of the lineup, the Imperial returned—as an ultra-deluxe version of the latest Fifth Avenue sedan.

Resurrecting another familiar name, Chrysler launched a luxurious Town & Country minivan, wearing imitation-wood paneling. Minivans could have a new 3.3-liter V-6 (first of a family of corporate powerplants for the Nineties). This was the final year for Omni/Horizon, now with a standard driver-side air bag installed.

In fact, most 1990 Chrysler products had one—an ironic twist since Iacocca had previously been a vociferous opponent of air bags. Once more, Chrysler took the lead in an emerging technology, putting an air bag into every domestically built car except the new Eagle Talon and Plymouth Laser. Introduced as early '90 models, those two sport coupes were produced in Illinois, as a Chrysler/Mitsubishi joint venture.

Daytona got its first V-6 choice (Mitsubishi-built) in 1990, available with Chrysler's new five-speed gearbox. Dynasty added the *Chrysler*-built 3.3-liter V-6 as an option. Dodge dealers got a Monaco-badged variant of the Eagle Premier sedan. Neither would last long.

Not only did Chrysler's passenger-car market share dip to 9.3 percent, it barely beat American Honda in sales. Critics still insisted that Chrysler had been hanging on to aging models—and the K-car platform—far too long.

An even bigger 3.8-liter V-6 arrived in 1991, under Imperial hoods. Anti-lock braking made its way into more models. Caravan and Voyager—the best selling American minivans—gained their most sweeping overhaul, including new all-wheel-drive models.

Dodge Shadow added both a convertible and an entry-level "America" edition. Plymouth's equivalent, Sundance, was promoted as the least-expensive car with a standard air bag.

A new limited-edition, high-performance Dodge Spirit R/T carried a 224-bhp turbocharged engine, sold only with manual shift. Dodge dealers also got a new Japanese-built model, the Stealth 2+2 coupe, akin to the Mitsubishi 3000GT. Chrysler took credit for exterior styling, Mitsubishi for interior and mechanicals. Engine choices ranged all the way to an R/T Turbo, with twin turbochargers for an impressive 300 horsepower, plus four-wheel drive and four-wheel steering.

Recession was taking its toll on sales. The economic slowdown that began in

mid-1990 was expected to be over by '92. For millions of Americans, however, its impact lingered on and on, marked by both blue- and white-collar layoffs and cutbacks, which effectively drove many a young family out of the new-car market.

Transplants—foreign companies producing cars in the U.S.—were playing an ever-greater role. Chrysler had long been a leader, courtesy of its tie with Mitsubishi. Early in the decade, though, several hoped-for global connections had fallen through, including one with Fiat and another with Hyundai. Chrysler managed to sell Gulfstream Aerospace in 1990, for $825 million, but attempts to dispose of other subsidiaries failed to transpire. Now, the corporation was putting additional assets on the block—even including its 50-percent ownership in Diamond-Star Motors—in an attempt to raise much-needed capital.

Minivans could have integrated child safety seats in 1992, an industry first. They also contained a standard driver-side air bag—a first for minivans, phased in during '91. Daytonas earned a new nose with exposed aero headlights, plus a hot IROC R/T edition.

As for imports, a new Eagle Summit Wagon ranked as a "mini-minivan." Plymouth's version took the Colt Vista name. Plymouth borrowed a badge from the muscle-car era for a V-6 version of its Sundance; though frisky, this front-drive Duster was hardly a match for its burly ancestor.

Only 200 went on sale, but Dodge finally had a Viper ready—powered by a 400-horsepower V-10, no less. While not quite as blatant as the '89 show roadster, it inspired a frenzy of lust among performance-car zealots. Some speculators paid up to double the $50,000 sticker for the early production models.

Even bigger news than Viper wasn't a product, but the announcement that Lee Iacocca would depart as chairman. He retired in December. Earlier that year, Iacocca had earned headlines for critical remarks about Japanese automakers, during a trip to Japan with his GM and Ford counterparts, and President Bush.

An era was over, another one commencing. Over the course of a dozen years, Iacocca had restored Chrysler to life—then coped with further decline in the late Eighties. In doing so, he'd become America's most famous corporate executive. By now, several top executives had departed, including ace marketer Bennett Bidwell and vice-chairman Gerald Greenwald, once viewed by many as Iacocca's likeliest successor. In March 1992, Robert Eaton had been named vice-chairman and chief operating officer—a stepping-stone to the top spot.

Chrysler had taken the lead in high-efficiency engines, in safety, and in modern technology. Now, it was time for a different—if less charismatic—team of managers to take charge.

1988

Chrysler profits are down for the fourth straight year

Chrysler Corporation's model-year output begins a downward slide, dropping 15 percent this season

Passenger-car sales are up slightly, for Chrysler and the industry

Dynasty is Dodge's new family sedan—it's destined to become the corporation's top seller

Chrysler launches another New Yorker, with a new 3.0-liter V-6

Chrysler markets the departed AMC's Eagle line, the Canadian-built Premier, and French-made Medallion

The K-car-based Plymouth Caravelle and Dodge 600 are in their last year

The final Dodge Aries/Plymouth Reliant station wagons are built

A new Shelby Lancer carries the hot Turbo II engine

Anti-lock braking is available on several models

Chrysler is the first U.S. manufacturer to install an air bag as standard equipment

New concept vehicles include the Chrysler Portofino and Plymouth Slingshot

Dodge and Plymouth debut long-wheelbase Caravan and Voyager minivans; a 3.0-liter, Mitsubishi-built V-6 is now optional

Top and above: A new front-drive mid-size luxury sedan bore Chrysler's oldest model name. Sharing the new C-body design with the Dodge Dynasty, this New Yorker measured 6.4 inches longer than the E-body New Yorker Turbo. Beneath its hood sat a Mitsubishi 3.0-liter V-6 driving a three-speed automatic with lockup torque converter. A base and a $19,509 premium Landau version (*shown*) were offered, the latter with a landau vinyl roof—and 47,400 sales. *Left:* Tufted leather gave a New Yorker Landau extra zest; velour was standard. Landaus held an electronic instrument cluster. *Below:* Chrysler's $17,243 Fifth Avenue sedan wore a new padded vinyl roof and two-tone paint option. Now built at the former AMC plant in Kenosha, Wisconsin, it found 43,486 buyers.

More equipment went into the Chrysler LeBaron coupe (*top left*), such as a rear defogger and wider tires. The $13,830 Premium model added automatic temperature control, power heated mirrors, and an overhead console. The $11,286 LeBaron sedan (*top right*) got a stronger battery and redesigned air conditioning controls. Mid-year brought a sharp GTC edition of the LeBaron convertible (*above*). Premium models added two-tone paint, tilt wheel, and cruise control. The $12,971 LeBaron GTS Premium hatchback sedan (*above right*), of which 4604 were sold, added power locks and mirrors, and an optional power sunroof. The base $10,798 model didn't do much better—9607 units.

Dodge trimmed its Aries line to a single America series, reduced the number of individual options, and cut base prices by nearly $1300. The $6995 two-door (*above*) found just 6578 buyers, compared to 85,613 for the four-door, and 19,172 for the wagon. A five-speed stick was standard, but the optional three-speed automatic (required with the 2.5-liter) added a lockup torque converter. *Left:* Like most front-drive cars, the Dodge Caravan used a transverse-mounted engine—either a 2.5-liter four or 3.0-liter Mitsubishi V-6. New options included a 4000-pound towing package, rear-seat air conditioner, and sporty ES package. Starting at $10,887, standard-length Caravans came in base, SE, and LE guise. Long-wheelbase Grand Caravans, priced at $12,502 and up, carried SE and LE designations.

Dodge issued its 600 sedan (*right*) for the last time, in base and SE trim at $10,659 and $11,628. The 2.5-liter four was now standard in the 600 SE. Base 600s kept the 2.2-liter four, with the 2.5 (or turbo 2.2) optional. The automatic added a lockup torque converter, to boost fuel economy. This mid-size front-driver was related to the Chrysler New Yorker Turbo and Plymouth Caravelle.

The largest front-drive Dodge was the Dynasty sedan, based on the same C-body as the Chrysler New Yorker. The new four-door came in base trim, and as an LE (*left*). Less-equipped than the New Yorker, Dynasty was cheaper, starting at $11,666, and wore exposed aero head-lamps. *Below:* Dynasty's base engine was a 96-bhp, 2.5-liter four, hooked to a three-speed automatic. A 136-bhp Mitsubishi V-6 could be installed instead. Options included new all-disc anti-lock brakes, on the LE only, as well as automatic rear load leveling.

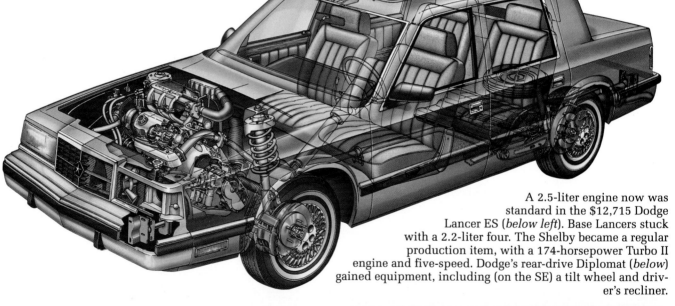

A 2.5-liter engine now was standard in the $12,715 Dodge Lancer ES (*below left*). Base Lancers stuck with a 2.2-liter four. The Shelby became a regular production item, with a 174-horsepower Turbo II engine and five-speed. Dodge's rear-drive Diplomat (*below*) gained equipment, including (on the SE) a tilt wheel and driver's recliner.

Changes to Dodge Shadows with the high-performance ES package (*above*) embraced a new front fascia with integral lower air dam and fog lamps, front fender flares, and a new rear spoiler. Base Shadows came in $7875 three- and $8075 five-door hatchback form; the ES package added about $2200. The base engine was a 2.2 four, but the ES got a turbo 2.2, or delete-option 2.5 four. The optional three-speed automatic transmission added a lockup torque converter. A hot 174-bhp Turbo II engine was the driving force in Dodge's $13,394 Daytona Shelby Z (*right*), wearing a modest rear spoiler. Base Daytonas made do with a 96-bhp, 2.5-liter four; Pacificas held a 146-horse Turbo I. The Turbo I was part of a new C/S Performance Package for base Daytonas. Daytona interiors (*inset*) looked inviting to performance fans, with well-bolstered front seats. Daytonas had door-mounted shoulder belts, and rode the same 97-inch wheelbase as the Shadow. The 2.0-liter engine in a Dodge Colt Vista 4x4 (*below*) got multi-point fuel injection and gained eight bhp. The $12,405 4WD Vista came only with a five-speed. The Mitsubishi-built Dodge Colt three-door hatchback (*bottom right*) and four-door sedan were joined by a wagon.

Right: Carroll Shelby worked wonders on various Chrysler vehicles. Now, the small Dodge Shadow drew the attention of his high-performance team. Those folks chose the new VNT (Variable Nozzle Turbocharged) 2.2-liter four, for use in a modified Shadow, the Shelby CXS (about 2250 were built 1988-89). A Dodge Dakota SE pickup (*below*) could haul 2550 pounds of cargo and tow 5500 pounds. "Not too big, not too small," Dodge claimed of its mid-sizer. The 2.2-liter four was standard, a 3.9 V-6 optional (standard with 4WD). SE pickups came on a 112- or 124-inch wheelbase, with 6½- or 8-foot bed.

Some auto-show visitors doubtless thought Dodge was joshing when they saw this concept convertible pickup (*right*). Responding to "positive reaction," though, the open truck would become a production item during 1989, as a "spring special." ASC Inc. got the nod to perform the conversion—the "first production convertible truck attempted in the industry." A new extended-wheelbase Mini Ram Van (*below*) debuted, able to carry a 2010-pound payload within its 160 cubic feet of cargo space. A one-piece liftgate was standard, but dual cargo doors could be ordered. *Below right:* With two-wheel drive, Dodge's Power Ram pickup got a D150 designation; 4WD versions took W150 badges. The 3.9-liter V-6 and 5.2-liter V-8 engines were fuel-injected.

Right: Extended-wheelbase Plymouth Grand Voyagers came as a $12,502 SE, or as a $15,509 LE (*shown*). Regular-size Voyagers, on a 112-inch wheelbase, came in base, SE, and LE trim. A standard 2.5-liter four replaced the 2.2-liter engine. With the V-6, Grand Voyagers could handle a 4000-pound trailer towing setup. A new optional LX appearance package included bright moldings and two-tone body trim. Grand Voyagers seated seven or eight passengers, while standard models carried five or seven. Only an automatic was available with the 136-horsepower V-6. Describing its similar Caravan, Dodge declared it "a touring sedan, family wagon, and spacious van all in one."

A sporty new RS (Rally Sport) package could be had on the Plymouth Sundance, $1390 extra on the $7975 three-door hatch (*left and above*). Featured were a 96-bhp 2.5 four, unique front fascia with integral fog lamps, luggage rack, and power locks. A removable glass sunroof added $377. Throttle-body fuel injection became standard on the 2.2 engine in the Horizon America (*below*), but the 93 rated bhp was down three.

Above: For $1438, an RS group for the Plymouth Sundance five-door hatchback featured new front bucket seats with a manual driver's lumbar support, stereo cassette player, leather-wrapped steering wheel, and a premium interior with a 60/40 folding rear seat. *Left:* Plymouth Colt four-doors came in E, DL, and Premier dress. The $8943 Premier (*shown*) featured a sport suspension, tach, and 14-inch tires on aluminum wheels. The carbureted 1.5-liter four-cylinder engine delivered 68 bhp (105 bhp optional). *Below:* Plymouth Reliants now came in one price series as the America (LE trim level), with most options grouped into two packages. The $6995 four-door (*shown*) with the Popular and Premium Equipment Discount packages plus air conditioning cost $10,303.

Developed by Renault and AMC before Chrysler's takeover, the new front-drive Eagle Premier sedan, styled by Giorgetto Giugiaro, was built in Canada. It had fully independent suspension and a 111-bhp 2.5 four, or a 150-bhp 3.0 V-6.

1988 Production

Chrysler

LeBaron	113,446
LeBaron GTS	14,211
New Yorker Turbo	8,805
New Yorker	70,968
Fifth Avenue	43,486
Total	**250,916**

Dodge

Omni	59,867
Daytona	66,407
Shadow	92,309
Aries America	111,363
Lancer	9,343
600	17,090
Dynasty	55,550
Diplomat	19,173
Caravan	205,223 *
Total	**636,325**

* Calendar year

Eagle*

Premier	59,068
Total	**73,780**

* Calendar year

Jeep

Wrangler	52,691
Cherokee	187,136
Total	**293,827**

Plymouth

Horizon	61,715
Sundance	88,348
Reliant	125,307
Caravelle	16,889
Gran Fury	11,421
Voyager	187,715 *
Total	**491,395**

* Calendar year

Imports*

Dodge/Plymouth Colt	79,885
Dodge/Plymouth Colt Vista	19,439
Chrysler Conquest TSi	9,873
Medallion	14,712

* Calendar year

1988 Engine Availability

Chrysler

No. Cyl.	Disp., cid	bhp	Availability
I-4	135.0	93	S-LeBaron sedan, GTS
I-4T	135.0	146	S-NY Turbo; O-LeBaron/GTS
I-4	153.0	96	S-LeBaron GTS Premium; O-LeBaron GTS
I-4	153.0	100	S-LeBaron cpe/cvt/wgn
V-6	181.4	136	S-NY
V-8	318.0	140	S-Fifth Avenue

Dodge

No. Cyl.	Disp., cid	bhp	Availability
I-4	135.0	93	S-Omni, Aries, Shadow, Lancer, 600
I-4T	135.0	146	S-Daytona Pacifica; O-Daytona, Shadow, Lancer, 600
I-4T	135.0	174	S-Daytona Shelby Z, Lancer Shelby
I-4	153.0	96	S-Daytona, Dynasty, Lancer ES, Caravan; O-Aries, Shadow, Lancer, 600
V-6	181.4	136	O-Dynasty, Caravan
V-8	318.0	140	S-Diplomat

Eagle

No. Cyl.	Disp., cid	bhp	Availability
I-4	132.0	103	S-Medallion
I-4	150.0	111	S-Premier LX
V-6	182.0	150	S-Premier ES; O-Premier LX

Jeep

No. Cyl.	Disp., cid	bhp	Availability
I-4	150.0	117	S-Wrangler
I-4	150.0	121	S-Cherokee
I-6	242.0	173	S-Cherokee Limited; O-Cherokee
I-6	256.0	112	O-Wrangler

Plymouth

No. Cyl.	Disp., cid	bhp	Availability
I-4	135.0	93	S-Horizon, Sundance, Reliant, Caravelle
I-4T	135.0	146	O-Sundance, Caravelle
I-4	153.0	96	S-Voyager; O-Sundance, Reliant, Caravelle
V-6	181.0	136	O-Voyager
V-8	318.0	140	S-Gran Fury

Imports

No. Cyl.	Disp., cid	bhp	Availability
I-4	90.0	68	S-Dodge/Plymouth Colt
I-4T	97.5	105	O-Dodge/Plymouth Colt
I-4	121.7	96	S-Dodge/Plymouth Colt Vista
I-4T	155.9	188	S-Chrysler Conquest TSi

1989

The decline in Chrysler Corporation's model-year output continues, down 12 percent this year

Industry car sales drop; Chrysler falls twice as much as the industry average

Spirit and Acclaim arrive—Dodge's and Plymouth's family sedans for the '90s

The long-lived 5.2-liter V-8 is in its last year; future Chrysler cars are all fours or V-6s

An electronically controlled four-speed automatic transmission is introduced

The long-delayed Chrysler's TC by Maserati is finally marketed, but doesn't catch on

Chrysler produces its last rear-drive Fifth Avenues

The Plymouth Reliant/Dodge Aries and Chrysler Conquest are sold for the last time

LeBarons are the first convertibles with a standard air bag

Experimental vehicles include the Dodge Viper, Plymouth Speedster, and Chrysler Millenium

Jeep-Eagle dealers continue to offer the Premier sedan, plus a variant of the restyled Dodge/Plymouth Colt badged Summit

The Dodge Diplomat and Plymouth Gran Fury—popular as police cars and taxi cabs—enter their last year

Chrysler closes the old AMC Kenosha, Wisconsin, plant where they were built

Top: Showgoers got their first gander at the Chrysler/Maserati creation back in 1986, when it was known as the "Q-Coupe." After many delays, Chrysler's TC by Maserati finally went on sale—Chrysler's first production two-seater in decades. By this time, Chrysler had taken a minority interest in Maserati, but the design was Chrysler's—yet another variant of the K-car, on a shortened 93.3-inch wheelbase, with a wedgy body not unlike LeBaron's. A special 200-bhp turbocharged 2.2 four with intercooler and port injection, plus a Maserati-designed 16-valve twin-cam head, mated with a five-speed. With the three-speed automatic, the engine was a single-cam, 160-bhp Turbo II. Sold fully equipped as a $30,000 "one-price" model, the TC offered no choices other than body color. Leather upholstery and lots of power assists were the rule, including all-disc anti-lock brakes. Made of sheet molding compound, the TC's removable hardtop (*center*) sported round portholes (like the 1956-57 Ford Thunderbird). The soft top operated manually. In its final season, with a driver-side air bag installed, Chrysler's $18,045 rear-drive Fifth Avenue sedan (*above*) kept its carbureted V-8 engine and automatic transmission. During its long life, this car had been very profitable to Chrysler.

Above: Only the high-performance 174-bhp, 2.2-liter turbo edition of the Chrysler Lebaron sport hatchback hung onto the GTS designation. Base and mid-range models were called LeBaron and Lebaron Premium. A new 2.5-liter turbo rated at 150 bhp was available in base and Premium LeBarons (a credit option in the GTS). No matter, total sales skidded to just 2946 for the calendar year. Regular LeBaron sedans and wagons were gone, but the $17,435 GTC coupe (*left*) had the 174-bhp turbo 2.2, or the 2.5-liter turbo as a credit option. LeBaron two-doors got a driver-side air bag and all-disc brakes.

For top performance, Chrysler LeBaron buyers could order the GTC convertible (*right*) with its handling suspension and 16-inch tires. The $19,666 GTC ragtop also came with electronic gauges, Turbo II engine, heavy-duty five-speed shift, and a decklid luggage rack. The $17,416 Chrysler New Yorker sedan (*below*) got a new four-speed automatic—the first with fully adaptive electronic shift control. New options included an anti-theft alarm and "memory" driver's seat. The $19,509 New Yorker Landau sedan (*below left*) came standard with a landau vinyl roof, automatic rear load leveling, and electronic instruments.

Little change was evident in the $18,974 Chrysler Conquest TSi sport coupe (*right*). Power windows got an automatic-down feature; rear passengers got shoulder belts. Turbocharged and intercooled, the 2.6-liter four could drive a five-speed or automatic. All-disc brakes had rear anti-locking. Thomas C. Gale (*below*), named vice-president of design in April 1985, had joined Chrysler Corporation in 1967, with degrees in arts and business. His talents helped keep Chrysler afloat into the '90s.

A new 150-horsepower, 2.5-liter four went into the $11,995 Dodge Daytona ES Turbo (*above*), replacing the Pacifica. The Shelby Z was renamed Daytona Shelby, with the same Turbo II engine, but with a graduated paint treatment and 16-inch tires. Daytonas had all-disc brakes and a driver-side air bag.

A new Spirit four-door sedan (*above left*) edged aside the Aries as the family Dodge. Roughly the same size as the departed 600, the mid-size notchback rode the same 103.3-inch platform as Plymouth's Acclaim. Base, LE, and sporty ES editions went on sale, the latter with a 2.5-liter turbo four. Base and LE Spirits had the 100-bhp, 2.5-liter engine. A 3.0-liter V-6 with automatic could be had only in an ES, which sported aero panels and integral fog lamps. The Shelby team was working on a special 16-valve four (*above*) for installation in Spirits. *Left:* A 150-bhp Turbo II engine was now standard with the ES package for the Dodge Shadow (replacing the 2.2 turbo). That engine also was included in a new Daytona-style competition package. Overwhelmingly, however, Shadow buyers were far more interested in economy.

Turbocharging became available for the Dodge Caravan, in the form of a 150-bhp, 2.5-liter turbo four, optional only in the standard-length SE (*above*) and LE. "Ultradrive" electrically controlled four-speed automatic was standard in the Grand Caravan LE, optional in the Grand SE and regular LE. Station wagons departed the Dodge Aries lineup in its final season, leaving only the two- and the four-door (*right*) America sedans, both $7595 and marketed with option groups. New paint markings identified underhood service points. A redesigned intake manifold and freer-flowing exhaust gave the V-6 in the $13,595 Dodge Dynasty LE sedan (*below*) five more horsepower to send to the new Ultradrive. Anti-lock braking had been phased in during '88.

Slight engine modifications quieted down the Dodge Omni America (*above*). Service points were highlighted with paint for easier use. All Omnis had a tach, oil pressure and voltage gauges, and tinted glass. *Left:* Formerly an option, Shelby was now a full Lancer model with a spoiler and intercooled 174-bhp Turbo II 2.2-liter engine. Racy body add-ons were reminiscent of earlier Pacifica and Shelby limited editions. The $17,395 Shelby had a sport-handling suspension and mono-chromatic paint, but reportedly only 279 were produced. This was the final year for the Lancer.

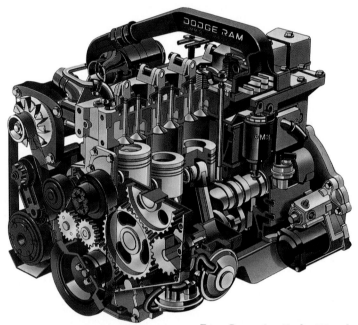

Ram Cummins Turbo Diesel

A heavy-duty Dodge Ram W350 pickup (*top*), with four-wheel drive on a 131-inch wheelbase, had a GVW rating of 8700 pounds. Standard engine was a 205-horsepower, 3.9-liter V-6 (a cut-down 5.2-V-8) that yielded 305 pounds/feet of torque. The mid-size Dakota got a bigger standard engine and rear anti-lock brakes. Standard in two-wheel-drive Dakotas, including this LE edition (*above*), the 2.5-liter four developed 100 horses. Foremost news for big Dodge Ram trucks was the option of a new 5.9-liter Turbo Diesel inline six-cylinder engine (*above right*). Built for Dodge by the Cummins company, the 160-horse motor could be installed in Ram 250 and 350 pickups with either two- or four-wheel drive. A Mitsubishi-built 3.0-liter V-6 could be installed in the Dodge Raider sport-utility (*right*), whether its purchaser had work or leisure in mind. Power windows and locks now were available.

Above: In the subcompact Plymouth Sundance lineup, a 150-horsepower turbo 2.5-liter engine replaced the turbo 2.2 as an option in the RS Turbo Sport Package. The regular RS engine added four horses, while the base motor remained a 93-bhp, 2.2-liter four. The facelifted Sundance exhibited a fresh face with flush aero headlights, a restyled grille, and new tail-lamps. *Right:* Like their Caravan counterparts, Plymouth Voyager minivans could be ordered with a sunroof and a new tur-bocharged engine. Turbos were available only for the short-wheelbase SE and LE, with a heavy-duty five-speed or three-speed automatic. Voyager LE and Grand Voyager models with a V-6 could get the new four-speed automatic transmission.

Now in its 12th season, the $6595 Plymouth Horizon America (*left*) showed only minor changes. The five-door hatch-back sedan's 93-horsepower, 2.2-liter engine gained some internal modifica-tions for quieter running. Such engine-bay items as the dipstick and coolant-overflow cap were highlighted with bright paint, for easier checking of fluid levels. Standard Horizon equipment included a tachometer, tinted glass, and a one-piece fold-down rear seat. An auto-matic transmission was optional, as part of a $776 option package that included power steering. *Bottom:* Plymouth's com-pact Acclaim four-door sedan, offered in $9920 base, $11,295 mid-range LE (*shown*), and $13,195 sporty LX trim, served as an upscale alternative to the aging Reliant America. Though its upright design and front-drive layout were simi-lar, the Acclaim offered more advanced engineering and performance, and a longer 103.3-inch wheelbase. The LE added such extras as cruise control and tilt wheel, with a standard 2.5-liter four and V-6 or turbo option. The LX came with the 3.0-liter V-6 as standard, plus a firmer touring suspension and larger 15-inch tires.

Above: Only a two- and four-door sedan remained in Plymouth's Reliant America line. The optional 2.5-liter four added four bhp. *Right:* A revised dashboard put controls closer to the driver of an Eagle Medallion sedan or wagon, but didn't include a glovebox. The French-built cars held a Renault 2.2-liter four-cylinder engine.

Marketed by Jeep-Eagle dealers, the Eagle Premier four-door sedan started the season in LX (*shown*) and upgraded ES trim, but a sporty ES Limited arrived later in the model year. Otherwise, changes were minor for '89. An LX sedan listed for $13,276, while the ES, with a touring suspension and slightly wider tires, commanded $15,259. Six-passenger Premiers were produced at a new (former AMC) plant near Toronto, Ontario. AMC's 2.5-liter four was standard in the LX, but an all-aluminum, 3.0-liter V-6 went into ES models. All had a four-speed overdrive automatic transmission and a fully independent suspension with 14-inch wheels, but the ES suspension was set for a firmer ride.

364

1989 Production

Chrysler

LeBaron	99,633
LeBaron Sedan	6,549
New Yorker	100,461
Fifth Avenue	17,454
Total	224,097

Dodge

Omni	46,239
Daytona	80,878
Shadow	99,743
Aries America	36,932
Lancer	5,019
Spirit	68,181
Dynasty	137,718
Diplomat	6,429
Caravan	248,852
Total	729,991

Eagle

Premier	32,720

Jeep

Wrangler	69,565
Cherokee	207,216
Total	276,781

Plymouth

Horizon	45,341
Sundance	104,150
Laser	21,098 *
Reliant	36,012
Acclaim	77,752
Voyager	219,229
Gran Fury	4,985
Total	508,567

* Calendar year

Imports*

Dodge/Plymouth Colt	58,299
Dodge/Plymouth Colt Vista	12,910
Chrysler Conquest TSi	5,026
Chrysler's TC by Maserati	2,924
Eagle Summit	19,121
Eagle Medallion	3,907

* Calendar year

Left: Summit was the name of the new entry-level Eagle subcompact sedan. Designed by Mitsubishi, it was a four-door variant of the Dodge/Plymouth Colt, also sold as the Mirage. Standard engine in the DL (*shown*) and LX was an 81-horsepower, 1.5-liter four. A DOHC performance package was available for the LX edition, featuring a 113-horsepower, dual-overhead-cam, 1.6-liter engine, sport suspension, four-wheel disc brakes, and 14-inch wheels. An LX DOHC could have a four-speed overdrive automatic transmission for $682 extra.

Topping the Jeep Cherokee line, the Limited (*right*) came in three- or five-door wagon form, at $23,130 and $24,058, versus as little as $12,160 for a 2WD basic wagon. Four-wheel anti-lock brakes were newly optional with the 173-horse, 4.0-liter, six-cylinder engine, equipped with an automatic transmission and Selec-Trac. The standard 4WD system in Cherokees was part-time Command-Trac. Power steering was now standard on base Cherokees, and the Limited added a remote entry system. The five-door Wagoneer Limited had the same body as the Cherokee, but different trim and a higher price.

1989 Engine Availability

Chrysler

No. Cyl.	Disp., cid	bhp	Availability
I-4	135.0	93	S-LeBaron sedan
I-4T	135.0	174	S-LeBaron GTC & GTS
I-4	153.0	100	S-LeBaron cpe/cvt & Premium sedan; O-LeBaron sedan
I-4T	153.0	150	O-LeBaron GTC & GTS
V-6	181.4	140	S-NY
V-8	318.0	140	S-Fifth Avenue

Dodge

No. Cyl.	Disp., cid	bhp	Availability
I-4	135.0	93	S-Omni, Aries, Shadow, Lancer
I-4T	135.0	174	S-Daytona Shelby, Lancer Shelby
I-4	153.0	100	S-Daytona, Dynasty, Spirit, Caravan; O-Aries, Shadow, Lancer
I-4T	153.0	150	S-Spirit ES, Lancer ES; O-Daytona, Lancer, Shadow ES, Spirit, Caravan

No. Cyl.	Disp., cid	bhp	Availability
V-6	181.4	141	S-Dynasty LE; Spirit ES, Caravan
V-8	318.0	140	S-Diplomat

Eagle

No. Cyl.	Disp., cid	bhp	Availability
I-4	90.0	81	S-Summit
I-4	97.5	113	O-Summit
I-4	132.0	103	S-Medallion
I-4	150.0	111	S-Premier LX
V-6	182.0	150	S-Premier ES; O-Premier LX

Jeep

No. Cyl.	Disp., cid	bhp	Availability
I-4	150.0	117	S-Wrangler
I-4	150.0	121	S-Cherokee
I-6	242.0	177	S-Cherokee Limited; O-Cherokee
I-6	256.0	112	O-Wrangler

Plymouth

No. Cyl.	Disp., cid	bhp	Availability
I-4	107.0	92	S-Laser
I-4	122.0	135	S-Laser RS
I-4T	122.0	190	S-Laser RS Turbo
I-4	135.0	93	S-Horizon, Sundance, Reliant

No. Cyl.	Disp., cid	bhp	Availability
I-4	153.0	100	S-Acclaim, Voyager; O-Sundance, Reliant
I-4T	153.0	150	O-Sundance, Acclaim, Voyager
V-6	181.4	141	S-Acclaim LX; O-Voyager
V-8	318.0	140	S-Gran Fury

Imports

No. Cyl.	Disp., cid	bhp	Availability
I-4	90.0	81	S-Dodge/Plymouth Colt, Eagle Summit
I-4T	97.5	135	O-Dodge/Plymouth Colt GT
I-4	110.0	87	S-Dodge/Plymouth Colt DL 4WD wagon
I-4	121.7	96	S-Dodge/Plymouth Colt Vista
I-4T	135.0	160	S-Chrysler TC w/auto trans
I-4T	135.0	200	S-Chrysler TC w/manual trans
I-4T	155.9	188	S-Chrysler Conquest TSi

1990

The auto industry suffers its worst year since 1983, as Iraq invades Kuwait

Chrysler Corporation's model-year production sinks to the early '80s level—under three-quarter million passenger cars

American Honda approaches Chrysler's Number Three spot in sales

Chrysler shows a modest $68 million profit, while Ford makes $860 million

Diamond-Star Motors in Illinois launches the Mitsubishi Eclipse sport coupe, plus its American-badged kin: Eagle Talon and Plymouth Laser

Driver-side air bags are standard in all American-built Chrysler products (except Talon/Laser)

Chrysler fields an upmarket Town & Country minivan

A front-drive Chrysler Fifth Avenue debuts, as does the posh Chrysler Imperial

A V-6 becomes available in the Dodge Daytona

The Plymouth Horizon and Dodge Omni enter their final year

The Dodge Monaco is a rebadged Eagle Premier, sold through 1991

Concept vehicles include the Chrysler Voyager III

Vice-chairman Gerald Greenwald, viewed as Iacocca's likely successor, leaves Chrysler; other executives also depart

Chrysler's new Y-body New Yorker Fifth Avenue sedan (*top*) replaced the old rear-driver of that name. This was essentially the front-drive New Yorker expanded to a 109.3-inch wheelbase—and $21,395 sticker. Formal styling included hidden headlamps. A deluxe version of the Fifth Avenue revived the Imperial name-plate (*above*). Four inches longer overall, it displayed an upright grille and eagle badges, plus a hefty $24,995 base price. A new port-injected, 147-bhp, 3.3-liter V-6 (*left*) went into the New Yorker, Fifth Avenue, and Imperial. Sales of Chrysler's TC by Maserati (*below*) never took off, so only about 7500 were built.

A Chrysler-built 3.3-liter V-6 replaced the Mitsubishi V-6 under the hood of the $18,795 New Yorker Landau (*above and left*). A driver-side air bag became standard, as did a one-touch driver's power window and rear outboard shoulder belts. At $16,395, the base New Yorker, now named Salon, was trimmed more like the similar Dodge Dynasty. It lacked even standard air conditioning and power windows, although options embraced all-disc anti-lock brakes. A $59 road-handling suspension was optional only on the Salon version.

In a bid to establish a strong presence in Europe and thereby become a "global" company (like Ford and GM), Chrysler had acquired a controlling interest in Simca of France in 1964 and then negotiated a similar deal with the Rootes Group of Great Britain. Much to its regret later, during one of its recurrent financial crises, Chrysler was forced to sell them off (to Peugeot). In the late Eighties, Chrysler set about to reestablish a toehold in Europe, this time mainly as an importer. One of the results was this Chrysler Saratoga (*right*), known to Americans as the LeBaron sedan. It didn't make much of an impression there, but Chrysler did find success selling Jeeps in Europe and formed a joint venture in Austria to build minivans for that vast market.

After half a dozen years of offering the popular Dodge Caravan and Plymouth Voyager minivans, Chrysler launched the luxurious Town & Country. Marketed in one top-of-the-line trim level, the T&C seated seven and had no options other than whitewall tires. Inside were leather upholstery and front/rear air conditioning. Beneath the hood sat the new corporate 3.3-liter V-6, developing 150 horsepower and driving a four-speed automatic transmission. Power windows, locks, driver's seat, mirrors—all were standard, for an even $25,000. All T&Cs strutted woodgrain appliqués and lower bodyside cladding, plus a roof rack.

At long last, a Chrysler LeBaron could get a V-6. The Mitsubishi-built, 3.0-liter engine made 141 horsepower and 171 lbs/ft torque. No matter, the $20,406 GTC convertible (*above*) and $18,238 GTC coupe (*right*) boasted a new 2.2-liter, 174-bhp intercooled VNT IV engine, plus a variable-damping suspension. The interior was also redesigned to be more user-friendly.

The $14,295 Dodge Daytona Shelby (*above*) got a new 2.2-liter, 174-bhp VNT motor for smoother running. Optional in a C/S competition package as well, it came only with a five-speed. Electronic variable suspension—with firm, normal, or soft shock-absorber damping—was new. The ES (*right*) and base Daytonas offered their first V-6 (for $700 extra), the same 3.0-liter engine used in other Chrysler products, available with a new five-speed gearbox. Daytonas also added a driver-side air bag.

Dodge's popular $14,395 Dynasty LE sedan (*top and above*) got Chrysler's new 3.3-liter V-6, which could also replace the standard 100-bhp four in a base Dynasty. Like all domestically built Chrysler cars, the Dynasty gained an air bag. The six-passenger sedan was Dodge's version of the C-body used for Chrysler's New Yorker. A swoopy Daytona R/T concept car (*left*) blended aggressive ground-effects trim with a glass roof, flush side glass, and enormous air scoops ahead of the rear wheels. A 2.2-liter VNT four lurked beneath the hood, and massive Goodyear experimental 275/40VR17 tires met the pavement.

In 1988, this sleek and low Intrepid concept car (*right*) had toured the auto-show circuit as a "Dodge of Tomorrow." Chrysler's "design team worked to express all the excitement, power, and spirited fun of a high performance sports car," the company explained this year. That design, with "sweeping lines and dramatic shape," served as inspiration for the soon-to-arrive Dodge Stealth coupe. While the concept vehicle had a mid-engine configuration, the production Mitsubishi-built Stealth would mount its V-6 up front.

The Dodge Caravan got the new 3.3-liter V-6 option, here (*above*) a $16,125 LE with optional ES Decor Package sporting "warm silver fascia and bodyside moldings." Seven-passenger seating (formerly optional) was now standard in the regular-length LE. A convert-a-bed option was available in standard models, and air conditioners delivered more rapid cooldown. In addition to an air bag, the $13,145 Dodge Spirit ES (for Euro-Sport) sedan (*right*) gained all-disc brakes. The Mitsubishi V-6 was available on all models, and new self-restoring bumpers could handle five-mph collisions. The facelifted Shadow coupe cost $8735. This one (*below*) has the ES package, with new fascias (with fog lamps up front), ground-effects panels, and the reworked instruments found on all Shadows. The Turbo II engine lurked under the hood of many ES Shadows.

Dodge dropped the America label from its subcompact Omni (*above*). Now in its final year, it added a driver-side air bag as well as rear-seat shoulder belts. This year's new instrument panel held revised climate-control ducts. As before, the 93-horsepower 2.2 four mated with a standard five-speed manual or optional three-speed automatic transmission. Once again, too, few options were offered, and those mainly in groups. Riders in a full-size Dodge pickup (*second from top*) did not have to be alone—new Club Cab versions of the D150 and its heavier-duty mates added two side-facing folding seats in the rear. This was accomplished by adding 18 inches to the length of the cab. Note the roof lights and bracing on this tough-guy D150 pickup. Mid-size Dodge Dakota pickups also got a Club Cab edition. Dodge's $8863 Colt GT DOHC three-door hatchback (*third from top*) zipped along with a twin-cam, 1.6-liter engine, rated at 113 bhp. Other three-doors and the 2WD wagon made do with an 81-horse, 1.5-liter four, but the 4WD wagon ran with a 1.8-liter motor. The formerly optional turbo engine was dropped. Built by Mitsubishi, Colts were sold as virtually identical Dodges and Plymouths. Three-doors came in base, GL, and GT form. The wagon continued with only minor trim changes.

The eagerly awaited, front-drive Plymouth Laser 2+2 hatchback (*right*)—assembled by Diamond-Star Motors in Normal, Illinois—surfaced in January 1989 as an early '90 model. The sporty coupe was also marketed as the Mitsubishi Eclipse and Eagle Talon, but only the Laser lacked an all-wheel-drive version. A 92-horsepower, 1.8-liter four went into the base Laser and better-equipped RS. Optional in the RS was a 135-bhp, 16-valve, dual-cam, 2.0-liter four. The RS Turbo carried the hot version of that motor, delivering 190 horses. Each model, except the turbo, could have a four-speed automatic as an option. All Lasers stopped with all-disc brakes, but anti-lock brakes weren't offered. Both the RS and RS Turbo rode 16-inch tires. Note the prominent hood bulge.

Top: Chrysler's new 3.3-liter V-6 became standard (and welcome) in the $18,325 extended-wheelbase Plymouth Grand Voyager with four-speed automatic. A unique two-in-one Voyager III concept vehicle (*above*) appeared at auto shows. The propane-powered front module could be used for urban driving, seating three. The rear unit added a 2.2-liter motor. Overall length was comparable to a Grand Voyager.

All three versions of the Plymouth Acclaim sedan, including this $13,805 LX (*above*), could have Mitsubishi's 141-bhp, 3.0 V-6 mated to a new four-speed automatic. A new instrument cluster and driver-side air bag went into the Sundance (*right*), here in RS trim.

1990 Production	
Chrysler	
LeBaron	65,220
LeBaron Sedan	8,074
New Yorker	41,581
New Yorker Fifth Avenue	44,423
Imperial	14,968
Town & Country	3,615
Total	177,881
Dodge	
Omni	16,733
Daytona	43,785
Shadow	93,660
Spirit	99,319
Monaco	7,154
Dynasty	112,833
Caravan	260,799
Total	634,283
Eagle	
Talon	28,227
Premier	15,077
Total	43,304
* Calendar year	
Jeep	
Wrangler	58,184
Cherokee	151,230
Total	209,414
Plymouth	
Horizon	16,397
Sundance	79,562
Laser	40,177 *
Acclaim	110,330
Voyager	221,108
Total	467,574
* Calendar year	
Imports*	
Dodge/Plymouth Colt	39,602
Eagle Summit	12,735
Dodge/Plymouth Colt Vista	5,430
Chrysler's TC by Maserati	3,298
* Calendar year	

Chrysler launched one of the products of its Diamond-Star joint venture under the Eagle Talon badge. The top model, the $16,437 TSi AWD (*right*) boasted a turbocharged/intercooled 2.0-liter, four-valve mill, churning out its 190 horses through all four wheels. The base engine was a 135-bhp, dual-cam four. This 2+2, also sold as a Plymouth Laser and Mitsubishi Eclipse, skipped the base 1.8-liter four. Except for a new overhead console, the Jeep Grand Wagoneer (*below*) showed little change. Neither did the Cherokee sport-utility, which differed mainly in trim and equipment. The sportiest Eagle Premier was the $20,272 ES Limited (*below right*), with its firmer touring suspension. Premiers now had all-disc brakes and a floor-mounted shift lever. Dodge launched a similar Monaco, but neither did very well in the marketplace.

1990 Engine Availability

Chrysler

No. Cyl.	Disp., cid	bhp	Availability
I-4T	135.0	174	S-LeBaron GTC
I-4	153.0	100	S-LeBaron cpe/cvt
I-4T	153.0	150	O-LeBaron cpe/cvt
V-6	181.4	141	S-LeBaron sdn, LeBaron Premium and GT cpe/cvt
V-6	201.0	147	S-Imperial, NY, NY Fifth Avenue
V-6	201.0	150	S-Town & Country

Dodge

No. Cyl.	Disp., cid	bhp	Availability
I-4	135.0	93	S-Omni, Aries, Shadow, Lancer
I-4T	135.0	174	S-Daytona Shelby; O-Shadow
I-4	153.0	100	S-Daytona, Dynasty, Spirit, Caravan; O-Shadow
I-4T	153.0	150	S-Spirit ES; O-Spirit, Shadow, Daytona, Caravan
V-6	181.4	141	O-Dynasty LE; O-Dynasty, Daytona, Spirit
V-6	181.4	142	O-Caravan
V-6	182.0	150	S-Monaco
V-6	201.0	147	O-Dynasty
V-6	201.0	150	O-Caravan

Eagle

No. Cyl.	Disp., cid	bhp	Availability
I-4	122.0	135	S-Talon
I-4T	122.0	190	S-Talon TSi/AWD
V-6	182.0	150	S-Premier

Jeep

No. Cyl.	Disp., cid	bhp	Availability
I-4	150.0	117	S-Wrangler
I-4	150.0	121	S-Cherokee
I-6	242.0	177	S-Cherokee Limited; O-Cherokee
I-6	256.0	112	O-Wrangler

Plymouth

No. Cyl.	Disp., cid	bhp	Availability
I-4	107.0	92	S-Laser
I-4	122.0	135	S-Laser RS
I-4T	122.0	190	S-Laser RS Turbo
I-4	135.0	93	S-Horizon, Sundance
I-4	153.0	100	S-Acclaim, Voyager; O-Sundance
I-4T	153.0	150	O-Sundance, Acclaim, Voyager
V-6	181.4	141	S-Acclaim LX
V-6	181.4	142	O-Voyager
V-6	201.0	150	O-Voyager

Imports

No. Cyl.	Disp., cid	bhp	Availability
I-4	90.0	81	S-Dodge/Plymouth Colt, Eagle Summit
I-4	97.5	113	O-Dodge/Plymouth Colt GT, Eagle Summit
I-4	110.0	87	S-Dodge/Plymouth Colt DL 4WD wagon
I-4	121.7	96	S-Dodge/Plymouth Colt Vista
I-4T	135.0	200	S-Chrysler TC w/manual trans
V-6	181.0	141	S-Chrysler TC w/auto trans

1991

The Persian Gulf war signals another bad year for the auto industry

American Honda and Toyota beat Chrysler's sales as the domestic company sinks to an ignominious fifth place

The Big Three show a combined net loss of $7.5 billion—the worst year ever

Chrysler loses $795 million for the fiscal year

Chrysler's model-year output declines nearly 17 percent

Iacocca warns that if Japan keeps taking market share, Chrysler could be "gone"

The Big Three chairmen seek concessions on the Clean Air Act, and also oppose threatened tightened fuel-economy restrictions

Dodge Shadow now comes as a convertible; the Spirit R/T carries a 224-horsepower turbocharged engine

Dodge launches the Mitsubishi-built Stealth sport coupe

The minivans are reworked, and now come with a driver-side air bag

All-wheel-drive Dodge and Plymouth minivan models become available

Chrysler sells its 50-percent share of Diamond-Star Motors

Growing sales of nearly new "program" cars is harming the new-car market

A new larger, 150-horsepower, 3.8-liter V-6 engine went into the $26,925 Chrysler Imperial four-door sedan (*above*), which halted with all-disc anti-lock brakes. Cloth upholstery substituted for the former leather, but a $649 Mark Cross leather interior became available. The new 3.8-liter V-6 was optional in the $20,875 New Yorker Fifth Avenue (*below*), priced $262 higher than the standard 3.3 V-6. Its landau vinyl roof, covering part of the back-door window, imparted a formal look.

The Landau edition of the Chrysler New Yorker, with its neo-classic vinyl rear roof section, disappeared this season. Still on sale was the New Yorker Salon (*above*), with some of the former Landau's equipment— but no padded roof. *Left:* One of this season's concept vehicles borrowed the heralded Chrysler 300 name to tour the auto-show circuit. The long-wheelbase, ultra-sleek, pillarless four-door, with rear-hinged back doors, held a powerful 8.0-liter "Copperhead" V-10.

Chrysler trimmed the lineup of the LeBaron convertible (*above*). The $15,925 base models lost their Highline name, but kept the 100-horsepower, 2.5-liter engine as standard. What had been called Premium got an LX badge, along with the 141-bhp V-6, but a little less standard equipment than before. The sporty GT version departed, and the hot GTC traded its sizzling turbo for V-6 power—with a tamer 2.5-liter turbo optional on either base or GTC models. The LeBaron sport coupe (*right*) underwent the same lineup changes as the convertible. Anti-lock brakes were available for the first time on the $16,450 LeBaron four-door sedan (*below right and below*).

Chrysler's Town & Country minivan (*right*) got a new interior and a smoother look, featuring a lower hood and greater glass area. Woodgrain trim remained standard, as did lace-patterned alloy wheels. Formerly optional, anti-lock brakes were now standard, but no four-wheel-drive version went on sale. All T&C minivans rode the long 119.3-inch wheelbase, comparable to the Grand Caravan/Voyager, but with a full load of standard equipment. The limited options list included Quad Command seating, rear air conditioning, and cloth/leather upholstery. The $23,905 T&C was the only Chrysler minivan with digital instruments. A vertical-bar grille provided instant identification.

Dodge dealers got an all-new model, the Japanese-built Stealth, here (*top*) the $18,056 ES—kin to Mitsubishi's 3000GT. Chrysler took credit for styling the front-drive 2+2 coupe, Mitsubishi for the interior and mechanicals (*above left*). The platform was similar to the Eclipse's, on a 97.2-inch chassis. Four models, each with a 3.0-liter V-6, were listed: base, ES, R/T, and R/T Turbo. The base engine developed 164 bhp, but the ES and R/T got a twin-cam version with 24 valves and 222 bhp. Note the spoiler at the base of the backlight of the $24,155 Stealth R/T (*above*). The $29,267 R/T Turbo got twin intercooled turbochargers for an impressive 300 bhp, plus four-wheel drive and four-wheel steering.

Anti-lock brakes joined the options list of the Dodge Spirit, shown (*above*) in $13,709 ES trim. Base and LE Spirits came with a 100-bhp four, but the ES carried a 152-bhp turbo. A limited-edition, high-performance, $17,820 R/T Turbo went on sale, packing a 224-bhp dual-cam, four-valve turbo engine mated to a five-speed manual gearbox. No other Chrysler products shared this power-plant, which delivered startling acceleration—accompanied by noticeable "torque-steer." Only 1400 R/Ts were to be built. Dodge debuted a Shadow convertible (*right*), as well as an entry-level America model. The manual-top ragtop (produced by ASC) started at $12,995 for the Highline, $14,068 for the ES.

Dodge's $17,595 Monaco ES four-door (*right*) carried a touring suspension, air conditioning, and all-disc brakes—items that were optional on the $14,995 Monaco LE. Anti-lock braking became optional during the model year. Monaco sales never took off, and the similar Eagle Premier wasn't exactly a hot item either. Sole powertrain was a 150-bhp, 3.0-liter V-6 with a four-speed automatic.

Left: Except for newly optional leather seat trim, in a choice of two colors, the Dynasty sedan—Dodge's top-selling car—carried on with little change. A new security alarm could be installed. A 2.5-liter four remained standard in the base Dynasty, but the $15,085 LE held a Mitsubishi-built, 3.0-liter V-6. A 3.3-liter V-6, made by Chrysler, could go into either model. *Below:* Dodge Ram Wagons, spacious enough to hold 15 people, gained new cast aluminum and styled steel wheels, plus a full-sized spare tire. Engine choices included the faithful 5.2- and 5.9-liter V-8s.

Full-size Dodge Ram pickups, including this D150 Club Cab (*above*), got a new grille, body moldings, and bumpers. The Dodge Caravan, here the $19,255 Grand Caravan LE (*below*), earned its greatest overhaul since its '84 debut. Changes included a restyled body, new interior, AWD models, and optional anti-lock brakes.

Turbocharged versions of the Plymouth Laser hatchback coupe could now have a four-speed overdrive automatic transmission, and all Lasers could get anti-lock braking, via a unit supplied by Mitsubishi. Unlike the similar Eagle Talon and Mitsubishi Eclipse, which offered four-wheel-drive models, Lasers were front-drive only. Base Lasers again held a 92-horsepower, four-cylinder engine, while the RS (*above and left*) contained a 135-horsepower, dual-overhead-cam 2.0-liter four, which had initially been optional. RS Turbos used a turbocharged rendition of the 2.0-liter engine. A security alarm joined the options list, but only when ordered in conjunction with ABS. Laser prices began at $10,864.

Optional all-disc anti-lock braking became available in the compact Acclaim sedan, shown in $12,880 LE trim (*right*). Turbocharged engines faded away. A 141-horsepower, 3.0-liter V-6, standard in the top-of-the-line LX, could also be installed in a base or LE Acclaim. Plymouth's imported Colt line dipped to a single three-door body style, with a 92-bhp, 1.5-liter four. A five-speed gearbox was standard on the $7845 GL (*below*), but base Colts had a four-speed. Plymouth's Colt Vista high-roofed, seven-seat wagon (*below right*) came in $11,941 front-drive or $13,167 all-wheel-drive form, powered by a 2.0-liter, 96-bhp four.

A new entry-level "America" version of the Plymouth Sundance bowed, starting at $7699. A five-door RS (*top*) cost $10,425 with the 2.5-liter, 100-bhp four and five-speed stick ($11,042 with automatic). Chrysler hyped the America as the least-expensive car with a standard air bag. The 2.5-liter turbo four (only in RS models) produced an extra 30 lbs/ft of torque, now 210. The RS interior (*above*) held a console, tach, and split-folding rear seat.

Above: A 1984 Plymouth Voyager joined the automotive collection at the Henry Ford Museum in October. Here, former Chrysler Motors president Bennett E. Bidwell (*left*) presents the keys to museum president Harold K. Skramstad, Jr. Chrysler's minivan was recognized for its role in beginning an entirely new automotive market segment. *Left:* New inside and out, the Voyager now came with either front- or all-wheel drive, with anti-lock brakes optional. All body panels were new, except for the roof, but the overall appearance didn't change dramatically. A glove box was installed for the first time in the minivans.

A four-speed automatic transmission became available for turbocharged Eagle Talons, including this $16,513 TSi AWD (*top*). Talons could now have anti-lock brakes, too. Anti-lock braking was standard on the top-of-the-line, $19,495 Eagle Premier ES Limited (*above*), optional on the LX and mid-level ES. The futuristic-looking Jeep Wagoneer 2000 concept vehicle (*right*) featured a versatile bench-or-bucket interior and a pop-up roof rack.

1991 Production	
Chrysler	
LeBaron	43,907
New Yorker Salon	15,108
New Yorker Fifth Avenue	44,464
Imperial	11,601
Town & Country	6,414
Total	121,494
Dodge	
Shadow	77,084
Daytona	20,443
Spirit	97,696
Monaco	7,303
Dynasty	126,025
Caravan	266,924
Total	595,475
Eagle	
Talon	NA
Premier	10,810
Total	10,810
Jeep	
Wrangler	65,135
Cherokee	151,578
Total	216,713
Plymouth	
Laser	28,201 *
Sundance	70,769
Acclaim	113,434
Voyager	207,260
Total	419,664
* Calendar year	
Imports*	
Dodge/Plymouth Colt	27,280
Eagle Summit	18,211
Dodge/Plymouth Colt Vista	8,884
Dodge Stealth	NA
Chrysler's TC by Maserati	1,077
* Calendar year	

A $6949 three-door hatchback (*above*) joined the Eagle Summit line, with a shorter wheelbase (93.9 inches) than that used by the four-door (96.7 inches). Base and sporty ES models gained a more powerful 92-bhp engine with three valves per cylinder. The new grille was designed to impart greater identity to the Eagle brand, which suffered from a lack of public recognition. The step-up Summit ES sedan (*left*) also got the 92-bhp four, as the former dual-cam engine departed. Mid-range models (DL and LX) were also dropped, but this year's $9623 ES sedan was equipped similar to the prior LX. Some sedans were assembled in Illinois.

1991 Engine Availability

Chrysler

No. Cyl.	Disp., cid	bhp	Availability
I-4	153.0	100	S-LeBaron cpe/cvt
I-4T	153.0	152	O-LeBaron/GTC
V-6	181.4	141	S-LeBaron LX, GTC, and sedan
V-6	201.0	147	S-NY Fifth Ave, NY Salon, Town & Country
V-6	230.0	150	S-Imperial; O-New Yorker Fifth Ave

Dodge

No. Cyl.	Disp., cid	bhp	Availability
I-4	135.0	93	S-Shadow
I-4T	135.0	224	S-Spirit R/T
I-4	153.0	100	S-Daytona, Dynasty, Shadow ES and cvt, Spirit, Caravan; O-Shadow
I-4T	153.0	152	S-Daytona Shelby, Spirit ES; O-Daytona, Shadow, Spirit
V-6	181.4	141	S-Dynasty LE; O-Daytona, Spirit, Caravan

No. Cyl.	Disp., cid	bhp	Availability
V-6	182.0	150	S-Monaco
V-6	201.0	147	O-Dynasty
V-6	201.0	150	S-Grand Caravan, Caravan AWD; O-Caravan

Eagle

No. Cyl.	Disp., cid	bhp	Availability
I-4	122.0	135	S-Talon
I-4T	122.0	190	S-Talon TSi/AWD
V-6	182.0	150	S-Premier

Jeep

No. Cyl.	Disp., cid	bhp	Availability
I-4	150.0	123	S-Wrangler
I-4	150.0	130	S-Cherokee
I-6	242.0	180	O-Wrangler
I-6	242.0	190	S-Cherokee Limited; O-Cherokee

Plymouth

No. Cyl.	Disp., cid	bhp	Availability
I-4	107.0	92	S-Laser
I-4	122.0	135	S-Laser RS
I-4T	122.0	190	S-Laser RS Turbo

No. Cyl.	Disp., cid	bhp	Availability
I-4	135.0	93	S-Sundance
I-4	153.0	100	S-Acclaim, Voyager
V-6	181.4	141	S-Acclaim LX; O-Acclaim, Caravan
V-6	201.0	150	S-Grand Voyager, Voyager AWD; O-Voyager

Imports

No. Cyl.	Disp., cid	bhp	Availability
I-4	90.0	92	S-Dodge/Plymouth Colt, Eagle Summit
I-4	121.7	96	S-Dodge/Plymouth Colt Vista
I-4T	135.0	200	S-Chrysler TC w/manual trans
V-6	181.0	141	S-Chrysler TC w/auto trans
V-6	181.0	164	S-Dodge Stealth
V-6	181.0	222	S-Dodge Stealth ES and R/T
V-6T	181.0	300	S-Dodge Stealth R/T Turbo

1992

The auto market is stable—8.2 million cars are sold, 6.2 million domestically built

Chrysler Corporation ends the year with a healthy $723 million net profit

After a series of bad seasons, Chrysler captures nearly 13 percent of the domestic new-car market

Dodge releases the eagerly awaited "retro" Viper roadster, with a 400-bhp V-10; only 200 go on sale this season

The hot Dodge Daytona IROC R/T sport coupe replaces the Shelby edition

Plymouth's Sundance Duster gets a 141-bhp V-6

The Chrysler-marketed Jeep Grand Cherokee is the only sport-utility vehicle with a driver-side air bag

Robert Eaton, formerly from GM, is named Chrysler vice-chairman in March

Lee Iacocca—hailed as one of top auto executives of all time—retires as chairman of Chrysler Corporation

Chrysler president Robert Lutz is favored to take over the chairmanship, but will lose the post to outsider Eaton

Much of the gain in overall profit is attributed to continued cost-cutting

Minivans can have integrated child safety seats—an industry first

An all-wheel-drive Town & Country minivan bows

Chrysler's $18,849 New Yorker Salon near-luxury sedan (*top and above*) gained rounded front/rear styling, plus an optional landau vinyl roof (absent in '91). Plush was the word for a New Yorker interior (*right*), especially when fitted with tufted leather. A floor console with cassette storage became available, as did an electrochromic rear-view mirror. The $21,874 Chrysler New Yorker Fifth Avenue sedan (*below*) wore similarly revised styling, with a slightly rounded nose and tail. As a result, it had a more distinct look when compared to the Imperial, which retained its straight-edged profile.

Chrysler's LeBaron four-door sedan (*above*) expanded its range, adding engine and transmission choices. A 100-horsepower, 2.5-liter four with three-speed automatic transmission was standard on the $13,998 base model. The $15,287 LX sedan and $15,710 Landau used a V-6 hooked to a four-speed automatic (optional on the base model). A 3.0-liter, port fuel-injected V-6, rated at 141 bhp, remained standard in the LeBaron GTC coupe and convertible. Anti-lock braking (including rear discs) was a new—and desirable—option. This top-line LeBaron GTC coupe (*right*) stickered at $16,164. With the five-speed manual gearbox came a starter interlock that prevented the engine from starting unless the clutch pedal was pushed all the way to the floor. Automatic-transmission LeBarons added an interlock that required the application of the brake before shifting.

A driver-side air bag was installed in the $24,716 Chrysler Town & Country minivan (*above*), now available with all-wheel drive. For the first time, the luxury T&C could be ordered without woodgrain bodyside trim. The Chrysler 300 concept car (*above right*) appeared at auto shows in 1991. Although rumored to be under consideration for production, it soon faded from public memory. Chrysler first used the Cirrus name for a '92 concept car (*right*). Like the Cirrus sedan that debuted for 1995, it featured cab-forward design. All four doors opened from the center on the pillarless car, which held a two-stroke turbo motor.

After attracting scads of attention at auto shows in 1989, the Viper RT/10 roadster, patterned loosely after the old Shelby Cobra, headed for actual production—complete with a V-10 engine. Shown with the Viper production team (*top*) is the car that paced the 75th Indianapolis 500 race. The Viper's 8.0-liter (488-cid) V-10 (*above*) developed a whopping 400 horsepower, plus 462 pounds/feet of grunting, stump-pulling torque. All Vipers had a six-speed manual transmission, with a forced first-to-fourth-gear shift when taking off under light throttle—like that employed in Corvettes. Each of the first-year Vipers was red (*above right*). The two-seat roadster went on sale in early summer of 1992, and the entire 200-car run sold out immediately—some bringing far more than the $50,000 list price. Traditional-style white gauges with black lettering (*right*) enhanced the visceral experience of piloting a Viper. Farther down the Dodge high-performance scale, an $18,532 Daytona IROC R/T debuted at mid-year, replacing the Shelby and shod with Z-rated tires, good for 149+ mph.

In its second year, the Dodge Stealth (*above*) showed few changes, apart from late availability of a tilt/removable glass sunroof. Dodge Daytonas (*right*) wore a new nose with exposed aero headlamps, and could get anti-lock braking.

New body colors were the only notable changes in the Dodge Monaco sedan, kin to the Eagle Premier, both now in their final year. The $14,354 LE and the step-up $17,203 ES edition (*above*) had front bucket seats with a floor lever for the automatic transmission. Dodge's top-selling model, the Dynasty four-door sedan (*right*), added a floor console with slots for tape cassettes and child-proof rear door locks, plus an optional overhead console. Three engine choices were available, a four and two V-6s. A 152-bhp turbo motor powered the $14,441 Dodge Spirit ES sedan (*below*), but three other engines went into Spirit models—topped by the high-performance, 224-horse R/T. The only changes were in transmission availability and gear ratios.

This year's Dodge Caravan, here the $15,624 SE (*above*), gained a driver-side air bag and an optional bench seat with integrated child seats. The popular mini-vans added flush door handles and restyled wheels, and a 3.0-liter V-6 was now offered in Grand Caravans. After a year's absence, base models could have a manual shift, although it wasn't very popular. *Left:* This EPIC (Electric Power Interurban Commuter) concept minivan, Dodge claimed, "begins the thesis for the future design of Chrysler minivans." The TEVan program was investigating the feasibility of electric vehicles.

Full-size Dodge pickups gained more powerful Magnum 3.9-liter V-6 and 5.2-liter V-8 engines, delivering 180 and 230 bhp, respectively. Both engines now featured more precise sequential multi-point fuel injection. A new, heavy-duty five-speed manual gearbox also became available in Ram pickups, including this D150 "S" (*right*) with two-wheel drive. Dodge Caravans were best known as people-carriers, but cargo-hauling versions (*below*) saw plenty of service, too. The compact cargo vans came on both 112- and 119-inch wheelbases.

Magnum 3.9-liter V-6   Magnum 5.2-liter V-8

A Plymouth Laser with all-wheel drive finally became available, matching what had been offered in the Eagle Talon and Mitsubishi Eclipse lines since the beginning. The new $16,853 Laser RS Turbo AWD (*above*) had permanently engaged four-wheel-drive and, unlike Talon/Eclipse, came only with a five-speed manual. Cosmetic revisions gave the Laser a fresh look, led by newly exposed aero headlamps and front/rear styling modifications that made it visually distinct from the Talon. Plymouth slashed its compact Acclaim sedan lineup to a single $11,470 model (*right*)—mainly because 85 percent of cars sold had been base models. In another consumer-oriented move, the optional 3.0-liter V-6 engine might now drive either a lower-cost three-speed automatic transmission, or the more flexible four-speed unit.

Plymouth dropped the sporty RS edition of its subcompact Sundance, leaving only the budget-priced America version (*left*) and the Highline, which started at $7992 and $9336, respectively. Highlines added body-color bumpers and new front/rear fascias. Sundance never got a convertible, like that offered in the Dodge Shadow line, but a sporty Sundance Duster arrived late in the model year. Borrowing a high-performance badge from the past, the $9849 Duster got exclusive use of a 141-bhp V-6. A driver-side air bag went into all Plymouth Voyagers (*below*). It had been an option since early 1991. A new integrated child safety seat was optional. Regular- and long-wheelbase Grand Voyagers were again available with front-drive or all-wheel drive. Voyager/Caravan sales showed no signs of letting up.

A completely different version of the Plymouth Colt Vista emerged for '92 (*below*), nearly identical to the new Mitsubishi Expo LRV "mini-mini-van." The $11,397 five-passenger wagon had a van-like sliding rear side door. Both the front-drive and a $13,469 all-wheel-drive variant were offered, with either a 113-bhp, 1.8-liter engine, or an optional 116-bhp, 2.4-liter four (with 136 lbs/ft torque). Anti-lock brakes were optional. Sales, however, were disappointing.

Like its Eclipse/Laser mates, the Eagle Talon sport coupe earned a fresh face, with exposed aero headlamps (replacing the hidden units) and a new hood that dipped into the nose. Restyled taillamps and rear spoiler rounded out the revisions. The sporty, top-line TSi (*top*) now came in monochromatic paint schemes, with front-wheel drive or full-time four-wheel drive (AWD). Save for the availability of cloth-faced seats on the base hatchback, the Eagle Summit soldiered on with little change. The four-door (*above*) started at $9067, and topped out at $12,210. New to Eagle, the $13,469 AWD wagon (*below*) ran with a port fuel-injected, 2.4-liter four.

1992 Production

Chrysler

LeBaron	44,437
New Yorker Salon	19,779
New Yorker Fifth Avenue	37,884
Imperial	7,643
Town & Country	18,181
Total	127,924

Dodge

Shadow	89,987
Daytona	13,478
Spirit	78,740
Dynasty	96,403
Monaco	2,118
Viper	162
Caravan	285,865
Total	566,753

Eagle

Talon	29,618
Premier	4,747
Total	34,365

Jeep

Wrangler	59,690
Cherokee	137,826
Total	197,516

Plymouth

Sundance	66,557
Laser	25,119
Acclaim	77,105
Voyager	218,089
Total	386,870

Imports*

Dodge/Plymouth Colt	28,817
Eagle Summit/Summit Wagon	21,073
Plymouth Colt Vista	7,948
Dodge Stealth	16,926

* Calendar year

A new look hit the Jeep Wrangler Sahara (*left*)—a $2499/$3004 package option—featuring low-lustre paints and color-coordinated hub covers. Note the heavy roll-bar structure on this one, ready for serious off-roading. Sahara, Renegade, and Islander "models" held a 4.0-liter Power Tech Six yielding 180 horses, while base and S Wranglers came with a 2.5-liter four. The hard-to-miss Jeep Comanche pickup with the Eliminator package (*below left*) carried the 190-bhp Power Tech Six, as did its Pioneer mate. Lesser Comanches made do with the 130-bhp four. Two new colors were available for the $25,484 Jeep Cherokee Limited 4x4 wagon (*below*)—one of five series in the 44-model Cherokee line. All except the base series employed Jeep's 190-bhp Power Tech Six. At the Detroit Auto Show, Chrysler introduced the new Grand Cherokee, due as a '93 model.

1992 Engine Availability

Chrysler

No. Cyl.	Disp., cid	bhp	Availability
I-4	153.0	100	S-LeBaron cpe/cvt
I-4T	153.0	152	O-LeBaron cpe/cvt
V-6	181.4	141	S-LeBaron LX, GTC, and sedan
V-6	201.0	147	S-NY Fifth Ave, NY Salon
V-6	201.0	150	S-Town & Country
V-6	230.0	150	S-Imperial; O-New Yorker Fifth Ave

Dodge

No. Cyl.	Disp., cid	bhp	Availability
I-4	135.0	93	S-Shadow
I-4T	135.0	224	S-Spirit R/T
I-4	153.0	100	S-Daytona, Dynasty, Shadow ES and cvt, Spirit, Caravan; O-Shadow
I-4T	153.0	152	S-Daytona Shelby, Spirit ES; O-Daytona, Shadow, Spirit
V-6	180.0	150	S-Monaco

No. Cyl.	Disp., cid	bhp	Availability
V-6	181.4	141	S-Dynasty LE; O-Daytona, Spirit, Caravan
V-6	201.0	147	O-Dynasty
V-6	201.0	150	S-Grand Caravan, Caravan AWD; O-Caravan
V-10	488.0	400	S-Viper

Eagle

No. Cyl.	Disp., cid	bhp	Availability
I-4	122.0	135	S-Talon
I-4T	122.0	195	S-Talon TSi/AWD
V-6	182.0	150	S-Premier

Jeep

No. Cyl.	Disp., cid	bhp	Availability
I-4	150.0	123	S-Wrangler
I-4	150.0	130	S-Cherokee O-Wrangler
I-6	242.0	180	S-Cherokee
I-6	242.0	190	S-Cherokee Limited; O-Cherokee

Plymouth

No. Cyl.	Disp., cid	bhp	Availability
I-4	107.0	92	S-Laser
I-4	122.0	135	S-Laser RS

No. Cyl.	Disp., cid	bhp	Availability
I-4T	122.0	195	S-Laser RS Turbo
I-4	135.0	93	S-Sundance
I-4	153.0	100	S-Acclaim, Voyager
V-6	181.4	141	O-Acclaim
V-6	181.4	142	O-Voyager
V-6	201.0	150	S-Grand Voyager, Voyager AWD; O-Voyager

Imports

No. Cyl.	Disp., cid	bhp	Availability
I-4	90.0	92	S-Dodge/Plymouth Colt, Eagle Summit
I-4	112.0	113	S-Plymouth Colt Vista, Eagle Summit Wagon
I-4	143.0	116	O-Plymouth Colt Vista, Eagle Summit Wagon
V-6	181.0	164	S-Dodge Stealth
V-6	181.0	222	S-Dodge Stealth ES and R/T
V-6T	181.0	300	S-Dodge Stealth R/T Turbo

Chapter 17

Beyond Rebirth; Taking Aim at Tomorrow: 1993-96

Out with the old, in with the new. That could well have been Chrysler's motto for the mid-Nineties. The remaining relatives of the crucial-but-antiquated K-car family—the vehicles that had virtually saved Chrysler Corporation from extinction—either were gone already, or on their way out. In their place would come an impressive progression of truly modern machines—rounded in line, technically advanced, paving the way to yet another rejuvenation for the company. By mid-decade, nearly all the vestiges of the past would be extinct, elbowed aside by fresh faces.

The first to arrive was the "LH" trio of front-drive sedans, measuring between mid- and full-size, and reveling in a flurry of favorable publicity. Chrysler's Concorde, issued in a single body style, took aim at such rivals as the Acura Legend and Lexus ES 300. Dodge named its version Intrepid, focusing on the family market—but with an ES edition on hand for those who favored a little more flavor. Rounding out the trio was the Eagle Vision, considered the sporti-est member of the group. In fact, each of the three had a model or an option with a touring suspension and 16-inch tires.

All LH sedans were Canadian-built, riding a 113-inch wheelbase. As that long span implies, the wheels sat con-siderably closer to the car's corners than usual, exhibiting what came to be known as "cab-forward" styling. Ostensibly replacing the New Yorker Fifth Avenue/Salon (and Imperial), the three bore scant kinship to those soon-to-be-extinct models.

Both LH engines, 3.3- and 3.5-liter V-6s, drove a new four-speed electronic automatic transmission. The hot one put out a vigorous 214 horsepower. Major options included traction control and a

child safety seat that folded out from the middle of the rear bench.

Because the first run of 200 Vipers—issued late in the '92 season—had sold immediately, Dodge planned to produce 3000 this time. Most of those, too, were spoken for before the model year began.

Before the '93 season got very far, though, a problem with the fit of the large hood (made by an outside suppli-er) delayed production. So only about half the expected number rolled out the door. While that sales total did little to reinforce Chrysler's financial coffers, the "back-to-basics" Viper drew scads of comment, and lured hordes of potential buyers for *other* models into Dodge showrooms.

Although Jeep Cherokees and Wranglers carried on with only modest changes, Chrysler had a surprise in store for four-wheel-drive fans, too. When president Robert Lutz drove the first Grand Cherokee up the steps of Detroit's Cobo Hall, dramatically crashing through a glass door during the auto-show preview, it signaled a focus on both brawn and luxury in the 4WD seg-ment. Now, Chrysler unabashedly tar-geted those customers who rarely—if ever—took their vehicles off-road.

The imported Mitsubishi-built Colt earned a major redesign for 1993. Now offered only in notchback body styles, the car was sold by both Dodge and Plymouth dealers, and also under the Eagle Summit nameplate.

In the alternative-fuel arena, some 4600 Dodge Spirits were built to run on gas/methanol blends, for government and private-fleet use. Some Plymouth Acclaims were similarly fitted.

As part of a continuous program of refocusing and restoring its cash flow, Chrysler Corporation began to divest some of its acquisitions. Lamborghini

The all-new 1996 Dodge Grand Caravan ES took a more aerody-namic stance.

SpA, the Italian sports-car maker, was among those that were sent off on their own. Chrysler sold its Snappy rental-car division, and even the last of its stake in the Japanese Mitsubishi company. By then, its holdings in Mitsubishi had shrunk to just 2.7 percent, down from 24 percent in 1985. The two companies parted amicably, agreeing to continued cooperation—especially in terms of the Diamond-Star operation in Illinois.

Stretching the basic LH body produced a pair of luxury models for 1994, bearing old and new names: New Yorker and LHS. With its Jaguaresque side profile, the LHS served as the company's new flagship, now that the Imperial nameplate had been retired yet again.

Dodge Ram trucks had long been favorites of the cargo-hauling bunch. Not until the debut of the restyled Ram for 1994, though, did full-size pickups command the attention of folks who'd never given trucks a second glance before. How could they avoid doing so, with the Ram's brazenly brawny front end virtually *daring* them to approach with caution? Customers were known to dash heedlessly across busy streets to catch a close look at a Ram when it first appeared on dealership lots.

Distribution problems surfaced during the 1994 model year, causing the corporation to be stuck with orders for 273,534 vehicles that never were delivered to dealers. A more equitable distribution system was promised, with more attention given to retail customers.

After almost expiring in 1979-80, and nearing bankruptcy in 1991, Chrysler was obviously back on track in the financial markets. Record first-quarter earnings in 1994 were exceeded in the second quarter, which showed a total of $956 million. For the first half of '94, Chrysler turned in a net profit of $1.9 billion—58 percent above the prior year's half-season figure. Another $651 million in the third quarter brought the nine-month total past $2.5 billion. Even better, Chrysler held a whopping $6 billion in cash on hand.

"Strong consumer demands for Chrysler cars and trucks—both in North America and the world—once again generated solid quarterly financial results," proclaimed chairman Robert J. Eaton. "We are carefully adding increased capacity over the next three years in response to this demand." Eaton anticipated capacity of 3.5 million units—more than twice the number sold in 1991.

From 1994 through the decade's end, Chrysler was planning to invest some $1.5 billion in upgrading its factory facilities. The list of improvements encompassed everything from computerized control technology to road-test simulators and heightened worker training. Despite the startling recent financial success, Chrysler president Robert A. Lutz, for one, planned to focus his team efforts on further cost-cutting and improvements in quality.

Not many cars have enjoyed promotion nearly as heavy as that granted to the new Neon—a replacement for the aging Shadow and Sundance. Nor have many vehicles experienced so much praise—albeit mixed with an occasional grumble. Not quite everyone agreed that Neon was the greatest automotive achievement of the age, or believed it wise to launch the car so early: by February 1994, as a '95 model. Nevertheless, the winter debut let Neon buyers feel that they owned a new car for far longer than a single year. Targeted shoppers tended to be twenty-somethings, likely to appreciate the car's for-the-price value and advanced technology. Two early recalls threatened to squelch the publicity parade, but Chrysler weathered that storm.

Neon was just the beginning of an all-out blitz of new 1995 models. Autumn '94 brought the Chrysler Cirrus "JA" sedan, shrinking the LH cars' "cab-forward" theme to compact dimensions. Aiming even more than before at upscale "baby boomers," who might otherwise favor imports, the urbane Cirrus sedan proffered such simple but significant details as an easy-to-replace battery (mounted behind the fender). Ashtrays were an option, not standard gear. In addition to conventional advertising, Chrysler promoted the Cirrus via computer on-line services, VIP and resort-guest test drives, and special theater and sporting events.

After a year with no sport coupe to market, Dodge introduced the belligerently named Avenger. Produced alongside the fully redesigned Eagle Talon, at the Diamond-Star plant in Normal, Illinois, the Avenger had one feature lacking in most sport coupes: a back seat big enough for real people's legs. It also featured some familiar design cues, borrowed from the Viper and Stealth.

Not until early in calendar 1995 did the final pair of all-new models emerge: the Dodge Stratus, another JA sedan, and the Chrysler Sebring coupe. With the Stratus—like the related Chrysler Cirrus—Dodge expected to offer "midsize car room in a compact car." Sebring was the Chrysler version of Dodge's Avenger, bringing those two makes into close kinship—to the detriment, at least temporarily, of Plymouth and Eagle. With the Sebring, Chrysler wanted to tempt "a new generation of luxury buyers," said Steve Torok, Chrysler-Plymouth general manager.

Introduced as an early '95 model, the reworked Eagle Talon's wheelbase grew a bit. No Plymouth Laser version was marketed this time, but the Talon was again similar to Mitsubishi's Eclipse—with a turbocharged engine and all-wheel drive available. Meanwhile, Eagle Vision sedan prices shrank in response to sluggish sales, as Chrysler tried to establish a stronger presence for the Eagle brand. To help in that quest, marketing duties for Jeep and Eagle were split into two groups.

Despite a history dating back to 1928, the Plymouth name, like the far-newer Eagle, had been rumored to face possible extinction—largely because each of its models differed from a Dodge only in details and badging. Now, with no Laser on sale, Plymouth was reduced to just three models: Neon, Voyager, and Acclaim. The last was about to expire, but word was that a Plymouth JA with a "Breeze" badge was on the way.

The biggest news for 1996 arrived at auto-show previews early in 1995: wholly redesigned minivans, codenamed "NS." Chrysler had little choice but to rework its popular people-carriers. A decade earlier, the competition had been minimal. Ever since, Chrysler had experienced little trouble in selling loads of Caravans, Voyagers, and even the plusher Town & Country Chryslers.

Now, however, Ford had launched a seductive new front-drive Windstar. The Mercury Villager and similar Nissan Quest were capturing minivan customers. GM's minivan trio had never quite caught on strongly, but still managed to grab a modest share of that market segment.

Chrysler, then, couldn't rest on past laurels—even if its minivans had been the hottest items in that niche, year after year, for better than a decade. Having seen 44-percent of the minivan market in its camp, Chrysler wasn't about to let the late Nineties go by without another full-scale assault.

Ever since its appearance at 1993 auto shows, a hardtop Dodge Viper was anticipated. The Viper GTS coupe, coming soon, is expected to have a top speed even higher than that of the roadster, "for the enthusiast who wants more of an all-weather performance car."

Chrysler also is readying a convertible for the late Nineties, to take the place of the departing LeBaron, the last of the K-car derivatives.

After retirement, Lee Iacocca stayed on as a consultant to Chrysler. He also took on a series of auxiliary endeavors—including banking for the gaming industry. Iacocca had earned credit for "saving" Chrysler via loan guarantees and the K-car, then seeing it through hard times a decade later. Merely playing golf wasn't enough to suit his energies.

To carry on into the 21st century, Chrysler has a strong assemblage of creative executives: from visionary engineer Francois Castaing and his gathering of platform teams, to master stylist Tom Gale and his inventive crew, up to Bob Eaton and Bob Lutz at the helm. With a full complement of attractive products on the market, a low-cost manufacturing operation, and profits reaching an awesome five percent, the road ahead looks wide open. Walter P. Chrysler would have been proud to see what his successors had accomplished, and to know the obstacles they'd hurdled.

391

1993

Chrysler launches "cab-forward" LH sedans: a posh Chrysler Concorde, family Dodge Intrepid, and sporty Eagle Vision

All three LH cars have dual air bags and a choice of two V-6 engines, with traction control available

The final Chrysler New Yorker Fifth Avenue/Salons and Imperials are built

Dodge drops the hot Spirit R/T sedan, but expects to produce 800 similarly turbo-powered Daytona IROC R/T sport coupes

Dodge's Dynasty sedan goes on sale for the last time

The imported Dodge/Plymouth Colt is redesigned, and also sold as an Eagle Summit

Anti-lock braking is now available in the subcompact Shadow/Sundance duo

Some 3000 Dodge Vipers are expected to go on sale, but production halts temporarily because of a serious flaw in the massive hood

A luxurious Jeep Grand Cherokee debuts

The Grand Cherokee is the first sport-utility with a driver-side air bag

Chrysler sells its Snappy rental-car division, and the Lamborghini company goes to an Indonesian-led group

Chrysler sells the last of its stake in Mitsubishi

Some 48 electric-powered minivans are sold this year, all to fleet customers

Concorde (*top and above*) was the name of Chrysler's luxury version of the new mid-size "LH" sedan trio. It had the same basic front-drive, four-door notchback design as the Dodge Intrepid and Eagle Vision. For the $18,341 base price, a Concorde had dual air bags and anti-lock disc brakes. A 3.5-liter dohc, 24-valve V-6 (*right*) was optional, cranking out 214 horsepower, but Concordes had a standard 153-bhp, 3.3-liter V-6. Concorde interiors (*below*) showed a functional, businesslike dashboard layout.

The $19,815 Chrysler LeBaron GTC convertible (*right*), like all LeBaron ragtops and coupes, sported a new grille. Turbochargers faded away, and exposed aero headlamps replaced the pop-up versions. GTC badging again identified the top-line LeBarons, here the $16,840 coupe (*below*). The LeBaron sedan, on a longer 103.5-inch chassis, wore a new rear fascia and taillamps. The mid-line LX model was gone, leaving the base LE and step-up $17,119 Landau (*below right*), which kept its rear vinyl top and slim quarter windows.

In its last year, Chrysler's $18,705 mid-size New Yorker Salon (*right*) stuck with its hidden headlights, but earned upgraded interior trim. A new power six-way driver's seat could replace the standard 50/50 front bench. The sole engine was a 147-bhp, 3.3-liter V-6 with four-speed automatic. Prestige leader of the New Yorker lineup was the $21,948 Fifth Avenue (*below*), with its formal-looking rear end. The 3.3-liter V-6 was again standard, with a 150-bhp 3.8 V-6 optional. A new premium radio had either a cassette or CD player.

An all-wheel-drive Chrysler Town & Country minivan (*above*) stickered for $27,529, versus $25,538 for the front-drive version. New alloy wheels and minor interior revisions were the only changes, along with adjustable-height front shoulder belts. T&Cs came only in the extended-length body. Touted as "one vision of a possible flagship" for Chrysler, the Thunderbolt (*left*) was one of the sleekest sport coupes on the 1993 show-car circuit. Harking back to the '41 Thunderbolt concept car, it employed modern cab-forward styling for stability and spaciousness. The rear-drive, four-seat coupe held a 4.0-liter aluminum V-8, rated at 270 horsepower.

In addition to the original red, this year's Dodge Viper RT/10 (*right and below*) could be ordered in black. Chrysler insisted that Vipers had "no peers." Note the exposed side-exhaust system. Billed as "a no-excuses car for no-excuses people," the Viper could accelerate to 60 mph in 4.5 seconds, and dash from a standstill to 100 mph—and then brake to zero—in just 14.5 seconds. The Viper's burly 8.0-liter V-10 (*below right*) blasted out 400 horses and 465 lbs/ft torque. Composite body panels were bonded and bolted to a tubular steel frame. Neither an air bag nor ABS was offered, but the $50,000 roadster carried a $2600 gas guzzler tax.

Introduced in spring 1992, the limited-edition Dodge Daytona IROC R/T (*right*) carried a 224-horsepower, 2.2-liter intercooled Turbo III four (as in the departed Spirit R/T), which boasted over 100 bhp per liter. It also wore Z-rated tires good for 149+ mph. Only 800 (with five-speed only) were to be built at $19,185 apiece. An R/T, Dodge claimed, "lives up to its racing heritage." Turbocharging was gone, but the Mitsubishi 141-bhp V-6 powered the Daytona IROC coupe (*below right*), which rode a performance-tuned suspension.

Apart from trim-appearance changes, the Dodge Stealth changed little for '92. Four models were available: base, ES, R/T, and this $31,185 R/T Turbo (*above left and left*). It featured full-time all-wheel drive and four-wheel steering, plus a twin-turbo version of the 3.0-liter V-6 yielding 300 horsepower and 307 lbs/ft torque. Base models, starting at $17,321, gained the ES's lower body cladding, and base and ES Stealths could get the R/T's distinctive rear spoiler. New options included remote keyless entry and a trunk-mounted CD changer. While all Stealths got the 3.0 V-6, output stared at 164 bhp on the base model, and escalated to 222 on the ES and R/T versions.

The most affordable new LH sedan was the Dodge Intrepid. At $17,189, the sporty ES (*above*) got all-disc brakes and 16-inch touring tires, with a "Performance Suspension" optional. Base Intrepids could be ordered with a front bench seat instead of the standard buckets. Dodge Grand Caravans, here the $17,935 SE (*right*), earned minor trim changes. Front shoulder belts were now height-adjustable. Anti-lock brakes became optional in the Shadow (*below*), and the "America" designation was gone. Dodge's Spirit sedan (*below right*) wore revised body trim, but lost the turbo engine and two models, including the hot R/T.

Fully redesigned, the subcompact Dodge Colt (*above left*) was now available only as a two- or four-door notchback. Anti-lock braking became optional, but only on the GL four-door. No air bag was offered. A new 113-horsepower, 16-valve, 1.8-liter four was optional on base four-doors and standard on the GL. A new 5.9-liter V-8 could be installed in the full-size Dodge Ramcharger sport-utility (*above*), whether two- or four-wheel drive. The standard engine was the 5.2-liter Magnum. *Left:* Like other full-size pickups, Dodge's D350 Club Cab (*foreground*) and 4x4 W250 could have a 5.9-liter Turbo Diesel, or the 5.9-liter gasoline V-8.

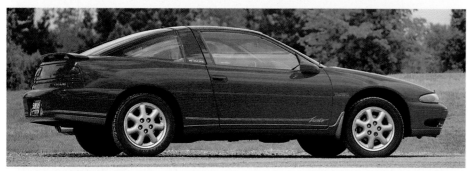

For the first time (and $857 extra), an automatic gearbox could be installed in the $17,371 all-wheel-drive version of the Plymouth Laser RS Turbo sport coupe (*left and above left*). Turbo models gained gas-filled shock absorbers and improved braking, and new seven-spoke alloy wheels became available. The turbo's rear spoiler was now standard on the RS, optional on base Lasers. All but the base model could get anti-lock brakes. The dual-overhead-cam, 2.0-liter Laser RS Turbo AWD engine (*above*) developed 195 horsepower, versus 135 for the non-turbo equivalent and 92 for the entry-level, 1.8-liter four. A new "Gold Decor Package" could be ordered for Lasers, and manual gearshift knobs became more ergonomic in shape.

Minor trim changes for the Plymouth Acclaim sedan (*above*) included a revised grille and a flush-mounted Pentastar hood ornament. All glass was now tinted, and the exhaust system was made of stainless steel. A compact-disc player joined the options list. This best-selling Plymouth came only in one $11,941 model, with a 2.5-liter four or a $725 3.0-liter V-6. Automatic four-cylinder models gained a higher-performance torque converter. Duster (*left*) was again the sporty Sundance coupe, with exclusive use of a 141-bhp, 3.0-liter V-6. Note the modest rear spoiler. Duster, as a $10,498 three-door or $10,898 five-door, also sported integral fog lamps, lower bodyside appliqués, and a hood power bulge. An anti-lock braking system was newly optional.

Regular-size and Grand Plymouth Voyagers again came in base, SE, and LE form—here the $17,935 Grand SE (*top*). Only detail changes were seen inside and out. A driver-side air bag came standard, anti-lock braking was optional with the 3.3-liter V-6. A 142-bhp 3.0 V-6 went into this $20,703 Voyager LE (*above left*) and into base Grand Voyagers, while the 150-bhp 3.3 V-6 was standard in the Grand SE and LE, and in AWD models. A 2.5-liter four was standard in regular-length models. *Above:* A Voyager AWD with an LX Decor Group cost $24,179. It had a body-colored grille, fog lamps, and a sport handling package.

Again marketed under Dodge and Plymouth names, the Colt (*above*) was redesigned for 1993, now a notchback only starting at $7806. Though longer in wheelbase and overall, it was no more spacious. Base and GL two- and four-doors were offered, with a 92-bhp, 1.5-liter four or 1.8-liter with 113 horses. ABS was optional in GL sedans. Inspired by traditional street rods, the Prowler concept car (*right*) drew so much attention at auto shows that it was considered for production. Many of its components came from Chrysler parts bins. A 3.5-liter, 24-valve V-6 sent about 240 horses to a rear-mounted transaxle. Aluminum was used for the chassis and body panels. Note the pointed nose, tapered running boards, and cycle-style fenders.

A new $11,752 base-model Talon DL (*right*)—with a 92-bhp, 1.8-liter four—gave Eagle a match for Eclipse and Laser. The former base Talon, renamed ES, carried a 135-bhp, twin-cam, 2.0-liter four. The $17,772 Talon TSi AWD (*below right*) had a 195-bhp turbo 2.0-liter (180 with automatic). The new Eagle Vision showed the same "cab-forward" design as Intrepid/Concorde. The hotter V-6 was standard in the $21,104 TSi (*below*), while the ESi got a 3.3 V-6. The TSi also boasted anti-lock brakes and a firmed-up touring suspension.

Redesigned as a notchback two- or four-door, the Eagle Summit came in DL and $11,860 ES (*far left*) guise, with a 1.5- or 1.8-liter engine. Anti-lock braking was now available. The five-seat Eagle Summit Wagon (*left*) had a sliding curbside door and either front drive or AWD.

Both the $16,895 Jeep Cherokee Sport (*above*) and new Country model ran with a standard 4.0-liter inline six and part-time Command-Trac four-wheel drive. Though Jeep's most popular series, Cherokees were repositioned a tier below the new upscale Grand Cherokee. Bowing in the spring of 1992 as a '93 model, the Grand Cherokee was the first sport-utility with a driver-side air bag. Standard anti-lock braking operated in both 2WD and 4WD. Base, Laredo, and Limited editions were joined in the fall by a new top-line, $29,471 Grand Wagoneer (*above right*) with a 220-bhp, 5.2-liter V-8. The Jeep Wrangler came in $10,925 "S" (*right*) and $13,343 base trim, the first mini 4x4 with available anti-lock brakes. Sahara and Renegade option groups were listed, the latter including wraparound fenders and integral running boards.

Above: Jeep Wranglers could be ordered with a Sport package that sported striping and side steps. Inline four- and six-cylinder engines were used. The ECCO concept vehicle (*above right*) aimed to bring traditional Jeep virtues to a "more environmentally aware generation." An advanced lean-burn two-stroke engine sat amidships. Components were recyclable aluminum and plastic.

1993 Production

Chrysler

LeBaron cpe/conv	35,260
LeBaron sdn	22,499
New Yorker Salon	22,323
Concorde	56,218
New Yorker Fifth Avenue	29,805
Imperial	7,064
Town & Country	26,451
Total	199,620

Dodge

Shadow	103,035
Daytona	9,677
Spirit	62,956
Dynasty	65,805
Intrepid	81,236
Caravan	300,666
Viper	1,043
Total	624,418

Eagle

Talon	28,070 *
Vision	30,676
Total	NA

* Model year sales

Jeep

Wrangler	69,329
Cherokee	145,013
Grand Cherokee	214,406
Total	428,748

Plymouth

Laser	18,488 *
Sundance	85,756
Acclaim	55,531
Voyager	237,875
Total	397,650

* Model year sales

Imports*

Dodge/Plymouth Colt	28,817
Dodge/Plymouth Colt Vista	6,175
Eagle Summit/Wagon	19,436
Dodge Stealth	14,556

* Calendar year

1993 Engine Availability

Chrysler

No. Cyl.	Disp., cid	bhp	Availability
I-4	153.0	100	S-LeBaron cpe/cvt
V-6	181.4	141	S-LeBaron LX, GTC, and sedan
V-6	201.0	147	S-NY Fifth Ave, NY Salon
V-6	201.0	150	S-Town & Country
V-6	201.0	153	S-Concorde
V-6	215.0	214	O-Concorde
V-6	230.0	150	S-Imperial; O-New Yorker Fifth Ave

Dodge

No. Cyl.	Disp., cid	bhp	Availability
I-4	135.0	93	S-Shadow
I-4T	135.0	224	S-Daytona IROC R/T
I-4	153.0	100	S-Daytona, Dynasty, Shadow ES and cvt Spirit, Caravan; O-Shadow
I-4T	153.0	152	S-Daytona Shelby, Spirit ES; O-Daytona, Shadow, Spirit
V-6	181.4	141	S-Dynasty LE; O-Daytona, Shadow, Spirit
V-6	181.4	142	O-Caravan
V-6	201.0	147	S-NY Fifth Ave, NY Salon; O-Dynasty
V-6	201.0	150	O-Caravan
V-6	201.0	153	S-Intrepid
V-6	215.0	214	O-Intrepid
V-10	488.0	400	S-Viper

Eagle

No. Cyl.	Disp., cid	bhp	Availability
I-4	107.0	92	S-Talon DL
I-4	122.0	135	S-Talon ES
I-4T	122.0	180/195	S-Talon TSi and TSi AWD auto/manual
V-6	201.0	153	S-Vision ESi
V-6	215.0	214	S-Vision TSi

Jeep

No. Cyl.	Disp., cid	bhp	Availability
I-4	150.0	123	S-Wrangler
I-4	150.0	130	S-Cherokee
I-6	242.0	180	O-Wrangler
I-6	242.0	190	S-Grand Cherokee; O-Cherokee
V-8	318.0	220	O-Grand Cherokee

Plymouth

No. Cyl.	Disp., cid	bhp	Availability
I-4	107.0	92	S-Laser
I-4	122.0	135	S-Laser RS
I-4T	122.0	180/195	S-Laser RS Turbo, Laser RS Turbo AWD auto/manual
I-4	135.0	93	S-Sundance
I-4	153.0	100	S-Acclaim, Voyager; O-Sundance
V-6	181.4	141	S-Sundance Duster; O-Acclaim
V-6	181.4	142	O-Voyager
V-6	201.0	150	O-Voyager

Imports

No. Cyl.	Disp., cid	bhp	Availability
I-4	90.0	92	S-Colt/Summit cpes
I-4	112.0	113	S-Colt GL sdn, Summit ES sdn, Colt Vista, Summit Wagon
I-4	143.0	136	S-Summit Wagon LX, Colt Vista SE; O-Summit Wagon, Colt Vista
V-6	181.0	164	S-Stealth
V-6	181.0	222	S-Stealth ES, Stealth R/T
V-6T	181.0	300	S-Stealth R/T Turbo

1994

Chrysler launches a lengthened New Yorker and LHS as early '94 models

Traction control is standard on the more upmarket LHS

The Chrysler LeBaron convertible is reduced to one model, with dual air bags and a standard V-6

The LeBaron coupe is history, along with the Imperial and Dodge Dynasty; this is the last year for the LeBaron sedan

Chrysler's trio of minivans meet all safety requirements through 1998

Chrysler's LH sedans can be ordered with flex-fuel V-6 engines that run on a mix of gasoline and methanol

Dodge Shadow and Plymouth Sundance return for their final (partial) season

Shadow/Sundance are eclipsed by the all-new subcompact Dodge and Plymouth Neon sedans, launched as very early '95 models

Dodge drops the Shadow convertible

Dodge Ram trucks gain a robust restyle—pickups that are impossible not to notice

Chrysler Corporation posts record quarterly earnings of $956 million

Chrysler endures the 1994 model year with more than 273,000 unfilled orders

As part of global expansion, Chrysler seeks a foothold in the mushrooming Chinese market for motor vehicles

Top and above: Chrysler launched its latest incarnation of the New Yorker as an early '94 model based on the "LH" sedans, but measuring five inches longer overall. More spacious inside and in the trunk, the $25,386 New Yorker came only with the 214-bhp, 3.5-liter V-6 engine. Variable-assist power steering was added as the full '94 model year began, along with a touring suspension. *Left and below:* In its second season, the Chrysler Concorde's base engine added eight horsepower, a touring suspension became standard, and a front bench could be substituted for the bucket seats. A power moonroof became available. Base price was now $19,457, up $1116.

Like the New Yorker, the slightly sportier LHS (*left*), stickered at $30,283, went on sale as an early '94 model. Variable-assist power steering came later, plus an alarm and automatic headlamps. The only options were a CD player and cloth upholstery, in place of the usual leather.

Above: Only a $16,999 GTC convertible remained in the now eight-year-old two-door Chrysler LeBaron line. The coupe was gone. A passenger-side air bag joined the driver's bag. All LeBarons, including LE and Landau sedans, now ran with a 141-bhp, 3.0-liter V-6. *Right:* A bigger 3.8-liter, 162-bhp V-6 entered Chrysler Town & Country minivans, which started at $27,184. Dual air bags were installed, too. *Below:* Stylists kept busy at the Pacifica Design Center in California, pondering both concept and production vehicles. The Expresso concept vehicle (*below right*) looked like something Roger Rabbit might drive. Inspired by taxis, and mounted on a Neon platform, it stood a full 15 inches taller than a Neon.

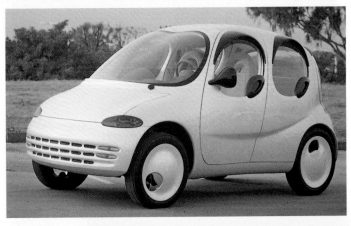

The new Dodge Neon spawned a group of concept vehicles, including this Venom coupe (*above*)—a modern rear-drive "muscle car" with six-speed gearshift. Rear wheels stretched away from the body in the Aviat concept coupe (*left*), forming huge scoops that helped aerodynamics.

Already a powerhouse, the engine in the $37,512 Dodge Stealth R/T Turbo (*above and right*) gained 20 horses, and a new six-speed manual gearbox took hold of all 320 of them. A passenger-side air bag joined the driver's bag. Just three models were sold, with minor styling changes that included the substitution of exposed headlamps for the prior hidden units. The ES departed. *Below right:* Note the narrowed roof in this overhead view of a Stealth 2+2 coupe.

Above left: Dodge Viper occupants could now enjoy "factory" air, rather than relying on their dealer to install a cooling unit. A new mechanism prevented shifting into reverse when the car was moving forward. Vipers could be painted yellow or emerald green, with a new black/tan interior available. The folding top had plastic side curtains. *Left:* As before, a mighty 8.0-liter, 400-bhp V-10 sent the Viper on its way.

Officially a '95 model, the subcompact Dodge Neon four-door sedan (*right*) debuted early in 1994, ready to replace the Shadow. Neons used a scaled-down version of the LH sedan's "cab-forward" profile, and carried a new 2.0-liter four that developed 132 horsepower. Dual air bags were standard, anti-lock brakes optional. Dodge Shadows remained in production for one last season, in base and ES (*below*) trim. Only the two- and four-door hatchbacks hung on—the convertible was gone. Just one $12,470 model of the Dodge Spirit sedan (*below right*) remained on sale, adding a motorized front-passenger seatbelt.

Safety got the nod in the Dodge Caravan (*right*), which added a passenger-side air bag and side door guard beams, thus meeting all passenger-car safety requirements through 1998. Only the longer-bodied Grand Caravan was still available with all-wheel drive, at $21,882 and up. A 3.8-liter V-6 could now be ordered. Viper wasn't the only Dodge with a V-10 engine—this full-size Ram 3500 4x2 pickup truck (*below*) has one, giving it plenty of brawn for heavy hauling.

Above: The base engine for the $19,191 Dodge Intrepid ES (and the base model) gained eight horsepower, to 161, and power steering now provided variable-assist. This year, both models had a touring suspension and standard air conditioning. New options included a power moonroof and a security alarm. *Left:* Chrysler's roster of alternative-fuel vehicles included (*left to right*): CNG full-size vans, electric-powered Dodge TEVans, and flexible-fuel Intrepids. Sold nationwide except in California, FFV Intrepid sedans ran on blends of gasoline and methanol.

403

The Plymouth Duster (*top and above*), again the "performance" edition of the soon-to-expire Sundance lineup, came in $10,946 three- and $11,346 five-door hatchback form. Four-door Sundances faded away during the '94 model year, replaced by the new Neon. Note the hood bulge on this Duster, suggesting the strength of its 141-horsepower, 3.0-liter V-6. Except for badging, Plymouth's version of the new subcompact Neon sedan (*above right*) rode a 104-inch wheelbase, and was virtually identical to Dodge's. The overhead-cam, 2.0-liter four made 132 bhp. Base price started at $8975.

A motorized shoulder belt for the front passenger was just about the sole change for the compact '94 Plymouth Acclaim sedan (*above*), closely related to the Dodge Spirit and Chrysler LeBaron. Only one $12,470 model was sold, with most options grouped in packages. Power came from a 2.5-liter four or 3.0-liter V-6. *Left:* Plymouth Colts added a driver-side air bag, following their redesign for 1993. From $9120 to $12,181, the Mitsubishi-built subcompact coupe and sedan, also sold by Dodge, were kissing cousins to the Mitsubishi Mirage and Eagle Summit. Power steering was now standard on Colt sedans. Plymouth also continued to offer the Colt Vista "mini-minivan," with front- or permanent all-wheel drive. Prices started at $12,979.

Only the Plymouth Grand Voyager minivan could have all-wheel drive this season. Regular-length Voyagers were all front-wheel-drive models. Voyagers gained a passenger-side air bag and side door guard beams, meeting all passenger-car safety requirements through 1998. Dashboards were redesigned (*above*), as in this $22,783 Grand Voyager LE (*top*), the upmarket long-wheelbase model. The optional bench seat, with integrated child seats, had a reclining seatback. All Voyagers gained new bumper fascias and body moldings. Regular-length Voyagers (*above left*) came in $14,819 base, $18,039 SE (*shown*), $21,863 LE, and $22,372 LX versions.

On the market for a decade, the Plymouth Voyager and Dodge Caravan had long been America's top-selling minivans. At $22,372, the most costly short-wheelbase Plymouth minivan was the Voyager LX (*above*). That model featured body-color fascias, grille, and bodyside trim; fog lights; sunscreen glass; and a sport handling group with P205/70R15 tires on aluminum wheels. *Right:* Short-bodied minivans rode a 112.3-inch wheelbase; Grand Voyagers spanned 119.3 inches. A four-cylinder engine remained standard in this base Voyager, but a 3.0-liter V-6 could be ordered. A limited number of Voyagers were equipped to run on compressed natural gas (CNG).

The standard 3.3-liter engine in an Eagle Vision ESi sedan (*left*) gained eight horsepower, while its body adopted the same cladding and fascias as the sportier—and more powerful—TSi edition. Flexible-fuel Visions also went on sale. Because a new model was anticipated as an early '95, the Eagle Talon sport coupe showed little change. Top dog, once again, was this $17,978 TSi AWD (*below left*), with a 195-horsepower turbo four and all-wheel drive. A driver-side air bag entered this year's Eagle Summit. The top-line ES sedan (*below*) cost $12,181, $753 more than a plainer LX.

Topping the Jeep Grand Cherokee line was the $29,618 Limited (*above*). The Grand Wagoneer departed. All Grand Cherokee models, including the popular Laredo (*left*), could get an optional 220-horsepower V-8 in place of the 190-bhp six. New safety features for the Jeep Cherokee, shown in $16,469 Sport form (*below*), included side door guard beams and a high-mounted stoplamp.

A soft-top Jeep Wrangler "S" (*above*) started at $11,390, while the step-up SE brought $3064 more. Note the tough-looking roof structure. An automatic transmission could now be had in four-cylinder Wranglers, as well as those with the inline six. A $2423 Sahara group for the Wrangler (*right*) added black trim, fog lights, fender flares, and side steps, among other goodies.

1994 Production

(All production figures for 1994 are model-year sales)

Chrysler
LeBaron cvt	37,844
LeBaron sdn	21,072
Concorde	85,636
New Yorker	35,582
LHS	48,036
Town & Country	38,356
Total	266,526

Dodge
Shadow	75,000 *
Neon	69,214
Spirit	42,431
Intrepid	155,170
Caravan	321,476
Viper	3,083
Total	666,374

* Estimated

Eagle
Talon	28,038
Vision	31,271
Total	59,309

Jeep
Wrangler	75,865
Cherokee	153,902
Grand Cherokee	257,557
Total	487,324

Plymouth
Laser	5,284
Sundance	70,438
Neon	67,315
Acclaim	40,294
Voyager	255,922
Total	439,253

Imports*
Dodge Colt	4,487
Plymouth Colt	3,603
Plymouth Vista	2,154
Eagle Summit	10,317
Dodge Stealth	6,753

* Sales January-November 1994

1994 Engine Availability

Chrysler

No. Cyl.	Disp., cid	bhp	Availability
V-6	181.4	141	S-LeBaron
V-6	201.0	161	S-Concorde
V-6	215.0	214	S-NY, LHS; O-Concorde
V-6	230.0	162	S-Town & Country

Dodge

No. Cyl.	Disp., cid	bhp	Availability
I-4	121.0	132	S-Neon
I-4	135.0	93	S-Shadow
I-4	153.0	100	S-Shadow ES, Spirit, Caravan; O-Shadow
V-6	181.4	141	O-Shadow, Spirit
V-6	181.4	142	O-Caravan
V-6	201.0	162	O-Caravan
V-6	201.0	161	S-Intrepid
V-6	215.0	214	O-Intrepid
V-6	230.0	162	O-Caravan
V-10	488.0	400	S-Viper

Eagle

No. Cyl.	Disp., cid	bhp	Availability
I-4	107.0	92	S-Talon DL
I-4	122.0	135	S-Talon ES
I-4T	122.0	180/195	S-Talon TSi and TSi AWD auto/manual
V-6	201.0	161	S-Vision ESi
V-6	215.0	214	S-Vision TSi

Jeep

No. Cyl.	Disp., cid	bhp	Availability
I-4	150.0	123	S-Wrangler
I-4	150.0	130	S-Cherokee
I-6	242.0	180	O-Wrangler
I-6	242.0	190	S-Grand Cherokee; O-Cherokee

No. Cyl.	Disp., cid	bhp	Availability
V-8	318.0	220	O-Grand Cherokee

Plymouth

No. Cyl.	Disp., cid	bhp	Availability
I-4	107.0	92	S-Laser
I-4	121.0	132	S-Neon
I-4	122.0	135	S-Laser RS
I-4	122.0	180/195	S-Laser RS Turbo, Laser RS Turbo AWD auto/manual
I-4	135.0	93	S-Sundance
I-4	153.0	100	S-Acclaim, Voyager; O-Sundance
V-6	181.4	141	S-Sundance Duster; O-Acclaim
V-6	181.4	142	O-Voyager
V-6	201.0	162	O-Voyager
V-6	230.0	162	O-Voyager

Imports

No. Cyl.	Disp., cid	bhp	Availability
I-4	90.0	92	S-Colt/Summit cpes
I-4	112.0	113	S-Colt GL sdn, Summit ES sdn, Colt Vista, Summit Wagon
I-4	143.0	136	S-Summit Wagon LX, Colt Vista SE/AWD; O-Summit Wagon, Colt Vista
V-6	181.0	164	S-Stealth
V-6	181.0	222	S-Stealth R/T
V-6T	181.0	320	S-Stealth R/T Turbo

1995-96

Chrysler issues six fresh models—five all-new

Some new-for-1995 models are early, while others arrive late; some critics fault Chrysler for issuing the '95 Neon so early in 1994

Technically sophisticated Neons come only in four-door form at first; '95 coupes arrive later

A performance-oriented Neon Sport engine appears after the start of the 1995 model year

The redesigned Eagle Talon no longer is accompanied by a Plymouth Laser mate

The '95 Chrysler Cirrus sedan is launched in fall '94; a related Dodge Stratus follows later

Dodge's Avenger sport coupe arrives in fall 1994, trailed by Chrysler's comparable Sebring

The Dodge Spirit and Plymouth Acclaim linger briefly in the '95 lineup

Advertising intensifies for Eagles, in an effort to keep the sagging brand alive

All cars get the same warranty—the choice of two plans is discontinued

Fully redesigned Chrysler minivans emerge early in 1995, as '96 models

Modernized '96 minivans are sleeker and rounder, taking aim at Ford's Windstar

Chrysler expects to have electric-powered minivans on sale, to meet a 1998 requirement in California

Chrysler launched an all-new "JA" model for 1995. Replacing the LeBaron sedan, the stylish front-drive Cirrus (*top*) ranked between compact and mid-size. "Cab-forward" styling and a 108-inch wheelbase created a spacious interior. A 2.5-liter Mitsubishi V-6 sent 164 bhp to an electronic automatic gearbox. The $19,365 Cirrus LXi (*above*) was the step-up model, with a sport suspension and other extras. Cirrus LX controls (*left*) were easy to reach. Dual air bags, anti-lock brakes, and cloth upholstery came standard. The '95 New Yorker (*below*) changed little, except for a new corporate hood badge.

Like the New Yorker, the 1995 Chrysler LHS sedan (*above*) measured six inches longer than the Concorde on which it was based. An LHS, with its body-colored grille, stickered for $3999 more than a New Yorker, but came fully loaded, including traction control and leather front bucket seats. Chrysler introduced its all-new Sebring luxury sport coupe (*right*) early in 1995, a cousin to the also-new Dodge Avenger. Both were built by Mitsubishi, at the Diamond-Star plant in Illinois. LX Sebrings held a 140-bhp four, while this LXi got a 161-bhp V-6.

Left: After a decade of minivan market success, Chrysler stylists were busy penning a suitable replacement. Meanwhile, the '95 Chrysler Town & Country (*below left*) carried on, with little change other than a modified keyless entry system. *Below:* Ready for auto-show appearances early in '95, the '96 Chrysler Town & Country LXi showed a more rounded profile than its long-lived predecessor, but kept its spacious interior and car-like qualities.

After the demise of the long-lived Daytona, Dodge dealers had no sport coupe to offer. Now, for 1995, came the all-new Avenger (*above and right*), shown in step-up ES trim with a subtle rear spoiler and 16-inch aluminum wheels. Styled by Chrysler, the new coupe was produced by Mitsubishi, in Illinois, on a modified Mitsubishi Galant sedan platform. Base Avengers held a Chrysler-built, 2.0-liter, dual-cam four, but the ES got a 155-horse, 2.5-liter V-6 made by Mitsubishi. Unlike most sporty coupes, which tend to be cramped in back, the Avenger offered ample rear-seat legroom. Anti-lock braking came as standard on the ES, optional on the base model, but both Avengers featured dual air bags as well as a height-adjustable driver's seat.

Dodge's all-new replacement for the Spirit sedan, named Stratus, arrived well after the 1995 model year began. Close kin to the Chrysler Cirrus, the Stratus came in base guise, and as an ES (*above left and left*). The latter carried a Mitsubishi 2.5-liter V-6 that made 164 horsepower. Base models used a 2.0-liter four, evolved from the Neon's, rated at 132 bhp. An optional 2.4-liter four gave 140 horses. Prices began at $13,965. The more costly ES included a sport suspension and power gadgets. *Above:* Stratus controls were designed for easy access. A "smoker's package" could be dealer-installed.

410

Even before the 1994 model year was over, orders were being taken for the '95 Dodge Viper (*above*)—sold in a selection of colors, including yellow. The "no-holds-barred" $56,000 roadster kept its 400-bhp V-10 and six-speed gearbox. In 1994, Chrysler president Robert A. Lutz announced that Dodge would develop a Viper GTS coupe (*left*), based on the show car that was first seen a year earlier. "Positive response from the public" was the reason for the decision, Lutz added, as had been the case with the original Viper roadster. Anticipated features included twin blisters on the hardtop, an air scoop, integrated spoiler, rear exhaust—plus power windows instead of side curtains.

A Dodge Neon coupe (*above*) went on sale in fall 1994, joining the original sedan. Neon Sport four-doors (*above right*) had anti-lock braking, but the same engine as other Neons. *Left:* A stronger 16-valve, dual-cam, 2.0-liter engine, rated at 150 bhp, went into the Neon Sport coupe. *Right:* Chrysler shaved 500 pounds by using aluminum parts in the Neon Lite concept car.

Above: Interior features of the redesigned '96 Dodge Grand Caravan ES weren't dramatically different from its predecessor. *Top right:* Despite the fact that Caravans were about to be redesigned, new Sport and SE Decor option groups could be installed on the 1995 model. The Sport package included blackout window trim, sunscreen glass, sport suspension, and wider tires. The SE Decor Group featured two-tone paint and striping. *Above right:* Power steering and a rear step bumper became standard in the 1995 Dodge Dakota mid-size pickup truck, available as a 4x2 or 4x4. Three engines were offered: four, V-6, or V-8. *Right:* A Club Cab version of the brawny Dodge Ram pickup went on sale for the 1995 model year, shown here in the one-ton 3500 series.

Left: Black-out window treatment made the side glass in a 1996 Plymouth Grand Voyager so dark it almost looked like a cargo van. Redesigning gave the popular minivan a rounded profile, plus the first-time option of dual sliding side doors. A new Rallye Group for the 1995 Plymouth Grand Voyager SE (*below left*) consisted of special striping and script, two-tone paint, sunscreen glass, and wider tires on aluminum wheels. The optional remote-entry system was modified, and Voyagers could be ordered with a V-6 engine that ran on compressed natural gas. Manual shift was no longer available on any Voyager model.

Right: Only a single-cam, 132-horsepower, 2.0-liter engine powered the subcompact Plymouth Neon sedan when it first went on sale early in 1994. Aiming at the youth market, Neons were loaded with technical innovations, from a weight-saving plastic intake manifold to water-based paint and recyclable components. Later in the '95 model year came a Neon Sport coupe with a dual-cam engine, domed hood, rear spoiler, stiffer suspension, and 14-inch cast-aluminum wheels.

Above: Stiffer-bodied than before, the 1995 Eagle Talon TSi packed a 210-bhp turbo four. A low cowl and new instrument panel highlighted the interior, featuring dual air bags. Talons went racing.

Chrysler has seemed unsure what to do about the Plymouth brand name since the late '70s, and in the early '90s, it even seemed as though Plymouth might be dropped. Reduced to just Neon and Acclaim (and minivans) for '95, Plymouth needed help, so Chrysler reversed its original plan not to offer a Plymouth-badged "JA." With the Acclaim about to disappear, a last-minute decision was made to give Plymouth its own JA, seen here (*top*) as the "Breeze" show car at the '95 Detroit Auto Show. The production model will be ready for '96, and would carry the same name. The inset shows Plymouth's new "post-modern" version of the original Mayflower badge worn by the very first 1929 model. Little-changed for '95, the $22,871 Eagle Vision TSi (*above*) still aimed at import-oriented buyers.

Left and above: A new Orvis Edition trim group for the 1995 Jeep Grand Cherokee included Moss Green paint and champagne/green leather upholstery.

The 1995 Jeep Cherokee lineup included SE, two-toned Sport (*above*), and Country models. Sport and Country editions had six-cylinder power. *Below:* A new Rio Grande option for the Jeep Wrangler "S" gave a Southwestern look.

1995 Model Lineup

Chrysler	Jeep
LeBaron conv	Wrangler
Sebring	Cherokee
Cirrus	Grand Cherokee
Concorde	
New Yorker	**Plymouth**
LHS	Neon
Town & Country	Acclaim
	Voyager
Dodge	
Neon	**Imports**
Spirit	Eagle Summit
Avenger	Eagle Summit Wagon
Stratus	Dodge Stealth
Intrepid	
Caravan	
Viper	

Eagle
Talon
Vision

1995 Engine Availability

Chrysler

No. Cyl.	Disp., cid	bhp	Availability
I-4	121.0	140	S-Sebring LX
V-6	153.0	164	S-Cirrus LXi, Sebring LXi
V-6	181.4	141	S-LeBaron
V-6	201.0	161	S-Concorde
V-6	215.0	214	S-NY, LHS; O-Concorde
V-6	230.0	162	S-Town & Country

Dodge

No. Cyl.	Disp., cid	bhp	Availability
I-4	121.0	132	S-Neon
I-4	121.0	132	S-Stratus manual
I-4	121.0	140	S-Avenger
I-4	121.0	150	S-Neon Sport cpe
I-4	147.0	140	S-Stratus auto
I-4	153.0	100	S-Spirit, Caravan
V-6	153.0	164	S-Stratus ES, Avenger, ES
V-6	181.4	141	O-Spirit
V-6	181.4	142	O-Caravan
V-6	201.0	162	O-Caravan
V-6	201.0	161	S-Intrepid
V-6	215.0	214	O-Intrepid
V-6	230.0	162	O-Caravan
V-10	488.0	400	S-Viper

Eagle

No. Cyl.	Disp., cid	bhp	Availability
I-4	121.0	140	S-Talon ESi
I-4T	122.0	210	S-Talon TSi and TSi AWD
V-6	201.0	161	S-Vision ESi
V-6	215.0	214	S-Vision TSi

Jeep

No. Cyl.	Disp., cid	bhp	Availability
I-4	150.0	123	S-Wrangler
I-4	150.0	130	S-Cherokee
I-6	242.0	180	O-Wrangler
I-6	242.0	190	S-Grand Cherokee; O-Cherokee
V-8	318.0	220	O-Grand Cherokee

Plymouth

No. Cyl.	Disp., cid	bhp	Availability
I-4	121.0	132	S-Neon
I-4	121.0	150	S-Neon Sport cpe
I-4	153.0	100	S-Acclaim, Voyager
V-6	181.4	141	O-Acclaim
V-6	181.4	142	O-Voyager
V-6	201.0	162	O-Voyager
V-6	230.0	162	O-Voyager

Imports

No. Cyl.	Disp., cid	bhp	Availability
I-4	90.0	92	S-Summit cpes
I-4	112.0	113	S-Summit sdn, Summit Wagon; O-Summit ES cpe
I-4	143.0	136	S-Summit Wagon LX/AWD; O-Summit Wagon
V-6	181.0	164	S-Stealth
V-6	181.0	222	S-Stealth R/T
V-6T	181.0	320	S-Stealth R/T Turbo

INDEX

INDEX

416